Martin Lutterjohann
Klaudia & Eberhard Homann

Malaysia & Singapore

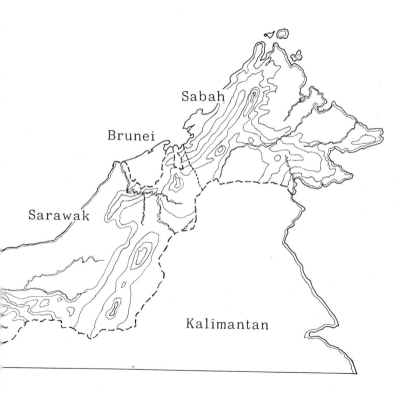

M. Lutterjohann, K. & E. Homann
Malaysia & Singapore
Published by

Peter Rump Publishing Co.
Hauptstr. 198
D-4800 Bielefeld 14

© **Peter Rump, 1991**

ISBN: 3-89416-331-3

Design:
Cover: M. Schömann, P. Rump
Contents: P. Rump
Maps: B. Steffen
Photos: see page 405
Typesetting:
digitron, Bielefeld
Translated
by Neil Platt from the 2nd German edition
Edited by: David Henley and Patricia Maguire
Printed by: Polygraphic Marketing Sdn. Bhd., Cheras, Malaysia

PRINTED IN MALAYSIA

Distributors:
Travel Bug guides are available in the countries listed below. If you can't find them, ask your bookshop to order them from one of the listed distributors. For countries not listed, write to Peter Rump in Germany.

Austria: Robo, Postfach 601, 1060 Wien
Germany: Prolit, Postfach 6301, Fernwald (Annerod)
India and Nepal: India Book Distributor, 107/108, Arcadia, 195, Nariman Point, Bombay 400021
Malaysia and Singapore: S. Abdul Majeed & Co.; 2210, Malayan Mansion, Jl. Masjid India; 50100 Kuala Lumpur
Netherlands: Nilsson & Lamm bv. Postbus 195, Pampuslaan 212, 1380 AD Weesp
Switzerland: AVA-buch 2000, Postfach, 3910 Affoltern
Thailand: Bangkok Book Distributor Co. LTD., 302-4 Siam Square Soi 4 Phatumwan, Bangkok 10330
USA: SCB Distributors, P.O. Box 5446, Carson, CA 90749-5446

Send 17 US$ for a copy of the **Malaysia & Singapore Handbook** to P.R.-Distribution, Heidekampstr. 18, D-4450 Lingen, Germany, and the book will be airmailed anywhere in the world.

Foreword

Malaysia, it seems, is destined to remain in the shadows of her better-known neighbors, Thailand, Indonesia and Singapore. Many Westerners have no idea about this wonderful country, except, perhaps, that it is somewhere in the tropics, that Islam is the state religion, and that the death penalty awaits drug traffickers.

But there are advantages to this dearth of knowledge. It is a fresh country, relatively new to Western tourists. There are no obligatory sights and so here, more so than in many other places, visitors are free to create their own experiences. The riches of Malaysia lie in her people - both in the cities and the *kampongs* - and in nature.

Though Malaysia has few old cultural monuments to entice the traveler, it does have an incredible variety of natural attractions. Half of the Peninsula and most of Sabah and Sarawak are still covered by jungle. There are hundreds of inviting offshore islands, offering great opportunities for swimming, snorkeling, diving or just relaxing. And since many of these islands are uninhabited, visitors can easily escape the crowds. The close proximity of nature is surely one of Malaysia's greatest attractions.

Another attraction of Malaysia is the chance to meet the different ethnic groups – Islamic Malays, Buddhist and Christian Chinese, Hindu and Christian Indians, and the animist Orang Asli, the original inhabitants of the Peninsula and Borneo.

It is easy to meet people as you travel around the country. Most Malaysians have few inhibitions about getting to know foreigners. They are proud of their country and want to know how you like it. Friendliness and hospitality are greatly valued here. Even the strict Muslims on the East Coast welcome the chance to meet unbelievers, though they often consider westerners a bit indiscreet. The Orang Asli are harder to get to know, but if you are persistent, the experience can be very rewarding.

We wish you happy traveling and plenty of good experiences along the way, and hope that your choices of lodging, food and transportation are good ones. There will always be flops, but then, that's part of traveling.

We hope this book helps you get acquainted with this beautiful land so that you can come to know it and love it on your own terms.

Martin Lutterjohann,
Klaudia and Eberhard Homann

Malaysia: General Information

Getting There 18
Visas 20
Money 21
Costs 23
Health 24
Security 24
Power / Measurements 25
Government Offices 25
Media 26
Nightlife 27
Accomodation 27
Food 30
Shopping 36
Public Transportation 38

Peninsular Malaysia

Land and People
Geography 49
Climate 52
Flora and Fauna 54
The People of
   Peninsular Malaysia 59
National Language 64
History 64
Current Politics 71
Economy 74
Religion 77
Festivals and Holidays 87
Arts and Culture 92
Rules of Behavior 95
Tourism 100
Travel 101
Suggested Travel routes 110
The West Coast 113
The East Coast 225
Central Malaysia 255
Taman Negara 259

Foreword 7

Preparations

Costs 12
Vaccines 12
Health 13
Clothing 14
Equipment 14
Photography 15

Sarawak and Sabah

Getting to Sabah and Sarawak 276
Traveling between Sabah and
   Sarawak 277
Special Customs Regulations for
   Sarawak 279
Climate 280
Equipment 281
Transporation 281
Accomodation 283
Costs 283
Flora and Fauna 284

Sarawak 285
History 286
Economy 287
Religion 288
People 288
National Parks 294
Travel 295

Sabah 325
Geography 325
History 326
Economy 327
Religion 327
Language 328
People 328
Travel 330

Singapore

Land and People 365
Geography 367
Climate 367
Population 367
Language 367
History 368
About the State 369
Religion 370
Behavior 372

In Singapore 373
Money 375
Health 376
Security 376
Accommodation 376
Food 377
What to See 382
Further Travel 396

Appendix

Information 400
Bahasa Malaysia 401
Outdoor Activities 403
Literature 404
List of Photos 405
Help! 408
Flight Prices 410
Ship Fares 412
Train Fares 413
Notes 415
General Index 425
Geographical Index 427
Maps 430
Metric Conversion 431
The Authors 432

Preparations

Costs

Malaysia, though cheaper than most Western countries, is not an incredibly cheap place, especially in comparison to other Southeast Asian countries.

Figure on a minimum of M$ 12 a night for accommodation. The price is usually the same for one or two people. Some Chinese hotels can be a bit cheaper if you can fit two people into a smaller room. These rooms are usually rented as a single, but many hotels do not have them.

For food and drink, the minimum you can get by on is M$2 a person per meal, providing, of course, that you eat local food. Of course, if you are looking for luxury it is possible to spend much more. Prices for food and accommodation are slightly higher in Singapore and much higher in Sarawak and Sabah.

Additionally, you will have to figure costs for transportation. These are listed throughout the book.

As a rule of thumb, a bus trip the length of the Peninsula, from Johor Baru, through Kuantan and on to Kota Baru, costs M$ 40.

The prices in this book should be good through 1990, and after that, count on a 7% annual rate of inflation.

That rate might not apply for everything. Transportation, for example, might get cheaper as new roads are built and driving times decrease.

Vaccines

There are no vaccines required for Malaysia. Nonetheless, you should check with your doctor a few weeks before you depart to see if there have been any epidemics or other exceptions. If you are arriving from a yellow fever area (Latin America or Africa), you will need to show proof of vaccination against *yellow fever.*

Even though the World Health Organization (WHO) declared that *smallpox* had been eliminated in 1979, people who have been in Chad or Cambodia will need to show proof of vaccination.

Vaccination against *cholera* used to be recommended, but there is now some question as to its effectiveness, especially when considering its side-effects. Check with your doctor. The best protection against cholera is absolute cleanliness (washing your hands with soap before eating anything, peeling all fruits and vegetables, etc.) Cholera is more prevalent in Sarawak than in the rest of Malaysia.

You should get a vaccination for *typhoid*. As with cholera, cleanliness is very important in avoiding typhoid. Protection against *tetanus* and *polio* are also recommended.

Gamma globulin only offers partial protection from *hepatitis A*, but it does improve general immunity. There is a vaccine for *hepatitis B*, but it is not always recommended. Check with your doctor about all immunizations.

Malaria is a widespread and dangerous disease. It is a virus spread by infected mosquitoes and can be fatal in the worst circumstances. It is most prevalent in Sarawak, but is certainly not unknown in the rest of Malaysia. Unfortunately, there is no consensus on how to prevent malaria. Conditions and effective medicines and treatments are different all over the world, and even vary from region to region. The mosquitoes in one town might be malarial, while those in a town five miles away might not. Discuss it with your doctor before you go to Malaysia and then, if you are in rural areas, check with local health workers about the conditions in that particular area. If you do think you have malaria, characterized by a high fever and muscle pains, particularly in the evening, stay with a friend, and get medical help immediately!

Generally, the best protection against malaria is not to get bitten by mosquitoes, particularly in rural areas or near still water. Malarial mosquitoes come out at dusk; daytime mosquitoes do not usually carry the virus. Starting at dusk, wear clothes that do not expose a lot of skin. Use mosquito repellent on your clothes and hair as well as on your exposed skin. Burn mosquito coils, or if you do not have any, burn incense to keep away mosquitoes. Sleeping under a mosquito net is also highly recommended.

Above all, it is crucial that you check with your doctor before you go to Malaysia. It is a relatively safe country, despite the fact that this chapter might sound threatening, but the authors are not doctors and make no claim to be. Health conditions are subject to change, so make sure you are getting the most up-to-date information.

Health

In addition to the vaccinations and medicines needed to protect you from serious diseases, you should also carry medicines for minor ailments, like headaches and diarrhea. It is wise to see your dentist shortly before you leave, as nothing can ruin a trip more than a bad toothache.

Any medical kit should include medicine for the following:

- *Malaria*: As prescribed by your doctor.
- *Fever / Pain*: Aspirin (available all over Malaysia) or a substitute.
- *Diarrhea* : As recommended by your doctor.
- *Insect bites*: Hydrocortizone.
- *Muscle sprains*.
- *Small wounds*: Bandages, iodine, etc.
- *Purifying drinking water*: Potable Aqua or a substitute.
- *Miscellaneous*: Thermometer, sterile needles (2 and 5 ml), sterile tubes.

If you should become ill and require medical attention, do not worry – Malaysia has an excellent health care system, and almost all doctors speak English. All big towns (even in Sarawak) have a general hospital, staffed by capable personnel, using modern equipment. Usually, treatment is free, except for a negligible registration fee (M$ 1) . In addition to the hospitals, there are quite a few private clinics, which are normally less crowded than the public hospitals. These are more expensive. Be careful to get complete receipts for your health insurance program at home.

In Singapore, health care is even better, though it is more expensive. Here, you pay at the time of your visit. Again, do not forget to get receipts. If you need sophisticated medical attention that cannot be given in Malaysia (most likely in Sarawak), you should go immediately to Singapore.

A note on **snake bites**: In general, the danger of snake bites in the tropics is greatly overestimated by tourists. You need not worry about them as the chances of getting bitten are quite small. Obviously, if you are bitten, get medical help immediately.

Clothing

It is usually warm enough to wear shorts and a t-shirt all the time, though this is not considered respectable attire for Malaysians. In overwhelmingly Malay areas, like the east coast of the Peninsula, a skirt is far better for women.

On formal occasions, women wear dresses and men wear long pants and a long-sleeved white cotton or batik shirt. The batik shirts are beautiful and available everywhere. Jackets and ties are only worn in air-conditioned offices.

In the lowlands, the coldest places are invariably the air-conditioned buses and trains. Long pants or a skirt and a long-sleeved shirt are recommended for long trips. It can also get quite cool (enough for a warm sweater) in the highlands at night in the cool season. Many of the hotels in the *Cameron Highlands* have fireplaces in the rooms.

Equipment

The main thing to remember when packing is that you will have to carry everything yourself. The best thing for this is a **backpack**, preferably one with an internal frame. They are better than those with external frames as they keep things tidier and are easier to put on in a bus or a train.

Loose cotton **clothing** is the best choice for Malaysia. If you will be dealing with officials , it is best to have at least one "respectable" shirt. Men should take long pants and a long-sleeved shirt. Women should do the same, though a long skirt is better. Women should also have a light shirt or wrap to cover their arms in conservative settings such as visiting a mosque.

T-shirts are cheaper in Asia than anywhere else, so there is no need to bring many. Shorts are OK for relaxing on the beach, but are not normally worn by adults in public.

Of course, bring a bathing suit, as well as a wide-brimmed hat for the days at the beach, as the sun is very bright around the Equator. It can also protect against the rain. Bring both shoes and sandals, as each is suited to different purposes.

• *Sun-tan lotion* with a high protection factor is necessary for walking around during the day.
They are available only in big cities and are very expensive in Asia.
• *Detergent* in small packets is available everywhere.
• *Bed linen* is always provided, but is not always clean. If that bothers you, take a sheet or a sleeping bag liner.
• A *flashlight (torch)* is very important, since many places do not have electricity. Batteries are no problem to replace.
• Bring a good *padlock* to secure your luggage, as well as your room door.
• *Sunglasses* and a spare pair of glasses, if you wear them, are necessary.
• In addition to your backpack, you should have a *day pack* or similar bag. This is useful for a day or an overnight trip when you do not want to carry everything with you.
• *Money belts* and other places to hide your money can be useful, too.
• Other important things are *a sewing kit, tissues / toilet paper, a water bottle, eating utensils, a pocket knife* and *pens*. Take all the *tampons* you need as they are very expensive - if you can find them.

Maps

It is a good idea to take maps with you. If you have trouble finding good maps at home, you can get them from the Malaysian Tourist Development Corporation (TDC), or in Singapore once you arrive.

If you need detailed maps of a specific area, get an **ONC (Operational Navigation Chart)** or a **TPC (Tactical Pilot Chart)**. They have complete topographic information. The ONC are of a larger scale (i.e. 1 ONC is divided into 4 TPCs.)

The best map for driving in the area is published by the United Nations, the *Asian Highway Route Map (Singapore - Malaysia - Thailand)*.

Photography

Cameras and equipment must be protected from water, especially in the rainforest or during the rainy season.

When flying, it is best to have your camera and film in a lead bag, to protect them from accidental exposure from X-rays. Always carry your camera and film with you; never check them through as luggage.

For regular shots, ASA 64-100 film is good, but in the rainforest it is much darker, so plan on using ASA 200 or even 400. It used to be expensive to buy film in Asia, but now it is reasonably priced. Since film is not always well-kept in Malaysia, it is better to buy at a reputable store before you depart. Always check the expiry date on the package.

Taking Pictures of People

1. When taking photos, go alone or in pairs. Too many people will attract too much attention and make people around you uneasy.

2. Take your time. People are hard to photograph in a hurry. It is better to wait in one place for a good opportunity than to run around and take indiscriminate shots.

3. Make eye-contact (but not with people of the opposite sex!) Use a combination of body language, friendliness and spontaneity to get good results.

4. Learn the words for "please," "thank you" and "excuse me" in the language of the people you are addressing.

Always ask permission to photograph a person.

5. Respect the wishes of the people as to how they would like to be photographed. A posed group portrait is typical, but after one of those, people will loosen up and you can get some good, more informal shots.

6. Before photographing people in their own environment, try and give them the opportunity to get to know you a bit. Smiles and a few friendly words will get you everywhere, but do not be too forthcoming or immediately offer to give money. Subtlety is appreciated in Malaysia.

7. Once you have decided to take a picture and have permission, do not waste time. Make sure the film is already wound on and focus quickly. The perfect moment waits for no one.

8. All photographers say, "Smile," but not too many smile themselves. Once, on a street in Africa, I saw a photographer who started to grin just before he was ready to shoot. As if planned, his models smiled right back at him.

9. Once finished, do not leave immediately, but take the time to thank your subjects, and leave politely.

10. When photographing a sight, it is far better to take a head and shoulders shot of a person with the sight in the background than it is to shoot their whole body in front of the sight.

Malaysia: General Information

Getting There

From Neighboring Countries

From Bangkok, you can travel to Peninsular Malaysia by plane, train or bus.

From Singapore, you can take city bus 170 or the Johor-Singapore Express from Queen St. to Johor Baru, and then go from there to other points in Malaysia by taxi or bus. From the Golden Mile Shopping Center, there are buses going all over Malaysia and even to Thailand. There are also trains and planes from Singapore to Malaysia.

You can also get to Malaysia **from Indonesia**, either by air from Bali or Jakarta to Kuala Lumpur or from Medan to Penang. There is also a connection between Pekanbaru, Sumatra to Malacca. From the island of Batam, near Singapore, there are boats to Singapore and Malaysia.

Kuala Lumpur is a big international hub, though not as big as Bangkok or Singapore. It is fully accessible **from other cities in Asia** like Tokyo, Hong Kong, Manila, etc.

Further Travel from Malaysia

There are **international airports** in Kuala Lumpur and Penang, and of course Singapore is easily accessible. Kuala Lumpur has far more flights than Penang. Depending on exchange rates, Penang can be an even bigger bargain center for flights around Southeast Asia than Bangkok.

If you have an *International Student ID Card (ISIC)*, you might be able to get special rates on some flights. Contact any of the following travel agents, who also have special excursion fares for non-students:

Penang:
MSL Travel
Lebuh Chulia 340
Ming Court Hotel
Tel.   04-24748 / 9 (main office), 616112.

Let's Travel & Tours
428 Chulia St.
10200 Penang
Tel. 04-613087, 622384.

Kuala Lumpur:
MSL Travel
South East Asia Hotel
69 Jalan Haji Hussein
Tel. 03-2989049.

Singapore:
Holiday Tours & Travel
Ming Court Hotel
Mezzanine Floor
Tel. for student fares, 02-7345681
other inquiries, 7322388.

It is difficult to say which travel agencies have the best service and prices. Ask other travelers and shop around.

There are many others on the same street.

Sample **one-way fares from Penang** (all prices in M$, student prices in parentheses):
Medan   109;
Bangkok   311 (250);
Hong Kong 718 (495);
Madras   590 (580).

From Kuala Lumpur there is a greater selection. (All prices in M$)

	Round-trip	One-way	Student
Manila	778	611	495
Taipei	1099	964	710
Tokyo	1429	1272	935
Seoul	1264	1321	875
Hong Kong	858	717	545
Bangkok	550	352	300
Jakarta	495	372	265
Madras	990	580	580
Sydney	1255	970	900

If you are buying tickets in Malaysia for further travel, you can put together some interesting combinations. I have a friend who bought a one-way ticket in Penang for around US$ 700 from Singapore to Jakarta to Denpasar to Sydney to Papeete (or Hawaii) and Los Angeles.

Keep an eye out for cheap *excursion tickets*, or heavily discounted round-trip tickets. Even if you are not planning on returning, a heavily discounted round-trip ticket can sometimes be cheaper than a one-way ticket!

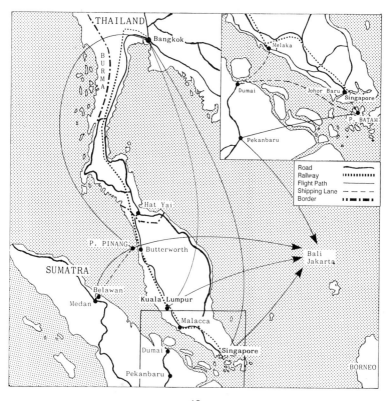

Airport Taxes for domestic flights cost M$ 3 (usually included in the purchase price); for flights to Singapore and Brunei, M$ 5; and for other international flights, M$ 15.

Visas

A passport is necessary for entry and it must be valid for at least another 6 months at the time of entry.

●No visa is needed by citizens of the Commonwealth, Pakistan, Ireland, Liechtenstein, the Netherlands, San Marino, Switzerland and the United States. This is providing, of course, you do not work during your visit.

●Citizens of the following countries may stay a maximum of three months with no visa: Belgium, Luxembourg, France, Italy, Germany, Austria and the Scandinavian countries.

●Citizens of ASEAN nations may stay for one month without a visa.

●Citizens of Eastern European countries may normally stay for only one week without a visa.

●Citizens of Israel and South Africa are not allowed to enter Malaysia.

All over Asia, questionable-looking travelers are not exactly welcomed with open arms, and that applies here as well. Dress neatly and look respectable when you enter, or officials could just stamp a two-week permit in your passport or deny you entry altogether. This happens rarely.

If you would like to **extend your visa**, you will have to go to the nearest Immigration office (there is one in the capital of every state.) The naturally suspicious officials like to see precise addresses on forms rather than just, "Hotel, Penang."

Tourist (Social) Visa

People coming from countries with no visa requirements generally receive an extension of three months on request. There is a fee of M$ 5 per month. If you want, you might ask for more than three months at once and they might give it to you. If not, you can always leave the country for a short while and reenter. With this visa, you may not work, do business or engage in political activity.

Business Visa

This visa is good for one month and is given free to people visiting companies or attending conferences and meetings. It may be extended for up to three months for free. After that, there is a charge of M$ 5 per month.

20

Professional Visa

This visa must be arranged before arrival in Malaysia and is reserved for experts, artists, performers and others who are bringing their professional expertise to Malaysia. It costs M$ 45 for the duration of the visa (either six months or one year.)

Temporary Employment Visa

This visa is granted for up to three years and is, in general, only given to professionals invited to Malaysia by a company or organization. It costs M$ 20 for the duration.
If you do have a special, long-term visa and wish to leave and reenter the country, you must get a **multiple reentry visa** or get an entirely new visa every time you reenter. It costs M$ 9.60, payable only in postage stamps, which you have to buy beforehand. It is valid for up to six months, or until the main visa expires, whichever comes first.

Customs

There is nothing special about customs in Malaysia. The **duty-free allowance** is the following:
- 200 cigarettes, 60 cigars or 225 g of tobacco.
- 1 liter of alcohol.
- Perfume for personal use.
- Up to 100 matches (!).
- Gifts worth up to M$ 200.
- Travel items for personal use including cameras, hair dryers, etc.

- A car or other vehicle can be taken in for three months duty-free; after that there is a charge.
- **Permission** is needed for hunting weapons.

Theoretically, officials could charge duty for bringing in computers, video cameras and similar items, which they should return when you leave. If you are charged, be careful to get a complete receipt, so that you get your refund.
- **Prohibited items** are pornography, sharp weapons, and drugs (the death penalty is *mandatory* for even small quantities of heroin, opium or cannabis!)
- **Animals** must have a clean bill of health from their country of origin. At the point of entry, the *Director General of Veterinary Services* can give permission to import animals.
- The import and export of **currency** is unrestricted. Address of Customs:
 Royal Malaysian Customs & Excise
 Blok 11, Kompleks Kerajaan
 Jalan Duta
 50596 Kuala Lumpur
 Tel. 03-2546088.

Money

What to Bring

Travelers' checks are widely accepted by banks, including Maybank (Malayan Banking Berhad), Kwong Yik, OCBC, and UBMC, among others. The best place to exchange them is either at a foreign bank like *Amex (American Express)* or a large local bank. In the Amex offices in Penang, Kuala Lumpur and Singapore, you can also buy new checks, either with cash or with your credit card (Amex, of course.) Banks give a slightly better rate for travelers' checks than cash, but the reverse is true for money changers, if they take travelers' checks at all. In out-of-the-way places, it can take a while to change travelers' checks, sometimes up to 30 minutes. In tourist centers, it is much faster.

Eurochecks are not widely accepted. Only European banks and a few money changers on Lebuh Pitt in Penang will change them for you including the *European Asian Bank*, Yee Seng Building, 15 Jalan. Raja Chulan, Kuala Lumpur.

Credit cards, including Visa, American Express, and others are worth taking. They are widely accepted in tourist areas. You can also use them for the purchase of plane tickets. If you run out of money, the quickest way to get more is to get a cash advance on your card.

Cash, preferably U.S. dollars, is accepted everywhere, and usually the moneychangers give the best rates. Nonetheless, for security reasons, travelers' checks are recommended.

Malaysian Currency

Officially the Malaysian Dollar is known as the *ringgit* and is made up of 100 *sen*. The Chinese call dollars *man,* and there are other names as

well. Often people say dollars and *sen*. In practice dollars and *ringgit* are interchangeable.

●The **coins** come in denominations of 1, 5, 10, 20, 50 *sen* and M$ 1.

●**Bills** come in denominations of M$ 1, 5, 10, 20, 50, 100, 500 and 1000. If you pay with bills of M$ 50 or more, shop owners may well check to see if they are genuine.

Money Transfers

If you are going to be in Malaysia for a long time, find a bank in your home country that has a branch in Malaysia or Singapore, or at least one that can send your money there. Then you will have to arrange for the bank to send you money or, better still, have a friend or relative send you money. If you are receiving money at a local bank, you might have to open an **external account** to get money. Send the telex number of the bank in Malaysia to your bank at home and money transfers will be easy.

Rate of Exchange

The *ringgit* is stable and there is no black market. The **inflation rate** is almost negligible at 1.5-2%.

The Malaysian Dollar is tied to the U.S. Dollar. So if the U.S. dollar is strong, the *ringgit* will be as well.

Sample exchange rates from April 1991:

1	US $	M$ 2.74
1	Australian $	2.07
1	British	5.06
1	Singapore $	1.58
1	Brunei $	1.44
1	German Mark	1.73
1	Swiss Franc	1.99
1	Dutch Guilder	1.54
1	Canadian $	2.36
1	Danish Kr	0.45
1	Swedish Kr	0.47
1	Norwegian Kr	0.44
1	New Zealand $	1.62
1	Indian Rp	0.14
100	Japanese Yen	1.99
100	Hong Kong $	34.99
100	Indonesian Rupiah	0.14
100	Thai Baht	10.64
100	Philippine Pesos	9.83
100	Austrian Schillings	24.55

Costs

If you stay in the cheapest places, **rooms** will cost between M$ 10-15 a night for two.

Food can be quite cheap if you eat at food stalls and in cheap restaurants. Plan on between M$ 2-5 a meal, per person. Depending on how much and how often you eat, you can spend US $ 3-7 a day on food.

Transportation is also inexpensive. Traveling the entire length of the Malay Peninsula by bus only costs around US $ 20.

A good minimum guideline for budget travel in Malaysia is US $ 15 / day. However that can vary, depending on where you are and what you are doing. If you are just sitting around on the beach and staying at a rudimentary bungalow, you might only spend half that. If you are traveling around the region, Singapore is more expensive than Malaysia, though Thailand is somewhat cheaper and Indonesia is cheaper still.

Prices in Sarawak and Sabah are a good deal more expensive. See the appropriate chapters.

Tipping is not necessary. Ordering a plate of fruit is regarded as a tip. You can also leave a portion of the change. There is no need to tip at food stalls or food centers.

Health

There are lots of doctors and pharmacies of all types in Malaysia. The Chinese are well-known for their medical skills, and Western medical care is also widely available.

For many, the **Chinese pharmacy** is the first line of relief. If you are not feeling too well , stop by one of these and consult the pharmacist. Even if you do not opt for treatment, it is interesting to see all the herbs and preserved plants they have on hand.

Western medicine is available at pharmacies in every town. You do not need prescriptions. If you go to a doctor, you can buy the necessary medicine there, the consultation fee is between M$ 10-20.

Dentists are also very cheap. A visit to a private clinic will not set you back more than M$ 25. A dentist or a doctor in a public hospital will be even cheaper, only a few dollars, everything included. All doctors must work for a time in a public hospital. If you have time, false teeth are far cheaper in Malaysia than in the West.

Good deals are to be found in **glasses** and **contact lenses**. American-made soft contact lenses cost around US $ 70 and glasses are even cheaper. Look for American, Japanese or European brands for the highest quality.

Security

"Beware of Pickpockets" is a warning sign that greets you at almost every bus station. While crime is not overwhelming, it is wise to keep a watchful eye on your wallet, especially in crowded places. Though I've never had a bad experience, my wife, loaded down with shopping bags, had her purse snatched by a motorcyclist.

Houses and apartments are broken into all the time. In upperclass districts, you will see gates, guards, dogs, and alarms, and even then, there are robberies. Everywhere you go, doors are protected by gates and windows by gratings. Most people try never to leave their homes unattended.

Despite this, tourists have little to fear in Malaysia, certainly less than in Thailand and Indonesia. So just be careful about your money and valuables.

There is the reality of **organized crime** in Malaysia, mostly in the form of Chinese *triads*, or secret societies. Though not much is known about them, they engage in various mafia-like activities like gambling, prostitution, protection, drugs, etc. They do not concern themselves with tourists at all.

There is some **overcharging**, but not nearly as much as in some parts of Indonesia. Naturally, people might be inclined to make a few extra *sen* from a *kwailo* or *orang putih*, but there is a reasonable limit. Always ask for prices before you buy if nothing is listed in stores or restaurants. Even if there is a fixed price, you may be able to bargain. Be careful of taxi drivers in Kuala Lumpur who want to avoid using the meter, because often they will offer you an inflated "special price." Always insist on the meter. Of course, if they do use the meter, they can always take you for a long detour. But they won't dare if you act as if you know your way around.

Power / Measurements

Power: The voltage in Malaysia is 220 volts and uses a three-pronged plug. If you are from the U.S. or Canada, you will need a converter and a plug converter. If you are from Europe, all you will need is a plug converter, available in Malaysia.

Measurements: Though the metric system is the official system of measurements, many people prefer to use the Imperial system.

Metric conversion, see appendix.

Government Offices

Opening Hours

Offices:
Monday-Thursday:
8:00-12:45 and 14:00-16:15
Friday:
8:00-12:15 and 14:45-16:15
Saturday:
8:00-12:45.
●In *Kedah, Perlis, Kelantan, Terengganu* and *Johor*, the weekend is Thursday and Friday, so the times are different:
Thursday:
8:00-12:45
Friday:
closed
Saturday-Wednesday:
8:00-12:45 and 14:00-16:15.

Banks:
Monday-Friday:
10:00-15:00
Saturday:
9:30-11:30.
●In *Kedah, Perlis, Kelantan, Terengganu* and *Johor*:
Saturday-Wednesday:
10:00-15:00
Thursday:
9:30-11:30.

There are over 40 banks with some 600 branches.

- **Area Codes:**
  - 02 = Singapore
  - 03 = Kuala Lumpur / Selangor
  - 04 = Kedah, Perlis, Penang
  - 05 = Perak
  - 06 = Negeri Sembilan, Malacca
  - 07 = Johor
  - 08 = Sabah / Sarawak
  - 09 = Pahang, Terengganu, Kelantan

- **Overseas Calls**

*Every big city has a telecommunications office or STM (*Syarikat Telecom Malaysia *or* Kedai Telecom*), open 24 hours.* You can make international calls, either operator-assisted or direct-dial, collect, person-to-person or station-to-station. You can also send telexes and telegrams from here. Only cash is accepted as payment. There are instructions in the offices on how to dial. Rates are significantly cheaper at night and during off-hours. Singapore is a domestic call.

Businesses:
There are no official hours. They usually open around 9:00 and close around 18:00 or 19:00.
- Small businesses close around 17:00.
- Shopping centers and supermarkets are usually open from 10:00-22:00.

Post Offices:
Monday-Saturday:
9:00-17:00.

Postal Rates

- **Domestic:**

Postcards:	15 *sen*
Letters (to 20 g):	20 *sen*

- **Foreign:**

SE Asia:	20 / 40 *sen*
Asia:	25 / 50 *sen*
Pacific, Mid-East, Europe:	40 / 80 *sen*
Africa / America:	55 *sen* / M$ 1.10
Aerograms:	40 *sen*

- **Telegrams / Telex / Fax:**
  These can be handled at some large post offices and hotels.
- **Telephone**
  One local three-minute call costs 10 *sen*. Press the square metal button to speak.

There are only five **telephone books** for Malaysia: North, Central, South, East, Sabah & Sarawak and the phone books do not sort out names by city. Government offices, ministries, hospitals, etc., are listed at the front. Businesses are listed in the yellow pages at the back of the book.

Media

Newspapers

THE STAR was a paper of national note financed by the *Malaysian Chinese Association*. In 1987 it was closed down and 106 writers and editors were arrested by the government under the International Security Act. It has recently reopened, but it has had to practice an extremely rigorous form of self-censorship.

The other English papers are all quite boring and financed by the old UMNO, the ruling party. There is THE NEW STRAITS TIMES, the standard national paper, and the sensationalist tabloid, THE MALAY

MAIL. There is also a financial paper out of Penang, the KONSUMER UTUSAN, which keeps itself out of politics.

English political and critical news monthlies are THE ROCKET, published by the opposition, and ALIRAN.

Radio

There are four state-run stations, with some broadcasts in English. In Kuala Lumpur, there is a local English station.

Television

There are three channels that offer various programs in Malay, Cantonese, Mandarin, Tamil and English. RTM 1 and 2 are state-run and TV3 is private. There is daily news in English at 18:00 on TV3 and 21:30 on RTM 2.

Movies

The popularity of films in Malaysia is due in part to the privacy dark movie theaters provide in a very non-private society.

International films are usually shown in English with Malay subtitles. There are also locally-made and Indonesian films. Prices are around M$ 3-4.

There are also many *video* rental shops. The cost for a few days is around M$ 2. They usually cater to one ethnic group and have movies in that language, though many of them have English movies as well.

Nightlife

Clubs and Discos

Discos are found in virtually every city. Do not go to a disco expecting to meet people; Malaysians usually go in groups or in pairs. They are not pick-up bars.

Night clubs usually refer to hostess bars, where men go to drink, chat and dance with the women who work there. They are not cheap.

Accommodation

There is accommodation for every taste and in every price range in Peninsular Malaysia. Anywhere travelers go, there are *guest houses*. Every single town seems to have at least one. There are even more **Chinese hotels**, *rumah tumpangan* in Malay. Every big city has luxury hotels. There are also cheap **bungalows** along the beaches and even some opportunities to stay as a paying guest in a Malaysian household.

Guest Houses are often just collections of simple apartments, including perhaps a dormitory and some double rooms with a shared bathroom. The atmosphere is, to say the least, very informal. Most have cupboards to lock bags and valuables away in. Beds usually cost about M$ 5-6.

Bungalows, found primarily on the east coast, often refer to very simple wooden huts with a mattress on the

floor. The cheaper bungalows do not have running water or bathrooms. They cost between M$ 10-20 per room. Better bungalows with a bathroom included go for around M$ 30 per night.

There are even **cheaper places to stay**, like Khoo's Minicamp on *Pangkor Island*, which attracts many local students on the weekends. They cost around M$ 4 for nothing more than a fragile hut with a mattress.

Always take mosquito coils with you if you are planning on staying somewhere cheap. Mosquito nets are an alternative, but you cannot always count on them being there when you need them.

Be prepared for a standard of cleanliness in some accommodation that is not the same as that in the West. Though places may not always be spotless, they should not be filthy, and if they are, go elsewhere.

Most cheap accommodation comes with Asian-style squat toilets (squat, don't sit – you'll figure it out) and *mandis*, or traditional spoon-showers. To take a shower, you scoop water out of the big container with the ladle provided. Be careful not to get soap, or anything else in the container, as everyone must use it. Also be sure to carry your own toilet paper with you wherever you go.

For M$ 20-30, you can find a double room with a shower and toilet in the room. This is about the price of a room in an inexpensive *hotel*. For M$ 30-40, you are already talking about a degree of luxury in a mid-priced hotel. Prices in Kuala Lumpur are higher. It costs at least M$ 50 for a room in a good location with a Western bathroom, TV, etc.

You can also stay at a *government resthouse*. These were once operated by the colonial administration to house officials and dignitaries on arduous trips through the wilderness. Today, they are operated by the government for government employees. When they are not full (usually anytime but a holiday), they also welcome tourists. The quality varies. Some, like the one in *Kuala Lipis* are very good while others, like in *Merapoh*, are comparable with simple mountain huts. The tourist information center in Kuala Lumpur has a list of the 16 resthouses. Prices vary between M$ 20 and 50.

The Malaysian Youth Hostel Association operates 11 *youth hostels*. There are two each in *Kuala Lumpur* and the *Cameron Highlands* and one in *Penang*, *Pangkor Island*, *Fraser's Hill*, *Port Dickson*, *Kota Baru*, *Kuantan* and *Kota Kinabalu* (Sabah).

There are *many classes of better hotels*, particularly in Kuala Lumpur. Since the building boom has leveled off, prices have dropped a bit. Like Singapore, fancy hotels in Kuala Lumpur sometimes offer big discounts, which can be fine for a bit of luxury. For example. M$ 25++ (meaning plus tax and service, or around + 25%) per person, double

occupancy for a modern room with full services. Though it might seem expensive, the price comes to less than you pay for a cheap motel in the U.S.

Malaysia also has a few government-owned *prestige hotels* that are so expensive they attract only the very rich. It is said that only 20% of rooms are occupied at any one time. Often, they wind up in the hands of private owners who try to bring the prices down, while improving the service. These hotels include:

- *Mutiara* on Langkawi
- *Golden Sands* and *Rasa Sayang* on Batu Ferringhi on Penang
- *Pangkor Island Resort* / *Pan-Pacific*
- *Tanjung Jara* near Rantau Abang, Rantau Abang Visitors' Center
- *Merlin Samudra* on Tioman.

These hotels all have one thing in common: they are not worth the considerable expense. It is a shame, considering some of them are in beautiful locations. In addition, the staff often seem unconcerned with

The author in the Eastern & Oriental

providing the service you might expect for so much money.

The natural alternative for the luxury-conscious are the few hotels left over from the colonial era. The names themselves conjure up nostalgia: The *Strand* in Rangoon, the *Oriental* in Bangkok (now a huge modern complex), and *Raffles* in Singapore (now more of a tourist attraction than a true first-class hotel). In Malaysia, there is the *E&O* (*Eastern & Oriental*) in Penang and the *Station Hotel* in Ipoh and Kuala Lumpur. Time seems to have stood still for the past hundred years in these hotels.

Food

Where to Eat

Malaysia's three main ethnic groups have remained relatively independent. Though this has led to a series of racial and political problems, it has also led to one of the most varied and interesting national cuisines in the world. In almost every part of the Peninsula, you can choose between Chinese, Indian and Malay food.

Every city has its **hawker food**, which is cheap and often quite tasty. Though originally most hawkers operated portable food stands, there are now more and more food centers springing up. These centers bring a dozen or more hawkers together in one place.

Coffee shops (*kedai kopi*) are a good alternative to eating on the streets because they provide a roof over your head, an important consideration in rainy Malaysia. They are open rooms with tables and chairs where you order drinks from the owners and food from the hawkers that operate inside. In most locales, there will be some kind of Western food available.

Indian hawkers offer *chapatis* (flat bread made from wheat flour and water) with curry side-dishes. Some have *roti canai*, another kind of flat bread. It is fun watching them make the various breads.

Malay hawkers make great *satay*, or little skewers of cooked meat with a hot, sweet peanut sauce (*lembu* = beef, *kambing* = goat, *ayam* = chicken). *Ikan panggang* is also popular: fish, spiced and wrapped in a banana leaf and cooked over a coal fire.

Chinese food includes fried *kueytiaw* (other spellings might apply) and *Hokka mee* (both are noodle dishes, *kueytiaw* are wide, white noodles and *bihun / mihun* are thin noodles.) There is also duck and chicken rice, *dim sum* and many other fascinating foods.

If you want to **eat cheaply** you should have no problem in the food centers or *kedai kopi*.

Drinks are cheap, though beer is quite expensive, M$ 4-5 a bottle, while soft drinks are around 60 *sen*.

Meals do not have to cost more than M$ 5, or about US$ 2, including drinks. It is possible to get by for half that if you are on a really tight budget. If you are especially hungry, you can order a selection of different dishes from various hawkers in one area. **Restaurants** are more expensive, and four people can get a great meal for around US$ 15.

In Malaysia and Singapore, food is a constant topic of conversation and of dispute – everyone is always looking for the best food and local pride runs high. Ask around in Penang or Singapore – it's a good way to get to talk to the local people as well as to find some really good food. Many Chinese maintain that Ipoh has the best food in Malaysia. Penang is renowned for its hawker food and Kuala Lumpur is the only place with a complete selection of international food.

For those who cannot live without it, there is plenty of Western **fast-food** in Malaysia. Surprisingly, Kentucky Fried Chicken has quite a following. Perhaps this is due to chicken being a common food to all three ethnic groups in Malaysia.

Let me assure those afraid of dysentery or hepatitis that I have eaten street food all over Southeast Asia, including salad, raw vegetables and shaved ice, and have never

been sick. Just eat food that looks fresh and well-cooked, and you won't do any better or worse than in fine restaurants.

How to Eat

Most Malaysians eat with a spoon in their right hand, helped by a fork in their left. Malays and Indians often eat with their right hands (but never with their unclean left!) Watch their perfect technique. The Chinese often eat with chopsticks, made of either wood or plastic, and a spoon, which is normally made of plastic.

What to Eat

Malay Food is delightfully varied, and also heavily spiced. Fresh ingredients include chili peppers, garlic, onions, ginger, lemon grass, lemon leaves, coriander, tamarind and most importantly, coconut milk (pressed coconut pulp or *santan*.) Shrimp paste (*belacan*) and chili paste (*sambal*) are frequently used in cooking.

In Malay restaurants, or even at bus stops, food is laid out so you can see everything before you decide. There is usually chicken, beef, shrimp, fish and vegetables. These are eaten with white rice (*nasi puteh*). You can also order fried rice or noodles (*nasi goreng / mee goreng*) just about anywhere.

These are rice or noodles, stir-fried with chili peppers, vegetables, beef, spices, and other ingredients. It tastes a bit different everywhere you go. **Malay specialties** include:

- *Kari Ikan* – fish curry with coconut milk.
- *Gulai Kepala Ikan* – fish head curry.
- *Ikan / Udang / Sotong Goreng* – grilled fish / shrimps / squid.
- *Pagedel Daging* – beef meatballs.
- *Daging Rendang* – ground beef cooked in coconut milk.
- *Ayam masak / Goreng* – steamed / roasted chicken.
- *Telur Bungkus* – stuffed omelette.
- *Masak Lemak Nangka* – young jackfruit in coconut milk.
- *Sayur Campur* – mixed vegetables.
- *Pasembur Rojak* – salad and tofu with a spicy sauce.
- *Sup Sayur* – vegetable soup.

In the morning, Malays like to eat *Nasi Lemak* (fatty rice). This sounds less appetizing than it actually is. A better description would be rice cooked in coconut milk with side dishes like pickles, peanuts, *Ikan Bilis* (little dried fish), eggs, etc. Often it is served in a banana leaf.

If you like sweet things try the desserts (*kueh-mueh*). Many are prepared with coconut milk. If you are here in the fasting month (*puasa*), you will see a wide variety of desserts in the evening, though they are available all year. They come in a variety of outrageous colors, but are not as sweet as they look.

A desert popular all over Southeast Asia is ABC, or *Ais Batu Campur*, also called *Ais Kacang*. It comprises of shaved ice in a bowl, with coconut milk, rice, beans, *Agar* (a distant relative of gumdrops) and other things. Just pick out what you want from the jars on display. One portion costs 60 *sen* or so (minimum 80 *sen* in Kuala Lumpur). *Cendol* is a variation on this: shaved ice with *Gula Melaka* (brown palm sugar).

Nyonya food is a variant of Malay food. The first Chinese to arrive in Malaysia in the 16th century mixed freely with the Malays. The result was a mixed culture known as *Peranakan Chinese* or *Baba Nyonya*.

The food is a more refined version of Malay with Chinese overtones. *Ikan Panggang* and *Laksa* are both Nyonya dishes (a famous one is *Penang Laksa*, a delicious soup made from fish paste, fresh vegetables, coriander, noodles, and other spices). The Nyonya especially love *kueh*. (Note: In Indonesia, *Nyonya* is a polite way to address a married woman, but it is not used here; *Puan* is the proper word.)

Favorite drinks include *Air Limau* (lemon water) and *Air Bandung* (rose water).

Chinese Food: Generalizing about Chinese food is a bit like generalizing about European food. Though most people have eaten Chinese food in their home countries, it is often quite unlike the "real thing" in Malaysia and elsewhere. One of the best aspects of Chinese food is its variety. People prefer to eat in large groups so they can sample as many dishes as possible. As a rule of thumb, one dish per person is about right. A well-laid table will include fish, meat, fowl and vegetable dishes.

Most Malaysian Chinese come from Guangdong (Canton) province, though most of Penang's population is from Hokkien. Other immigrants came from southern Chinese provinces neighboring Guangdong: Swatow (Chiu Chow), Haklo, Fukien, and Hainan. To varying degrees they have all influenced the cuisine.

Though Chinese food is prepared to please the eye as well as the mouth, Chinese people do not care much about the decor of restaurants. Many Chinese restaurants in Malaysia look like canteens, but the ambience has no bearing on the food.

Ingredients are incredibly varied and should be fresh. Staples include herbs, spices, soy sauce, oyster sauce, vinegar, mustard, sesame oil, ginger, garlic, shallots, dried mushrooms, and vegetables.

The four main regional cuisines are the following:

Peking: Heavily spiced with lots of paprika, garlic, ginger, leeks and coriander. Noodles, pancakes and breads often replace rice. A northern cuisine made to warm the body. Peking Duck is the most familiar offering.

Shanghai: Stronger tasting, sweeter and oilier than Peking or Cantonese food. A lot is done with vegetables and preserved meats. More noodles than rice.

Szechuan: Very spicy and tasty. Simmering and smoking are the two most popular ways to prepare food. Smoked duck is a very good, representative dish.

Cantonese: This is the most well-known form of Chinese food. Chinese restaurants in the West specialize in Cantonese food. It is also very popular within China. The ingredients are usually fresh, and spices and oil are kept to a minimum. Famous dishes include shark's fin soup, sweet and sour pork, roast pigeon, fried crab claws, scrambled eggs with crabmeat, and red bean soup.

A Cantonese specialty is *dim sum*, usually served as brunch. There is no menu, just sit down and little dishes of food are brought around on carts. Just point to the ones you want. Steamed and fried foods, particularly dumplings, are popular.

Indian Food: The word 'curry' is inseparable from the idea of Indian food. Curry is a catch phrase for any combination of spices used to prepare a sauce for vegetables, fish, chicken, lamb and other meats. In Malaysia, there is a lot of vegetarian Tamil food from the south of India. This is traditionally eaten with the right hand off a banana leaf.

●In the morning, many people eat *thosays* (omelettes) or *roti canai* with curries.

●*Fish head curry* is very good and one portion is usually enough for 3-4 people.

●*Murtabak*, is a pan-cooked bread stuffed with egg, onions and vegetables. A favorite for breakfast or a light snack.

●Those wanting something milder should try *roti canai pisang*, filled with bananas. While the roti is cooking, some bananas are cut up and thrown on top. The roti is then folded. The bananas are a soft filling by the time the roti is cooked. This dish was invented for travelers, you can find it on the east coast and also in the Cameron Highlands.

Drinks: All restaurants serve water free of charge. Chinese restaurants always have warm jasmine or another kind of tea, usually for a small fee.

The favorite drink of Chinese men is cognac (brandy), and Malaysia is one of the principal importers of the stuff. Despite this, it is still very expensive, though there is always a lot at weddings and other festivities.

●Indian plantation workers drink *toddy*, a light coconut beer as well as *samsu*. Samsu is the general term for alcoholic beverages, but also refers to a cheap whiskey, similar to Mekhong in Thailand. *Toddy* mixed with stout is quite good.

●Malays are not supposed to drink alcohol. Instead, they drink fruit juices, soft drinks, rose water or just ice water. *Kopi* and *teh* are coffee and tea with sweetened condensed milk.

●*Kopi / teh ais* are the same, but served iced.

●*Kopi / teh oh* are without anything and ●*kopi / teh oh manis* are with sugar, but without milk.

● Milo and Ovaltine are chocolate drinks available everywhere, served hot or cold.

● Food stands usually have iced drinks available in plastic bags to carry away for around 60 *sen*.

●Do not miss *air tebu* (sugar cane juice, not too sweet) and *kelapa muda* (young coconut juice).

Malaysian Tropical Fruit

While we consider tropical fruits a great luxury, the Malaysians think the same of fruits from more temperate climes like apples, pears, strawberries, nectarines, grapes and oranges.

Here is a partial list of the tropical fruits available in Malaysia:

Banana: There are around 40 varieties, but they are not grown for export. Varieties eaten raw include *pisang* (Malay for banana) *mas, pisang embun*, and *pisang rastali*. Some, like the *pisang abu, pisang awak* and *pisang tanduk* must be cooked first.

Cempedak: Similar to the giant jackfruit. It can grow 20 to 50 cm long and 10 to 15 cm wide. Eat it raw or cooked. The trees grow up to 20 m high and take five years to bear "fruit.

Ciku: An egg-like fruit, which can be anything from brown to pink, depending on how ripe it is. The flesh is soft, white and sweet.

Durian: Durians stink! Literally. This king of fruits, widely praised throughout Southeast Asia, has a soft, sweet, custard-like flesh. This flesh lets off a pungent odor similar to rotting eggs. You will see signs everywhere (hotels, stations, etc.) prohibiting "strong-smelling fruits" (you will understand this once you smell one). Durian is a jungle fruit that grows on high trees. When ripe, they fall to the ground and should be eaten within 24 hours. They are in season from November to February and from June to August. Durians are not cheap: for a whole fruit, people will pay up to US$ 30 or so. Fortunately smaller pieces are available for around M$ 1.50.

Guava: The guava has an irregular green skin and a soft white inside. It contains 2 to 5 times as much vitamin C as an orange, though it tastes more like an apple. They contain hard black seeds, though seedless varieties (*tampa biji*) are becoming popular. A good place to get them is Bidor on the Ipoh-Kuala Lumpur road.

Langsat / Duku: A small fruit with sweet-sour, juicy white flesh. It takes 15 years for trees to bear fruit.

Mandarin: A smaller version of a tangerine. Not as intense a flavor as those grown in more temperate climes.

Mango: There are all kinds of mangoes in Malaysia – big ones, little ones, sweet ones, sour ones. Some of the best-known are apple mangoes, *harumanis*, Indian papaya mangoes and coconut mangoes.

Mangosteen / Manggis: A round purple fruit, 5 to 7 cm in diameter with a wonder-

fully sweet, juicy white flesh. Be careful when you open them – the purple dye of the skin never comes out of clothes. Trees take 15 years to bear fruit. They have the same season as *durian*.

Muskat: If you want to try this fruit (not the dried nut), the best place to do so is Penang, where they are grown. They are on sale in plastic bags on the way up to the Kek Lok Si temple.

Nangka / Jackfruit: These grow up to 40 by 25-50 cm and grow year-round. The best months are June and December.

Papaya: These grow year-round and are rich in vitamins A and C. Though Malaysians eat them plain, I prefer the Philippine method of adding lemon juice and a bit of salt.

Passionfruit: They have a wonderfully sweet-sour juice.

Pineapple: There are three sorts eaten fresh, and one (Singapore Spanish) used mainly in preserves.
Sarawak is a big source of pineapples.

Pomelo: The largest of the citrus fruits. Its pink flesh under a thick yellow skin is reminiscent of a grapefruit, but is milder and drier. The pomelos (*bali limau*) from Tambun near Ipoh are the best-known. They cost around M$ 2-3 each.

Rambutan: A hairy cousin of the lychee. Best eaten between June and September.

Sourswop: Often served as a dessert or made into preserves.

Starfruit / Belimbing: About the size of, and vaguely reminiscent of a yellow pepper. When sliced down the middle, it looks like a star. It tastes a little like an apple and is available all year.

Cashew Nuts: Though not a fruit, they are worth mentioning. They grow in Kelantan, Terengganu and Pahang. Though they are quite cheap by our standards, they are still a lot more expensive than in Thailand, and many Malaysians prefer to go there to buy them.

Watermelon: Can be eaten 100 days after seeding and is always refreshing. The seeds are often chewed.

Shopping

There are some opportunities to buy gifts in Malaysia, though the shopping is not as rich as in Thailand or Indonesia.

Kelantan is known as the center of handiwork in Malaysia. You can buy **silverwork, Batik, brocade**, and **kites** (*Wau*, up to 2.50 m across), **tops** (*Gasing*), **Wayang Kulit** figures, and **Kris**. A good place for a complete selection is on the road from *Kota Baru* to the "Beach of Passionate Love" (*Pantai Cinta Berahi*).

Tin products are typical souvenirs, including figures and tin-plated or golden orchids.

Batik is widely available, in characteristic Malaysian style. The selection is not as large as in Indonesia, but many prefer the bold, rustic colors of Kelantan-style batik.

On the east coast there are lots of **bamboo** and **rattan** products available. East coast **Keropok / Krupuk** (shrimp toast) or dried fish might make a good present for someone who likes food.

Orang Asli carvings are interesting, too. Look in the government
resthouse in *Jerantut* on the way to
Taman Negara for abstracted spirit
figures by *Jah Hut*. There are very
good ones for around M$ 30. The
Mah Meri Orang Asli who live on
Carey Island (near *Port Klang* in
Selangor), are known for their wood
carvings. If you are interested, you
can go and see them work; they
have established a mini-industry.
The *Orang Asli Department* sells the
finished carvings at the Orang Asli
Museum and the Hospital in
Gombak near *Mimaland*, outside
Kuala Lumpur. You can find more
expensive carvings for sale in the
Central Market of Kuala Lumpur or
in *Kuala Tembeling*.

Another native souvenir is a ***blow
gun***, available all over the *Cameron
Highlands*. They even have collaps-
ible ones you can fit in your luggage.
With a quiver and arrows, they cost
around M$ 12-15.

There are other souvenirs – just
look around and see what is available including Chinese and Indian
temple figures and other religious
objects. There are some good
antiques available in Malacca, but if
you want authenticity, don't look for
bargains.

There are also ***government-run
souvenir stores***, such as *Karyaneka*, near the *Bukit Bintang* shopping
district in Kuala Lumpur. Some
streets, like the road to the Kek Lok
Si Temple in Penang, sell nothing
but souvenirs.

You might also want to pick up
some ***cassette tapes***. Some stores
in Kuala Lumpur and Penang will
make custom tapes with songs you
select. They cost between M$ 6-12,
depending on your choices, but
cassettes are even cheaper in
Thailand and Indonesia if you are
going there next.

There is good modern handiwork
like ***batik*** and ***hand-painted t-shirts***
in the Central Market in Kuala
Lumpur.

Public Transportation

Malaysia probably has the best transportation network in Southeast Asia. So getting around Peninsular Malaysia poses no great problems.

Airplanes

Domestic flights are conducted by MAS, short for *Malaysian Airline System*. Destinations on the peninsula are *Langkawi, Alor Setar, Penang, Ipoh, Kota Baru, Kuala Terengganu, Kerteh, Kuantan, Tioman, Johor Baru, Singapore, Malacca* and of course, *Kuala Lumpur*.

There are discounts for some night flights (e.g. *Kuala Lumpur - Penang- Alor Setar - Kota Baru*) as well as special rates for families, students, the handicapped and the elderly. There are also standby and group fares for 3 or more people.

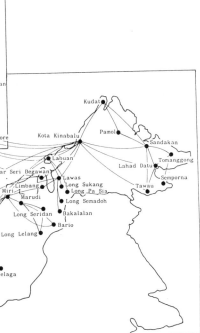

MAS Domestic Routes

Short domestic flights are flown on Fokker Friend-ships and Boeing 737's. Flights to Tioman are on De Haviland Twin Otters.

International Flights that stop in Penang are sometimes on Airbus A 300's, Boeing 737's or DC 10's.

Trains

The good old Malaysian railway, the **Keretapi Tanah Melayu** (KTM) is something of a colonial relic. It is still mostly manned by Indians. The big mosque-like station in Kuala Lumpur and the station palace in Ipoh, with its colonial hotel, are living memories of days gone by. The KTM is modernizing, but very slowly, though a computer ticketing system has just recently been introduced.

You can reserve **sleepers** up to one month beforehand (2nd class without air-conditioning, 1st class with air-conditioning). Often, they are fully booked as soon as they are available, especially on weekends, so get your tickets early.

Trains do not always run on time, so do not plan any close connections, especially flights, at your destination. It is better to go a day earlier to be on the safe side.

In general, trains are more expensive (unless you go 3rd class), and slower than buses, but they are more comfortable. They also offer a good way to see the countryside.

Since 1989, there have been additional rail buses (*Rel Bas*) between Butterworth, Ipoh, Kuala Lumpur and Port Klang.

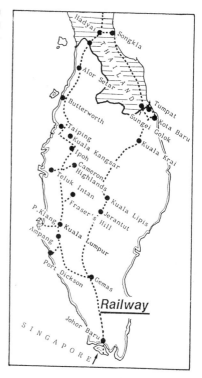

Railway

General information on **train** schedules is as follows:

Butterworth-Bangkok (via Bukit Mertajam, Alor Setar, Padang Besar, Haad Yai). The train departs Butterworth at 13.35 and arrives in Bangkok at 8:30 the next morning. Return: The train leaves Bangkok at 15:15 and gets to Butterworth at 12:10 (reserve tickets in Bangkok).

Butterworth-Kuala Lumpur (via Bt. Mertajam, Taiping, Kuala Kangsar, Ipoh, Batu Gajah, Kampar, Tapah Rd., Tanjung Malim). Trains run all day and the trip takes about 6 hours, or 8-9 hours at night.

Kuala Lumpur - Singapore (via Kajang, Seremban, Tampin, Gemas, Segamat, Kluang, Kulai, Johor Baru). The trip takes 7-9 hours.

Gemas - Tumpat (via Mentakab, Kuala Krau, Jerantut, Mela, Kuala Lipis, Gua Musang, Krai, Pasir Mas, Wakaf Baru). The trip takes around 13 hours. In Gemas there are connections to Kuala Lumpur and Singapore.

The train line from *Gemas* to *Tumpat* is still sometimes called the "Jungle Railway," though that is no longer the case. There was formerly no road along the tracks, and the train cut straight through the jungle, but it is being logged more and more.

There is now a road connection, opened in 1987, connecting Kuala Lumpur and Kota Baru. Since the train has to go all the way south to *Gemas* to make this trip, the bus is about 7 hours faster.

A few Malay words *dealing with train travel:*

kereta api	locomotive
keretapi	railway
tren	train
tren-tren	trains
ke utara	northbound
ke selanta	southbound
keluar	exit
tandas	toilet
stesen	station
pejabat	office
ketua besar	station master
pejabat ketua besar stesen	
	station master's office

Buses and Long-Distance Taxis

A well developed **road network** exists in Peninsular Malaysia. There are 27,000 km of roads, 80% of them paved. The north-south highway is mostly finished, but will not be entirely complete until 1992.

All over Malaysia, there are **long-distance taxis** going from one city to another. They often follow the same routes as buses, and cost slightly more, but are generally faster. They usually wait until they have four passengers, and then leave, rather than go at set times. At night, or when there is little traffic, these taxis might travel with fewer than four passengers, but will cost more.

Most overland travel in Malaysia is done by bus. There is a very good network of **express buses** that make long, non-stop trips. They connect virtually every major city on the Peninsula, as well as Singapore, and destinations in Thailand (usually Haad Yai.)

There are also **local buses** that make shorter trips, usually under two hours. Using these, you can go anywhere in Malaysia, with time and patience.

There are both **private and government bus companies**. The best one is *Ekpres Nasional*, whose buses leave from the *Puduraya Bus Station* in Kuala Lumpur. There might be several bus lines operating the same route. In bus stations you will find touts (or rather, they will find you) directing people to the proper ticket offices for their destinations. The system works quite well. The touts get a few pennies from the bus companies. The only drawbacks are that you could be overcharged, or that you might not be taken to the next bus to leave. Normally though, there are no big ripoffs. If you have time, you can go to all the different offices by yourself and check out times and prices. Some buses have reserved seats, and some do not. Statistically, the safest seats are on the driver's side in the middle of the bus.

On **local buses** be sure to get a ticket from the conductor as soon as

you get on. Usually, he or she will come to you, but if the bus is crowded, you might not be noticed. Tickets are important if an inspector gets on the bus to check everyone's tickets. Actually he's most likely checking on the conductor, not you.

Rental Cars

All of the international chains, like *Avis* and *Hertz*, have many offices in Malaysia. So it is possible to return a rented car to a city other than the one you rented it in. It is usually cheaper, however, to rent from a local company. These usually require that you bring the car back to where you started. If you are in a large group, renting a car can be a good alternative to public transportation because it gives you a lot more freedom. Normal costs are around M$ 125 a day for a sedan or M$ 300 for a luxury model, with unlimited mileage.

While driving in Malaysia is not as crazy as in other Asian countries, it can still be a bit unnerving, especially on long stretches of highway. Oncoming buses appear to want to force you off the road. Motorcycles seem to pop out of nowhere, often on the wrong side of the road. Also remember that most bicycles do not have lights and are practically invisible after dark. Drive carefully!

Unlike Thailand, **seat belts** and **motorcycle helmets** are mandatory in Malaysia. There are frequent

Distances in Peninsular Malaysia (km)

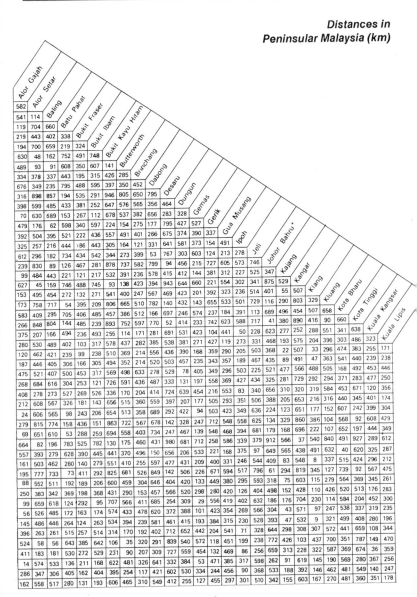

By booking a car at a travel agency before you get to Malaysia, you can save as much as 40%.

police checkpoints along the road. If you don't comply, you can be fined from M$ 50-200, and get up to six weeks in prison.

Gas is reasonably priced at 92 *sen* per liter. The government fixes all prices. Some gas stations are open all night, but not in rural areas.

Distances on road signs are stated in kilometers (miles are bracketed in red). The Malay word for mile is *batu*, abbreviated as *b*.

Many smaller roads have milestones along their sides. New blue signs with white writing are always in kilometers.

Police cars have blue lights and **ambulances** and **fire engines** use red lights. If a motorcade approaches, get to the left and wait until it passes. Here are a few more **Malaysian rules of the road:**

- If the car in front of you flashes its right blinker, it means, "Do not pass." If it flashes its left blinker, it means, "Pass carefully, at your own risk."
- If an oncoming car flashes its headlights, get out of the way!
- In the ubiquitous British traffic circles (roundabouts), the car in the circle (to the right), has the right-of-way.
- There are still some roads closed at night due to the *curfew laws*, particularly in the interior.

From \ To	Kuala Lumpur	Kuala Selangor	Kuala Terengganu	Kuantan	Lumut	Maran	Melaka	Mersing	Muar	Padang Besar	Pasir Puteh	Pelabuhan Klang	Pontian Kechil	Port Dickson	Sabak Bernam	Segamat	Seremban	Shah Alam	Sitiawan	Sungai Petani	Taiping	Tampin	Teluk Intan
Kuala Selangor	67																						
Kuala Terengganu	455	522																					
Kuantan	259	326	209																				
Lumut	288	272	586	510																			
Maran	183	250	272	76	434																		
Melaka	144	211	508	292	432	236																	
Mersing	353	420	401	191	641	253	255																
Muar	189	256	544	336	477	281	45	210															
Padang Besar	544	528	603	760	360	690	688	897	733														
Pasir Puteh	458	525	128	337	437	400	581	528	626	475													
Pelabuhan Klang	41	55	496	300	329	224	185	394	230	585	483												
Pontian Kechil	312	379	571	375	600	399	171	184	126	859	699	337											
Port Dickson	90	162	503	291	384	231	94	321	139	634	554	123	265										
Sabak Bernam	130	63	585	389	209	313	274	550	318	465	501	118	514	226									
Segamat	197	264	376	180	485	202	120	218	168	741	504	238	197	165	327								
Seremban	64	131	471	259	352	199	80	289	125	608	522	105	251	32	194	133							
Shah Alam	25	56	480	284	313	208	169	378	214	568	483	17	337	121	118	222	90						
Sitiawan	276	260	574	498	12	422	420	629	465	348	425	317	588	372	197	473	340	301					
Sungai Petani	404	388	463	626	218	550	548	757	593	140	335	780	716	494	325	601	468	429	206				
Taiping	291	275	481	513	104	437	435	644	480	265	353	332	603	387	212	488	355	316	92	125			
Tampin	112	179	461	254	400	198	38	294	83	656	543	154	209	80	242	85	48	137	388	516	403		
Teluk Intan	166	99	593	402	173	326	310	514	355	320	465	154	478	262	36	363	230	155	161	278	176	278	
Temerloh	133	200	322	126	384	50	186	305	231	640	450	174	357	181	263	156	149	158	372	500	387	148	276

Road Signs

Normally, all traffic signs are international, though there are a few exceptions, like the yellow rhombus with 9 red dots that means 'Caution'. Other signs are normally only in Malay. Here are a few:

Awas	Caution
Beri Laluan	Yield to Traffic
Berhenti	Stop
Kanak-Kanak Melintas	Children Crossing
Jalan Mati	Dead End
Jalan Sa-Hala	One Way
Ikut Kiri	Keep Left
Kawasan Kemalangan	Danger
Get Automatic	Automatic Gate
Kurangkan Laju	Reduce Speed
Jalan Pelahan-Pelahan	Go Slow
Pusat Bandar	City Center
Utara	North
Selatan	South
Timor	East
Barat	West

Hitchhiking

Though hitchhiking is possible here, it is not widespread.

Taxis

Though taxi meters are mandatory in some cities, many drivers prefer not to use theirs. In Kuala Lumpur, this is especially the case, and if you do not know where you are going, you might find yourself being taken on long detours. If you are unsure of your destination, ask around first and see what the price should be, then fix a price with a taxi driver.

The same is true in Penang, where there are a number of private cars acting as illegal taxis. These do not have meters and you'll have to bargain. Legal taxis are either yellow and black, or red and white with a taxi sign on top. Ipoh also has a law mandating taxi meters, but it is not always followed. Most other cities do not have metered taxis.

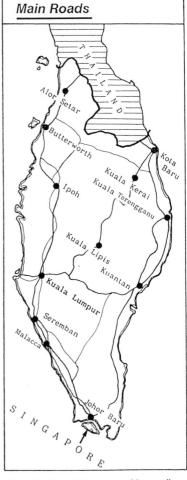

Main Roads

Many cities also have **collective taxis**, which go along certain routes, making only small detours at the request of the passengers. Along with 3-4 other passengers, I paid M$ 1.50 for a trip that would have cost me at least M$ 10 if I were alone.

Bicycle Rickshaws (Trishaws)

You will find these relics of another time in many cities (though not in Kuala Lumpur). Locals use them for short trips in the city. Tourists will pay more than for a taxi, but many like to try a trishaw at least once. The cost is around M$ 1 a km, but set a price beforehand. Quite often old rickshaw drivers are opium addicts, especially those in Penang.

City Buses

There are usually several bus companies operating in the same city. In Kuala Lumpur, there are an additional 400 **minibuses**. Unlike in Bangkok and Singapore, in Malaysia you cannot find a city map with all the bus routes written on it. You simply have to ask which buses go where. It is worth finding out, since buses are quite a bit cheaper than taxis, especially if you are alone.

Boats

Although there are some wide rivers, there is little river transportation in Peninsular Malaysia. The exceptions are the long-boats from *Tembe-*

ling to *Kuala Tahan* and within the national park of Taman Negara. Of course, East Malaysia has a vast river transportation network.

There are boats which travel to most of the offshore islands including *Langkawi, Penang, Pangkor, Tioman, Rawa, Kapas, Berhentian, Redang* and others.

There is also a boat connection between *Penang* and *Langkawi* and from *Port Klang* and *Singapore* to *Kuching, Kota Kinabalu* and back to *Kuantan*.

For information about ships to *Medan, Indonesia*, see the section on Penang. For information on ships to *Sabah* and *Sarawak*, refer to those sections.

Peninsular Malaysia: Land and People

The hustle and bustle of the town amazed me. It was a far cry from my kampung days.

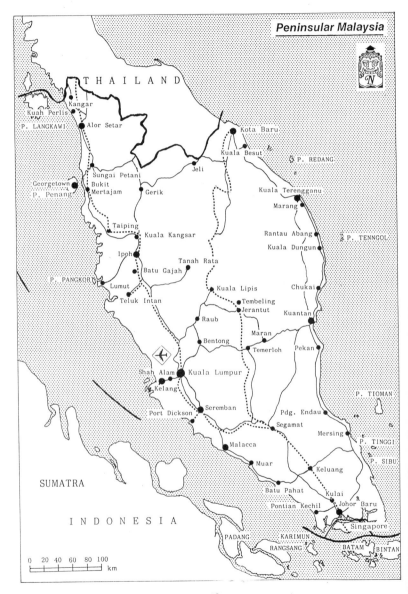

Peninsular Malaysia

THAILAND

Kuah Perlis
P. LANGKAWI
Kangar
Alor Setar

Kota Baru
Kuala Besut
P. REDANG

Georgetown
P. Penang
Sungai Petani
Bukit
Mertajam
Jeli
Gerik

Kuala Terengganu
Marang

Taiping
Kuala Kangsar

Rantau Abang
Kuala Dungun
P. TENNGOL

Ipoh
Batu Gajah
Tanah Rata

P. PANGKOR
Lumut
Teluk Intan

Kuala Lipis
Chukai

Tembeling
Jerantut
Kuantan

Raub
Maran

Bentong
Temerloh
Pekan

Shah Alam
Kuala Lumpur
Kelang

P. TIOMAN

Port Dickson
Seremban
Pdg. Endau
Segamat
Mersing
P. TINGGI

Malacca
P. SIBU

Muar
Keluang

SUMATRA

Batu Pahat
Kulai

Pontian Kechil
Johor Baru

INDONESIA
Singapore

PADANG
KARIMUN
RANGSANG
BATAM
BINTAN

0 20 40 60 80 100
km

Malaysia consists of two separate land masses, with a 640 to 750 km stretch of the South China Sea between them. Were it not for British colonial rule, the two would never have come together. Combined, the entire country has an area of 330,433 km^2, 40% of which consists of Peninsular Malaysia, known previously as Malaya. The remainder consists of *Sabah* and *Sarawak*, the northern and northwestern portions of the island of *Borneo* (the third largest island in the world).

The Gunung Tahan Range

Geography

Peninsular Malaysia covers the southern part of the Malay Peninsula, a 1500 km long, narrow strip of land that forms the southernmost part of the Asian mainland.

Peninsular Malaysia has an area of 131,587 km^2, and is about the size of Greece. It lies between 100 and 105 degrees east longitude and between 7 and 1 degrees north latitude, between the Equator and the Tropic of Cancer.

Peninsular Malaysia measures 740 km at its longest point and has a coastline of 1930 km. From the southernmost point, it is a little more than 100 km to the Equator.

To the north lies Thailand, to the east the South China Sea and to the south, the island of Singapore. The Straits of Malacca are found to the west and southwest.

Peninsular Malaysia and Indonesian Sumatra are at one point as close as 40 km – within visual range, weather permitting.

The Malay Peninsula has a 10 to 60 km wide plain along the west coast and a narrow strip of lowlands along the east coast. The interior is predominantly mountainous, consisting of old folded mountain ranges. They run in a north-south direction, approximately parallel to each other, but with different lengths.

The longest mountain range is the *Big Titiwangsa Range* (*Banjaran* or *Barisan Titiwangsa*), which begins in Thailand and runs all the way to Negeri Sembilan.

The highest point along this range is *Gunung Korbu* (2182 m). Not far from Ipoh, it

is the second highest peak on the Malay Peninsula. The *Cameron Highlands*, the *Genting Highlands* and *Fraser's Hill* are all part of the Titiwangsa range.

West of this range, in the northern part of the country, above Penang, lies the *Bintang Range* (*Banjaran Bintang*). It is named after *Gunung Bintang* the area's highest peak (1862 m). The drive south from Penang passes in between Taiping (Maxwell Hill) and Kuala Kangsar.

East of the main mountains, the *Gunung Tahan Range* (*Banjaran Gunung Tahan*) breaks through the wide central highlands. It is named after *Gunung Tahan*, the highest point on the peninsula with an altitude of 2187 m. The peak lies in the northwest corner of a 4350 km^2 national park (*Taman Negara*).

Above Raub is the short *Gunung Benom Range* (2108 m).

Parallel to the east coast runs the *Eastern Range* with its highest point at *Gunung Lawit* (1519 m).

The south is not mountainous, and is comprised mostly of *hills and swampland*. An example is the *Endau Rompin* National Park, south of Pekan, the residence of the Sultan of Pahang. Best seen from a plane, it is crisscrossed with wide meandering rivers that are constantly forming new estuaries with their mud. The south is not completely without mountains, however. *Gunung Ledang* in Johor (1276 m) is the first mountain on the way up from Singapore.

Something of a curiosity are the **karst formations**, that suddenly appear in the landscape. Particularly common around Ipoh, they recall the bizarre landscape of the Guilin Mountains in southern China. These cave-filled hills were once underwater limestone deposits. They can be found in the area near the border between Thailand and Malaysia, in *Taman Negara* and in the middle of the peninsula near Merapoh. Again and again, groups of these wooded hills keep popping up. They are quite remarkable in *Templer Park*, in *Bukit Takun*, and at the *Batu Caves* near Kuala Lumpur.

The mountains are, for the most part, still covered with **virgin forest**. The thick jungle that only a hundred years ago covered all of Malaysia is today limited to the areas of *Taman Negara* and *Endau Rompin*, and some smaller forest reserves. In its place, especially along the west coast, are large rubber and palm oil plantations.

Rice paddies are found in northern Malaysia, on the plains that form the border

areas with Thailand. In northwestern Kedah (the rice bowl of Malaysia), Perlis, and north and south of Butterworth. Recently the Malays have begun growing rice in Perak and Selangor. In the northeast, the low-lying land of North Kelantan is the only large rice-producing area.

To the west of the *Titiwangs. Range*, are two of the world's most important sources of **tin**. The first is the *Kinta Valley* (where Ipoh is located). The second, the densely populated *Klang River Valley* (Kuala Lumpur, Petaling Jaya, Shah Alam, Klang, Port Klang). When viewed from above, the effects of tin mining on the land are all too clear; naked earth stripped of its topsoil and numerous mining pools. Around Kuala Lumpur, some of these pools have been transformed into attractive parks and this beautification process is still going on. *Lake View Garden* in Taiping is a good example.

Those not flying over the landscape can get a good impression of the damage wrought by tin mining by climbing *Kledang Hill* (808 m) near Ipoh. The summit offers an excellent view of the Kinta Valley with Ipoh and the many lakes and ponds nearby. Its abundance has made tin Malaysia's most important mineral, but iron ore, bauxite, and gold are also mined.

Along the east coast, the plains are very narrow. With the notable exception of the northern part, the main crops are coconut palms and simple plants like tapioca.

Deep jungle and extensive mangrove swamps dominate the southeast, but new plantations keep springing up, for example, in the area between Kota Tinggi and Desaru. Because the east coast is unprotected from the northeast monsoon, it boasts a famous 500 km (not completely continuous) stretch of **sandy beach**. In contrast, mangrove forests run all the way to the ocean on the west coast, which is protected from the southwest monsoon by Sumatra.

Malaysia's largest **lakes** have been formed by dams: *Tasek Temengor* in upper Perak (Hulu Perak), the larger of the two

dammed lakes in Perak; and *Terengganu Lake*, formed by the *Kenyir Dam* and the convergence of several rivers. The largest lake south of the Pahang river is the *Tasek Berak / Tasek Dampar*.

The powerful *Sungai Pahang* or Pahang River (475 km including the source), is the longest **river** in Peninsular Malaysia. With the exception of Penang (*Pulau Pinang* = betelnut island) and the Federal Territory (*Wilayah Persekutuan*), the states of Malaysia take their names from rivers.

The fact that the largest rivers are so short is due to the width of the peninsula which is never greater than 300 km. With all the mud they carry along, the largest rivers tend to silt up at their mouths like at Kuala Terengganu.

For 130 million years, the climate and composition of the peninsula have not changed very much. Since there was no Ice Age to interrupt the growth of the lush vegetation, these Southeast Asian jungles –

what remains of them – are the oldest forests in the world. This is also the case in Sabah and Sarawak.

Malay geographical terms:

alor	channel of a river
ampang	dam
air	water, river, stream
anak air	brook
air mati	dead river
air terjun	waterfall
atap	roof
bajang	a spirit (with the body of a weasel)
batang	major river
batas	low bank separating rice paddies
bagan	landing field
bandar	port town
batu	mile, milestone
bendang	wet rice- field
beting	sand bank
bukit	hill (30 m to 500 m)
buluh	bamboo
bumbun	hide, blind (national park)
changkat	rocky elevation
darat	dry land
dusun	orchard
genting	mountain pass
gua / goa	cave
gurun	wasteland
hilir	lower waters of a river
hantu	spirit, demon
hutan	jungle, forest
istana	palace
jalan	street, road
jenut	salt lick *jeram* rapids
kali	river
kampung	village
kangkar	Chinese settlement (from Kang Chu)
kárang	coral reef
kelian	(tin) mine
khemah	camp
kota	fort, city
kramat	a place of miracles
kuala	estuary, river mouth
kubang	watering hole, mud bath
kubu	stockade
labuhan	anchorage
ladang	plantation, planting
langsuir	vampire

laut	sea
lembah	lowland, valley
lobok	deep pool
mata air	source, spring
muara	estuary, delta
mukim	Muslim parish
padang	field, village green
pantai	beach
parit	irrigation canal
pawang	magician
paya	swamp
pekan	market, town
pengkalan	jetty
permatang	bank between rice-fields
pulau	island
putera	prince (son)
puteri	princess (daughter)
rantau	straight coastline
rentis	jungle trail
rimba	jungle
rumah api	lighthouse
sawah	paddy field
seberang	opposite bank of a river
selat	strait
simpang	intersection
semenanjung	peninsula, peninsula Malaysia
sungei / sungai	river
tamu	guest
tanah	land, earth, ground
tanjung	cape, promontory
tasik	lake
tebing	bank of a river
teluk	bay
titi	bridge
ujung / hujung	cape, endpoint
ulu / hulu	upper waters of a river

Climate

A tropical climate promises heat and humidity. That is what to expect in Malaysia and that is how it is, but it is not as bad as one might imagine. An extremely hot summer day in New York can be hotter than it ever gets in Malaysia. In general, the temperature in this tropical country never rises above 35°C, while such temperatures are not uncommon in the United States and Australia. In Malaysia the **temperature** generally hovers between 30°C and 34°C every day, with the **humidity** usually hovering around 60%.

Staying in the tropics for any length of time, one gets accustomed to the temperature surprisingly fast. I would never have believed that temperatures of 21°C to 23°C (that is how "cold" it gets at night and before dawn) would seem refreshingly cool to me. The evening temperature in the *Cameron Highlands* and other hill stations goes down to a pleasant 13°C to 15°C, which after a long time in the tropics, seems downright cold. The English fireplaces found in many hotels seem well-suited indeed. My nights spent in longhouses in Bario in the Kelabit Highlands in Sarawak, at 1300 m, are the most miserably cold I can remember. Even with a warm-up suit and a tarp for a blanket, I was chilled to the bone. It was not much different in the hill station of *Taman Negara* on the way to *Gunung Tahan*. This *padang* two hours under the Tahan peak is presumed to be the coldest spot on the peninsula, excluding refrigerators. Though only 1500 m high, the temperature there is said to fall as low as 4°C. So if you find the lowlands too hot and oppressive, you can always go to the mountains to relearn quickly what it means to be cold.

The temperature does not vary much over the course of the year. When it does not rain for a few days, the air gets hot and muggy. With overcast skies or rain, the air feels cooler.

There are no seasons in Malaysia, but the year is not the same day in and day out.

When a particular fruit is in season, like durian or mango, it marks the beginning of a new season.

There are however, significant variations in the weather from one time of year to another. There are times when it rarely rains, and times when it rains every day. Rain in the tropics often falls during thunderstorms, which are known for the massive quantities of water they release in a short time. Streets become impassable and everyone must put up with long detours and delays.

The climate is affected by two monsoons. The **northeast monsoon** comes from the South China Sea and affects the east coast from November to April. It is at its strongest between December and February. The **southwest monsoon** affects the west coast, but only in a weakened form, thanks to the protection offered by Sumatra. The rain comes to the west coast during April and May and September and October.

This is actually just a side-effect of the southwest monsoon, which blows from May to October, as there is really no noteworthy increase in precipitation.

During January and February, there is very little **rain** in the **northwest of the Malay Peninsula.** The northeast monsoon does not reach this area. Penang, in particular, is dry for much of the year. In 1987, there was a six-week period when not a single drop fell and the grass there withered away. Strangely enough, Taiping is known for its daily downpour in the late afternoon at the same time of year. And Taiping is only 70 km away!

During the rains on the **west coast**, there are no really heavy downpours. It does rain every day, usually in the late afternoon, but it is rarely more than a short shower. Then it clears, and the air is fresher. Because of this, many find the rain in Malaysia to be comfortable. And there is another important difference between tropical rain and North

Climate: A Summary

		JAN	FEB	MAR	APR	MAY	JUNE	JULY	AUG	SEP	OCT	NOV	DEC
Kuala	max	31°	32°	33°	32°	32°	32°	32°	32°	31°	31°	31°	31°
Lumpur	min	21°	22°	22°	23°	23°	22°	22°	22°	22°	22°	22°	22°
	pcp	168	145	213	302	179	129	112	132	167	270	259	225
	sun	6	6	7	6	6	6	6	6	5	5	4	5
Penang	max	31°	32°	32°	31°	31°	31°	31°	31°	30°	30°	30°	31°
	min	23°	23°	23°	24°	24°	23°	23°	23°	23°	23°	23°	23°
	pcp	67	93	139	214	248	177	203	231	344	375	251	107
	sun	8	8	7	7	6	6	6	6	5	5	5	6
Kuala	max	28°	29°	30°	31°	32°	31°	31°	31°	30°	30°	28°	28°
Tereng-	min	22°	22°	22°	23°	23°	23°	23°	23°	22°	23°	22°	22°
ganu	pcp	174	99	109	101	103	108	110	141	184	266	643	559
	sun	6	7	8	8	6	6	6	6	6	5	4	4
Johor Baru	max	30°	31°	32°	32°	32°	31°	31°	31°	31°	31°	30°	30°
Singapur	min	21°	21°	21°	22°	22°	22°	22°	22°	22°	22°	22°	22°
	pcp	114	141	172	242	212	158	170	148	183	215	277	252
	sun	6	6	6	5	5	5	5	5	4	4	4	4
Cameron	max	21°	22°	22°	23°	22°	22°	22°	22°	21°	21°	21°	21°
Highlands	min	13°	14°	14°	15°	15°	14°	14°	14°	14°	15°	14°	14°
	pcp	120	109	197	290	271	137	162	172	24	338	303	201
	sun	5	5	5	4	4	4	4	4	3	3	3	3
Kota	max	29°	30°	30°	31°	31°	31°	31°	31°	30°	30°	30°	30°
Kinabalu	min	22°	22°	23°	23°	24°	23°	23°	23°	23°	23°	23°	23°
	pcp	139	66	71	118	209	317	273	262	305	336	297	240
	sun	6	7	7	8	7	6	6	6	6	6	6	6
Kuching	max	29°	30°	31°	32°	32°	32°	32°	32°	32°	32°	31°	30°
	min	22°	22°	23°	23°	23°	23°	22°	22°	22°	22°	22°	22°
	pcp	664	532	334	289	256	200	191	209	274	335	339	466
	sun	3	3	4	5	6	6	6	5	4	4	4	3
Langkawi	max	32°	33°	33°	32°	31°	32°	31°	31°	30°	30°	31°	31°
	min	23°	23°	24°	24°	23°	23°	23°	23°	23°	23°	23°	23°
	pcp	27	27	72	169	233	261	292	304	361	340	222	588
	sun	9	9	9	8	7	6	6	6	5	6	6	7

(key: max = maximum temperature, min = minimum temperature, pcp = precipitation in mm, sun = sunshine in hours per day)

American or European rainstorms: there the rain is always cool or cold; in the tropics, the rain is warm, which makes a big difference.

In the **central part of the west coast**, around Kuala Lumpur, there is neither a rainy nor a distinctly dry period. At any time it might rain a great deal and cause flooding. Many city streets are impassable during these episodes and up to a meter underwater. (Watch out for the monsoon drains along the curbs. You cannot see them during floods!)

In **the south**, (Johor), the climate is very much the same as in Singapore, neither rainy nor dry.

Flora and Fauna

Nowhere in the world is there as great a variety of flora and fauna as there is in the rainforests of Southeast Asia. For 130 million years, there has been no change in the climate, leaving species to evolve undisturbed. Some illustrative figures are:

*40,000 species of flowering plants (8000 on the peninsula).

*5000 species of trees (in all of Europe there are only 160 species; 2500 are found on the peninsula, or about one hundred different varieties in a hectare of forest).

*400 species of dipterocarp (up to 40 m tall, large trees with smooth cylindrical trunks and large flowering tops which account for a majority of the commercial lumber).

There are **four different categories of vegetation** in Malaysia:

1. **Coastal and Swamp Vegetation** (swamps, moors, mangroves, thorny rattan and palms without trunks). On the west coast, mangroves dominate. The east coast in marked mainly by casuarina trees, and coconut palms planted by man, which thrive on salt water.

2. **Dipterocarp Forests** (rainforests in lowlands, hills, and low mountains, 0-1300 m).

3. **Oak and Laurel Rainforests** (1300-3000 m) and Mountain Forests with their parasites and lush moss and lichens (2000-3500 m). Rhododendron and other shrubs grow here too.

4. *Dwarf Plants and Grasses* (in Malaysia only found on *Mount Kinabalu*).

Taman Negara the large national park in the heart of the peninsula is a well-preserved jungle. Along with some forests in neighboring Southeast Asian countries, it is representative of the world's oldest forests.

The ***animal kingdom*** of Malaysia is no less varied. As the country used to be mostly forest, its animals developed in the jungle and fully half the species are tree-dwellers, as compared to only one-sixth of the species in Europe.

On the peninsula, there are about 200 varieties of ***mammals***. They include various apes like the gibbon and orangutan (found only in East Malaysia), elephants, tigers, leopards, panthers and other wild cats. The Sumatran rhinoceros, *Seladang* (a wild cow-like animal), barking deer, *kanchil* (miniature goats, 20 cm high, symbolic of courage and cleverness, to compensate for their diminutive size). There are also wild pigs, tapirs, wild dogs, bears, otters, porcupines, bats, and lemurs.

There are more species of ***birds*** than mammals. Over six hundred, including kingfishers, woodpeckers, falcons, goshawks, herons, cranes, storks, ibis, ducks, pheasants, snipes, seagulls, pigeons, cuckoos, parrots, owls, swallows, orioles, sparrows, finches, and many others. The rhinoceros-bird is important as the state symbol of Sarawak.

There are about 100 species of ***freshwater fish*** including the catfish, which can grow up to 1.8 m long and 45 kg in weight. There is also the unique Siamese fighting fish. Fishing is quite popular in Malaysia and there is no need for any kind of license.

There are 111 different kinds of ***snakes*** on the Malay Peninsula. 16 of these are poisonous, though only 5 are really dangerous to people. The most fearsome is the King Cobra, which grows up to 6 m long, and can attack unprovoked. Also deadly are the poisons of the pit viper (Wagler's Pit Viper is on view in the Snake Temple of Penang), the black cobra, the coral snake, and the banded krait: Giant snakes are also common, like the reticulated python, which can grow up to 10 m long.

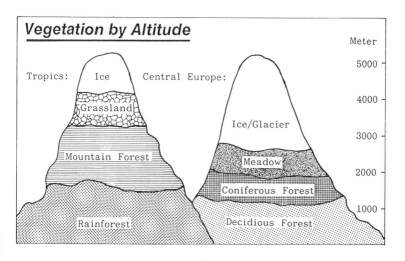

Vegetation by Altitude

Meter

Tropics: Ice   Central Europe:

5000

Grassland

Ice/Glacier

4000

Mountain Forest

3000

Meadow

Coniferous Forest

2000

Rainforest   Decidious Forest

1000

everywhere. There are mosquitoes, which can carry malaria in rural areas; the inevitable cockroaches, which inhabit every household; ants (from little sugar ants that can immediately locate the sweets in any kitchen to giant forest ants that can be up to 2.5 cm long); crickets, grasshoppers and various beetles like the stag and rhinoceros--beetle.

Care should be taken to avoid hornets' nests, scorpions, centipedes (millipedes are completely harmless, however) and certain spiders.

For various reasons (destruction of their natural habitats, earlier unchecked hunting, etc.) the larger mammals are in danger of extinction. Apart from survival artists like rats, mosquitoes and cockroaches, other animals are also endangered.

Unfortunately, the living area for all these animals is continually getting smaller.

Reptiles include various crocodiles, saurians and lizards, some of which are airborne. Most houses contain geckos, or house-lizards. Malaysia is well-known as a home of the giant sea turtles. They regularly ply the beach at Rantau Abang (between Kuala Terengganu and Dungun) to lay their eggs. There are also several other varieties of sea turtles that choose to lay their eggs on Malaysian beaches. Also interesting are the terrapins, fresh-water turtles, which can grow up to a meter long. There is a terrapin breeding farm in Perak.

Malaysia is also famous for its **butterflies**. Varieties include the *Raja Brooke*, the Atlas moth, among many others. Like most natural things, they are far more beautiful when alive and in their natural habitat.

There are over 100,000 species of insects in Malaysia and you can certainly find them

Previously, over 80% of the peninsula was forested. Now the percentage is far less. (For more information, read the section on the lumber economy in the appendix.)

What There is to See

What is commonplace in the Malaysian rainforest, an ecosystem left undisturbed for 130 million years, is a source of wonder to residents of more temperate climes. In one hectare around the Tahan River, there are more than 200 identifiable varieties of trees.

The giant trees dominate the jungle with their smooth cylindrical trunks and spectacular leafy crowns.

Next come the trees with long narrow crowns which do not require as much light. Still lower are the palms and, of course, the younger trees. Tall palms like rattan can reach heights of 60 m and liana can reach the tops of the tallest trees. Vines and orchids grow on boughs.

On the slopes of *Bukit Teresek* in Taman Negara, many of the trees have numbers that correspond to the list in the park brochure.

Rousseau paints a naive picture of a jungle where all sorts of exotic animals are practically stepping on people's feet. The same with the stories of Kipling and others. In reality, the jungle can seem quite empty to the eyes and ears of the visitor. You might hear monkeys, birds or crickets, but do not count on seeing them.

Marine Parks

Since 1985, most islands on the west coast south of Langkawi and the east coast have been declared marine parks. They include *Pulau Perhentian, Kecil* and *Besar, Lang Tengah, Redang, Kapas, Tenggol* off the Kelantan and Terengganu coasts, as well as *Pulau Chebeh, Tualai, Tioman, Sembilang, Seri Buat, Rawa, Babi Hujung / Tengah / Besar, Tinggi, Mentinggi* and *Sibu.* The reasons for setting up these marine parks

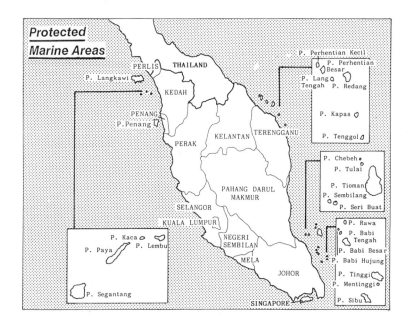

Protected Marine Areas

includes the protection of coral, the recovery of the marine ecosystem, and the protection of wildlife.

There are two kinds of marine parks. One for science and the other for tourism. In the tourist parks, underwater photography, swimming, snorkeling and diving are permitted, but **the following activities are forbidden:**

*Water-skiing, speedboating, harpooning, breaking coral and removing wildlife.
*Anchoring boats in coral reef areas.
*Using weapons to hunt wildlife.
*Fishing nearby.

For **more information**, write to:

Department of Fisheries,
Ministry of Agriculture,
Wisma Tani,
Jalan Mahameru,
50628 Kuala Lumpur,
Tel. 03-298011,

Malaysian Society of Marine Sciences
P.O. Box 250,
Jalan Sultan Post Office,
46730 Petaling Jaya, Selangor.

The People of Peninsular Malaysia

There are 68 different ethnic groups in Malaysia and of these, 36 live on the Malay Peninsula. Officially they are divided into the *Bumiputera* and the *non-Bumiputera*. "Bumis", as the "sons of the earth" are often called, are further divided into three groups:

The Bumiputeras

The *Orang Asli* (aboriginal, or literally, *original people*).

The oldest group are the nomadic **Semang** (sometimes called *Negritos*, due to their appearance). They belong to the Melanesian-Negroid race and live in the Andaman Islands, and remote parts of the Philippines, Indonesia and New Guinea. There are only around 2000 Semang in Malaysia.

The Semang are sub-divided into six different linguistic groups and live in the interior in Perak, Kelantan, Terengganu and Pahang.

As their name implies, they are dark-skinned, small and have other Negroid characteristics. It is not known how long they have lived on the peninsula, but certainly for many thousands of years and very likely since the early Neolithic age. They live mostly in secluded jungles or swampy areas, near small mountains (300 to 600 m). In Kuala Tahan, at the entrance to Taman Negara, one can occasionally see their huts near the river, next to the park buildings.

The Semang live not so much in organized groups as in loose bands of extended families, rarely containing more than 30 people. There is an elected, but impeachable leader, who is usually the oldest in the group. They share everything they use or consume. Their only real possessions are blowguns, which are passed on from generation to generation, and durian trees, whose produce they

share. They conduct a kind of silent business with the Malays. They deposit certain jungle products (roots, tubers, fruits, honey, etc.) at predetermined locations near Malay settlements and return a few days later to pick up what the Malays have deposited for them. In this way they get their favorite goods like salt, *parangs* (bush knives) and pearls, which they use for ornaments.

Since they have a strong incest taboo, people must leave their own groups to find spouses in other groups. The nomadic Semang build lean-tos, while those who are settled live in simple huts. You can see both forms of dwellings in the national park.

The greatest percentage of Orang Asli are light-skinned **Senoi** ("people", or "mountain people"), of which the **Semai** and the **Temar** form the largest sub-groups. The Senoi,

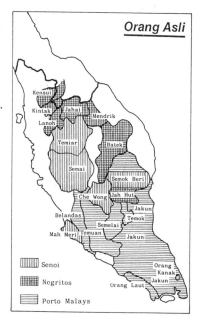

Orang Asli

Kensui
Kintak Jahai
Lanoh Mendrik
Temiar Batek
Semai
Semok Beri
Che Wong Jah Hut
Belandas Jakun
Semelai Temok
Mah Meri Temuan Jakun
Orang Kanak
Orang Laut Jakun

||||| Senoi

▦ Negritos

☰ Porto Malays

Breakdown of Orang Asli by ethnic group, areas of settlement and population (as of 1980.)

Group	Area of Settlement	Population
Negritos		
Batek	Kelantan, Pahang, Terengganu	702
Jahai	Kelantan, Perak	740
Kensiu	Kedah	130
Kintak	Perak	103
Lanoh	Perak	224
Mendrik	Kelantan	144
Senoi		
Che Wong	Pahang	203
Jah Hut	Pahang	2442
Mah Meri	Selangor	1389
Semai	Pahang, Perak, Selangor	17789
Semok Beri	Kelantan, Pahang, Terengganu	1746
Temiar	Kelantan, Pahang, Perak	12365
Proto-Malaien		
Jakun	Johor, Pahang	9605
Kanak	Johor	37
Orang Laut	Johor	1625
Orang Selitar	Johor	497
Semelai	Negeri Sembilan, Pahang	3096
Temok	Pahang	?
Temuan	Johor, Melaka, Pahang, Negeri Sembilan, Selangor	9449

about 36,000 people, came to Malaysia sometime after the *Semang*, but before the *Proto-Malays*. While many groups live today on the edge of the jungle, their original settlements were near sources of the large rivers, at altitudes around 800 to 1000 m.

The Senoi are non-nomadic and originally lived by growing simple crops like mountain rice, sweet potatoes, tapioca, millet, chilies, papaya and tobacco.

Today they are still small-time farmers growing tapioca, bananas, a few durian trees and the products mentioned above. They also raise chickens, goats, sheep and cows, and fish the rivers with baskets and nets. In addition, they gather and sell jungle products like roots, fruits, beans and rattan. Some live in government-established reservations.

The third official group is the **Proto-Malays**, who arrived on the Peninsula before the Malays and live predominantly in the south. Together, there are about 25,000 Proto-Malays. They prefer to live around the middle and lower tributaries of the major rivers at altitudes of about 300 m. They may therefore be considered lowland dwellers. Some live in the coastal mangrove swamps. The Proto-Malays, of whom the *Jakun* are the largest sub-group, are non-nomadic. They grow the same useful crops as the *Senoi*, and cultivate fruit trees, including durian, mangosteen, rambutan and other trees native to the jungle. They also produce small quantities of cash crops like rubber, palm oil, coconuts and catch fish. They build houses in the fashion of the Malays, while the Senoi prefer to use bamboo. Unlike the Senoi, the Proto-Malays no longer hunt with blowguns.

Common to all Orang Asli is the **belief in the animation of nature.** They seek the favor of spirits, demons and deities through blood sacrifices and other rituals.

There are a number of strong taboos against incest, disrespect for elders, torture of animals, etc. The most important deities are the god of sky or thunder, *Karei*, and the

Earth goddess, *TaPed'n*. When the two come together, there is lightning. Priests or medicine men called *Hala* form the link between the human and divine worlds.

The Orang Asli were often used in the past as slaves by the Malays, even into this century, though the British passed anti-slavery laws at the end of the last century, the first in 1878 in Perak.

The Malay name for Orang Asli today is the deprecating term *Sakai*, which means slave or hillbil-ly. During slave hunts, the Orang Asli died by the thousands. Many also lost their lives during the *Emergency*, the guerrilla war that followed World War II, in which they fought on both sides. Whenever they helped the forces of either side who were injured or lost in the jungle, they often got dragged into the fighting.

The **Malays** are the people most often associated with Malaysia. They are the largest ethnic group, and the country is

Hindu influence is still apparent in marriage customs ("*King for a Day*") among other things. In many ancient traditions, Islam plays little or no part.

There are more than 8 million Malays in Malaysia and they make up around 48% of the total population of 16 million. They form a majority on the peninsula: 7 out of 13 million.

In addition to the *Orang Asli*, the **people of Sabah and Sarawak** (the Bajauh, Bidayuh, Iban, Kadazan, Kedazan, Kelabit, Kenyah, Metanu and others) are also considered *Bumiputeras*. Only a very few are Moslem. Due to the work of Christian missionaries however, many are Christian. The effort to promote Malay culture in East Malaysia is very intense. Further information may be found in the section on Sarawak and Sabah.

named after them. Their skin is brown, at its lightest, the color of light coffee. Their faces are Southeast Asian with large eyes and non-folded eyelids. Their hair is black and the men have light beard growth.

Their *language*, Malay, belongs to the Austronesian language group, which reaches from Malaysia to Polynesia. Tagalog, the national language of the Philippines, is part of the same group as are the Indonesian languages of Sundanese, Javanese and other less common languages.

In contrast, the languages of the Orang Asli belong to the Austroasiatic language group. This group includes Tibetan, Burmese, Thai and the languages of the people in the Golden Triangle. "Bazaar Malay" has been the common language of merchants and sailors for centuries, and this explains why it is understood elsewhere. For this reason Indonesia was able to make it the national language.

Malay culture is derived from *adat* (traditional customs) and especially from Islam. However, the Malays were formerly Hindus and Buddhists.

King and Queen for a Day *(Raja Sehari)*

This ceremony is a leftover from the Hindu past. It is a common Malay custom which allows newlyweds to spend their first day of marriage as a royal couple. This day is the most important day of their lives and is celebrated accordingly. The ceremony costs a lot of money and many couples are married a long time before they can afford it. The ceremony combines elements of Hinduism, Islam and even animism (which some people believe in even today).

Before the official wedding day, the couple are symbolically cleansed. Three days before the event the bride has her hair cut in a particular style and has her teeth filed. Both are done to get rid of spirits that might be in her hair or between her teeth. Two days before, her fingernails are painted with henna. On the final day, the bridegroom also takes part in the painting ceremony. After this, both smell good and their blood is considered to be "sweet".

The wedding day is called *"Bersanding"*. The bridegroom, dressed as a sultan, with a *kris* in his brocade sarong to show his status, goes to the house of the bride. On his arrival, he is sprinkled with saffron rice and rose water. He then sits down in the "throne room" (the converted living room) with the bride at his right side. In the afternoon or evening, the dinner is served. They eat Malay food, such as chicken curry, fried chicken, goat meat, fish, and Rendang beef in coconut milk. At most weddings the participants drink rose water. The couple sits at a specially-decorated table where the bride must feed the groom, much to the amusement of the other guests. After the meal they might pose for photographs, sitting on their bed. Most guests come only for the meal and to have a good look at the one-day-only "Royal Couple" in the "Throne Hall."

One day after the *Bersanding*, at the end of the ceremony, the couple bathes together in lemon water, usually in front of the house. Finally, the guests are also sprinkled with the lemon bath water - for fun and as a blessing. There are regional differences to the ceremony.

Guests are welcomed in large numbers and foreigners enhance the prestige. So if you turn up at a wedding, count on being warmly welcomed. Leave a little donation in an envelope with the person who invited you, but do not worry if you don't have any money on you. Just by being there, you contribute to the good mood.

The Non-Bumiputeras

Bumiputera status requires two things: being Moslem and embracing Malay culture. Thus, Indonesian immigrants from Sumatra who arrived a dozen years ago and are ethnically close to the Malays, are considered Bumiputeras. Chinese families who have been here for centuries are not.

Chinese came to the peninsula as traders almost two thousand years ago. The fact that the emperor of China named *Parameswara* King of Malacca attests to the close relationship between the peninsula and China. Since that time, Chinese have lived in Malacca (*Baba Nyona*) where they have mixed with the Malays, but still maintained many Chinese cultural influences.

In the 19th century, a massive Chinese immigration was promoted by the British to supply labor for the tin mines. The immigration was slowed down in 1931 and was cut off completely during the Japanese occupation. The Chinese (approximately 5 million) are mostly from South China and primarily from the Cantonese, Hokkien and Hakka groups.

Indians compose around 10% of the population of Peninsular Malaysia. Most of them arrived this century first to work on tea plantations, and later to work on rubber and palm oil plantations. The largest groups are Tamils, Sikhs and Malayalees.

National Language

Bahasa Malaysia (Malay) is the official language of the country. Since the early 70's, the government has tried to purify the language and lessen the influence of English. In the 70's, many schools taught in English, but today (with the exception of a few international schools), all middle and secondary schools use only Malay. Some primary schools teach in Chinese and Tamil.

The national and state governments, as well as all administrative bodies, must use Malay. Official correspondence, even concerning business matters, must be made available in Malay. Since 3 out of 4 official positions must be filled by Malays, these regulations do not pose much of a problem.

In general, Malays and Indians usually speak Malay to each other. The Chinese and Indians usually speak English to each other. Both groups also speak English among themselves when there are differences in dialect. Today, Chinese and Malays also speak Malay to each other, though many Chinese, particularly the older people, do not speak it very well. Since Malay is now the official language of instruction, young people speak it very well.

The language, however, remains in a state of flux. Currently, *Bahasa Buku* is being promoted. This is the pronunciation of Malay as it is written. This raises a problem: it makes *Bahasa Malaysia* sound like *Bahasa Indonesia*. Still, the standard is the *Johor Riau dialect*, in which *saya* is not pronounced like *saya*, but like *saye* (with a short e). The origins of some orthographic problems lie in *Yawi*, Malay written in Arabic script. In this form, the short vowels are not written.

On one hand, Malaysia encourages the two *bahasas* to become more similar, but out of national pride, the smaller nation does not want to appear that it is carrying the whole burden.

In principle, Indonesian and Malay are the same language, and are both very easy to learn. Though there are some differences, an Indonesian speaker will have no trouble conversing with Malaysians.

History

Malaysia's location at the south of the Malay Peninsula, where the northeast and southwest monsoons come together, brought many seafarers to her coasts. The Chinese came from the South China Sea,

while the Indian Ocean brought Indians, Arabs and later, the harbingers of European colonialism.

Early Settlement: No one knows for sure where the first human settlers came from. The oldest human bones (the skull of *Homo sapiens*) were found in the *Niah* caves in Sarawak and are about 40,000 years old. The oldest found on the peninsula go back "only" 10,000 years. The warm climate encouraged early settlement. People lived in caves in the limestone mountains and similar groups are still found today on Palawan in the Philippines. The vast forests and rivers offered a steady supply of food. The *Negritos*, who today number just over 2000 people, might be descendants of the original inhabitants.

The *Proto-Malays* probably migrated from Yunnan in southern China, through Burma and Thailand to the Malay Peninsula around 2500 B.C. They came from Tibeto-Burman stock, which includes the peoples of the "Golden Triangle," the majority of the Orang Asli and Filipino peoples like the *Igoroten*. Unlike the earliest stone-age people, the newcomers cultivated the land and took to the ocean.

Like the Negritos before them, the Proto-Malays were driven into the interior by the *Deutero-Malays* (Malays), who came around 300 B.C. and settled on the coast. Thus the residence patterns that persist

today were established very early. The Negritos and Proto-Malays lived in the remote and mountainous interior, while the Malays lived in small settlements on the coast or near the mouths of rivers. Small federations developed among the settlements, which later became the sultanates.

Separated by impassable jungle, the settlements had little contact with one another. Everything they needed to live on was present in their immediate environment. This hindered the development of an urban society, normally formed by river cultures in the fight against flooding. Instead, people lived from agriculture and fishing. Decisions in the loose village federations were reached by consensus. People believed in the power of the spirit world, a system of animism that has still not been entirely replaced by Islam.

Hindu-Buddhist Kingdoms: By the first century A.D., the west coast of the Malay peninsula was being visited regularly by Indian and later, Arab sailors and merchants. The east coast was probably reached even earlier by the Chinese. In his remarkable world map of A.D. 160, Ptolemy recorded the peninsula as *"Chersoneus Aurea"* (Golden Peninsula). He noted the harbor of *Takola* on the west coast as part of the Roman Empire. Today this is thought to be *Takua Pa* in Thailand.

In the 4th century, according to the logs of Indian, Arab and Chinese ships, there was a gold rush in *Sungei Patani* (now in Kedah). The sailors brought religion, writing, new knowledge and cultures. Small Hindu kingdoms sprang up.

Kalah, which was possibly the most important settlement of the time, founded by Tamils, has been reconstructed. It was located at the ruins of the Hindu temple in the *Bujang Valley* (near *Kedah Peak*) which have been excavated and restored. There was at that time a land route from *Kedah* to the east coast. Traveling in elephant caravans, merchants from Kalah could reach the other side of the peninsula through the jungle. This avoided the long voyage around the southern tip, and also the feared pirates of the Straits of Malacca. Around the year 300, Kalah replaced Takola as the major town on the peninsula.

During the Liang Dynasty (502-28), Kalah paid tribute to China and thus came under the protection of the Middle Kingdom.

Indian merchants (and from the 9th century, Arab merchants) sailed with the southwest monsoon to trade with the Chinese who arrived with the northeast monsoon. Trade continued in Kalah until the 15th century, when Malacca was founded, and assumed the leading role. Marco Polo, who sailed through the Straits of Malacca in 1292 on behalf of Kublai Khan, did not mention Kalah, indicating that the town might have already started to decline.

Between the 7th and 14th centuries, the Malay Peninsula came under the influence of *Sri Vijaya*, the Hindu Buddhist kingdom of

Malay
Kris

Sumatra. Following that, the Javanese *Maja-pahit* Kingdom ruled the entire Southeast Asian island world.

At this time, the Malays were heavily influenced by Indian culture, an influence which remains highly visible today. Men's hats, jackets and *songkets* are all Indian, as are the marriage rituals. In the small Hindu kingdoms, court life was adapted from Brahmin rituals and the rulers called themselves Rajahs.

The Rise of Malacca: Parameswara, the first ruler of Malacca, originally came from Palembang on Sumatra (the capital of Sri Vijaya). He left Sumatra because of attacks by the Javanese. Then in 1398, the Thais forced him to flee the island of Tumasek (Singapore), which he then ruled. After a short time in Muar, he finally wound up in Malacca. It was an inviting place with no mangrove swamps, and water deep enough for a large harbor.

Though he made his fortune through piracy on Tumasek, Malacca made Parameswara a more honorable man. He sold trading concessions and, in return, offered protection for the merchants. He fended off his Malay neighbors with help from the Thais.

In 1403, the Emperor of China sent his ambassador *Admiral Cheng Ho* to Malacca and conveyed upon Parameswara the title of King (in 1411, the Admiral took him back to China.) In return, Parameswara pledged loyalty to and accepted the patronage of China. Malacca became a protectorate of the Middle Kingdom, which was a wise move as the Thais to the north were expanding continually. At that time, the city had just over 2000 residents and was one of the most cosmopolitan cities in the world. At the beginning of the year, the northeast monsoon would bring Chinese, Thais, Javanese and Bugis (from Sulawesi) while Indians, Burmese and Arabs arrived in May with the southwest monsoon.

Malacca prospered with a tremendous variety of goods: Chinese silk, brocade and porcelain; spices from the

Minangkabau House, circa 1850

Southeast Asian islands; woodcuts from India; precious stones from Burma; gold, herbs, fruit, from the nearby forests. In addition, tin was mined even at that early time.

Malacca quickly became known as a safe port. The rulers made a treaty with the *Orang Laut*, or sea-gypsies, which effectively controlled the threat of pirates in the Straits of Malacca. The sphere of influence of the city-state grew along with its riches. By 1488 Malacca controlled the west coast of the Malay Peninsula, a large part of the east coast of Sumatra (thus, the Straits of Malacca) and Pahang.

Meanwhile, there were changes taking place in the rest of the world. Like the Arabs before them, the Indian sailors were converted to Islam (at the time, India was ruled by the Moghul Emperors.) The rulers of Malacca liked the new religion – not surprisingly, since Islam's strict laws and prohibitions made it easier to maintain control over the people. There were also tactical advantages to Islam. Almost all the merchants were Moslem, including the Chinese Admiral Cheng Ho and his wife, the daughter of a Sumatran prince from Pasai. In 1414, Parameswara converted and changed his name to *Sultan Magat Iskandar Shah*. The term "Sultan" had religious over-tones which made the title seem divine.

Under him were the *Bendahara* (the senior minister and commander of the army), the *Temenggong* (minister of the interior), and the *Penghulu Bendahari* (head of the court). Also the *Mentri Paduka Tuan* (the national judiciary), the *Maharaja Lela* (head of the port and customs) and the *Imam Paduka Tuan* (chief Imam) functioned under his leadership. All were chosen from the ruling family.

67

Islam also brought Arabic script to Malaya. Malay was no longer written in the *Devanagari* script of Sanskrit, but with Arabic letters. The new script was called *Yawi*, though it was not widely used. Islam introduced radical changes not only in religion and writing but also in spiritual and cultural values.

The Malays' first contact with **Islam** was actually in the 7th century, with the first Arab traders. Though Moslems, they did not engage in any missionary activity. The oldest written evidence of Islam in Malaya, the *Terengganu Stone* (on view in the Negara Museum in Kuala Lumpur) dates back to 1303. Islam did not become widespread, however, until it was adopted by the rulers of Malacca. In 1446, there was fighting between Moslems and Hindus for dominance. The Moslems were successful, and Islam became the official religion under *Muzaffar Shah* (1446-58).

The Golden Age of Malacca lasted one hundred years, and the city flourished with a population of 40,000. These hundred years are considered the high point of Malaysia's civilization. Almost all of Malaysia's ruling houses trace their roots to Malacca.

Arrival of the Europeans (Colonialism)

The first Europeans with the intention to conquer Malaysia were the Portuguese. The Arab *Shibab al-Din Ahmad ibn Majid* guided *Vasco de Gama* over the Indian Ocean and into the Straits of Malacca. Thus began the race for the valuable spices of Malacca as the Arab and Indian traders' monopoly was broken. The Portuguese also managed to fit in a bit of missionary work in a crusade to contain the growth of Islam. At first they tried to establish themselves peacefully and set up a trading settlement. But the locals and the Moslem Arabs and Indians were suspicious and tried to seize control of the Portuguese fleet. All but twenty Portuguese escaped, but the incident gave the Portuguese a reason to return.

In 1511, *Alfonso de Albuquerque* laid siege to Malacca. Sultan *Mahmud* was powerless

against the enemy guns and cannon, despite his large army and war elephants. Malacca fell on August 24, 1511.

The Portuguese built a fortress, *A Famosa*, whose walls protected them for 130 years. They established a monopoly over the lucrative spice trade (spices could be resold in Europe for a 400 to 500% profit). In addition, they established a steep port tax and permitted only specially authorized ships to sail through the Straits of Malacca. Their missionaries (*Francis Xavier*, was particularly active from 1545 and made it all the way to Japan) were not very successful, however. In 1580, the Motherland was annexed by Spain, and the colony went slowly downhill.

The next to arrive were the **Dutch**, with their "*United East India Company.*" They arrived in the area in 1602 with the intention of dominating the spice trade. In 1621 they established a base at *Batavia* (Jakarta). In 1641, after a seven-month blockade, they seized the fortress and with it, the city of

Malacca. To the Dutch, Malacca was an important outpost, but the center of their operations was still Batavia.

More and more non-Dutch traders shunned Malacca in favor of *Johor*, where the younger son of Mahmud had established a sultanate. The city had local rivalries with Aceh in northern Sumatra, the Minangkabau from central Sumatra and the Bugis from Sulawesi. *Johor* lost a great deal of its influence in 1673 after an attack from Sumatra. At the same time, *Perak*, where the older son of Mahmud fled to, became an important center for tin.

The next and final step of European colonialism came from the **British**. The *East India Company*, which primarily imported tea from China, needed a safe harbor near the Bight of Bengal. In 1785, *Francis Light* talked the Sultan of Kedah into letting them use the

Opposite page: Santiago gate, from the time of the Portuguese. Above: An old Dutch headstone.

island of *Penang* as a trading base. The Sultan was hoping, in vain, for British support in his fight against the Thais to the north.

When the British did not support him, he tried to take the island back, but the British had different ideas. They attacked the Sultan's fleet. That left the East India Company free to lease out the island and within a short time, the harbor blossomed. Francis Light died of malaria on Penang in 1794.

The British took over Malacca in 1795 because the French had defeated the Dutch in a war at home. Both the British and the Dutch wanted to prevent the French from taking the trading outpost. Naturally, the Dutch wanted Malacca back after the war. After another period of Dutch rule, Malacca reverted to British control in a trade for *Bencoolen* on Sumatra.

In 1819, *Stamford Raffles* came to Singapore where he found only a few thousand Malays and Orang Laut, and established a trading colony to, "...finally break the Dutch monopoly." In 1824 (the population had already reached 11,000), the Sultan of Johor gave the whole island to the British. The free port was a complete success from the very start.

In 1826, the three British bases at Penang, Malacca and Singapore were united under the "*Straits Settlement*." In 1867, their collective status was promoted to Crown Colony.

In order to conserve strength, the group agreed not to interfere with intra-Malay affairs. But when strife erupted in the tin industry, which was expanding rapidly due to the development of canned food this promise was broken. The thousands of Chinese immigrants who worked as miners or entrepreneurs were forming into secret societies. These societies were seen as potential rivals to the power of the Sultans. In order to protect their sizable investments in the tin industry, the British interceded. In the *Treaty of Pangkor* (1874), they agreed that the Sultan of Perak would take on a British "adviser". He would have

Babas from the
Straits Settlements

Shoemaker (opium eater)
from Singapore

production) as the mainstay of the economy. Many Indians, mostly Tamils, came over willingly as plantation workers because Malays did not want to work in the plantations. Thus a situation arose where different trades were dominated by different races.

For the most part, the situation remains the same today. In 1931, Malaya had a population of almost 4 million: 49% Malay; 34% Chinese, and the remainder consisting of Indians, indigenous people, Europeans and other minorities.

The Japanese Interlude: In December, 1941, Japanese troops occupied Malaya. The British surrendered in February 1942. They were busy fighting Germany in Europe and had more important things to do than defend Malaya. In addition, they were not accustomed to jungle warfare.

Japanese rule was brutal. Especially so for the Chinese, whom the Japanese were convinced were on the side of the British (because of Japan's war against China.) To avoid being massacred, many Chinese fled to the jungle and formed the communist-leaning *"Malayan People's Anti-Japanese Army"* (MPAJA). Many of the Europeans were taken to work on the Burma death-railway in Thailand ("The Bridge on the River Kwai").

The Road to Independence: The Japanese nightmare came to an end in September, 1945. The British were in control once again and wanted to form a more centralized *Malayan Union*. This plan was opposed by the Malays. The opposition movement formed the *United Malay National Organization* (UMNO) in March, 1946 under the leadership of *Dato Onn Jaafar*. This led to the founding of the Malay Federation on April 1, 1948. The federation recognized the sovereignty of the individual sultans.

Singapore remained a British Crown Colony. Sarawak, ruled by the *Brooke* family of "White Rajahs" since 1841, and Sabah, governed by the *"British North Borneo*

the final word in all matters outside of religion and Adat (the traditional Malay morals).

Later, the states of Selangor and Negeri Sembilan also took on British advisers. Pahang accepted one only after a war (1891), which became a proud milestone in the Malay struggle for independence.

In 1896, the Malay Confederacy of States was founded. Kuala Lumpur became the capital and the federation became tighter. After some resistance, Johor also joined in 1914. The northern states of Kedah, Kelantan and Terengganu which were subordinate to the King of Siam until that year, finally came under British authority.

At the beginning of the 20th century, the invention of the automobile led to the rapid development of the rubber industry. The first seedlings were smuggled out of Brazil through England to Singapore and Kuala Kangsar. The jungle was cleared and rubber became even more important than tin (Malaya accounted for half the worlds'

Company" since 1881, both became colonies in 1946. The Chinese, Malays and British who fought the Japanese in the jungle under the MPAJA wanted to establish a republic. Under the leadership of *Chin Peng*, they organized strikes, attempted assassinations of European mine and plantation owners and managers, and caused unrest, with the aim of crippling the economy. Thus began the Emergency, a "War of Nerves" which lasted officially until July 31, 1960.

The communists were well-organized and forced many villagers living on the edge of the jungle to work with them. *Sir Harold Briggs* devised a system to relocate 500 villages in secure areas. Here they could not be used as supply bases, and this weakened the communists considerably. They lost most of their power in 1955, but the Emergency continued for another five years.

In 1951, UMNO joined together with the anti-communist and anti-colonial *"Malayan Chinese Association"* (MCA). Then in 1954, it joined the *"Malayan Indian Congress"* (MIC), forming the *Alliance of Barisan*. This alliance was under the leadership of the pioneer of independence, *Tunku Abdul Rahman*, son of the Sultan of Kedah. After successful negotiations with the British in London, necessary preparations were made, and on August 31, 1957, Malaya declared her independence. Tunku Abdul Rahman became the first prime minister and also the hero of independence.

The Birth of Malaysia: In 1959, under the leadership of *Lee Kwan Yew*, Singapore decided it wanted to join Malaya in order to gain independence from Great Britain. Tunku Abdul Rahman agreed, partly in order to dilute the communist influence with the addition of more than one million Singaporean Chinese to the population. However, with the addition of that many Chinese, the Malays would no longer be the majority. So they insisted on the addition of Sabah and Sarawak to the union. Brunei wanted nothing to do with it (the little kingdom was

content enough with its large petroleum reserves), but Sarawak and Sabah agreed. Indonesia and the Philippines did not like the arrangement. The latter had old claims to Sabah (which was earlier part of the territory of the Sultan of Sulu). And under the leadership of *Sukarno*, Indonesia dreamed of building a regional super-state including all of Malaysia and Brunei.

Even before the founding of Malaysia on September 16, 1963, the *"Confrontation"* had already started in Kalimantan, the Indonesian half of Borneo. The *"Konfrontasi"* ended in 1965 with the fall of Sukarno. Diplomatic relations were resumed with the Philippines and Indonesia.

A year earlier, Singapore seceded from Malaysia and formed an independent republic.

The government of Malaysia adopted a policy of *New Economic Politics* which guaranteed the Malays a greater role in the economy, previously dominated by the Chinese. Laws were passed that favored the Malays in all areas. On May 13, 1969, the anger over the repression of other races exploded in bloody riots in Kuala Lumpur in which hundreds lost their lives.

Today, Malaysia is fairly stable. Much of this stability derives from Malaysia's membership (since 1967) of the *Association of Southeast Asian Nations* (ASEAN).

In the first years of the *Mahathir* era, the country was already well-developed. The expansion of the tin and rubber industries, the increased attention to palm oil, petroleum and lumber production and the expansion of other industry turned a developing country into a regional economic power.

Current Politics

Today, Malaysia is a unique constitutional monarchy in which a new king, *Yang di-Pertuan Agong,* is elected every five years from the nine sultans. In 1989, the Sultan of Perak took over the title from the Sultan of Johor.

The king rules with the help of Parliament, which is composed of an elected house of representatives and a Senate of appointed members.

Since the founding of the nation, the government has been controlled by the so-called *Alliance*. The Alliance has been called the *National Front (Barisan Nasional)* since 1971.

The president of UMNO, which is always the strongest political party, automatically becomes the prime minister. After *Tunku Abdul Rahman, Tun Abdul Razak* ruled from 1970 to 1976. After his death he was succeeded by *Tun Hussein Onn*, and since 1981, *Datuk Seri Dr. Mahathir Mohamad* has led the country.

The Mahathir government promotes itself as a "clean (free of corruption), effective and trustworthy" leadership. Characteristic of its bold initiatives are strong economic partnerships with Japan ("Look East Policy"),and the development of heavy industry.

Political Structure

Malaysia is officially a constitutional monarchy.

The Head of State is the king, or the *Yang di-Pertuan Agong*, elected from among the Malay sultans for a term of five years. The current king, since 1989, is the Sultan of Perak, *Azlan Shah*. He is an intelligent and outgoing man, very much liked by the people. Politically, he does not always see eye-to-eye with the Mahathir government which led some to doubt that he would be elected.

The king's position is largely ceremonial, but he does have some influence on the government. He signs all laws, but has to act on the government's advice. He also officially presides over Parliament, much like the Queen of England.

The **government** is structured similarly to that of a Western parliamentary democracy. There are two chambers in the **Parliament**, the **Senate** (*Dewan Negara*), with 96 members, and the **House of Representatives** (*Dewan Rakyat*).

40 members of the **Senate** (upper house) are appointed by the king and the other 29 are sent from the states. The Senate can make recommendations on bills about to become laws, and can slow down decisions, but it does not have the power to vote down laws. A senator serves for three years and must be at least 30 years old.

The **House of Representatives** (lower house) is based on the British House of Commons. It is made up of 177 members, each of whom is elected by a district. They serve five year terms and must be at least 21 years old. The House of Representatives is where laws and policies are argued.

The **cabinet** is officially named by the king. In reality, the king names the head of the cabinet, the elected **Prime Minister**. The Prime Minister then picks his own cabinet ministers, who are appointed by the king. One of the duties of the cabinet is to support the king in his tasks.

The official head of each state is the **sultan** except in Penang and Malacca, which have **governors** (*Yang di-Pertua Negeri*) who serve four-year terms.

Each state also has its own parliament, which has only one house. The head of the cabinet of each state is the *Menteri Besar*. In Sabah and Sarawak, the position is called the "Chief Minister," or the *Kertua Menteri*.

The states are divided into **districts** (*Daerah*), administered by **District Officers** (*Pegawai Daerah*). Kuala Lumpur, Penang, Ipoh and Kuching all have City status. These **cities** (*Bandaraya*) are administered by mayors or *Datuk Bandar*. All other cities are controlled by the state governments.

National Symbols

The flag consists of 14 red and white stripes with a blue field in the upper left corner. The field contains a yellow crescent moon and a 14-pointed star. The meanings are as follows:

● The stripes represent the equality of the 13 states and the Federal Territory.
● The blue field represents the unity of the Malaysian people.
● The moon is the symbol of Islam, the state religion.
● The star represents the unity of the states.
● Yellow is the color of the sultans.

The Coat of Arms is crowned by a 14-pointed star over a crescent moon. The shield itself has a row of 5 *kris* (Malaysian daggers), which stand for the old Unfederated Malay States: Johor, Kedah, Kelantan, Perlis, and Terengganu.

The four colored fields (red, black, white, yellow) in the middle stand for the old Federated Malay States: Negeri Sembilan, Pahan, Perak, and Selangor.

Penang is to the left (betelnut tree and bridge), Malacca is to the right (Melaka tree). Sabah is to the lower left, Sarawak is to the lower right and the national flower, the *bunga raya* (hibiscus) is in the center. The tigers on either side are from the old Malayan coat of arms.

The **royal flag** is a yellow field with the coat of arms, surrounded by a chocolate-brown flower wreath.

The national flower is the *bunga raya* or a red hibiscus with five petals. The flower was brought to Malaysia in the 12th century by merchants from either China, Japan or the Pacific.

Hibiscus

The national anthem is based on a melody from the Seychelles, where the ex-Sultan of Perak was sent in exile by the British.

Negara ku,
tanah tumpahnya darah ku
Rayat hidup bersatu dan maju:
Rahmat bahgia tuhan kurniyakan
Raja kita selamat bertakhda.

In our nation,
the land of our birth,
may the people live together in unity and wealth;
God protect our land,
Long live the King.

Other symbols of nationalism are the National Mosque, the National Monument and Parliament, all in Kuala Lumpur. And of course, there is the national language.

Economy

The Malaysian economy is heavily based on a few natural resources. These vary tremendously on the world market and therefore introduce a degree of instability to the national economy. The government is actively trying to change this condition, which is, unfortunately, typical for developing countries. This is being done by promoting light industry, including electronics, and heavy industry, automobile manufacturing and actively diversifying agriculture.

Tin: The crash of world tin prices began on October 24, 1985. From the start of large-scale food preservation in the last century up through the mid-1980's, the procurement of tin was one of the world's most important industries. In this, Malaysia led the world. The Kinta Valley around Ipoh is still the richest tin mining area in the world. Nonetheless, when the crash brought prices down below production costs, it spelled disaster for the industry and for Malaysia.

Production dropped from 40,000 metric tons in 1983 to about half that in 1987. In the same period, the number of open mines went from 500 to 200, and more than half of the 25,000 employees lost their jobs. Ipoh, which had come to be known as the "City of Millionaires," has borne the brunt of the crisis.

Rubber: This agricultural product was introduced by the British. It never really took off until the beginning of this century when automobiles with rubber tires first came into widespread use. Now, as worldwide

A new landscape: Tin mines in the Kinta Valley.

Rubber: The condom originates in the jungle.

any usable product. An oil palm, on the other hand, produces oil after only three years. Right now, there are 988,000 more acres of rubber plantations than of oil palm plantations. But the difference is getting smaller every year as more and more land is converted.

Palm Oil: Malaysia produces over 60% of the world's crude palm oil. Over the past five years, production has shot up from 3 to 5 million metric tons. The largest producer, as with rubber, is the *Federal Land Development Authority* or FELDA, which has incorporated 100,000 small farmers.

The world price for palm oil has dropped sharply in the past few years. Nonetheless, new oil palm plantations are being carved out of the jungle all the time.

Palm oil, rich in vitamin E, has many uses. Cooking oil, margarine, cosmetics and even fuel have been manufactured from it. The government is determined to demonstrate the usefulness of palm oil to the

demand has fallen, this industry is slowly declining. It seems only a matter of time before synthetic products replace natural rubber. Malaysia is the world's largest producer of rubber, though production is being cut back every year. Currently only about 1.6 million metric tons are produced. Malaysia's share of the world market has dropped from 39% to 36%. The government is making an effort to increase the production of palm oil while cutting back on rubber. Of Malaysia's 1.6 million tons of rubber produced annually, about 1 million is produced by small plantations under 150 acres. The rest is produced by the huge family-owned plantations of up to 9900 acres.

The worldwide AIDS crisis has increased the demand for rubber condoms and surgical gloves. However, it is difficult to say how the industry will respond, since it takes seven years for a rubber tree to produce

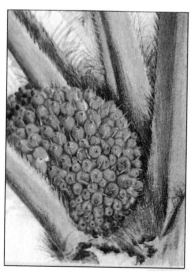

world. In the U.S., there has been a campaign against the use of palm oil by the domestic soy bean industry.

As with rubber, Malaysia faces competition from neighboring Thailand and, especially, Indonesia, as wages there are lower.

Rice: Rice production is around 1.6 million metric tons a year, a decrease of around 18% from 1985. Less land in the traditional rice growing areas of the northern Peninsula is being devoted to rice, though more land in Sabah is being cultivated. In the last few years, there has been a controversial shift from the wonder rice, *IR42* (high yield, low quality)) to *MR 84 / 85* (low yield, high quality).

Cocoa: Malaysia is the world's fourth largest producer of cocoa after the Ivory Coast, Brazil and Ghana. Sabah is responsible for 61% of domestic production, which was 165,000 tons in 1988. Production has doubled over the past 5 years.

Pepper: The world price for pepper has gone up lately, as demand grows faster than supply. Malaysia produces 17,000 metric tons annually. Pepper is a very easy crop to grow in Malaysia, particularly in Sarawak.

Pineapple: Annual production is around 130,000 metric tons, a decrease of 13% since 1985.

Tobacco: 12,000 metric tons are grown annually, mainly for the domestic market, twice the quantity grown in 1984.

Meat: About 500,000 metric tons of meat are produced annually, 10% more than in 1985. Sheep are popular, since they can be raised on rubber plantations. Chicken production is almost too high. In 1988, 12 million of them were exported.

Fish: 600,000 metric tons of fish were caught in 1986. The number of deep sea fleets has increased, but all over the world,

coastal supplies are dwindling and Malaysia is no exception. Fish and shrimp are raised in freshwater farms.

Tropical Wood: Though world prices are falling and supply is too high for demand, Malaysia has not cut back production, now at over 30 million cubic meters a year. Of these, some 12 million come from Sarawak, and the rest is divided equally between Sabah and the Peninsula. The harvested area has been enlarged by 160 hectares.

Oil and Natural Gas: Malaysia has about 3 billion metric tons of oil reserves, and ranks 22nd in the world. It also has 40 billion tons of natural gas reserves, and ranks 13th in the world. There is great demand for the light, low-sulfur Malaysian oil. Oil and natural gas bring more money to Malaysia than any other exports.

Most wells are located on islands in the South China Sea. There are others on the east coast of the Peninsula and along the northwest coasts of Sarawak and Sabah. Daily production is over 500,000 barrels.

Coal: Coal has been mined for 140 years in Sabah and for 70 years on the Peninsula. The reserves, mostly in Sarawak, are estimated at around 500 million metric tons, though coal is not being mined at present.

Other Resources: There are nine iron mines in Kedah, Perak and Johor. Johor also has two bauxite mines. Silica, antimony, tungsten and kaolin are mined in small quantities as is gold, primarily in the Gua Musang area.

Hydroelectric Power: Since Malaysia gets some 250 cm of rainfall a year, the government is understandably eager to develop hydroelectric power. However, to do so means altering the courses of rivers, an enormous task which can have tragic consequences for the environment unless done properly. The country has the potential of producing 123,000 gigawatt-hours per year. Some 70% of these would come from

Sarawak, with its huge river systems, the Rajang and the Baram. There is currently a project in Sarawak that will bring power to the mainland. It will be by way of 2 or 3 underwater cables, some 600 km long, each with a capacity of 375 megawatts. It will not be ready until the end of this decade. In addition, over 100 smaller power plants are being planned, each with a capacity of 50-500 kilowatts.

Income Levels

Though Malaysia is growing fast, it still has quite a way to go until it catches up with the *Four Tigers*, Hong Kong, Singapore, South Korea and Taiwan. It is still a developing, third-world country, and the government realizes this.

The income level varies. In rural areas, it is often not more than M$ 100-200 per month, though the average salary of government officials is M$ 1000. Even though most of the wealth is concentrated in the hands of a select few, the average person makes about twice as much as his counterparts in Indonesia or Thailand. A saleswoman or secretary makes M$ 250-300, a rubber tapper on a plantation makes about the same, and a policeman makes M$ 450-600. Taxi drivers make about the same as policemen if they do not own their cars, and more if they do. A teacher makes between M$ 600 and 1500, depending on seniority, which is as much as a mid-level bureaucrat. Young doctors begin at M$ 1000, as assistants during their internships.

Religion

As a multi-cultural and multi-racial country, Malaysia is home to many of the world's great religions. Throughout the entire country, you will find Islamic mosques, Buddhist, Hindu and Taoist temples and Christian churches.

Not only is religious freedom guaranteed by law, the Malaysian people are also very tolerant. All of the major religions have national holidays in their honor. The religious affiliations of the various ethnic groups are as follows:

●*Orang Asli*
Animists, or converted Christians or Muslims.
●*Malays*
Originally animists, then Buddhists or Hindus, but Mus-lims since the 15th century. Today, a non-Muslim Malay is unthinkable, though animist and other traditions are thoroughly integrated with Islam.
●*Chinese*
Buddhism, Taoism, Confucianism and ancestor worship are all practiced. There are also some Chinese Christians and Muslims.
●*Indians*
There are Hindu Tamils, Sikhs (sometimes called Punjabis), Muslim Pakistanis and many Christians.

Islam

As the state religion, Islam has played an important part in the history of Malaysia. The first evidence of Islam in Southeast Asia is a gravestone in Gerik on Java from the year 1082. The oldest written proof of Islam in Malaysia is an inscription from Kuala Brang in Terengganu from the 14th century. It is now on display in the National Museum in Kuala Lumpur.

Islam is based on the teachings of the prophet Mohammed, who lived in what is now Saudi Arabia from 571-632. *Allah* is the one God of Islam and a line of Judeo-Christian prophets are recognized: Adam, Abraham (*Ibrahim*), David (*Daud*), Moses (*Musa*) and Jesus (*Issa*). The central book is called the Koran or (*Quran*).

In Islamic thinking, the Koran is the perfect teaching and therefore it must never be changed. Also within an Islamic society, the spiritual and secular powers become one. The concept of equality is an integral part of Islamic thought.

These are the **Five Pillars of Islam,** by which all Muslims should live:

●First duty: **The Confession of Faith,** expressed by the prayer of affirmation, "There is no God but Allah, and Mohammed is his prophet." In Arabic: *Ash-hadu allaahilaaha illallah, Wa-ash-hadu anna Muhammadar Rasuulullah..*

Moslems do not recognize the Christian idea of the trinity. To a Muslim there is only one God. There is a prohibition against physical images of God which also applies to Mohammed. This stricture applies to all living things except plants. For this reason, Arabic art has concentrated on arabesque and calligraphic styles.

●Second duty: **Daily Prayers,** which take place five times a day. *Salat* is the ritual prayer, with prescribed words and body movements. *Doa* is a personal prayer, performed afterwards. The times of prayer are dictated by the sun:

Subuh: Just before dawn.
Zuhur: From midday to late afternoon.
Asar: From late afternoon to just before dusk.
Maghrib: From dusk until an hour after dusk.
Isyak: From an hour after dusk until the next morning.

Before praying, the faithful must wash their bodies in the following order: Hands, mouth, face, underarms, forehead (the front of the hair), ears, feet.

To pray, men must cover their bodies from the navel to below the knees. Most people wear a sarong or a Malay suit. Women must keep their entire bodies, including their hair, covered, leaving only their faces and hands exposed.

The sequence of positions for prayer are as follows:
1. Standing up, hands beside legs.
2. Standing, hands at ear level with palms facing forward.
3. Standing, hands crossed in front of the stomach.
4. Bent over, hands on knees.
5. Standing, hands as 2.
6. Kneeling, face touching the carpet.

In Malaysia, the **Muezzin** calls the people to prayer himself, without using an amplified recording. The *Azan*, or call-to-prayer, is as follows, with each phrase repeated twice:
1. *Allahu akbar, Allaahu akbar.*
   Allah is great.
2. *Ash-hadu allaa ilaaha illallaah.*
   I declare that no one other than Allah should be worshiped.
3. *Ash-hadu anna Muhammadar rasuulullah.*
   I declare that Mohammed is the prophet of Allah.
4. *Haiya 'alasw-swalaah.*
   Hurry to the prayers.
5. *Haiya 'alal falaah.*
   Hurry to the progress.
6. *Allaahu akbar*
   Same as 1.
7. *Laa ilaaha illallah.*
   Same as 2 without "I declare that..."

اَللهُ اَكْبَرْ ۔ اَللهُ اَكْبَرْ
اَللهُ اَكْبَرْ ۔ اَللهُ اَكْبَرْ
اَشْهَدُاَنْ لَاإِلَهَ إِلَّا اللهْ
اَشْهَدُاَنْ لَاإِلَهَ إِلَّا اللهْ
اَشْهَدُاَنَّ مُحَمَّدًا رَسُوْلُ اللهْ
اَشْهَدُاَنَّ مُحَمَّدًا رَسُوْلُ اللهْ
حَيَّ عَلَى الصَّلَاةِ
حَيَّ عَلَى الصَّلَاةِ
حَيَّ عَلَى الْفَلَاحْ
حَيَّ عَلَى الْفَلَاحْ
اَللهُ اَكْبَرْ ۔ اَللهُ اَكْبَرْ
لَاإِلَهَ إِلَّا اللهْ

7. Sitting back on the heels.
8. Same as 6.
9. Stand up, repeat 2 to 8, remain seated.
10. Look right and left, stand up.

There are specific prayers to be recited in each position.

●Third duty: **Giving Alms**. *Zakat Fitrah* is a donation given every year after the fasting month, *Puasa* and consists of 2.5% of personal savings.

●Fourth duty: **Fasting** from dawn to dusk during the month of *Ramadan* (*Puasa* in Malay.)

●Fifth duty: a **Pilgrimage to Mecca** at least once in one's life. Pilgrims take the honorary title of *Haji* (*Hajjah* for women.)

There are several **prohibitions** in Islam, the 114 *Suren* of the Koran, as they are known. Eating pork is prohibited and there is no sex outside of marriage. Even a kiss is prohibited if it is not with a family member.

There is a special court to enforce Islamic rules and prohibitions. It seems only a matter of time before Islamic law will be binding for all Malays. Other groups are worried that they, too, might be forced to follow Islamic traditions.

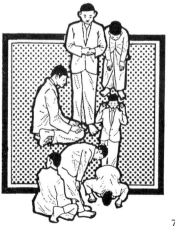

During my first visit to Malaysia, in 1981, I only rarely saw *tudungs* (the nun-like head coverings). Now they are no longer a rare sight, especially in the universities. More and more states have declared Friday to be the day of rest including Kedah, Perlis, Kelantan, Terengganu and Johor.

There are a great many fundamentalist *Dakwah* missionaries from Pakistan in the country. They are known by their turbans and green shirts. The *Parti Islam* (PAS) is becoming a potent political force, particularly on the east coast.

Sarawak, incidentally, is an exception; Islam is not the state religion there.

Buddhism

There were Buddhists in Malaysia long before the first Muslims arrived. The Sumatran kingdom of *Sri Vijaya* ruled over parts of the Peninsula during its height from the 7th to the 14th centuries. Nonetheless, Buddhism took no permanent foothold here as it did in Thailand.

It was Chinese immigrants who really brought Buddhism in its contemporary form to Malaysia. Most of these immigrants came in the 19th century, but the oldest Buddhist temple is in Malacca, built in the 15th century by *Chen Hoon Teng*.

Chinese practice *Mahayana Buddhism* (the Greater Vehicle), in which the *Boddhisattvas* help people to achieve *Nirvana*. The other form of Buddhism is *Hinayana* or *Thereveda* (the Lesser Vehicle) in which the people try to emulate the Buddha himself. This form of Buddhism is practiced in Sri Lanka, Burma, Cambodia and Thailand.

There are Thai Thereveda temples in Kelantan (Wat Putharamaran, Repek, Pasir Mas), Kedah, Perlis, Penang (right next to a Burmese temple on Jalan Burmah), Taiping, Ipoh and Kuala Lumpur. The north of Malaysia once belonged to Thailand, which explains the lasting influence. Sinhalese immigrants from Sri Lanka have founded

additional Therevada temples. Therevada Buddhism is practiced through **three main principles:**

1. Enlightenment is within all beings and needs only be developed.

2. *Dharma* is the teaching that leads to acquaintance with Buddha's nature, which is enlightenment or *Bodhi Nirvana*.

3. The *Sangha* is the community of monks, *Arhats* (the enlightened), or *Boddhisattvas* (who help others on the path to enlightenment.)

Therevada Buddhism is closer to original Buddhism than Mahayana. Chinese Buddhism is closely linked with Confucian social theory and Taoist philosophy and moral theory.

Though there are technically no gods in Buddhism, there are certain people who are honored, including the female form of *Boddhisattva Avalokiteshvara*, or the Goddess of Mercy (*Kuan Yin*). A large statue of her can be found in *Kek Lok See* Temple in Penang. *Kuan Ti*, the God of War,

doubles as the God of Business in peaceful times and is naturally quite important for those seeking success.

Other favorite "gods" in Malaysia include *Sam Po Shan* or *Sam Poh Tai Shen*, the spirit of Admiral Cheng Ho. He first came to Malacca as the ambassador of the Emperor of China at the beginning of the 15th century. He is the protector of travelers. Another god favored by immigrant Chinese is *Toh Peh Kong* or *Ta Pai Kung*, the protector of pioneers.

The Chinese Pantheon includes not only beneficent gods (*shen*), but malevolent spirits and demons (*kuei*), who must be placated or kept in check.

Chinese people may also worship the souls of their departed ancestors, who can be beneficent or dangerous. These beliefs are essential to the strength of the family-clan among the Chinese.

There are more than 3500 Buddhist temples and societies in Malaysia. The umbrella organization is the *Malaysian Buddhist Association*.

Hinduism

Like Buddhism, Hinduism arrived on the Malay Peninsula centuries before Islam. It has left a stronger mark on the Malays than Buddhism and many aspects of Malay culture can be traced back to India. From language and literature to clothing (the Malay suit and hat are Indian in origin), to customs like the Malay wedding or *Bersanding*. Physically, there are far fewer reminders of that past. Aside from the ruins in the Bujang Valley and in Kedah at the mouth of the Merbok River, there is nothing left.

Indian plantation laborers who came to Malaya in the last half of the previous century and the first half of this century brought their regional forms of Hinduism with them. Since the majority of Indians in Malaysia are Tamils, southern Indian Hinduism is the most widespread.

The temples are dedicated to the gods *Mariamman* and *Subramaniam* or *Murugan*. The latter is the god of the *Chettyar* caste, who seem to run all the money changers' offices. Hindu national organizations include the *Malaysia Hindu Bangam*, the *Divine Life Society*, the *Society for the Krishna Consciousness* and the *Sai Baba Foundation*. Over 80% of Malaysian Indians are Hindus.

The caste system is an integral part of Hinduism. It was developed some 3000 years ago in India by Indo-Aryan invaders who made themselves and their followers members of the highest caste, *Brahmin*. In Malaysia today, caste is not very important. Since most of the Indians in Malaysia came to the country as plantation workers, they were originally from the lower castes.

Hindus believe in reincarnation of the soul in another body. Unlike Islam, Christianity and Buddhism, it is not an evangelical religion. There is no real dogma, but there are ritual hymns, the *Vedas* and epics, the *Mahabharata* and the *Ramayana*. Hinduism is subject to great regional differences.

Hinduism stresses love of all living things, selflessness and non-violence. People are judged based on their soul's accumulation of good or bad deeds, or *karma*. The *dhamma* are the rules for leading a good life.

You can encounter the divine world at the entrance to any south Indian Hindu temple in the tower of the gods, or *gopuram*. Behind that is the *mandapa*, a hall containing a small chamber facing east, the *garbha griha*, which is the home of the god of the temple. The altar is crowned with a tower or cupola, called the *sikhara*, which symbolizes *meru*, the divine mountain.

Worshipers clean their hands, smear their faces, and give five offerings (including coconuts, fruit and rice), representing the five senses, to the priests. They then pass these gifts along to the gods. During the

ritual, the worshipers keep their eyes on the altar. Finally, they take their gifts back and circle the tower.

The Indian gods have very human characteristics and they are feared as much as they are honored. The characteristic gods of Malaysian Hindus are Subramaniam, the son of *Shiva* and *Parvati*. (Shiva is one of the three main gods, the creator and destroyer; *Brahma* is also a creator and *Vishnu* is the preserver).

Subramaniam is the god of war and imparts power, strength and victory.

The other temples are dedicated to Mariamman. She protects against illness and provides rain.

Sikhism

Sikhs should not be confused with Hindus, for though the two religions are related, they are not the same. Sikh men have beards and wear turbans. Their last name always has the word *Singh* (lion) in it. Women's last names always contain the word *Kaur* (princess).

There are 40-50,000 Sikhs in Malaysia, divided up into three groups, *Malway*, *Majaha* and *Dhoaba*. They came to Malaysia as soldiers and policemen in the service of the British, but they have since moved into many other fields.

Sikhs celebrate the birthdays and deaths of their gurus, the most notable being *Guru Nanak* and *Govind Singh*. They have a new year's festival in the middle of our year. The holy book of the Sikhs is called the *Granth*. Sikhism was once supposed to serve as a synthesis of India's two main religions, but it was never really possible to reconcile Hinduism and Islam. Now, within India, militant Sikhs want to secede and form their own state.

This is not something to fear in Malaysia however. All minority religions have recently banded together in the *Malaysian Consultative Council for Buddhism, Christianity, Hinduism and Sikhism*.

Christianity

Christianity came to Malacca during colonial times. The Portuguese brought Catholicism and the Dutch brought Protestantism. Of the two, the Portuguese promoted missionary activity while the Dutch preferred to concentrate solely on business. Catholic and Methodist missionaries in the 19th century were the first to arrive in great numbers. Many of Malaysia's elite schools are still nominally Christian, recalling the work of the missionaries. There are about 1 million Christians in Malaysia. Christmas is an official national holiday and Good Friday is a state holiday in Sarawak.

In addition to Catholics and Methodists, there are also Presbyterians, Baptists and Adventists. Church life tends to be very lively and services can be quite emotional.

Animism

Animism, the original indigenous religion of East and Southeast Asia, predates all other religions in Malaysia. It is still the religion of many of the Orang Asli.

Animism is the belief that all things have spirits or souls. There are good and bad spirits and part of the quest for mankind is to cater to the good spirits, while warding off the bad ones.

The Senoi believe – a very modern and beautiful notion – that each human being has his own soul, but that this is merely a part of the collective world soul. When a ghost takes possession of someone's soul, that person gets sick. A *hala*, or priest, must go and find the soul. When he does, he must convince it to come back to the body.

The Senoi sit together each morning (or at least, they used to) and share their dreams from the previous night with one another. They give advice and guidance to those who have had bad dreams so that next time their dreams will be better. They believe that a great part of life takes place in dreams, so dreams must be positive. This is a kind of imagination training that is used in Western psychotherapy.

Some groups, like the Jah Hut and the Mah Meri, maintain the custom of carving ghost-images out of wood in certain circumstances:

●when a sickness must be lifted from a spirit.

●during harvest ceremonies.

●during purification ceremonies (when an area has been taken over by bad spirits).

●when a shaman passes on his power to a successor.

There are many strong taboos to protect against offending spirits.

Customs, Taboos and Superstitions

Like all Southeast Asian peoples, Malays were at one time animists, and their culture maintains a lot of animist influences. Traditionally, spirits had certain forms and characteristics. They could eat and drink, be pleasant or malicious. People can call them, chase them away or even destroy them.

Spirits live in trees, forests, water, mountains and swamps. They live in all animals including people, mostly in the head, but also in other parts of the body. There are hair, teeth, tongue, saliva, finger and fingernail spirits. These spirits are part of the reason Malays are so physically respectful of other people. They would not want to risk angering another person's spirits.

Naturally, many of these traditions and beliefs have been altered over the years by Islam. But since spirits are not incompatible with Islam, many of them have been strengthened and preserved as well. Islam also provides a strong way to intervene in the spirit world – with the help of certain Koranic verses. Since Allah is all-powerful, he can control the spirit world as well as the physical one.

Many people still put faith in *dukun* (conjurers), *pawang* (traditional healers) and *bomohs* (spirit healers). In the past, important deals were never made without consulting a *dukun*. Even today they are

consulted when building a house or before a marriage or birth, particularly in the countryside.

In the cities, not surprisingly, many of the traditional beliefs are no longer thought important and many of the once-important taboos are not observed. That is not the case in the *kampongs*, where nobody would question their existence. Vampire movies are discussed like documentaries. Spirits are invoked to protect women during pregnancy and to heal the sick, usually in conjunction with Islamic teaching.

Understanding the animistic background of Malay culture helps explain some of the customs and rules of behavior Westerners might find a little puzzling. People really do believe them. For example, **children** may not...

●play hide-and-seek in the dark, or spirits might follow them home.

●sit on pillows, or their rear ends will get burned.

●eat sugarcane in the evening, or their mother will have her blood sucked out, and die.

●climb on the kitchen cabinet, or they will stop growing.

●whistle at night, because it will attract spirits.

There are quite a few taboos that protect *infants*:

●The bib may not be soaked, or the baby will get a stomachache and cry.

●No one may sit near a baby's head, or the child will develop epilepsy.

●No one should call a baby fat, or it will lose weight.

Instead, say that it has a "healthy body."

●A baby must never be looked at in a mirror, or it will drown one day.

●A baby should not play with fire (a universal taboo, but with an unusual consequence) or it will soil its pants as an adult.

●A baby that eats sticky rice will have a stutter forever.

●Do not stroke the cheek or the stomach of a baby, or it will lose its appetite.

●If a baby eats its own excrement, the

parents must immediately get a handful of rice from the neighbors or else the baby will become an imbecile.

●If a baby eats fish, it will get worms in its stomach.

Of course, there are also taboos that apply **before birth**:

●The mother may not eat any rice stuck on the bottom of the pot, or the baby will stick coming out.

●In preparing fish, the mother may not cut the mouth or the child will have a hare-lip.

●Candles or lanterns must be carried behind a pregnant woman or she will lose too much blood giving birth.

●If a pregnant woman runs around the house too much, the baby will be born feet-first.

An **unmarried woman** should not sing in the kitchen when preparing meals, or she will not find a husband.

●If she changes her seat while eating, she will have more than one man, but not one for her entire life.

●If she sleeps past dawn, she will have to wait a long time for a husband.

●If she cuts fabric on a Sunday, it will one day burn.

Although unmarried women are better "protected" by taboos than men, there are taboos for **bachelors** as well:

●They should not cut holes in coconuts, or they will only find "used" women.

●If they sit on a coconut, their testicles will swell.

●If a young man reacts to an elder in an angry or aggressive way, he will be struck by lightning.

Some **general taboos** are the following:

●Anyone eating out of a pot will have an ugly or crippled spouse.

●Anyone who passes under a wash line will contract incurable rheumatism.

●Anyone who cuts his nails by daylight will have trouble making a living.

●Anyone who says he has no money will not be able to cover his own costs of living.

●Putting too much sauce on rice invites floods.

●A house door that opens to the street will bring bad luck.

Malay customs

Pregnancy and Birth: The *Bath of the Womb* is for mothers pregnant for the first time. It takes place in the 7th or 8th month of pregnancy, on the 12th, 19th or 23rd of the Islamic calendar, preferably on a Wednesday or a Saturday. The midwife recites magical verses, cuts the pregnant mother's hair along her forehead, paints her face with rice paste and puts saffron rice over her body. Then she bathes the mother with lime water, sticks an egg in her sarong and sits her on a stool with a hen tied to its leg. Then the mother is once again bathed with water so that the egg falls to the floor, a symbol to bring about an easy birth.

Next, the mother looks in the mirror and hopes the baby is at least as beautiful as she. Now it is clear that her hair was cut so that the baby will not be hairy.

Next, the mother lies down on seven layers of fabric, the bottom layer of which is white. The midwife recites some more magic spells and touches the mother's stomach. Three threads are tied around her stomach with rice, saffron and ginger and gold, silver and bronze rings. Then a smooth coconut is spun on her stomach and rolled down toward her feet. If the eye of the coconut is facing up, the child will be a boy.

Next, the mother gets up and puts on her best dress and bathes herself in sandalwood and coconut oil. Then she pays the midwife M$ 2.25 along with 2.5 m of white fabric, the sarong she was bathed in and the hen that was tied to the stool. Either before or after this ceremony, the midwife is formally asked to attend the birth.

In addition to the midwife, a *pawang* also attends the birth. Ingredients for his magic include, the tail of a manta, a bees' nest, an old fishing net, bitter grass and some bread.

The midwife bathes the newborn baby with betelnut juice to protect it from evil spirits and demons. She cuts the umbilical cord with sharp bamboo and ties the end in a knot. Then bathes it with saffron and lime juice and covers it with a betel leaf. Afterwards, the father or grandfather whispers a prayer into the baby's right ear. The midwife makes a cross on the baby's forehead with saffron and puts a drop of honey or date juice on its tongue. Finally, she massages the young mother. Once again, the midwife gets certain gifts for her services.

On the seventh day following the birth, there are more ceremonies. Often, it is on this day that the umbilical cord is fully cut. Then a chicken (a hen for boys, a rooster for girls) is let loose on the spot where blood fell a week earlier. The mother and baby are ceremonially bathed.

Another ceremony is the sweetening of the tongue. A gold ring is dipped in betelnut juice, syrup or date juice, and then in salt water. It is then touched to the baby's tongue. At the same time, the following prayer is spoken:

"In the name of Allah the almighty and all powerful, may this child have a long life; may he be wise enough to speak with a prince; may his voice be sweet as sugar and may his words bring joy to the hearts of men, as pleasant as betelnut and as compelling as salt."

On the same day, the baby's hair is cut and the child is carried around outside by an odd number of men, each of whom paint the baby's face with some rice paste and give it some saffron and rice, as well as a lock of hair. The hair is put in water inside a decorated coconut shell. The baby is named during this ceremony.

Next, the midwife shaves the baby and puts the hair in the coconut shell. This is buried along with a coco-nut or similar seedling. The plant, which grows along with the baby, is intended to commemorate the birth.

The mother must stay inside her house for the first 44 days after the birth. She must stay in bed for the first seven, even if she is feeling fine. She may not do any housework, or leave the house at all. She is also not allowed to eat what she wants. Everyday,

she takes traditional medicine and warms her stomach. On the 45th day, the midwife returns and once again bathes the mother in lime water, after which the mother may go out. The baby's siblings celebrate with a feast.

Circumcision: Islam requires the circumcision of both sexes. This is an old Arab practice that actually predates Islam. Today, circumcision of boys is routine in many parts of the world, including North America, for hygienic reasons. Female circumcision, or clitoridectomy, is the symbolic removal of a piece of skin from the clitoris. (In some parts of Africa, this is more extensive, with the intention of killing female lust.) The traditional male circumcision ceremony is described here, though in much of Malaysia it takes place unceremoniously in a hospital under total or local anesthesia.

The boys are usually between 10 and 12 years old and must have finished reading the Koran in religious school. Usually, they await the day with a mixture of excitement and apprehension. The day before the ceremony, the last Koran lesson is taught.

In the morning of the ceremony, the *Tok Mudim* (circumciser) and other guests come to the boy's house. The *Tok Mudim* is sprinkled with wet rice and invited inside. He

In two minutes it was over! It was not very painful. Just like antbite!

is given a betelnut box containing betelnuts, betel leaves, limes, tobacco, a gold ring and some money. Normally, the Imam, the Muezzin and other religious men attend as well. The circumcision is formally their responsibility, though it is passed on to the *Tok Mudim* by passing on the betelnut box.

Next, the boy sits down in front of the *Tok Mudim*, who gives him an amulet and recites holy words. Friends of the boy then lead the two to a nearby river where the *Tok Mudim* throws a spear in the water to ward off demons. The boy sits down in a boat that is then filled with water. He stays there for two or three hours, after which his penis should be nearly numb. During this time, he is supposed to remain in a good mood. The boy is then bathed with lime water, again to protect him from spirits. Then he goes into his house, which has been blessed with prayers and strewn with wet rice.

Now it is time for the actual act. The front of the house is blocked off with a curtain and the necessary tools are laid out for the *Tok Mudim*: A branch from a banana tree, a banana leaf, ashes, a razor, forceps and medicine. The circumcision takes place on the yard-long banana tree branch. At the command of the *Tok Mudim*, the boy recites two prayers. As soon as he is finished, the *Tok Mudim* quickly and skillfully cuts off the boy's foreskin. All the while, friends and relatives stand outside the curtains reciting verses from the Koran, which partially drown out the boy's scream. Sometimes, the parents of the boy prefer to be away. Afterwards, the *Tok Mudim* gives the boy back to his father and prays one more time before leaving.

The boy is then put to bed. A small bamboo stick is put between his legs so that his thighs will not touch the wound. A blanket is hung from a pole, like a tent.

After three days, the bandages come off. At first, there are a lot of taboos for the boy: he may have no second helpings at meals; he may not cut anything sharp (or the foreskin will grow back); he may not go barefoot in the chicken run (or his penis will rot); and he may neither drink coconut juice nor eat fatty food (or he will get a pimple on his penis). The main point of these taboos is to keep the boy from running around until he is fully healed.

House Building Ceremony: Before a house may be built, it must be determined whether or not the site is acceptable. A *Dukun* summons the spirits to ask if their descendants may build a house there. This takes place at dusk when saffron rice and rice water are laid out on the ground. At the same time, the woman of the house measures the area of the house with a stick the span of her arms. Then she inserts the stick in the ground in the middle of the site. Next to it is placed a glass filled with water and covered with a leaf. The *Dukun* then asks the spirit of the place if the family may build a house there.

Everyone returns to the site early the next morning. Unless the glass has overflowed or the stick is longer than the woman's arm, there are no objections to building the house. After a small meal, the *Dukun* scatters saffron rice on the site and sprinkles special water on the wood to be used for construction.

When the central pillar of the house is put into place, a coin is buried with it, as a sort of rent for the land. The column is covered with colored fabric, usually red, white and black, while magic words are recited. Two green coconuts covered in rice paste are left at the foot of the column. The coconuts are left there for about two months until they start to sprout. If they both sprout at the same time, it is a sign of good luck.

On the day of the official opening of the house, the *Dukun* returns and symbolically opens the door, scattering rice and sprinkling water. A few days later, the family invites the children of the *kampong* and their teacher for a special dinner. The pot from which rice and coconut milk are served is then hung on the central column for good luck.

Burial: When someone dies, the first person to be informed is the *Imam*, and then the rest of the village. A person who dies in the morning is buried that evening, and a person who dies in the afternoon is buried the next day. Not only is this an Islamic tradition, but it is generally a good idea in the tropics. Before burial, the body is laid out in the middle of the house on a bed made with fine cloth. Another cloth is laid over the body to keep it clean.

The arms are folded over the chest and the body is covered with blankets, the face with thin fabric. A betelnut box is placed over the stomach to scare spirits. Some incense is placed on the floor, where it remains for three days after the burial.

Friends and relatives now say goodbye. At a set time, the body is taken outside and bathed with sandalwood and camphor. Cotton is laid on the body. It is then taken back inside the house and dressed in an unsewn shirt and pants, then wrapped in cotton. Before the head is finally covered, the family of the deceased sprinkle sandalwood powder on it. The body is then laid in a coffin lined with fabric. The coffin is then covered with cloth and carried to the mosque, where special prayers are recited. The relatives then give money to the assembly for their prayers.

The coffin is then taken to the grave where it is once again opened, and a little earth is put inside. Next, the coffin is buried and the spot is marked with wood until a stone is prepared. The *Imam* recites a few last prayers and flowers and sandalwood water are scattered on the grave. The *Imam* gets some money, the empty bottle, and the mat and umbrella he used during the ceremony.

There are special days of mourning on the 3rd, 7th, 14th, 40th and 100th days after the death and sometimes also on the yearly anniversary of the death.

Festivals and Holidays

There are few countries with as many holidays as Malaysia. This is the result of its having so many different ethnic groups and religions. Even though Islam is the state religion, other major religions have at least one or two nationally-recognized holidays of their own. In addition, the sultans each have holidays in their states on their birthdays. There is also a whole assortment of other national holidays. If you are (not) careful, you can wind up running into holidays all over the country. The advantage is that you might get to see something special. The disadvantage is that many sights and businesses are closed, including government offices. Most shops and restaurants stay open, except during Ramadan. If a holiday falls on a Sunday, it is moved to another day.

Islamic Festivals and Holidays

As they are based on a lunar calendar, Islamic holidays jump around on the Roman calendar. The lunar calendar moves in a 30-year cycle, where every second and third year has 355 instead of 354 days. Like other things Islamic, the names of the months are in Arabic. 1991 is the year 1411 / 12 after the Haj when Mohammed left Mecca for Medina in 622.

The following are Islamic national holidays:

Israk Mikraj: On the evening of the 27th of Rejab (an Islamic month). It commemorates the night when Mohammed went to heaven and received the 5 daily prayers from Allah. Only a holiday in Kedah and Negeri Sembilan.

Awal Ramadan: The start of the fasting month of Ramadan. Only a holiday in Johor.

Nuzul Quran: On the 7th day of Ramadan, Mohammed was shown the Surens of the Koran. A state holiday in Kelantan, Melaka, Perak, Perlis, Selangor and Terengganu.

Hari Raya Puasa: The end of the month of Ramadan, during which Muslims may not eat or drink between sunrise and sunset. Not even spittle may be swallowed during the day - so be careful when you walk below a Muslim's window. Sweets are popular in the evenings, so many people gain weight rather than losing. When the first sign of the new moon appears, the sultan of each state declares the official end of the fast. In the *kampongs*, the men go from house to house, praying, eating and wishing everyone well. The next day, *Hari Raya Puasa Day*, many people have open houses and invite their non-Muslim friends as well.

Hari Raya Haji: The 10th day of the 12th month (Zulhijah), when the pilgrims in Mecca visit *Baitullah*, the black stone. A day for prayer and visiting friends. Those who can, slaughter a goat or cow and give the meat to the poor.

Every year, thousands of Malaysian Moslems go on the pilgrimage to Saudi Arabia. At this time, you can see white-clad pilgrims all over the country, particularly in Suban Airport. Friends and relatives wish them off and welcome them back as new *Haji* or *Hajjah*. Every year some poor souls are cheated out of their life savings by operators who promise them a trip to Mecca and then disappear with their money. There is a special agency, *Tabung Haji*, to deter this abuse.

This holiday is extended by a day in Kedah, Kelantan, Pahang, Perlis and Terengganu.

Ma'al Hijrah / Awal Muharram: The Islamic New Year. The Islamic year 1411 began on July 23, 1990.

Birthday of the Prophet Mohammed: Koran readings, parades.

Chinese Holidays and Festivals

The Chinese' calendar is also based on the moon. The months are 29 or 30 days long. Every 30 months, another month is added. There is a 60 year repeating cycle made up of five 12-year blocks. Each of these 12 years is given the name of an animal. 1991 is the year of the goat.

1991:	Goat	1997:	Ox
1992:	Monkey	1998:	Tiger
1993:	Hen	1999:	Rabbit
1994:	Dog	2000:	Dragon
1995:	Pig	2001:	Snake
1996:	Rat	2002:	Horse

Chinese New Year: Takes place sometime between January 21 and February 19. Actually a month-long celebration for two weeks either side of New Year's day, but the official holiday lasts only for two days.

Many businesses are closed for the entire week of the new year, however. As during *Hari Raya Puasa*, people get together with their families which means heavy traffic, and fully booked flights, trains, buses and hotels. There are additional buses and trains run

The god of the sky is honored on the 9th day of the new year. The Hakka Chinese make offerings of sugar cane.

On the last day, *Chap Goh Meh*, young people throw mandarin oranges into water in order to find a good husband or wife.

There are lion and dragon dances everywhere during the New Year's celebrations.

Ang Pow

An important part of the Chinese New Year is giving unmarried people *ang pow*, or small red (for good luck) bags filled with money. Bills are usually given in pairs, for example, M$ 2, 4, 8, 20, etc., though it is acceptable to give one dollar bill and one ten *sen* piece. Some young people do quite well, and all children look forward to it.

Today, Malay children also get *ang pow* on Hari Raya in green (for Islam) bags. This is an interesting example of how the different cultures influence each other.

---

during the New Year. As you might expect, there are many rituals associated with this very important occasion. For example, seven days before the New Year, the kitchen god is honored. He looks after the well-being of the family. He is offered a candy so his mouth sticks together and only sweet things come out.

On the last day of the old year, most families have a big reunion dinner. Family and temple altars are full. Unmarried members of the family are given *ang pows* in red bags.

At 11 pm, the official start of the year, all the windows are opened to let the new year in. Then things get crazy as hundreds of tons of fireworks go off all over Malaysia. Officially, fireworks are only allowed on the 1st, 2nd and 15th days of the new year, but no one follows this. 1988 was the first time in years that fireworks were allowed again. In Singapore, Lee Kwan Yew has little patience for this kind of wastefulness, and fireworks remain banned.

The first few days of the year are for visiting friends and relatives. The exception being the 3rd day, when it is particularly important to avoid quarrels. People bring gifts of mandarin oranges in even numbers. The word for mandarin sounds like the word for "gold," so they are a symbol of prosperity. All Chinese must begin the new year in a completely new set of clothes.

Chinese age one year at the new year, so a baby born two months before would celebrate its second birthday. On its day of birth, a baby is considered one year old.

Qing Ming: Not an official holiday. The 8th day of the 3rd month. Families visit the graves of their ancestors. A few days beforehand, the graves are cleared and cleaned. On the actual day, families assemble at the graves, burn incense, kneel in prayer and show respect to their departed ancestors. They burn money as an offering and also offer pork, chickens, ducks, fruit, sweets, tea and wine. Finally, after the spirits have enjoyed it, the food is eaten. If the graves are inaccessible, then the whole ceremony can take place on the house altar or in a temple. The ceremony dates back to Confucius (551-449 BC). The graveyards, which lie still for an entire year, are for one day full of life.

Wesak Day: The most important Buddhist holiday, the celebration of the Buddha's birth, enlightenment and entry into Nirvana. Known in Thailand as *Visakha Buja*. There are candle processions in Thai temples. In all Buddhist temples, people pray and light incense. In Malacca there is a procession of decorated cars.

Tuan Wu Chieh: Not an official holiday. The 5th day of the 5th month. People honor the patriotic poet *Chu Yuan* (3rd century BC), who drowned himself rather than serve under a corrupt administration. At the time, people threw sticky rice into the river to confuse the fish so they would not eat his body. The festival is also known as the dragon boat festival. Some cities hold dragon boat races to honor the poet.

Festival of the Hungry Spirit: Not an official holiday. During the 7th month of the lunar year, the souls of the dead come back to wander the physical world. Offerings are prepared and incense is lit in the streets.

Moon Cake Festival: Not an official holiday. The commemoration of the victory over the Mongols on the 15th day of the 8th month. Children have parades, women pray to the moon god, and everyone eats rich moon cakes. They sometimes have unusual fillings of meat or lard.

Festival of the Nine Emperor Gods: Not an official holiday. Celebrated only in Penang and Kuala Lumpur. Takes place on the 9th day of the 9th month. Operas and parades mark this nine-day-long celebration honoring the gods, during which many people only eat vegetarian foods. On the 9th day, some people walk over hot coals near the temples. The same holiday as the *Vegetarian Festival* on Phuket, in Thailand.

Indian Festivals and Holidays

This is a list of Hindu festivals, but bear in mind that they are not celebrated by all Indians. There are many Muslims and Christians among Malaysia's Indian population.

Thaipusam: Sometime in February. An official holiday in Penang, Selangor, Kuala Lumpur and Sarawak. This festival, in its

Holy Smokes!: Giant sticks of incense.

Malay form banned in India, is devoted to *Lord Murugan / Subramaniam*, a son of *Shiva*. Pilgrims parade through the streets to the *Mariamman* or *Subramaniam* Temple, carrying offerings. Some men stick sharp hooks with weights and even long spears into their bodies in order to fulfill holy vows. Some thrust spears in one cheek and out the other.

The preparations for taking part are extensive, including a month-long vegetarian fast, sleeping on hard floors, and abstaining from sexual relations. On the day of the festival, the pilgrims go into a trance and they neither bleed nor feel any pain! And when the hooks and spears are withdrawn, there are no marks or scars. When the procession reaches the temple, and after circling it three times, the pilgrims give their offerings. Then they remove the spears and hooks and rub themselves with holy ashes.

There are also parades, processions, music, and other events. If you are in Kuala Lumpur and feel like celebrating with hundreds of thousands of others, go to the Batu Caves, where it gets really wild. In Penang, the trip to the temple is good, but it is becoming too much of a tourist attraction and losing its appeal. In Ipoh, there are seldom more than a dozen tourists and the holiday retains all of its traditional local flavor.

Mah Shiva Rathiri: Not an official holiday. End of February. All night prayers and songs are offered to Shiva.

Tasimagam: Not an official holiday. Mid-March. Similar to *Thaipusam*, especially in Cheng, 11 km north of Malacca.

Hindu New Year: Not an official holiday. Mid-April. The 1st day of the month of *Sitthirai*. Prayers are offered in temples and homes.

Chithra Paurnami: Not an official holiday. Celebrated in Negeri Sembilan, Perak and Selangor on the full moon in the Tamil month of Chithirai. Similar to *Thaipusam*.

Deepavali: In the month of Aippasi in mid-October. A celebration of the victory of good over evil, light over darkness and wisdom over ignorance. Prayers are offered in homes and temples, and many people have open houses for their friends and relatives.

Kanta Shashti: Not an official holiday. Also in the month of Aippasi. The festival lasts 6 days and is dedicated to *Subramaniam*, the champion over evil. The last day is the high point when the fight with *Sooran* is reenacted in pantomime in the temples. *Kandasamy Temple* in Kuala Lumpur is an especially good place to experience this holiday.

Christian Festivals and Holidays

Friday is a holiday in Sabah and Sarawak.

Fiesta San Pedro (June 29): The festival of the Portuguese fishermen of Malacca. They clean and fix up their boats and, of course, pray for a good catch.

The Feast of St. Anne (July 26-29): The Catholics of Malacca ask for good will. Ends with high mass and a candle procession.

Santa Cruz (September 13): Festival of the Holy Cross in the small chapel of the Holy Cross on Malim Hill in Malacca. There is a service and a lantern procession.

St. Xavier (December 3): Festival honoring St. Xavier, the patron saint of Malacca.

Christmas (December 25): Christians have their open-house parties on Christmas day. Christmas carols are very popular in Malaysia.

State Holidays

Each state has its sultan or governor. On his birthday, the state has an official holiday. If it falls on a Sunday, the following Monday is a holiday.

1 / 25	*Kedah*
3 / 8	*Selangor*
3 / 21	*Terengganu* (coronation of the sultan)
3 / 30,31	*Kelantan*
4 / 8	*Johor*
4 / 9	*Terengganu* (birthday of the sultan)
4 / 19	*Perak*
6 / 10	*Malacca*
7 / 16	*Penang*
7 / 19	*Negeri Sembilan*
9 / 25	*Perlis*
10 / 24	*Pahang*

1 / 1	New Year's Day (except in Kedah, Perlis, Kelantan, Terengganu, and Johor)
2 / 1	Federal Territory Day (only in K.L.)
5 / 1	Labor Day
6 / 3	The King's Birthday
8 / 31	Independence Day

Arts and Culture

If we were to go back a few hundred years and visit the Malay Peninsula, we would find a land completely covered by jungle. There were no cities. (Even Malacca, at the height of its glory, was never more than a big town).

Near the mouths of the big rivers were the wooden palaces and fortifications of the various sultans. Smaller settlements appeared along the riverbanks. The people lived from fishing the rivers and seas, and from whatever they grew in the small fields within the settlements and from what they could find in the forests.

Country life was simple. There was little problem raising enough food for everyone. Sometimes there were festivals, weddings, religious or other ceremonies to keep people entertained. If someone became sick, they consulted the *bomohs* whose magic was used to repel or counteract evil spirits. For fun, there were spinning tops, kites and sometimes, shadow puppet plays.

Court life was more elegant and formal. Courtly manners were important and well-defined. Nonetheless, life was far from ostentatious and the palaces themselves were quite simple.

Since Malaysians were never really an urban people, they never developed a formal high culture. The more sophisticated forms of Malay culture have developed in their neighbors, particularly the Javanese.

The Malays are skilled at handiwork. There are some nice wood carvings on houses and palaces, but Islam has inhibited the development of painting, since neither people nor animals can be portrayed.

Literature is similarly undeveloped. Even today, reading is not very popular in Malaysia. (According to new regulations, one can become a teacher only if he or she reads a minimum of three books a year!) Most of the books published in Malay are schoolbooks or religious texts, and there are few translations of world literature and local literature is not supported effectively.

Concerts and *theater* are seldom found, and usually confined to Kuala Lumpur when they are. In places like the central market of Kuala Lumpur, there are regular folklore performances. Despite its multi-cultural makeup, Malaysia has little to offer in terms of high culture.

Neither politicians nor ruling families are much concerned with promoting culture. Life is rather practical and materialistic. The Chinese and Indians came from rich cultural traditions, but they came to Malaysia as laborers who worked hard to become wealthy. Most of their free time is taken up by Mahjong and other games of chance. Of course, there are a few cultural societies that promote lion and dragon dances and traditional orchestras. The same is true for traditional Indian dance, which is usually religious in nature. But though high culture is preserved, it is in the same state it was a hundred years ago. There is no sense of advancing culture the way we think of it in the West, or for that matter, in other parts of Asia. In Japan for instance, artists search for new expressions all the time.

I have had contact with Malaysians from all cultural backgrounds and from all age groups. But I have never encountered any kind of intellectual culture – that never comes into discussion; philosophy is a foreign word. Obviously, this has advantages, like avoiding ideological disputes. People in Malaysia live in the middle of their lives, having a job, earning money and supporting a family are far more important than abstract concerns. It is quite easy to meet the basic needs of life, the desire to go beyond this is almost non-existent. Though most people have unfulfilled material desires, few people want for the basics in life. The high points of most people's lives are religious and family festivals.

So let us take a look at the few cultural specialties of Peninsular Malaysia:

Shadow Puppets (*Wayang Kulit*)

The Islamic Malays, particularly those in Kelantan, have a Hindu tradition of shadow puppet plays. They originated over 1000 years ago in Java and spread to India and Thailand, as well as to Malaysia. Epic stories are recounted by the puppets. The most popular themes are the **Mahabharata** and the **Ramayana**. The Thai influence is noticeable in the leather (=*kulit*) puppets and the accompanying gong music. The Malays were enjoying this forerun-ner to television long before Islam swept the country.

These Hindu epics deal with struggles between gods and demons. Although they are not Islamic, they are a completely indigenous part of Malay culture. The plays themselves are more than the retelling of old stories.

The *tok dalang*, or puppet master, entertains his audience with his skill and dynamism, and also his ability to interweave recent village events into the story. There are different styles and traditions in each town, and though the stories remain the same, no two performances are alike. Small villages have makeshift bamboo stages, about 2.5 x 3 m. They are usually open at the rear, allowing the audience to get a look at the puppet master at work, as well as at the multi-colored puppets. At the beginning of every performance, there is a brief ceremony in which the figures are "brought to life" by the gods and spirits.

A cycle of performances lasts a week (about 3-4 hours a night) and ends with the division of the earthly and the divine.

Malay Dance

As with shadow puppets, Javanese traditional dance evolved into Malay traditional dance, though Malay dance also shows considerable Indian influence. As in Indonesia and Thailand, the accompanying music is played by a *gamelan* orchestra. This consists of various gongs and drums – *gendang, deguk gedomabok* – accompanied by flute and three-stringed *rebab*.

There are harvest and fishing dances, candle and umbrella dances. In some, like the *Tari Piring* or *Plate Dance*, offerings are symbolically given to the gods. In others, dancers are supposed to be riding imaginary horses. Some dances (*Ronggeng*) resemble a contest between groups of men and women.

Now and then, you can find the *Makyong* dance drama being performed. All roles are played by women, apart from two clowns. It is a 12-part romance between a prince and a princess with demons and others taking part.

Malays are known as the most artistic cultural group within Malaysia – actors, musicians (they dominate the pop scene), dancers, painters (look for the cartoonist LAT), and even a few writers.

93

Indian Dance

Of the great variety of Indian dance, it is mostly southern Indian dance that we see in Malaysia. There are frequent contests between different groups of dancers so that they do not lose their artistic traditions.

Classical Indian music is not as widespread. The *Bangra* is a temperamental and lively group dance from the Punjab, home of the Sikhs.

Chinese Opera

The best time to see Chinese or Peking Opera is at temple festivals like the Festival of the 9 Emperor Gods in October. To us, this art form seems very foreign.

Every detail is standardized and individuality is forsaken. The actors either wear masks or are made up with colors to have the proper facial expression for their characters (gold = gods; green = spirits or demons; black = honesty; white = dishonesty). The dances are fully choreographed according to tradition, which also dictates the way the songs are to be sung. There is an orchestra with flutes, string instruments, cymbals, gongs, and other instruments.

The performance is often static. The actors deliver long speeches which we cannot understand. But the fight scenes and other dances are very dramatic. Usually, there is a moral. Good defeats evil. There are themes like love, loyalty, heroism, duty and honor, which conflict with intrigues and jealousy.

The older members of the audience know the story already. They are not there to find out what happens, but to experience the complete work of art.

Rules of Behavior

There are at least three different sets of standards, one for each of the three main ethnic groups. The following rules, however, are applicable for the entire country:

• Treat older people and people with high positions in society with respect. Children are expected to respect their parents unquestioningly. Asian cultures are hierarchical and everyone has his or her place. An older brother or sister is addressed as "older brother" or "older sister," rather than by his or her name. If a person has a title, like "doctor" or "professor," use the title to address him, rather than his name.

• Never point at anyone with your index finger. If you must point, either use your entire hand or make a fist and point with your thumb. If you are gesturing for someone to come to you, wave your hand with the palm down, not with the palm up as we do.

• In general, people do not like to give "no" as an answer. So if someone says "yes," it might only mean that they understand what you are saying, not that they necessarily agree with you. If you really need information, do not ask yes or no questions.

• The concept of "saving face" is very important all over Asia. Do not attempt to shame or embarrass anyone – you will never get what you want that way. The same goes for raising your voice or getting visibly agitated. This is more true for Malays than Chinese, who tend to be a bit more direct.

• Friendly, courteous behavior is always appreciated in Malaysia. No one expects foreigners to behave as Malaysians, but people will generally appreciate you more if you are polite and friendly. This is the most important rule of behavior.

• In general, Asian societies are more conservative than Western ones. Sexual promiscuity or openness is not tolerated. Dress respectfully. Women, for example, are expected to wear bras. Kissing in public is taboo, even for married couples. I have seen Chinese couples holding hands in public, but this is rare. Do not be fooled by modern, well-dressed young people, despite their appearance, they are sure to be more conservative than their Western counterparts. Touching members of the opposite sex in public is to be avoided. Women who do, only serve to encourage the stereotype of the promiscuous Western woman, something many Malays believe due to Western T.V., video and cinema.

• Do not wear shoes in anyone's house. Always take them off at the door, even when they tell you it is not necessary.

• In general, people use squat toilets, which are more biologically effective and sanitary than Western toilets. Malays and Indians use water and their left hands instead of toilet paper, so take your own toilet paper with you if you cannot get used to this practice.

• Accordingly, Malays and Indians eat only with the right hand, usually without utensils.

• There is no need to tip in restaurants in Malaysia. Though you might want to leave a portion of the change in places where no service charge is added to the bill. Hotel chambermaids get a small tip. There is no need to tip taxi drivers.

• Do not call out to waiters in restaurants, but try and catch their eye and motion to them.

It is not difficult to get along in Malaysia. The people are friendly and easy-going and like foreigners. Even dress restrictions are fairly relaxed in comparison with other Islamic countries. Remember that despite their present status, most of the Chinese and Indian immigrants came from the working classes. There was formerly no middle class and only a few Malay families formed the upper class. Now, there is a small, but growing middle class. It is not yet big enough to support the leisure activities that we usually associate with the middle class in the West. Most people work all day, usually for very little money. In the evening, they eat dinner, play cards or mahjong, watch TV and go to bed early. Day-to-day life has a relaxed and natural pace.

A particularly warm Malaysian tradition is that of the Open House on certain holidays, like *Hari Raya*, the end of Ramadan. On such days, you are welcome to go into the house of any Muslim. Ordinary people can also call on the king or prime minister.

During the Chinese New Year, you can visit some Chinese families (except on the 3rd day), and there is usually something to eat or drink. If you are invited, bring a gift of 4 oranges or mandarin oranges (for good luck) and give *ang pow* envelopes to the children (see section on Chinese Festivals and Holidays). Do not wear black or white, the colors of mourning.

Here are some of the *rules of behavior for the different ethnic groups:*

The Malays

Malay social life is governed by Islam and by the **Adat**, or traditional code of behavior and customs. There are several forms of *Adat*:

- *Adat Temenggong* – paternal organization (all over Malaysia);
- *Adat Perpateh* – maternal organization (in Negeri Sembilan and Minangkabau parts of Malacca;
- *Adat Istiadat di Raja* – the traditions and customs of the court.
- *Adat Resam* – customs and traditions dealing with specific parts of life like birth, weddings, funerals, etc. Malays expect and appreciate respect for parents and other elders, good neighborly relations and maintenance of harmony and order.

Malay society is group-oriented. The *kampong* is the most important social unit, with the *ketua kampong* or *penghulu* at the head. In general, Malays are not particularly well-to-do, but they rarely want for anything.

Malays love **status and prestige**. All over Malaysia, you will run across official titles, uniforms, awards, and other status-symbols. As a rule, Malays do not like to work for others outside of their family or *kampong*.

The English plantation owners realized this and were forced to import Indian labor. This might explain why so much of the tourism business is not in Malay hands.

Malays love **children**, fathers no less than mothers. Children are pretty much free to do whatever they want. Parents hit their children very rarely. Example and praise are the foundations of child-rearing.

The society is generally divided by sex. **Women** are not oppressed, especially on the east coast, where they have a lot more

(GU)

Buddha Under Glass: One of many in the Kek Lok Si Temple in Penang.

(KN)

Kuala Lumpur: A fascinating blend of old and new, tradition and progress: An open air

(WW)

(KN)

restaurant in Chinatown; colonial buildings in the shadows of gigantic skyscrapers.

(H

The Cameron Highlands: Fresh air, tea plantations, and the chance to cool off with

(KN)

(PR)

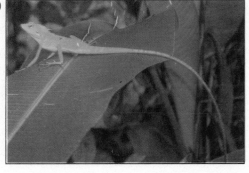

nature.

Religious Splendor: The Ubudiah Mosque in Kuala Kangsar; memorials in the Cheng

(KN)

(KN)

Hoon Teng Temple in Malacca; a statue of Ganesha in the Batu Caves near Kuala Lumpur.

(PR)

(PR)

Sun, Sea and Sand: The east coast and many offshore islands have a lot to offe

control over family affairs. They also control the markets, which has great bearing in a rural society.

Malays also put great value in politeness. This is evident in the language and in personal **greetings**. Men do not normally touch women as this would require a long cleaning ceremony before prayer, so do not expect to shake hands with members of the opposite sex. This prohibition is gradually disappear-ing, especially in the big cities, but it is better to err on the side of caution.

Men greet others by lightly touching both hands and then bringing them into the chest, which means, "I greet you by heart".

Women respond by bringing the right hand to the lips and then to the breast. This means, "I kiss your greeting, take it through the mouth and direct it to my heart".

With the resurgence of Islam, traditional Malay **clothing** is once again becoming popular. Men wear *sarongs* to Friday prayers even in the big cities. In the countryside, you see them often. Men wear black *songkoks* on their heads. For formal occasions, men wear a Malay shirt, or *baju melayu*, with pants and a sarong made of brocade tied around their hips.

Women usually wear *baju kurung*, a long loose-fitting blouse over a long skirt. It covers the body from shoulders to feet in a very elegant way. Most women also wear a scarf around their heads when outside.

There is also the *baju kebaya*, a tighter-fitting blouse, with a tight sarong. The stewardesses of SIA and MAS wear this combination. The nun-like *tudung* covers up all traces of the female form. It is worn by schoolgirls and university students, even during sports.

Malay names conform to the Islamic rule: The first name is followed by *bin* (son)or *binti* (daughter) and the name of the father. The *bin* or *binti* is often left out. Pilgrims who have made the trip to Mecca take the honorary title of *Haji* or *Hajjah*, before the first name. Converted Muslims whose parents did not have Islamic names are called by the last name *Abdullah* or *Abdul Rahman*. (*Tunku Abdul Rahman* is an "adoptive father" of converts.) The proper name always comes first. So Mohammed Rahman is known not as Mr. Rahman, but Mr. Mohammed. And if your name is John Brown, expect to be called Mr. John.

The Chinese

Chinese immigrants to Malaysia brought their customs and traditions with them from their homeland. Cantonese, Hokkien, Hakka, Teochew (Siu Chow) and Hainanese all have their own traditions. Many of these have stayed the same for centuries, but in Malaysia, as in the rest of the world, modern youth seems to have a mind of its own.

When black and white (traditional Chinese colors of mourning) were in fashion in 1987-88, young Chinese people wore these clothes to New Year's celebrations, much to the dismay of their elders. Other traditions are being broken as the world becomes a smaller place. The young Iban people in long-houses have similar tastes in pop music to the young Chinese in Malaysia.

The Chinese in Malaysia are the mer-chants, shopkeepers and entrepreneurs. Most of them live in cities, and city life in general is very Chinese-oriented. There is little interest for Chinese high culture as most of the immigrants were among the poorest Chinese. Money is the focus of life. The standard greeting among Chinese is "How's business?", and the usually understated answer is, "Business is so-so." Another universal greeting is, "Have you eaten yet?" "Yes, thanks" is the standard answer, whether or not it is true.

Chinese women may shake hands with men, but the women initiate it. Those higher in rank or senior in age are addressed first, as is the custom in the West. Men often greet each other with a pat on the arm.

Dress in Chinese culture is informal. Old women prefer the *sam foo*, a combination of blouse and pants. The *cheongsam*, or dress with a slit up the side, is becoming popular. The young Chinese tend to dress very stylishly.

Visiting a Chinese home, be aware that while people in some homes remove their shoes, people in others do not. So take a look at what your hosts are doing as you enter. As a guest, you are not expected to bring anything, though sweets for the children are a standard gift. They love chocolate with nuts, cookies, cakes and fruits (always bring an even number.) It is better not to bring flowers since they are inedible and are usually given to the sick or grieving.

Gifts are not opened in the presence of the giver, so as not to appear greedy. There are some taboos about appropriate gifts:

- do not give clocks or watches, since the Cantonese word for clock sounds like "going to a burial";
- do not give figures of storks as baby or shower gifts since the heron, which looks similar to a stork, represents the death of a woman;
- do not give anything sharp like knives or scissors (they can sever friendships);

- do not give flowers, especially not an uneven number;
- do not give anything black, white or blue (the colors of mourning); the same goes for wrapping paper.
- do not give handkerchiefs as they are a symbol of mourning.
- The best gifts are usually edible, as Chinese people are very practical.

People love to eat in restaurants, which is not surprising given the necessary preparations for a fine Chinese meal. Invitations to dinner often mean at a restaurant, not in someone's home.

In a culture that places such value on ancestor-worship, **burial customs** take on an especially important meaning. Parents, for example, may not honor their children as ancestors. If a child dies before his parents, he cannot have a place on the family altar as it is believed that the ghost would wander around hungry.

There are many other **taboos and customs associated with funerals and burials.**

● If you see a funeral, it might be a foot procession with a very heavy coffin on a wagon and a loud band, to ward off evil spirits.

● If you are invited into the house of a family in mourning, there are special rules to follow. You should wear dark colors, black, or white. You will be taken to the coffin, where you should bow three times. People discuss the deceased at the common meal. Bring an *ang pow* with an uneven sum of money (M$ 10.30) in a red envelope. Close friends and relatives will bring white or brown envelopes. Well-to-do families will usually give the money to a charity. It is permitted to send flowers at burials.

● Upon leaving the house, you will be given two pieces of red string, for good luck. Tie them to a button on your clothes and then throw them away when you get outside. You will also get an *ang pow* with 5 or 10 *sen*. Use this money to buy candy to "sweeten" the sorrow. If you do not use it, throw it away. In any case, do not take the money back home.

A word about **Chinese names.** The family or clan name comes first. The person is related by blood to all other people with this same name. Women, logically, do not change their names when they get married, her ancestors are different to her husbands. Some groups forbid marrying someone with the same family name. The second name is the middle name, often the same for all the children of one couple. The third name is the personal name.

The Indians

The Indian immigrants to Malaysia came from all over India. However, the majority are dark-skinned Tamils, from the south of India. Most Tamils are Hindus, but there are quite a few Christians. Other south Indian groups are also represented. In addition to Tamil, south Indian languages spoken in Malaysia include Malayalam and Telegu.

Other languages are Punjabi, the language of the Sikhs, and Urdu, a language similar to Hindi spoken by Muslim Indians and Pakistanis. So, as is the case with the Chinese, any statement about the group as a whole is necessarily a generalization. Their reasons for immigrating to Malaysia are varied. The Tamils came as plantation workers and the Sikhs as soldiers. Today, Indians often work in professions like law and medicine. They are also in railroad administration, the army, the police and in trade unions. And many still work on the plantations.

From an **Indian name**, you can tell what a person's ethnic background and religion are. Muslim Indians however, have Muslim-Arabic names similar to the Malays. Christian Indians often have Western Christian first names. Tamil names consist of a letter, which stands for the father's first name, followed by a personal name. Sikh men have the word *Singh* (lion) in their names and women have the word *Kaur* (princess). They also use clan names.

Indian society is traditionally structured with regard to sex roles and respect for elders. Men and women may not touch in public. As guests, men should sit in the place offered to them and not walk around the house. Shoes are not worn in the house. Female guests should help the women prepare the food. Men and women sit separately. The woman of the house will never eat with guests, even when the guests include women.

There is no need to bring **gifts** to an Indian home. If you choose to, bring something for the children, sari fabric, or fruit. Indians do not open gifts in the presence of guests. Gifts are given with the right hand and the left hand should never come into contact with other people.

Many Hindus are vegetarians. Even if they are not, they do not eat beef. Indians eat with the right hand, but in a slightly different manner than the Malays. Invitations to dine are very informal and Indians love good eaters.

There are many occasions to invite guests into the home, like puberty festivals for girls, marriages, births and deaths. There are set rules for each occasion.

There are some **strict taboos concerning death**. Do not visit a mourning family on a Monday, Tuesday or Thursday. Also, do not visit a mother recovering from birth on a Tuesday. After a funeral or period of mourning, Indians must go through a ritual cleansing before returning to daily life. Funerals and weddings may not be attended within the same period of time. Widows are barred from societal occasions for a year and may not enter temples during this time.

Tourism

Malaysia is in the middle of a huge campaign to promote tourism. It is already the nation's fourth-largest money-maker.

When tourism was controlled by the state, there was a limit to what tourists could do. Now, the government has realized that tourism is a real market, and to grow, it must be given over to the private sector.

The government is currently in the process of selling off its unprofitable, very expensive, resorts to private operators.

In my opinion, nature is the most interesting thing about Malaysia. In addition to Taman Negara, the big National Park, there are various smaller parks. More are being planned all the time, like the Endau - Rompin Reserve on the Pahang - Johor border. These parks are popular not only with foreign tourists, but with Malaysians as well.

The **state tourist office** is known as the TDC or the *Tourist Development Corporation*. It has offices in Asia, Europe, and America, in addition to those all over Malaysia.

Peninsular Malaysia Travel

There are many places listed here that have been recommended by both residents and travelers. But be warned:

Places change over time; management changes; prices go up; and what was once a great restaurant or hotel might now be a dump. You may have a terrible experience in a place that I recommend. Therefore the best way to use this book is as a rough guide. Consider the places I suggest, but make your own decisions when you get there, based on what you see and feel.

You can usually tell a good *restaurant* by its clientele. If a coffee shop is always packed, chances are it has pretty good food. Ask about local and house specialties to find out what to order. It quickly becomes boring to live completely out of a guide book, but I have still made several suggestions for ordering in different restaurants.

The same caution applies to *lodging*, but there is more regularity here. You might find delicious food for only a few dollars, but you will never find a luxury suite for the price of a hovel. Cheap hotels rarely have more than a bed, a washbasin, a ceiling fan, clean linen (always look first!) and a shared bathroom.

You generally get good value at inexpensive hotels that offer rooms with bathrooms. They may or may not have air-conditioning (AC). Double rooms generally go for around M$ 30, but as a rule, the more you pay, the better the room.

A double room in a fancier hotel with a TV, AC and a bathroom will cost around M$ 40. In general, the charge is by the room, not by the person. Often, the hotel will not ask how many people are staying in the room. In quite respectable hotels, locals will often fit a lot of people into one room, with some sleeping on the floor.

Single rooms are the exception, rather than the rule. They are cheaper and usually simpler. Sometimes there are rooms with more than one bed for larger groups (abbreviated: 3B, 5B).

Prices in Malaysia are fairly stable, but there will be differences between your expenses and the prices stated here. Very often, hotels may offer discounts. The actual prices may be nothing more than guidelines. Even at expensive hotels, discounts of 40-50% are not unheard of. It always pays to ask.

In Malaysia, almost all the *cheap hotels* are owned by Chinese. Chinese people are pragmatic. A clean room for the night and cold or hot water for tea is really all you need. These places do not usually have much atmosphere. In some places, like Kuala Lumpur and Penang, there is a real travelers' atmosphere. Here you can trade stories and get information in several languages, especially in ground-floor hotel restaurants.

However, in many towns and even some cities, you might be the only "*kweilo*" (Cantonese for "foreign devil") or "*orang putih*" (Malay for "white person.")

In general, there are fewer *travelers in Malaysia* than in Thailand or Indonesia. The country is also a lot smaller than its northern and southern neighbors. Lodging is somewhat more expensive here, and you will usually have to pay more for less. It is unreasonable to expect to find a double room with a bathroom and shower for M$ 6.00. The standard of living and prices are both higher in Malaysia than in neighboring countries. The salary of Indonesian workers, for example, is half that of their Malaysian counterparts.

As for *transportation*, it is also more expensive than on Sumatra, but it is also a lot more comfortable. In the travel sections, I have given prices, but not departure times for the long-distance taxis and buses. Obviously there are fixed times, but these change frequently. Whenever I was ready to go anywhere from Butterworth, Ipoh, Kuala Lumpur, Malacca, Johor Baru or Kuantan, I just went to the bus station and got on the next bus. That always works when traveling between major hubs. In the bus stations in large cities, there is always someone to help you find the right bus for your destination. Just tell a passerby where you want to go and they will point you in the correct direction. To go from Kuala Lumpur to Butterworth or Singapore, you can normally get a bus or long-distance taxi at any time of the day or night from *Pudu Raya*. But if you are going to less-traveled places, ask about the schedule beforehand and be sure to book your seat in advance.

As a rule of thumb, figure on travel taking about an hour for every 60 km, plus twenty minutes for every two hours. If a bus is not full and picks up people along the way, it can take even longer. Ask in advance how long it takes.

There are certain advantages to traveling to areas not often visited by tourists. There are no children begging, and you can get closer to the everyday life of the people. The smiles you will encounter are sincere signs of friendliness and hospitality.

Unlike Thailand and other Southeast Asian countries, Malaysia is a young nation. Everywhere, people will ask, "How do you like Malaysia?" Or more specifically, "What do you like about our country?" or "How do you like the food?"

An Overview of the Individual States

Because of the influence of their Sultans (except in Penang, Malacca and the Federal Territories), the states are all quite different and all offer variety to the tourist.

Perlis

Perlis is the smallest Malaysian state, with an area of 795 km^2. Originally, it was part of Kedah, which was taken over by Thailand in 1821. In 1842, when Thailand permitted the Sultan of Kedah to take the throne again, Perlis broke away and became established as a vassal state. The Thais gave Perlis to the British in 1909, but it was given back to Thailand by the Japanese during World War II. When the British returned, it became part of the Malay Union and later, Malaysia.

The majority of the people are Malay (78%), followed by Chinese (17%). The economy is based on rice, rubber and fishing.

What to See:
Padang Besar: Border crossing; good shopping on both sides; an active border trade.

Kaki Bukit: Tin mines with extensive tunnels.

Chuping: Spectacular limestone outcrops with prehistoric remains.

Batu Pahat: Golf and leisure center.

Arau: Sultan's Palace.

Kangar: Capital; many hotels.

Kuala Perlis: Fishing center; the best place to get a boat for the island of *Langkawi*, which is part of Kedah, though closer to Perlis.

Kedah

Kedah, the "rice bowl" of Malaysia is 9426 km^2. The majority of the people are Malay (72%), followed by Chinese (19%) and Indians (8%), for a total of over 1 million people. Kedah is Malaysia's oldest state.

The ruling family traces its origins to Hindu times, and Kedah is the only state that still has ruins from that period, in the *Bujang Valley*. The state was settled very early since it is located along old trade routes. This has made it a desirable place to possess. First *Sri Vijaya* from Sumatra, then the *Acehnese*, sought to secure a pepper monopoly.

The Portuguese, Thais, British and Japanese, were all in charge at one point before Kedah quietly became a Malay-sian state.

What to See:

Bujang Valley: Historical interest; located on the south side of the massive *Gunung Jerai* or *Kedah Peak* (1330 m). *Sungai Teroi Forest Park* is nearby.

Alor Setar: Has some interesting buildings.

Kuala Kedah: Remains of old fortifications; known for its seafood; there are also old forts in

Sipuleh, Kota Sena and Kubang Pasu.

Langkawi Island: A duty-free zone if you spend at least 72 hours there; developing into a major tourist center.

Sik: Waterfalls.

Baling: A large limestone outcropping overlooks the city.

Penang (Pulau Pinang)

This state occupies an island (285 km^2) and a part of the mainland, with a total area of 1031 km^2. The Chinese (55%) are the majority of the population at over 1 million, with Malays (33%) and Indians (11%).

The island is between 3 and 12 km from the mainland. It used to belong to Kedah, but the Sultan ceded it to the *British East India Company* in 1786, in return for a promise of help in a war against Thailand. The British did not keep their word. Not only did the Sultan never get his island back, but he had to give up an additional chunk of the mainland, known earlier as *Wellesley* Province. Though the island had barely

been settled before, it grew very fast under the British, and Georgetown became a cosmopolitan city.

Penang joined the Malay Union in 1948.

What to See:

Penang: A traditional tourism center.

Georgetown: Lovely; marred only by the disproportionately large *Komtar Tower* (65 stories). Nonetheless the tower does offer a great view over the town.

Penang Hill: Can be ascended by a cog-railway or by a steep road.

Botanical Gardens: Features a waterfall.

Beaches: Batu Ferringgi and many others.

On the **mainland** there is a lot of industry, but nothing really worth seeing.

Perak

The second-largest state in Peninsular Malaysia (21,005 km^2). Perak was the richest state during the tin boom. This is no longer the case, and since the world-wide drop in tin prices, most of the mines are no longer profitable.

For a long time, Ipoh was known as the city of millionaires. But today, the main economic and industrial center is Kuala Lumpur, along with other cities in the Klang Valley in Selangor.

Among the population of 1.8 million, the percentage of Malays (45%) and Chinese (41%) is almost the same. There are also quite a few Indians (14%).

Pineapples and rice are grown in the north, while the south has the typical Malaysian rubber and palm oil plantations. In upper Perak there is a large lumber industry. The largest Malaysian naval base is at Lumut, a few kilometers from Pangkor island.

The second-largest river in the Malay Peninsula, the 400 km long *Perak* (Silver) *River*, runs through the state. The oldest signs of human settlement on the peninsula were found on the river's upper reaches, near Longgong dated at some 10,000 years.

The oldest son of the Sultan of Malacca founded the Perak Dynasty in 1528. The state retained its independence despite many foreign invaders before the tin boom of 1874. It survived attacks by the aggressive Aceh, the Dutch, the Bugis, and the Thais. The fighting between rival Chinese tin mining groups in Landarut (today, Taiping) weakened the state. The British stepped in and gained the upper hand with the Treaty of Pangkor in 1874.

The first governor was murdered, but after that, the British remained in firm control until Malaysian independence.

What to See:
Gerik: Endpoint of the East-West Highway and the Temengor Lake Dam.

Taiping: The first capital of Perak (until 1933); neoclassical colonial architecture; the beautiful Lake Garden (converted mines); zoo; Perak Museum; point of departure for Maxwell· Hill or Bukit Larut; good jungle trekking.

Kuala Kangsar: Beautiful Ubudiah Mosque; classic *Istana Kenangan*; large sultan's palace; Malay College; pleasant Perak River.

Sayong: Village near Kuala Kangsar, known for black ceramics.

Ipoh: Capital; colonial architecture and Chinese shops; cave temple; prehistoric cave paintings; good Chinese food; beautiful landscape of the Kinta Valley; the highest point in the Central Mountain Range; lots of limestone outcrops.

Batu Gajah: Neoclassical colonial buildings; amusement park; *Kellie's Castle*; Hindu temple.

Bruas: Center of the old Malay kings, some ruins.

Pangkor: Good beaches; some snorkeling (Pangkor Laut, Emerald Bay – both better than Penang); cheap accommodation in simple huts (M$ 5 a night); Dutch fortifications.

Perak River Valley: (between Parit and Kampong Gajah) Sultans' tombs.

Teluk Intan (Teluk Anson): Chinese tower.

Tapah: Starting point for trips to the *Cameron Highlands*, which are actually part of Pahang.

Selangor Darul Ehsan

Selangor is the state that surrounds the Federal Territory of *Kuala Lumpur*. It has an area of 7956 km², and the total population is 1.5 million, composed of 44% Malays, 37% Chinese and 18% Indians. The Klang Valley is a big industrial center, containing the cities of Petaling Jaya (commuter suburb and industrial expansion of Kuala Lumpur), Shah Alam (the capital), Klang and Port Klang (the second-largest port in Malaysia.)

As in Perak, the tin-rich Klang Valley attracted many outsiders. *Bendahara Tun Perak* ruled here at the time of the Malacca Sultanate. Bugis rulers (originally from Celebes) then replaced the Malays. Their capital was at the mouth of the Selangor, in Kuala Selangor.

The mid-19th century was marked by wars between the Bugis, Malay and Chinese "tin barons". The disorder gave the British an excuse to invade in 1874. Under British rule, the state flourished. After World War II, it became part of the Federation of Malaya. In 1974, Seiangor gave up Kuala Lumpur, so that the capital would lie in the Federal Territory.

What to See:
Kuala Selangor: Nature park with a good assortment of birds and some rare monkeys; the magnificent view from the light beacon on *Bukit Selangor*; left-over Dutch fortifications (Kota Malawafi and Kota Tanjung Keramat).

Morib: On the ocean and quite beautiful; remains undeveloped as the water is not suitable for swimming.

Templer Park: A park with primary rain forest; there is a good bird preserve; the highest peak, Bukit Takun, is crowded with Malaysian hikers on the weekends.

Shah Alam: The splendid state mosque is the main attraction of the capital.

Kuala Lumpur *(Federal Territory)*

What started out as an up-country mining station has become the nation's capital. It was designated the *Federal Territory (Wilayah Persekutuan)* in 1974, and has an area of 244 km².

What to See:

Batu Caves: A Hindu temple in a large cave in the last big limestone hills on the peninsula. The *Thaipusam Festival* here attracts large crowds of people.

Zoo and **Lake Gardens**.

Buildings: Railway Station; Parliament; the Selangor Club; and the Secretariat.

Primary jungle: Can be found in the middle of the city (Bukit Nanas, for example).

Shopping Centers: Chinatown; the Night Market; the Central Market.

Negeri Sembilan

Negeri Sembilan is practically an inland state with only 48 km of coastline. It has an area of 6643 km² and a population of 547,000 of whom 46% are Malay, 36% are Chinese and 17% are Indian.

Negeri Sembilan is set on industrializing, as its agriculture has already been fully developed. Rice, cocoa, oil palms, rubber trees, livestock and fish (including shrimp) are all raised here.

The state's history has been determined by the other states. The name means "nine states," and Negeri Sembilan is already something of a federation. It was founded by Minangkabau settlers who came from Sumatra to the lands north of Malacca in the 15th century.

Once again, tin was at the root of civil disturbances in one of the sub-states, *Sungai Ujong*. As a result, the British invaded, but not without resistance. In 1895, Negeri Sembilan was reorganized from nine to six smaller states. The ruler of the group was later the first King of Malaysia.

What to See:

Sri Menanti: Residence of the Sultan; the traditional palace of the early rulers is now a museum.

Minangkabau Houses: Found all over the state.

Seremban: Some colonial buildings; modern museum.

Port Dickson: The best beach south of Pangkor.

Pengkalan Kempas: Megaliths.

Forest Reserves: Hiking.

Malacca (Melaka)

The state of Malacca has an area of 1650 km² and a population of 465,000 of whom 54% are Malay, 38% are Chinese and 8% are Indian. The state is industrializing very rapidly and offers special start-up incentives for investors. Agriculture is also being promoted.

The history of Malacca is long and complicated and is detailed in the section on History near the beginning of this book.

What to See:

Malacca Town: The Stadhuys; the gate of the old fortifications; the ruins of St. Paul's; the Chin Hoong Teng Temple; the old mosques; antique shops; the reconstruction of the old Sultan's palace which formerly occupied the site of St. Paul's. A light and sound show is planned for Paul's Hill.

Ayer Kroh: A Malaysian cultural village, about 7 miles from the center of town; there is also a park with jungle trails.

Durian Tunggal Reservoir: Camping; hiking; fishing.

Tanjung Bidara: Newly developed beach resort.

Pulau Besar or **Big Island:** Another new beach resort.

Gadek, Bemban: Hot springs.

Merliman: Traditional Malay houses.

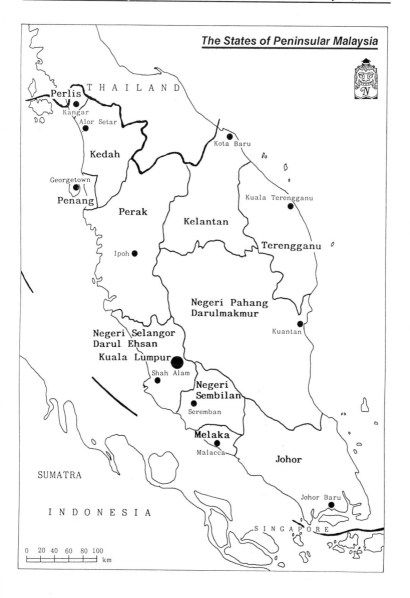

The States of Peninsular Malaysia

Johor (Johore)

The southernmost state on the peninsula has an area of 18,986 km^2. It has a population of 1.6 million, consisting of 55% Malays, 38% Chinese and only 6% Indians. Agriculture is well developed here, especially rubber, palm oil and pineapples. Johor is the leading agricultural state. New products include tea (near Kluang) and aquiculture (tiger prawns). A complete diversification of agriculture is in the works, which might become a model for the rest of Malaysia.

Johor is also industrializing rapidly. Its proximity to Singapore is a big factor. The new port of Pasir Gundang opposite Singapore is a modern container harbor that handles most of the traffic bound for East Malaysia.

Johor arose after the fall of the Sultanate of Malacca. In a sense, Johor was considered the successor to Malacca. In the 17th century, the Bugis took over.

In 1819, Stamford Raffles played on the rivalry between the Bugis and the Malays to grab the island of Tumasek, known today as Singapore. That was the end of the Johor Riau Kingdom. Riau became a Dutch protectorate and later, part of Indonesia. Johor came under British influence and later became part of Malaysia.

What to See:
Johor Baru (Old Johor): Abu Bakar Mosque and the large palace, which is now a museum; there are a few ruins of the old capital in Old Johor (*Johor Lama*).
Gunung Ledang: Mount Ophir, 1400 m, the best-known peak in Johor and a favorite of Singaporean hikers; development of tourism is planned for the area.
Endau: The best-preserved primary rain forest on the peninsula, which may soon become a legally protected nature preserve.
Desaru: Attractively developed beach resort with simple but expensive bungalows, a sandy beach, and good surf.
Mersing: Point of departure for *Tioman* (part of Pahang) and other islands.

Pulau Rawa: Private island with expensive accommodations.
Outer Islands: Pulau Aur, P. Pemanggil, P. Tinggi, P. Sibu, (all not yet developed).

Kelantan

Kelantan has an area of 14,943 km^2 and a population of 894,000. It has the second highest percentage of Malays with 93%. Chinese make up only 5% and Indians only 1% of the population. The people are mostly rice and tobacco farmers. Other products include rubber, palm oil, coconuts and fruit. Fishing is also an important industry.

Kelantan is known for traditional Malay handiwork, silverwork, brocade, batik.

Kelantan has been a state for 1000 years, but people have lived in the interior at least since the stone age. It was probably a vassal state of *Sri Vijaya*. Islam arrived during the Sultanate of Malacca. Kelantan remained independent for a long time after the fall of Malacca, but it eventually came under Thai domination.

The British took over in 1909, but the Thais regained control during World War II. In 1948, Kelantan joined the Malay Union.

What to See:
Kota Baru: Buildings like Istana Jabar (the state museum), Istana Balai Besar, and the European-influenced state mosque. Folklore shows with top spinning (*gasing*), kite flying (*wau*), drumming (*rebana*) and bird calling (*merbok*) competitions, shadow plays (*wayang kulit*), drama, dancing and music, handicrafts.
Nilam Puri: The mosque of Kampong Laut, one of the oldest in Malaysia.
Tumpat / Pasir Mas: Thai temples.
Pulai Chondong: Mosque with a wooden minaret.
Rantau Panjang / Sungai Golok: Lively border crossing and good shopping.
Gunung Reng: Spectacular stone age rocks of Batu Melintau.
Gua Musang: Stone age caves.

Taman Negara: Large national park, but it is not possible to enter it from Kelantan.

Sandy Beaches: The east coast is famous for these. The best in Kelantan are between Pengkalan Chapa and Kuala Best, the latter being the departure point for the *Perhentian Islands*. With Redang, the best snorkeling and diving on the east coast. Simple accommodation is available.

Terengganu

The most Malay of all the states. The population of 541,000 is 94% Malay and 5% Chinese. The total area is 12,955 km². Terengganu is the least developed state with an average yearly income of around US$ 800. At the beginning of this century, there were no roads leading into the state. People earn their livings from fishing, boat-building (for which they are famous), coconuts and rubber. The discovery of oil and natural gas along the coast has changed the landscape considerably – modern buildings in sleepy Kuala Terengganu, refineries, power plants, big dams, and a large harbor under construction.

Terengganu was exposed to Islamic influence before even Malacca (the Terengganu Stone is in the National Museum in Kuala Lumpur). The state was a vassal state of Malacca and later of Johor. From the 18th century, it was relatively independent, but had to pay tribute to Bangkok. From 1909 until the founding of the Malay Union, Terengganu was under British control.

What to See:

Beaches: The main attraction is the barely touched 240 km long stretch of beach; even the modern industrial complex is just a black dot on the white sandy coast.

Resorts: Besut, Marang, Rantau Abang (giant sea turtles).

Islands: Kapas, Berhentian, Redang.

Kuala Terengganu: A combination of a sleepy colonial capital and a modern oil town.

Kampong Rusila: Handicrafts.

Kuala Ibal: Silk weaving.

Pulau Duyong: Traditional boat building.

Kenyir Dam: Large forested area which should be developed for tourism soon with boat trips and other attractions.

Sekayu: Waterfall with hiking trails.

Pahang Darul Makmur

The largest state on the peninsula with an area of 35,965 km². The comparatively small population of 800,000 is 66% Malay, 26% Chinese and 7% Indian. Much of the state is still covered by forest, but it is being rapidly cut down (over 400,000 cubic meters a year). The main agricultural products are rubber and palm oil, but coconuts, cocoa, tea, fruit, coffee and rice are also grown.

Like Kelantan, Pahang was a vassal state first of *Sri Vijaya*, then later, Malacca. During the time of Johor-Riau, it enjoyed a short period of independence under the *Benda-haras* until 1888.

Then the British took over. They had to deal with considerable civil unrest between 1891 and 1896. Pahang later joined the Malaysian Federation.

What to See:

Pekan: Residence of the Sultan; museum; traditional Malay houses.

Kuala Lipis: Sleepy provincial town with neoclassical colonial architecture.

Cameron Highlands, Fraser's Hill, Genting Highlands: More or less developed hill stations. Cameron is the most interesting; Genting is more of a getaway from Kuala Lumpur.

Endau-Rompin Forest Reserve: Undisturbed lowland forest.

Tasek Chini / Tasek Bera: Interior lakes (Orang Asli).

Paya Bungor: New tourism area.

Taman Negara: National park with lowland and mountain jungle, 130 million years old.

Beaches: Cherating; Chendor to the north; Beserah and Tuluk Chempedak near Kuantan, the self-titled gateway to the east coast; Rompin in the south.

Tioman Island has been called one of the most beautiful islands in the world.

Sungai Lembing: Some underground tin mines, no longer in use.

Sarawak and Sabah

Covered in a separate section later in the book.

Suggested Travel Routes

From the North

Most travelers go through Malaysia from north to south, arriving with the **International Express** train from Thailand. If you do that, your first stop will be Butterworth, on the mainland of Penang. If you have more time you can take a train or bus from Hat Yai to Padang Besar. From there to Kangsar and Kuala Perlis, crossing over to Langkawi Island.

These islands are beautiful, similar to Phuket in Thailand, but not as developed. Malaysian tourism experts are doing their best to change that. Back on the mainland, you might take a look at Alor Setar. On the way south, go up the imposing Gunung Jerai / Kedah Peak, with a detour to see the Hindu ruins in the Bujang Valley.

Penang is certainly worth a few days. The Chinese-English city of Georgetown is lined with well-preserved Chinese shops and British colonial buildings. Beaches include the fully built-up Batu Ferringhi and the undeveloped Monkey Beach near Muka Head in the northwest of the island. You might visit carnation or nutmeg plantations in the south, and you should definitely go up Penang Hill.

If you decide not to go directly to the east coast (there are direct buses to Kota Baru that go over the East-West Highway), your next stop should be Taiping. If you are interested in birds, do make a detour to the bird preserve in the mangroves of Kuala Gula.

Along with the Botanical Gardens, the major attraction in **Taiping** is Maxwell Hill, the oldest of the hill stations. It is known today by its Malay name, Bukit Larut.

Kuala Kangsar, the seat of the Sultan of Perak, is worth a visit. You can see the Perak River, the Ubudiah Mosque, the somewhat pompous palace of Istana Iskanderiah, which is now a royal museum. The prestigious Malay College is also there, educating future sultans.

Next comes **Ipoh**, which has a lot more to offer than the cave temple. I find, for example, the prehistoric rock paintings to be very interesting, even though few locals know about them. Kledang Hill, a favorite with joggers and walkers, offers a good view of the Kinta Valley from 808 m up.

From Ipoh, you can see the high mountains of the central mountain range. Looking through binoculars on a clear day, you can make out the radio antennae on Gunung Batu Brinchang. It is part of the *Cameron Highlands*, a temperate area where the valleys are planted with tea, fruit and vegetables. There are good hiking trails here that do not take more than a few hours, Gunung Bereman, for example. The Highlands are worth one or two days at the least. There are some Orang Asli villages scattered around and it can be surprising to encounter a man in a loincloth with a blowgun. Farther south is Kuala Lumpur. To the left of the road to Kuala Lumpur, the hills are planted with rubber and oil palm plantations. Turn right in Rawang to get to Kuala Selangor, with its newly-established nature preserve. Templer Park, especially Bukit Takun, is worth a side trip. On the left just before Kuala Lumpur is the last big limestone hill on the peninsula. The Batu Caves are located here with their interesting vaults that house an Indian temple.

Kuala Lumpur has enough to offer for a few days, including perhaps a side-trip to the Genting Highlands and its modern casino. To go to the nearby coast, go through Shah Alam (don't miss the magnificent new mosque!) to Port Klang and on to Carey Island. Here the Mah Meri Orang Asli make abstracted, grotesque carvings of spirits. Then you could go through Morib, known for its seafood and Port Dickson (the

main beach near Kuala Lumpur) to Malacca. Do not leave out Negeri Sembilan and the Minangkabau culture. The interior of the state beckons with Sri Menanti, the royal city, and Pasoh, a protected jungle area.

Mountains worth seeing in Negeri Sembilan include Gunung Angsi and Telapak Burok, both not far from Seremban. True hiking enthusiasts will like Gunung Ledang (Mt. Ophir) and Gunung Besar near Segamat. By now, you are within reach of *Singapore*.

From the South

Coming from Singapore, you can do the same route in reverse. In which case your itinerary would be determined by whether or not you plan on visiting the *east coast*. For example, you may want to visit Desaru, Mersing with some islands and then through Kluang to Segamat and then continuing as above, in reverse.

An alternative would be a short trip across the peninsula from Kuala Lumpur to *Kuantan*. On the way, you might visit Fraser's Hill or make a detour from Temerloh through Jerantut to the Taman Negara National Park. Some 60 km before Kuantan, you can head off to Ulu Lepar and into a lowland jungle.

From Kuantan, there are many possibilities on the beautiful east coast, but remember that the season for the east coast is from April to September. From November to January is monsoon season, with lots of rain, flooding, and stormy seas.

Travelers enjoy the area around the bay of Cherating with its inexpensive and simple bungalows. Similarly affordable are those around Rantau Abang with its giant sea turtles (May-September, especially August.)

The islands farther north, Kapas, Redang, Perhentian, all have good snorkeling, simple accommodations and some good fishing (except Kapas.)

From **Kota Baru**, the center of Malay culture you can plan your trip in the following ways: a) Head north to Thailand and the wonderfully painted fishing boats along the Yala coast.

b) Take the East-West Highway to Penang and travel on from there. The highway goes over the mountains and jungle in the interior and by Temengor Lake. There are still curfew laws at night (the road was built partially to push back the communists.)

c) Take the new road from Kota Baru to Kuala Lumpur, or perhaps the "Jungle Railway" as far as Kuala Lipis. Here there are interesting jungle tours, some by boat, that wind up in Kuala Lumpur.

If you are coming from Singapore, you might want to go directly to the east coast. **Desaru** on the southeast tip is an expensive resort with a beautiful beach preferred by wealthy Singaporeans. Mersing is a point of departure for many islands like **Tio-man** and Rawa. Tioman has been well-developed for tourists. At the upper-end is the expensive Merlin Samudra, but there are also cheaper places to stay, great beaches, and a big mountain. (Snorkeling is not as good as on some of the other islands, listed above, like Kapas and Perhentian.)

Would-be explorers should certainly try and visit the **Endau-Rompin Nature Preserve**. You can paddle in on a boat along the Sungai Endau. This is for true adventurers with a lot of time.

In **Pekan**, take a look at the Istanas and mosques. Then you will be in Kuantan, the gateway to the east coast.

Many people want to know what the interior has to offer. Travel there is best done based on hints and tips picked up along the way. You could visit the lotus-lined **Tasek Chini** or the reed-filled **Tasek Bera**, on whose banks, the Semelai Orang Asli live. At one time, the lake was surrounded by forest. This is no longer the case and the Orang Asli have had to give up their centuries-old way of life. A visit to Tasek Bera will definitely open your eyes to the development of the interior. The jungle has been logged away and oil palms and rubber plantations now stand there at great cost to the Orang Asli. Tasek Chini is beginning to show the first signs of tourism. Be careful of the hints and tips you hear along the way.

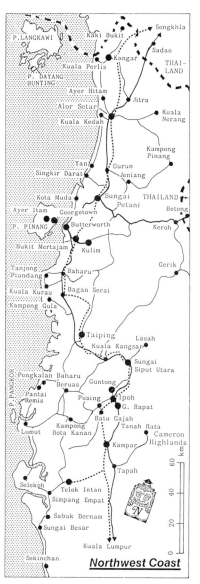

Northwest Coast

The West Coast

From North to South

The west coast is the most developed part of the country. The big tourist destinations of Kuala Lumpur and Penang are here, as are the big industrial centers. This part of the peninsula has the most to offer tourists.

Tourist Information

Outside of Kuala Lumpur and Penang, tourist information is available on the west coast in:

● **Kedah**

Kedah Information Center, Jalan Tunku Ibrahim, Alor Setar, Tel. 04-722455 / 722636.

● **Perak**

Perak Tourist Association, Jalan Panglima Bukit Gantang, Ipoh, Tel. 05-516180.

● **Negeri Sembilan**

Tourist Officer, State Economic Development Corporation, Jalan Paul, Seremban Tel. 06-73251.

● **Malacca**

Tourist Officer, State Economic Development Corporation, Jalan Kota, Malacca, Tel. 06-25711;

Melaka Tourist Information Center, Tel. 06-225895.

Kangar

The capital (20,000 people) of Perlis, the smallest state. There is not too much to see here except for the **Masjid Syed Alwi**, built in 1930. The curiously European **Sultan's Palace** and the **state mosque**, built in 1972, are located a kilometer or so east in the residential town of Arau. The international express train from Butterworth to Bangkok stops here.

Accommodation

●**Sri Perlis Inn**, Jalan Kangsar, Tel. 04-763266, 50 rooms, SR M$ 39-80, DR M$ 49-90.
●**Malaysia**, 67 Jalan Jubli Perak, Tel. 6761366, 26 rooms, SR M$ 20-33 (A / C, shower).
●**Ban Cheong**, 76A Main Rd, Tel.761184, 22 rooms, SR M$ 10, DR M$ 21 (A / C, bath / shower), comfortable.
●**Hotel Kangsar** near the bus station is less expensive.

Excursions

Arau:
Residential town with an attractive palace and mosque.

Kaki Bukit:
Tin mines that can be reached through a cave with interesting rock formations (stalagmites, stalactites). The main attraction is the walk through **Gua Kelam**, the "Dark Cave." This used to be an important tin mining area, but it is no longer mined. *Kaki Bukit* is some 30 km north on the road to Padang Besar.

Padang Besar:
This town on the Thai border is known and loved by locals as a shopping paradise. Traveling on the International Express, you will see heavily-laden people crossing the bridge when you get off to take care

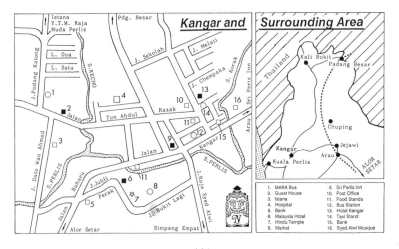

Kangar and Surrounding Area

1. MARA Bus
2. Guest House
3. Istana
4. Hospital
5. Bank
6. Malaysia Hotel
7. Hindu Temple
8. Market
9. Sri Perlis Inn
10. Post Office
11. Food Stands
12. Bus Station
13. Hotel Kangsar
14. Taxi Stand
15. Bank
16. Syed Alwi Mosque

of immigration formalities. Thai goods are more attractive to Malaysians than Malaysian goods are to Thais. Malaysians love imitation leather and shirts, but you will see regular household goods as well.

8 km from Kangar on the road to Pedang Besar is a snake farm, **Taman Ular** (open daily, except Mondays).

Chuping:

Another attraction in Perlis is Chuping, 15 km northeast of Kangar. Chuping is known for its huge limestone outcrops (up to 150 m) and ant hills (up to 2 m). On **Bukit Chuping**, archaeologists have found bones with marks from sharp tools that date back to the early stone age.

Kuala Perlis:

11 km west of Kangar, Kuala Perlis can be reached directly from Butterworth by express bus (M$ 5) or share-taxi (M$ 1.70). This picturesque fishing town is built on stilts and is surrounded by wooded hills.

There is a small hotel here, the Soon Hin (M$ 10). From here, you can get a ferry to *Langkawi* or a long-tailed boat (*hang yao*) to the Thai town of **Satun** (1.5 hours, M$ 3 or 30 Baht).

In K. Perlis, there are naturally a lot of good **seafood restaurants**. Local specialties include fried fish curry, seafood sambal and nasi lemak.

Langkawi

Langkawi refers both to the large island of that name and to the 98 other islands in the same group. They are actually part of a larger archipelago, the northern part of which is in the *Tarutao National Park* in Thailand. Like the Thai islands, Langkawi is being developed for tourism. Over 100 km north of Penang and almost 30 km from the mainland. This island group in the Andaman Sea has the best **swimming, snorkeling** and **diving** on the west coast. Malaysian tourism experts have big plans for this island, which used to be a pirate haven. Langkawi was declared a duty-free zone in 1987, providing you stay at least 72 hours. An international airport is planned and the roads are being expanded. You can find everything you might expect from a luxury resort here – golf, polo, waterskiing, boat trips, and many other activities.

The landscape is beautiful. There are all sorts of beaches, coves, and little coral islands, as well as a lake that supposedly encourages pregnancy. There are hot springs, an almost 1000 m mountain, and a lot more. The island is pretty big and it will be sometime before it becomes too built up.

Accommodation

●**Langkawi Island Resort** (previously, *Langkawi Country Club*). Too expensive for what it offers.

●*Pantal Dato' Syed Omar*, Tel. 04-788209, 100 rooms, SR M$ 95-150, DR M$ 115-170.
●*Mutiara Beach Hotel*, Tanjung Rhu, Tel. 788488, 68 rooms, M$ 70-120.
●*Government Rest House*, Kuah, Tel. 788335, 12 rooms, M$ 8-22 (2 rooms with A / C, shower, bath). Roomy.
●*Asia*, 1A Jalan Persiaran Putra, Tel. 788216, 15 rooms, M$ 26 (without A / C), or M$ 36 for two people, M$ 54 for 4 persons (A / C, bath, TV).

●*Langkawi*, 6-8 Pekan Kuah, Tel. 788248, 13 rooms, SR M$ 14, DR M$ 22, 35 (A / C, bath).
●The *Hotel Malaysia* is a travelers' meeting place run by the family of Mr. Velu, Kuah. Cheap and friendly.
●*Pulau Bumbon*, 3 bungalows, which you can rent for M$ 10. 15 minutes by boat from Kuah; two beaches. Look for the yellow boat with the word, "Bumbon."

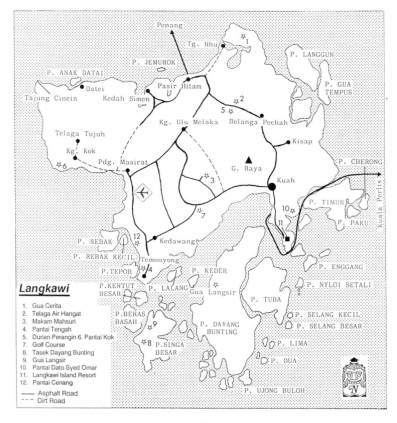

Langkawi

1. Gua Cerita
2. Telaga Air Hangat
3. Makam Mahsuri
4. Pantai Tengah
5. Durian Perangin 6. Pantai Kok
7. Golf Course
8. Tasek Dayang Bunting
9. Gua Langsir
10. Pantai Dato Syed Omar
11. Langkawi Island Resort
12. Pantai Cenang

— Asphalt Road
- - - Dirt Road

There are bungalows and guest houses on many beaches. On **Pantai Cenang**, and **Tengah**, some 20-22 km west of Kuah:

●**Sandy Beach**, on Pantai Cenang, with M$ 18 huts ($ 28 with bathroom). Good restaurant and rents canoes for M$ 5 / hour and motorcycles for M$ 20 / day. Traveler's favorite.

●**Semarak Langkawi**, on Pantai Cenang, rooms cost M$ 44 (with shower).

●Construction started on the large **Pelangi Beach Resort** at the end of 1988. The beach is flat and sandy.

Farther west near the *Talagah Tujuh* waterfall is Pantai Kok.

●**Country Beach Motel** has rooms for M$ 15 (SR) and 20 (DR) and bungalows for 2 people for M$ 60.

Tanjong Rhu, 22 km north of Kuah, is being developed into a big resort. The Promet company is building 1000 (!) bungalows next to a 500-bed eye hospital where Soviet experts will operate on the near-sighted. There are other bungalows nearby.

●A few kilometers southwest of the airport, near the road to Pantai Tengah is the **Inapan Desa Permai**, Pedang Wahid, Kedawang (Tel. 04-788085), DR M$ 15. Run by very nice people, it is popular with Malaysians coming for classes and seminars. The complex is in a *kampong* a kilometer or so from the beaches.

Kuah

Kuah, the biggest town, is in southeast Langkawi with 2000 people spread out along a 2 km long stretch of the main road. The good beaches are too far to reach on foot. You can rent **bicycles** (M$ 4 / day), **motorcycles** (M$ 20 / day) and **cars**.

There are also **taxis** and **mini-buses**. It is better to travel by taxi, since the buses only leave every hour or so for Pantai Tengah, Ewa (in the northwest) and Tanjong Rhu. They do not go to the best beaches. Taxi prices are listed on a sign at the taxi stand, mostly M$ 8, and M$ 40 for a sight-seeing tour. Drivers sometimes demand ridiculous fares, so watch out. The last buses leave Kuah at 17:30.

It is probably better for 2 people to rent a motorcycle. For example, at Chaun Hin in Kuah near the fire-house (M$ 15 / day) or at Jaya Motor on the left as you head towards Pantai Tengah (M$ 20 / day, M$ 15 / half day). Bring your driver's license.

Boats are also available for hire, for around M$ 100 / day, with room for 20 people. Contact Mr. Tan at the seaport, or book through the Hotel Asia. He does tours of 10 people for a full day of snorkeling, diving and swimming for M$ 12 / person.

Excursions

There is not much more in Kuah other than sunken fishing boats in the harbor and a Moorish-style mosque. It is best to spend one night at most here.

The Tomb of Mahsuri or *Makam Mahsuri* (12 km west of Kuah): A Malay princess was wrongly accused of adultery. Before her execution, she cursed the island for 7 generations, declaring that white blood would flow as proof of her innocence. That's why the sand here is so white!

Padang Masirat (19 km northwest of Kuah): After the death of *Mahsuri*, there was a Thai invasion during which the islanders burnt their rice rather than give it to the occupiers. They still follow this practice when it rains and at funerals.

Pantai Tengah / Pantai Cenang (18-20 km from Kuah, in the southwest of the island): Some bungalows; a protected cove, good for waterskiing; not many shady trees, but the huts are under the shade of coconut trees, right on the beach.

Telagah Tujuh or "Seven Springs" (30 km from Kuah, 8 km from Kuala Terjang Airport): A 90-meter high cascading fall with seven basins. You can slide down from basin to basin, but be careful, especially near the top. Good beach at Pantai Kok.

Pasir Hitam or "Black Beach" (20 km north of Kuah): Nothing special, except that the sand is black. The ferry from Penang, the Gadis Langkasusa lands here. There might also be boats going to Satun in Thailand.

Pantai Rhu, the beach of Tanjung Rhu (22 km north of Kuah): One of the island's best beaches, with nice shady trees, is being developed fast.

The **Gua (cave) Cerita** is at the tip of the cape and you can get there by boat. The tiny *ikan bilis* fish are dried there. They are used as seasoning or eaten as a snack with peanuts.

Gunung Raya: Over 800 m., this is the tallest mountain on the island. There is a nice picnic ground at the

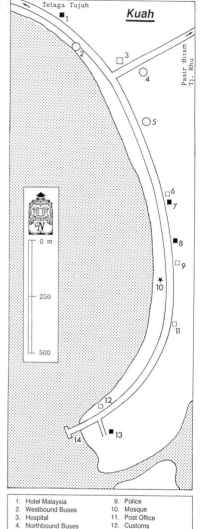

Kuah

Telaga Tujuh

Pasir Hitam
Tj. Rhu

1. Hotel Malaysia	9. Police
2. Westbound Buses	10. Mosque
3. Hospital	11. Post Office
4. Northbound Buses	12. Customs
5. Fish Market	13. Langkawi Island Resort
6. Bank	14. Ferry Landing
7. Langkawi Hotel	
8. Asia Hotel	

junction where the road from Kuah to Ulu Melaka joins the main road, right behind Kg. Ulu Melaka. Also some good places to swim in the nearby stream. There are a few huts here and some paths where the trees are identified. The path up Gunung Raya is hard to find and you will have to ask someone to show it to you. On Fridays (the Islamic rest day in Kedah), drinks are sold in the parking lot. Someone there will know the path. However there is a road to the telecommunications station at the top, so instead of turning left, follow the road to the right.

There is another **waterfall**, Durian Perangin, 15 km from Kuah. Turn left at the sign.

Pulau Dayang Bunting

Tasek Dayang Bunting or "Lake of the Pregnant Woman": A pretty lake in the south of **Dayang Bunting Island**. Childless couples make pilgrimages to the lake, which is said

to work wonders. The tradition began when a couple who had been trying to have children for 19 years came to the site. The wife drank the water and promptly got pregnant.

Gua Langsir or "Spirit Cave": North of the lake is a 90-m-high bat cave. The island is also a source of marble. A boat takes about 45 minutes to reach the island.

About 40 km south of Langkawi, there is a marine reserve, consisting of several islands, Pulau Segantang, Paya, and Lembu. The **snorkeling and diving** are exceptional, but the only way to get there is by rented boat from Kuah.

There is also some snorkeling between Pulau Bras Basah and Singa Besar.

Arrival / Departure for Langkawi

●Throughout the day, there are hourly boats between **Kuala Perlis** and **Kuah**, M$ 4.50, 1 3 / 4 hour trip.

●Express boats (M$ 10 / person, 180 person capacity) operate between 8.00 and 15.00, and take 25-45 minutes.
●Share taxis from the ferry landing to Kuah cost M$ 1 / person.
●The *Gadis Langkasusa* sails on weekends, leaving **Penang** Fridays at 23:00 and leaving **Langkawi** Saturdays at 9:00 (M$ 35.00, for information, call 04-379325, 03-2925622).
●A ferry between **Kuala Kedah** and **Kuah** is being planned.

Flights
●*Malaysian Air Charter* (MAC) from Penang: M$ 65.
●*MAS*: Kuala Lumpur-Penang-Langkawi, one flight a day, M$ 112 (from Penang, M$ 42).

Alor Setar / Alor Star

The capital of Kedah (population of 100,000) is located some 50 km from the Thai border crossing at Bukit Kayu. There is a rail connection through Padang Besar (border station) on to Hat Yai and Bangkok. Also through Butterworth on to Kuala Lumpur and Singapore. The International Express does not stop in Alor Setar.

What to See:

There are some interesting buildings in the center of town. The audience hall, **Balai Besar**, dates from 1898, and the home of the royal orchestra, Balai Nobat, both exhibit considerable Thai influence. Kedah was a Thai possession for a long time. Opposite is the **Zahir Mosque**, which dates from 1912 and is one of the most beautiful mosques in Malaysia. Behind the Balai Besar is the old **Sultan's Palace** where Tunku Abdul Rahman, the "Father of Malaysia" was born. His father, Sultan Abdul Hamid Halim Shah (1882-1943) was a supporter of the British. The present-day palace is 2 miles north of the center of town.

Other important buildings include the neoclassical **High Court** and the **Wisma Negeri** (state house), both built in modern Malaysian-Islamic style.

The **museum** (Muzium Kedah, Jalan Bakar Bata), is 2 km north of the town center. It has archaeological finds from the Bujang Valley, Chinese ceramics, and a Sultan's barge. Also a Bunga Mas made of gold and silver, an example of the elegant tributes that were paid to Thailand.

On Wednesdays, there is a big **market** opposite the government buildings.

Accommodation

In the eastern part of the city, near the train and bus stations, there are some **cheap Chinese hotels** (M$ 8-14).
●**Hai Pin**, 10 Pengkalan Kapal, Tel. 04-723650, 14 rooms, M$ 9-12 (with shower).
●**Lim Kung**, 36A Jalan Langgar, Tel. 722459, 13 rooms, M$ 9-12 (with shower).
●**Mandarin**, 109-111 Pekan China, Tel. 721321, 10 rooms, M$ 12-14 (with shower).
●**Tai Hock**, 1 Limbong Kapal, Tel. 732301, 14 rooms, M$ 8-11 (no shower).
●**Tye Tong**, 59 Pekan Melayu, Tel. 723186, 10 rooms, M$ 8 (no shower).
●**Station Hotel**, 74 Jalan Langgar, Tel. 723855, 53 rooms, M$ 14-20 (with shower).

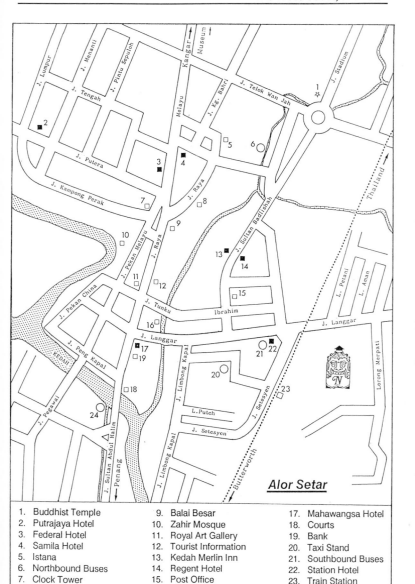

Alor Setar

1. Buddhist Temple	9. Balai Besar	17. Mahawangsa Hotel
2. Putrajaya Hotel	10. Zahir Mosque	18. Courts
3. Federal Hotel	11. Royal Art Gallery	19. Bank
4. Samila Hotel	12. Tourist Information	20. Taxi Stand
5. Istana	13. Kedah Merlin Inn	21. Southbound Buses
6. Northbound Buses	14. Regent Hotel	22. Station Hotel
7. Clock Tower	15. Post Office	23. Train Station
8. Wisma Negeri	16. Main Post Office	24. Market

●The **Government Rest House** is also a good deal. 75 Pumpong, 15 rooms, M$ 12-24 (with bathroom).

Somewhat more expensive:
●*Federal*, 429 Jalan Jancut, Tel. 730055, 43 rooms, M$ 22-27 (no shower).
●*Putra Jaya*, 250B Jalan Putra, Tel. 730344, M$ 24-36 with bathroom.
●*Mahawangsa*, 449 Jalan Raja, Tel. 721835, 54 rooms, M$ 24-36 (with bathroom).

Expensive:
●*Kedah Merlin Inn*, Lt. 134-141 Jalan Sultan Badlishah, Tel. 735917, 130 rooms, M$ 85-95, suites M$ 230-360.
●*Samila*, 27 Jalan Kancut, Tel. 722344, 52 rooms, M$ 58-66 (with bathroom).
●*Regent*, 1536 G.J. Sultan Badlishah, Tel. 721900, 28 rooms, M$ 48-66.

Excursions

To Kuala Kedah

An old town at the mouth of the Kedah River with some old 18th century fortifications and good seafood restaurants.

To Gunung Jerai (Kedah Peak)

The western part of Kedah is a big plain consisting of rice fields, interrupted occasionally by tree-covered limestone outcrops. Near the coast, 30 km south of Alor Setar and 25 km north of Sungai Petani, the 1217-meter-high Gunung Jerai or Kedah Peak rises high above the plains.

Kedah Peak beyond the rice fields

In antiquity, the mountain was known as an important navigational point for ships. It is no wonder, then that the oldest ruins in Malaysia are found in the adjoining **Bujang Valley**.

You can walk to just under the peak (where there is a radio antenna) to a **rest house** at 1000 meters. By taking the 13 km road (about a 3 hour walk) you can see the forest change little by little as you ascend.

A better hike begins some kilometers to the west by a stream that goes straight through the woods up to the rest house. This trail is hard to get to using public transportation.

You can also take a Landrover up and down the peak for M$ 5. These leave from a point about 1-2 km north of Gurum. It is clearly marked and if you arrive on the bus, get off at this point.

The summit is well laid out. There is an **English-style rest house** with some chalets, and a terraced house with rooms available. These cost M$ 50 for four people. The chalets are about M$ 104 for eight people. Individual travelers can usually join a group. You can also camp out.

The view from the privately-run rest house looks out to the north, northeast and northwest. When the sky is clear, the view is fantastic. You can see the west coast up to Thailand, west to Langkawi, and east to around Songkhla – a view to both oceans! Below, at the foot of the mountain, you can see the "rice bowl" of Malaysia.

On the way down the mountain, there are one or two good views of the undulating landscape to the southwest. The view of Penang, however, belongs to the military, which has a communications station on the summit. You can go up to the gate, but no farther. Call the rest house for **reservations:** 04-462046.

Getting There: You can get to Guar Chempedak or Gurun by car or by train (slow trains only). There is also a direct bus from Gunung Jerai Junction that makes a loop to the start of the road to the summit.

Around 800 meters, about 2-3 km before the rest house, there is a small **forest museum**. It is part of Taman Rimba (forest park). From the museum, there is a good path for 1 km up to a picnic area, and campground with a stream, a waterfall and a playground.

To the Bujang Valley

On Sungai Bujang, there are a few remains (foundation walls) of a 8th-9th century Hindu temple. This was the site of the once important Kalah / Kataha settlement that thrived for around 1000 years.

Visitors do not go into the Bujang Valley, but instead take the road into the Sg. Merbok Kecil River Valley to the *archaeological museum*. The museum gives a good overview of the 50 or so excavation sites and has some unearthed objects on display (the remainder are in the National Museum in Kuala Lumpur). Open daily from 9:30-17:00, closed Friday from 12:15-14:45, admission free.

Behind the museum are the reconstructed foundation walls, which with the exception of the main temple, were brought here from elsewhere. The place is really quite nice. There is a wide variety of plants and Gunung Jerai Mountain forms the background.

Marked trails go through the ruins. The most important ruin is *Candi Bukit Batu Pahat*. It is thought to have been a temple to Shiva, as a statue of Shiva was found here.

The simplicity of the ruins is striking, and the contrast of the green moss on the brown stones is quite beautiful. The blood of believers is still offered in the sanctuary (the elements of the temple are the same as in contemporary ones), so that the temple will endure. It is possible that this temple was part of an 8th century pilgrimage route to Gunung Herai, a route which no longer exists.

The nearby stream used to be a ritual bath, and is now a popular relaxation spot on the weekends.

There are a few good **side trips** from here, best made with your own transportation. The fishing village of

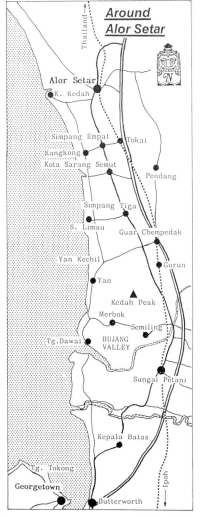

Around Alor Setar

Tanjung Dawai is located on the right bank of the short, but wide Sungai Merbok (on the road from Merbok). Here you can buy shrimp, salted fish or *belacan* (shrimp paste). There are a lot of goods from Terengganu like *Krupuk* (shrimp bread).

If you drive west past Gunung Jerai, you get to Yan. From here, you might go to **Song-Song Island**, a small coastal island with a beach (I discovered it from Kedah Peak).

Getting There: From **Sungai Petani** take a MARA bus for M$ 1.30.

From **Gurun** or **Bedong**, go to **Merbok** and from there, take a taxi (M$ 1.80) or walk the 2.5 km to the museum and temple ruins.

Further Travel

●There are **bus** and **share-taxi** connections in all directions.
Kuala Perlis: M$ 2.20
Penang: M$ 3.25, taxi: M$ 7.80
Kota Baru M$ 20, taxi: M$ 36.80
Ipoh: M$ 10, taxi: M$ 21.20
Kuala Lumpur: M$ 19.50 / 20, taxi: M$ 38
Singapore: M$ 34 / 40
●**Trains** go to Thailand or in the direction of Kuala Lumpur and Singapore.
●There are **flights** to Kota Baru (M$ 59), Kuala Lumpur (M$ 94) and Langkawi (M$ 47).

Penang (Pulau Pinang)

Penang, the self-christened "Pearl of the Orient," is the best known tourist destination in Malaysia. The city is a natural meeting place for travelers.

You can renew your Thai visa here or head south to Indonesia by way of Sumatra. That alone however, would hardly make a fascinating place. The over 1000 km^2 island, with altitudes of up to 830 meters, has enough to offer to keep anyone busy for a few days. There are rows and rows of Chinese and Indian shops. The popular, but somewhat boring beach, Batu Ferringhi. The interesting beaches near Telok Bahang and Muka Head. Malay fishing villages and *kampongs* under the shade of coconut palms on the west coast. Carnation, nutmeg and other plantations in the south. In short, Penang might be Malaysia in miniature.

There is a lot to see, with good walks and hikes, good food, and an incredible assortment of cheap guest houses and luxury hotels. The Hokkien Chinese (Fukien) who live in Penang are quite friendly. Georgetown has had a cosmopolitan character since the beginning of the previous century.

The **International Airport** has flights to and from Kuala Lumpur, Kota Baru, Singapore, Medan, Bangkok, Madras and Hong Kong. A new bridge provides direct access for cars. Trains and most buses stop in Butterworth, and you can take a ferry from there.

200 years ago, the island had only a few fishing villages and pirate hide-outs. Francis Light, a trading captain of the East India Company, arrived to occupy the island in 1876 and renamed it Prince of Wales

Penang merchand around 1870

Island. Light reached the island on August 11, the Prince's birthday.

Soon, Penang became a center for merchants, plantation owners, shipping magnates, and tin barons. Penang had more to offer than any other Malaysian city. Nowhere will you see as many stately colonial villas as in Penang.

Today, Penang is fast becoming a thriving center for modern industry. The harbor is still very busy, and the free trade zone has given rise to new industries, including electronics.

Accommodation

There are several dozen cheap Chinese hotels in Georgetown. If you want to stay in the city, there is a good selection on and around Chulia Street.

Near the ferry landing:

●*Noble*, 36 Lorong Pasar / Market Lane, 23 rooms, M$ 8 / 15 (as many people as you can fit), quiet, friendly. Tel. 04-612372.

●In Chulia Street, there is the popular *Tye Ann*, M$ 11.55 (fan), dorm M$ 5.25, good travelers' food in the restaurant. They sort out Thai visas for a M$ 5 service charge.

●Next door is the *Yee Hing*, with cheap rooms for M$ 8 / 9, friendly Chinese owners, good western food.

●To the right is Love Lane, and the *Pin Seng* is on the left. Try and stay in the old part. 23 rooms, SR M$ 11.50, DR 13,90, M$ 17.60 with four beds, M$ 23 with shower. Tel. 619004.

●A few feet down at No. 35 is the *Wan Hai*, under friendly Indian management, 12 rooms, M$ 12 / 16, including coffee and toast. Tel. 627676.

●A bit further is the unfriendly *Teong Wah*, M$ 11 for a room with a double bed.

●The *New China* on Lebuh Leith, is something of a legend among travelers. 35 rooms, double bed M$ 11, twin bed M$ 15.60 (both with shower), M$ 14,30 (without a shower), dorm M$ 4.40, 5.50 with a shower. Tel. 21852.

●Diagonally opposite is the stylish *Cathay*, a step up in quality. 32 rooms with a colonial atmosphere, SR with A / C and bathroom for M$ 27-46.

●At the corner of Lebuh Leith and Lebuh Muntri, is the *Modern Hotel*, 20 rooms, M$ 13-29, some with A / C and bathrooms. Tel. 25424.

●Behind it on Jalan Penang, there are a lot of mid-range hotels, and the somewhat expensive *White House*, 24 rooms, M$ 18-28, A / C and bathroom. Tel. 22385.

●Another street down at 3 Transfer Rd., is the *Num Keow*, 15 rooms, M$ 10 (fan), DR M$ 15 (A / C and bathroom), dorm M$ 5, clean and quiet. Tel. 24605.

●Back at 509 Lebuh Chulia is the *Eastern*, 21 rooms, M$ 12 / 16 (fan), M$ 20 (A / C, shower), clean. Tel. 614597.

●At No. 380, a bit further down on the left is the *Eng Aun*, 40 rooms, M$ 13.60 (no shower) / 16.80 (fan, shower). Tel. 372333.

●Across the street is the *Swiss Hotel*. Like the Eng Aun, it is set back a bit from the street and is therefore a bit quieter. 34 rooms, M$ 12 / 15-20, shower, dorm from M$ 6. Tel. 620133. Both hotels have lost a bit of their atmosphere because of too much success.

Everything is well organized (though there are lots of do's and don'ts in the Swiss). As for don'ts – don't even think about drugs here! Travelers' hotels do not have a great reputation, and they are the first places to be raided.

●Next to the Eng Aun is the quiet, friendly *Yeng Keng*, with big, cool rooms, M$ 11, with a double bed, M$ 13 with twin beds (no shower).

●The *Hang Chow* is at the corner of Lebuh Chulia and Penang Rd. DR M$ 14, with shower.

That should be enough of a selection, though there are many similar hotels throughout the city.

●There is also a *Youth Hostel*, next to the noble Eastern and Oriental, where you can get a bed for M$ 4 (for the first night) and then for M$ 3. You do not need an international hostel card.

●The *YMCA* is outside of the main hotel area, but in a good location, near the Thai consulate. 35 rooms, M$ 17-26. Tel. 362211.

●The *Paramount* is also good, 48F Northern Rd., 33 rooms, M$ 17-38 (A / C, bathroom). Tel. 363649.

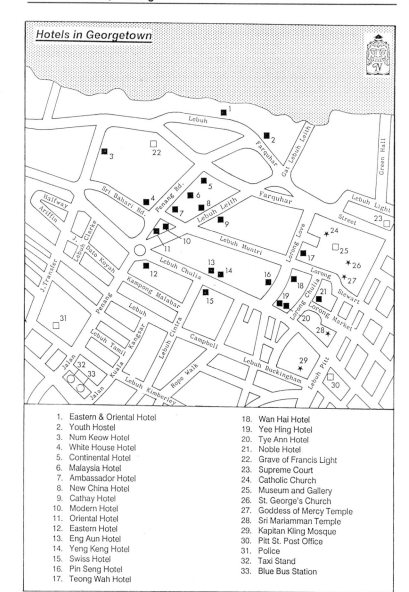

Hotels in Georgetown

1. Eastern & Oriental Hotel
2. Youth Hostel
3. Num Keow Hotel
4. White House Hotel
5. Continental Hotel
6. Malaysia Hotel
7. Ambassador Hotel
8. New China Hotel
9. Cathay Hotel
10. Modern Hotel
11. Oriental Hotel
12. Eastern Hotel
13. Eng Aun Hotel
14. Yeng Keng Hotel
15. Swiss Hotel
16. Pin Seng Hotel
17. Teong Wah Hotel
18. Wan Hai Hotel
19. Yee Hing Hotel
20. Tye Ann Hotel
21. Noble Hotel
22. Grave of Francis Light
23. Supreme Court
24. Catholic Church
25. Museum and Gallery
26. St. George's Church
27. Goddess of Mercy Temple
28. Sri Mariamman Temple
29. Kapitan Kling Mosque
30. Pitt St. Post Office
31. Police
32. Taxi Stand
33. Blue Bus Station

There is a good selection of *middle-range hotels* in the city. There are more than half a dozen on Jalan Pinang.

●*Oriental*, 94 rooms, M$ 60-66. Tel. 24211.
●*Town House*, 45 rooms, M$ 46-140. Tel. 368722.
●*Ambassador*, 78 rooms, M$ 65-180 Tel. 24101.
●*Federal, Peking*, 73 rooms, M$ 28-44 (once we stayed in a 6-bed room for M$ 40.) A / C and bathrooms. Tel. 29451.
●*Malaysia*, 126 rooms, M$ 66-172. Tel. 363311.
●The*Continental* is in the same price range. Tel. 263381.
●On Lebuh Leith, the *Waldorf* is nice and friendly. 57 rooms, M$ 30, DR 35-42 (A / C and bathroom). Tel. 26141.
●The *Golden City*, 12 Kinta Lane, 124 rooms, M$ 55-85. Tel. 27281.
●The *Garden Inn* is good, but a bit expensive. 41 Anson Rd., 60 rooms, M$ 74-148. Tel. 363655.
●One of the few fine old colonial hotels that has never lost its charm is the *Eastern & Oriental (E&O)*. On the ocean at 10 / 12 Jalan Farquhar, 100 rooms, M$ 120-400, in the new wing from M$ 85. Tel. 375322.

There are a few modern *luxury hotels* in the city.

●*Shangri La Inn*, next to the Komtar, 442 rooms, M$ 115-1260. Tel. 622622.
●*Merlin Inn*, Jalan Burma, 295 rooms, M$ 95-800, Tel. 376166.
●*Ming Court*, Jalan Macalister, 100 rooms, M$ 110-900. Tel. 26131.

Outside Georgetown

Hotels in *Batu Ferringhi*, a big tourist beach, are mostly taken up by tour groups. You will not be able to find anything for less than M$ 60.

●*Bayview*, 74 rooms, M$ 80-170. Tel. 81131.
●*Casuarina Beach*, 175 rooms, M$ 140-380. Tel. 811711.
●*Ferringhi Beach*, 136 rooms, M$ 170-400. Tel. 811289.

●*Golden Sands*, 39 rooms, M$ 165-400. Tel. 811911.
●*Holiday Inn*, 54 rooms, M$ 125-320. Tel. 811601.
●*Lone Pine*, 54 rooms, M$ 55-75, best value. Tel. 811511.
●*Palm Beach*, 145 rooms, M$ 90-140 Tel. 811621.
●*Rasa Sayang*, 320 rooms, M$ 130-2200 (!) Tel. 811811.

●Cheap food and rooms can be found at *Ali's Guest House*, on the beach west of the *Holiday Inn*.

In the *kampong* between the Holiday Inn and the Casuarina Beach Hotel, there are a lot of food stands, restaurants, bicycle and motorcycle rental shops, etc. You do not have to rely on the expensive hotel restaurants.

●If you are looking to get away from the big tourist scene, you might go west to the fishing village of *Teluk Bahang*. Places like *Rama's Guest House* have good, inexpensive lodging.
●If you are more partial to the mountains than the beach, you might try the *Bellevue Penang Hill*, on Penang Hill. It is not too far from the upper station of the cog railway. It has 12 rather expensive rooms for M$ 60-80. Tel. 892256.

City Transportation

●The *ferry landing* for Butterworth is a 10-15 minute walk from the cheap hotels.
●All *city buses* (M.P.P.P) stop at the terminal on Lebuh Victoria not far from the ferry landing. The ferries leave every 10 minutes and every 20 minutes at night. From Penang, its free. From Butterworth, 40 *sen*.
●The two *bus terminals* are on Lebuh Victoria (*M.P.P.P. buses*) and on Jalan Maxwell under the Komtar (blue, yellow and green buses).

Potentially useful routes are :
●*No. 1* to Ayer Itam (every 5 minutes, 55 *sen*);

129

•**No. 7** to the Botanical Gardens (every 30 minutes, 45 *sen*);
•**No. 8** from Ayer Itam village to the lower station of the Penang Hill railway (every 20 minutes, 30 *sen*);
•**No. 93** (Green Bus) from Jalan Maxwell to Ayer Itam.
•To get to the **airport**, take the **No. 83** (yellow bus) from the ferry landing (M$ 1.25) or from Jalan Maxwell (85 *sen*). Around M$ 15.00 with a coupon taxi.
•**Taxis:** The best thing for tourists to do is insist that taxis run on the meter (70 *sen* for the first mile, then 30 *sen* for each additional half-mile). Meters have been mandatory since 1988, and taxi drivers can theoretically be fined for not using them. But many will simply refuse to take you if you insist they use the meter. You can always take one of the 500 illegal taxis (*sapu*), that look like normal cars. They charge about M$ 1.00 a person and M$ 2.00 a taxi for trips within the city and M$ 4-5 for trips in a 5 mile zone. Trips outside the zone are an additional M$ 2, or more, a person.
•**Trishaws** are expensive, but they can be fun for a ride around the old part of town. Short distances are M$ 1.00, M$ 1.50-2.00 for rides of about a mile, or about M$ 6.00 / hour.

Be certain to fix the price beforehand, though you will probably have to pay more than the locals. They use the trishaws for short shopping trips, riding from store to store while the driver waits.

What to See

Start with a tour around the cape. Georgetown is known as *Tanjung* in Malay, which means "cape":

On August 11, 1786, Sir Francis Light first stepped ashore at **Kedah Pier** (there was no pier then, of course) and raised the first British flag over the island.

Right next to it is **Fort Cornwallis** (named for the then governor-general of India), built by Indian prisoners between 1804 and 1810. Before that, it was a single wooden fortification at the edge of a thick forest. The cannon is Dutch, and over 400 years old. It was a present for the Sultan of Johor.

Anyone with an interest in British colonial history should not miss the nearby **Museum** on Lebuh Farquhar, between Love Lane and Pitt Street. A statue of Francis Light stands in front. The museum building, which is one of the best examples of colonial architecture in Penang, was originally the Penang Free School (1907-1965). It was the first school in Penang to accept Malay students. Open daily 9:00-17:00, closed during Friday afternoon prayers from 12:15-14:45; admission free.

Nearby is a 60 meter **clock tower**, erected in 1897 in honor of Queen Victoria.

The **Penang Tourist Association** on Weld Pier is a good source of information. The nearby colonial buildings house many government offices and banks. **Immigra-**

tion is on the corner of Lebuh Light and Pantai. The main post office is on the corner of Lebuh Downing and Pengkalan Weld. Close by are the Harbor Commission, Customs, the High Court, the State Government and the old city offices (now located in the Komtar Tower.)

Walking from the ferry down Gat Lebuh Pasar, you will find yourself smack in the middle of the **Indian Quarter**. Many of Georgetown's 80,000 Indians live here.

At the intersection of Lebuh Victoria, is the **M.P.P.P. City Bus Terminal**.

Passing Lebuhs Pantai, Pinang, Raja and Queen brings you to Pitt Street. Here there are many **money changers**, and most change travelers' checks.

All four major Malaysian religions have houses of worship on this street. For example, near Lebuh Bishop is St. George's Anglican church.

Next door is one of Penang's most important, as well as her oldest Chinese temples. **Kuan Yin Yong** was dedicated to the goddess of mercy, Kuan Yin, in 1830. Fake paper money is burned in the two big iron stoves in the temple forecourt to help predict the future and grant wishes. Inside, incense is lit and the future is revealed by shaking joss sticks. The temple also honors laughing Mile Fo (Maitreya – the coming Buddha), Tuah Peh Kong (the god of prosperity), Kuan Ti (the god of war), and Wei To (the defender of Buddhism). You can watch people as they make their offerings – they are quite busy and barely notice your presence.

The **Sri Mariamann Temple** with its main entrance on Lebuh Queen is almost as old. It dates back to 1883, though it was renovated in 1980. It is in the south Indian style and has a remarkable *gopuram* which is symbolic of Meru, the mountain of the gods.

At the intersection of Chulia Street is the **Kapitan Kling Mosque**, which was already standing by 1800. Built in a Moorish-Indian style, it was donated by the Indian Moslem businessman, Cauder Mohudeen.

Continue down Pitt Street to Lebuh Cannon. On your left, hidden away down a side-street, at 18 Cannon Square, is the most famous and most striking Chinese clan house (*kongsi*) the **Khoo Kongsi**. The forefather of a clan whose members bear his name as their family name is honored like a deity. The *Kongsi* are thus related to temples and family shrines. The Khoo has an endless assortment of statues on its 25-ton roof. The building was first completed in 1894, but then burned down the night after the consecration. Supposedly because it too closely resembled the Emperor's Palace in Beijing. So a more modest version was built in 1902 and later renovated in 1955. Open Monday-Friday 9:00-17:00, Saturday 9:00-13:00.

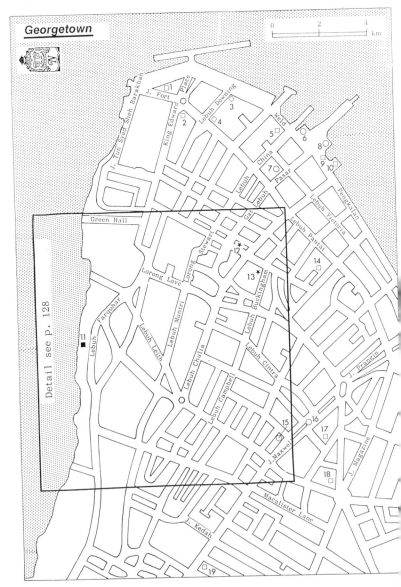

Georgetown

0   2   4
km

J. Tun Syed Sheh Barakbah
J. Fort
Lebuh Downing
King Edward Place
1
2
3
4
Weld
China
Pasar
5
6
8
9
10
7
Lebuh Gat
Lebuh Victoria
Lebuh Pengkalan
Lebuh Pantai
Green Hall
Lorong Love
Lorong Stewart
Lebuh Buckingham
12
13
14
Lebuh Muntri
Lebuh Leith
Lebuh Farquhar
Detail see p. 128
11
Lebuh Chulia
Lebuh Campbell
Lebuh Cintra
J. Prangin
J. Magazine
15
16
17
J. Maxwell
18
Macalister Lane
J. Kedah
19

1. Tourist Information
2. Immigration
3. Fort Cornwallis
4. State Government Buildings
5. Clock Tower / Bus Station
6. Sri Negara Bus Station
7. City Council Bus Station
8. Ferry Landing
9. Railway Booking Center
10. Customs
11. Eastern & Oriental Hotel
12. Sri Mariamman Temple
13. Kapitan Kling Mosque
14. Khoo Kongsi
15. Blue Bus Station / Taxi Stand
16. Green and Yellow Bus Station
17. KOMTAR Tower
18. U.S. Consulate
19. Super Department Store

There are other **clan houses** on neighboring Armenian Street (*Yap*), Jalan Burma (*Khaw, Lee*) and elsewhere.

On Weld Quay, or Pengkalan Weld, right next to the ferry landing, the *Lim* and *Chew* clans are in houses on the water. You can enter both houses, a privilege forbidden to clan members.

The **Mesjid Melayu**, built in 1820, is on Lebuh Aceh. Its builder Syed Hussain came from Aceh in north Sumatra.

As you walk through the **old city**, be sure to take a look at the shop houses. The facades reveal both Chinese and Victorian influence. Some good examples are found on Jalan Magazine near the Komtar. It is interesting to walk the streets and

see the traditional craftsmen at work, like the coffin makers on Lebuh Carnarvon.

On Lebuh Leith, opposite the Waldorf Hotel, are the oldest houses in Penang. They are around 200 years old and the property of Cheong Fatt Tze.

To get an excellent view over the city, go to the big cylinder – the **Komtar** (*Kompleks Tuanku Abdul Rahman*). There are six daily tours to the 55th floor: 11.00, 12.00, 14.00, 15.00, 16.00 and 17.00. There are some 600 visitors daily. Meet at the Tourist Information booth near McDonald's downstairs, the price is M$ 2. On a clear day, you can see Kedah Peak on the mainland. The Komtar is popular with locals for its big shopping center – shops, boutiques, restaurants.

Other interesting temples include the Thai temple **Wat Chaya Mang-kalaram**. It has guardians *(Yak)*, *Nagas*, and bird-women *(Kinnaree)* at the entrance and a 35 m-long reclining Buddha. Also take a look at the neighboring Burmese temple, **Dhammika Rama**, with a pair of elephants at the entrance and a typical Burmese pagoda.

To get there, take a No. 2 city bus from Lebuh Victoria to Jalan Kelawei or the blue bus from Jalan Maxwell (KOMTAR) to the Pulau-Tikus police station. The temples are on Lorong Burma.

You might combine your visit with a trip to Batu Ferringhi or a trip around the island (see below). Or, you can continue onto the Botanical

Garden. If so, go to Jalan Macalister and take a No. 7 city bus from there.

Gurney Drive, Pesiaran Gurney, on the water, is fine for a stroll. There are good food stands here, but a few rats on the beach. The view over the bay and the "North Channel" to the mainland makes up for this.

The **Botanical Garden** is also worth a visit (No. 7 city bus, 45 *sen* from Lebuh Victoria). Despite the interesting jungle trees and flowers, the rhesus monkeys wandering around can be something of a nuisance. The park is also the starting-point for some longer walks and hikes, like a nearby waterfall or up Penang Hill (see below).

About 1 km before the Botanical Gardens, on your left on Jalan Kebun Bunga or Waterfall Road is the tall Indian temple of **Nattukotai Chettiar**. This is a holy place for repentants during the Thaipusam festival.

Even if you are not interested in hiking, do not miss the trip up **Penang Hill** on the cog railway. Trains leave every 30 minutes between 6.30 and 21.30 (you have to change trains once). The round-trip costs M$ 3. To get to the lower station, take a No.1 city bus to Ayer Itam Village and then take a No.8 city bus from there.

The same No. 8 city bus also goes to Kek Lok Si temple. On the way there you pass the modern **State Mosque**. Late afternoon is the best time to go. That way, you can watch night fall over Penang. The cool, fresh air on top (often only 18°C) is a welcome change from the hot city below. At the summit there are restaurants, hotels, a police station, a post office, some houses and a mosque. For information on hiking, see "Excursions."

Ayer Itam is also the starting point for a visit to the spectacular *Kek Lok Si Temple*. On the path up to the temple, you will pass many souvenir stands. Since a road was built to the temple, the vendors do not see many tour groups anymore and have become dependent on individual visitors. They will complain that business has gone downhill, so be sure to bargain hard.

The temple complex, dedicated to Kuan Yin, consists of several areas. First, there is the *Giant Turtle Pool* where you can make merit by feeding the turtles. The other attractions are the *Hall of the Boddhisattva* and the *Hall of Devas* (deities), with the future Buddha Maitreya in the middle and

Wei To, the defender of Buddhism with the four kings of heaven. The next hall is dedicated to Buddha Shakyamuni, the historical Buddha. He is attended by his students Ananda and Kasyapa and 18 *arhats* or saints. In the *Library Tower*, there is a 1904 decree from the Emperor of China, announcing the completion of the temple.

The centerpiece is the 50-m-high *Pagoda of Ten Thousand Buddhas* (depicted on tiles), completed in 1930. The foundation is in the Chinese style, the middle part is Thai and the top is Burmese. You can climb to the top and enjoy the view from there. The upper sanctuary, where entry is forbidden, contains a valuable gold Buddha statue. The cornerstone of the pagoda was laid in 1915 by the Thai king, Rama VI (Vajiravudh).

Next to the pagoda is the *Shrine of Boddhisattva Tsi Tsang Wang*, one of the enlightened who declined to enter Nirvana so that he could bring others to salvation. The area around *Ayer Itam* also has some walks (see below).

There is a lot more to see in Georgetown. The **Shrine to Shiva** on Jalan Dato Kramat, and the **Sikh Temple** on Jalan Brickkiln are notable. There is also the **Penang Buddhist Association**, a villa-like building with statues of the Buddha and his disciples made from Carrera marble, with a small pagoda in front. The association spreads the teachings of the Buddha throughout Malaysia. It is on Jalan Anderson.

Food

Penang is one of Malaysia's best places to eat. The locals are certainly convinced of it. Be careful when eating at foodstalls, some can be less than hygienic. There have been cases of cholera, and though very rare, you are taking a slight risk when eating on the street. Penang **specialties** include:

● *Siam*: white noodle soup in a ground fish and fresh herb sauce. The taste is dominated by sour *assam* or tamarind. *Siam / lemak* has a coconut milk base.
● *Karp Kapitan* is a special kind of chicken curry.
● Beef noodles are known as *goo bak kway teow*.
● Another favorite is *nasi kandar*:
rice with beef, chicken, fish curry and vegetables.

Favorite **Indian restaurants** include *Dawood's* , 63 Queen Street, quite cheap (chicken biryani, kari kapitan, etc) , but to some extent it lives off its fame.

On Jalan Campbell, parallel to Chulia, there are two good places: *Hameediya* at 164A and *Taj* at 166.

The *Islamik* and the *Taj Mahal* are on the corner of Chulia and Penang. There is also good food at Chowrasta Square, including delicious *chendol*, at Jalan Penang.

In the *Veloo Villas* you can eat south Indian food from banana leaves.

One good little **Malaysian restaurant** in the area is the *Poshni* on the corner of Penang road and Lebuh Light.

A good **Malay-Indian** place is *Kassim Nasi Kandar* on Jalan Brickkiln. Also, *Minh* on Jalan Sg. Glugor.

There are many **Chinese restaurants**, and you are best off exploring them for yourselves. It is best to walk in and take a look. If the place is full, more than likely you have made a good choice. Two such places, both on Transfer Road, are *See Hong Hooi* and *Goh Swee Kee* at No. 110.

The *Kee Hong* on Jalan Campbell and places like *Hong Kong, Chup Seng, Sin Kuan Hiwa* and the foodstands on Lebuh Cintra, all have regular crowds.

In *Dragon King*, at the corner of Bishop and Pitt, you can try **Nyonya** specialties (Malay-Chinese food of the Straits Chinese).

Also good are *Chuan Lok Hoi*, on Jalan Macalister, *Prosperous* and *Dragon Inn* at 25C and 27B Jalan Gottlieb, respectively. *Foo Heong* and *Tai Hung* on Lebuh Cintra, and *Lok Thye Kee* at the beginning of Jalan Burma are also good.

Those looking for good *dim sum* should try *Haloman* on Jalan Anson.

Good **vegetarian restaurants** include *For You Yen* and *Eee Hoe Chai*, at 347 and 450 Jalan Kramat.

There is also a good selection of **Seafood** on the island. Try the *Oriental Cafe* on Jalan Macalister, the *Penang Seafood Restaurant* or *Dragon Gate* on Jalan Tanjung Tokong, north of Gurney Drive. Across from there on Tanjung Bungh, are *Hollywood, Sin Hai* and *Sri Batik*. The *Eden* is first-class, but also expensive.

You can always find a wide selection of good food at the **food centers**. For example, Gurney Drive, Jalan Syed Sheh Barakbah, the esplanade near the fort, Pulau Tikus near Jalan Burma, Jalan Cintra and the KOMTAR.

The cheap western hotels around Lebuh Chulia offer simple western food like omelettes, toast, sandwiches, porridge, etc. The *Eden* on Lorong Hutton has good steaks. Other **western restaurants** include: *Tip Top*, 294 Jalan Burma and *Wing Lock*, 300 Penang Road. *The Ship* on Jalan Sri Bahari has a good set lunch. For around M$ 7.00, you get shark's fin soup, steak and white snapper with salad and French fries, a dessert buffet, and coffee or tea.

Save a few dollars to splurge on a big **buffet**, which usually costs between M$ 15.00 and 20.00, even in expensive hotels. For example, Saturday evening in the *Batu Ferringhi Beach* – big barbecue, good salads and a very good dessert table. Or

Sunday brunch, in the *Palm Beach Hotel* (including six kinds of ice cream). At the big hotels, the food is a lot cheaper than the rooms, but drinks can be expensive. If you want to avoid this problem, just do as the locals do, drink the free cold water.

Shopping

Penang used to be a duty-free zone just like Singapore, but not any longer. There is a lot to buy and some good bargains can be found.

There are **souvenirs** of every sort on the way up to the Kek Lok Si Temple as well as on Jalan Penang. **Chowrasta Market** offers local delicacies. Chinese **jewelry** is found mostly on Lebuh Campbell, and Indian jewelry on Lebuh Pitt.

The Komtar is a modern shopping mall with a big department store and a lot of other shops and stores.

Cassettes are cheap. Sometimes you can mix and match songs on one tape – ask about it in the shops in the Chinese and Indian quarters.

You can have **clothes** made to order around Penang Rd.

There are still around 40 **Duty-Free Shops**, with good prices on alcohol, cigarettes, perfume and electronics. You can shop at these providing you leave the country within two weeks and leave the goods unopened until then.

Batik made in Penang can be bought in Batu Ferringhi, Teluk Bahang and Bagan Lapas.

For **books**, try the MPH Bookstore in the E&O hotel.

For **everyday goods** try Penang Bazaar. There are no real specialties in Penang, except perhaps nutmeg. Sometimes you can find some good buys on standard goods like American-made soft *contact lenses* at Lee Optics, 31 Level 3, Komtar for M$ 140.

Festivals

Thaipusam is one of Penang's biggest tourist attractions. Grandstands are set up for viewing the procession from Mariamman Temple on Queen Street to the temple on Waterfall Road (Jalan Kebun Bunga). A route lined by lovely colonial villas. Some orthodox Hindus have expressed regret over the dimensions of the spectacle. (Early-Mid February).

The Birthday of the Jade Emperor, Yu Huang is celebrated in Chinese temples. (February).

Penang International Boat Festival: Dragon boat races starting from Gurney Drive attract around 50,000 visitors. 27-man teams row the boats. (May and December).

Festival of St. Anna: Mass and candlelight procession. (July 24).

Penang Grand Prix: Motorcycle race through the city.

Festival of the Nine Emperor Gods: Prayers, Chinese Opera, parades, fire-walking, etc. (Usually in October).

Loy Kratong: A Thai holiday. Lotus blossom floats are set adrift on water, recalling the Buddha walking on the Narmada River. (November).

The Penang Festival: Sports, cultural and other events. The height of the tourist season in Penang. (Throughout December).

Addresses

Money Changers: Concentrated along Pitt Street, are generally open from 8.30 to 18.00.

●As in the rest of the country, *banks* are open Monday-Friday from 10.00 to 15.00 and Saturdays from 9.30 to 11.30.

●The *Royal Thai Consulate*, 1 Ayer Rajah Rd. Tel. 23352.

●The *Indonesian Consulate*, 467 Jalan Burma. Tel. 25162 / 3.

●You can use the pool at the *Penang Chinese Swimming Club* for M$ 1.00. Get there on the No.21 bus. When the horses are running, you can go to the races on weekends at the *Turf Club* for M$ 2.00.

●*Motorcycles* are available for rent at Sin Chuan Leong Moto at the corner of Lebuh Pasar and Pitt St. One day is M$ 30, two days, M$ 40, and three days, M$ 50.

●*Immigration* is located near the traffic circle on Lebuh Light. Tel. 365122.

●For medical care, go to either the *General Hospital* on Western Road, Tel. 364411, or the private *Penang Medical Center* on Pangkor Rd. Tel. 20731.

●In *case of an emergency*, for police, fire department or ambulance, call 999 throughout the country.

●The *Penang Tourist Association* on the Esplanade (Jalan Tun Syed Sheikh Barakbah) can answer your questions and help solve problems. Tel. 616663. Open Monday-Thursday from 8.30 to 12.45 and 14.00 to 16.30. Fridays from 8.30 to 12.30 and 14.45 to 16.30. Saturdays from 8.30 to 13.00. The *information booth at the airport* is open Monday-Friday from 8.30 to 16.30 and Saturdays from 8.30 to 13.00, Tel. 831501.

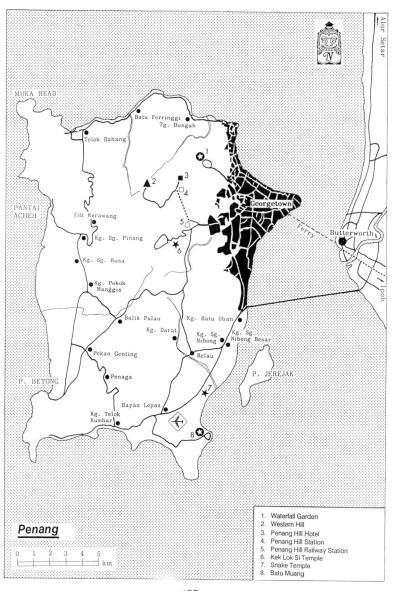

Penang

0 1 2 3 4 5
|___|___|___|___|___|___| km

1. Waterfall Garden
2. Western Hill
3. Penang Hill Hotel
4. Penang Hill Station
5. Penang Hill Railway Station
6. Kek Lok Si Temple
7. Snake Temple
8. Batu Muang

WARNING: As you probably know, Penang is a big center for illegal drugs. Drugs are serious business here and possession of even small quantities can mean **execution!** They love to get foreigners, so stay clean!

Excursions

A trip around the island:

The 75 km round-trip can be done with public transportation. Use *blue buses* for the northern part: Tanjung Tokong, Tanjung Bungah, and Batu Ferringhi to Teluk Bahang. Use *yellow buses* for the south and west parts of the island: Bukit Dumbar, Gelugor, the Snake Temple, Bayan Lepas, Airport, Balik Pulau, and Teluk Bahang.

The trip takes about 4-6 hours and costs around M$ 4. Leave from the Komtar or Jalan Maxwell on a No.66 yellow bus. You could also take a taxi for around M$ 40, or rent a car for a similar price and then drop it off elsewhere. (*Avis*, Tel. 04-361685, at the airport and E&O. *Hertz* near the E&O at 38 Lebuh Farquhar, Tel. 379914. *Sinlat* at the airport, Tel. 830958.

Traveling in a clockwise direction, the first stop could be a visit to the **Universiti Sains Malaysia** (USM), Penang's university. To the left of USM is the **Penang Bridge**, a 13.5 km-long, M$ 850 million prestige

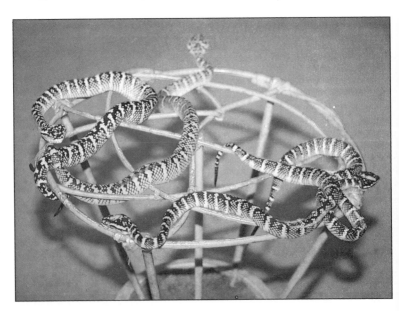

object. It is one of the longest bridges in the world and certainly one of the longest in Asia. Behind the bridge to the left is the fortified prison island of *Jerejak*.

Stop next at the 140 year-old *Snake Temple*. Souvenir stands line the way to the temple, which honors Choor Soo Kong. A monk bought the statue of the god here from China and it is said to have great powers. The god's servants are the highly poisonous green-yellow snakes lying motionless in branches on the altar. These vipers, Wagler's Pit Vipers, do nothing all day, perhaps numbed by the incense. At night , they indulge in chicken eggs left by the faithful. There are a few snakes that have had their fangs removed so that they can be draped around visitors necks for photographs. The snakes are bred and raised next to the temple.

A mile beyond the Snake Temple is the *Bayan Lepas Airport*. You can take a No.83 yellow bus direct from here to the ferry landing. Behind the airport is the fishing village of *Batu Maung*, in the southeast of the island. Here there is a small shrine to Cheng Ho (see the history of Malacca), with one of his footprints.

A little farther, in *Telak Kumbar*, you can take a detour to *Gertak Sanggol* with the No.78 / 80 yellow bus. This is where the best beaches are located. They are filled with locals on weekends and holidays.

On the way to *Balik Pulau* in the interior, you will see clove, nutmeg

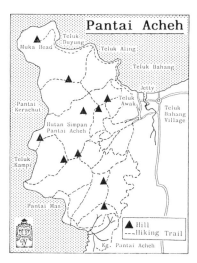

and rubber plantations. At Balik Pulau you have to change buses to continue north. A No.76 yellow bus will take you onto *Teluk Bahang*. The popular *Kitt Krawang Waterfall* is 12 km to the north of Balik Pulau.

You can make a detour to *Pantai Acheh* on the No.75 bus. The *Pantai Acheh Forest Reserve* is a 2000 hectare wood. It has marked trails and six good beaches between Kampong Pantai Acheh and the fishing village of Teluk Bahang. You can walk the whole stretch or take one of the rare No.76 buses or maybe hitch a ride. Near Pantai Acheh is a mangrove forest and *Pantai Mas* is to the north of that.

Pantai Kampi is a beautiful beach, but can be hard to get to. It is quite a way from both Teluk Bahang and Pantai Acheh. There is a path from

Teluk Bahang to the northwest tip of the island, **Muka Head** (a 2 to 2 1 / 2 hour walk).

Pantai Kerachut (Monkey Beach) is a one-hour hike. Start out on the path to Muka Head, but turn left at the fork at the end of the first beach, Teluk Awak / Teluk Bahang. Next, the path gets steep and hilly. Behind the narrow beach is a large lake. Sometimes turtles come up on the beach to lay their eggs on the coarse sand.

Behind the lighthouse on Muka Head lies **Teluk Ketapang**, a small beach, and then **Teluk Duyung**, which is actually private property. In about one hour, you can walk leisurely along the coast from Teluk Bahang to Teluk Aling. The university has a marine research station here.

South of Teluk Bahang is the **Teluk Bahang Forest Reserve**, 100 hectares with swimming holes, orchids, marked trails and a **Museum** (Muzim Perhutanan – a forest museum).

Also worth a visit is the **Butterfly Farm**, open Monday-Friday from 9.00 to 17.00, and until 18.00 on weekends, admission M$ 2.00. Here you can see many different butterflies, frogs, scorpions and other animals.

From Teluk Bahang, the blue bus goes back to Georgetown via Batu Ferringhi and Tanjung Bungah.

There are also **boat trips** around the island. Ask for details at Watertours, Tel. 623789.

Hiking on Penang Hill:

At the tourist information office, you can pick up a copy of *Trekking in Penang*, a pamphlet published by the Malayan Nature Society. It has information on various trails throughout the island and rough maps for orientation, since few of the trails are marked.

On **Strawberry Hill** or **Bukit Bendera**, which you can reach with the cog railway, there are quite a few trails. They start from the lower station or from the "Moon Gate" in the Botanical Gardens. Trails also begin from Batu Ferringhi (Chin Farm) over Bukit Laksamana (the longest and most strenuous way). Finally, from the reservoir to Western Hill (the island's highest point) then farther along to Strawberry Hill.

There are some good trails in and around the Botanical Gardens also. At the summit of **Strawberry / Penang Hill**, there are some good roads with fine views, including Tunnel Road, Viaduct Road, and Summit Road to Western Hill. At times, the hikes go through the jungle and at other times the land is developed on both sides of the path.

If you have your own transportation, a day-trip to **Kedah Peak** is possible (see Alor Setar, above).

You can also book **cheap package tours** in Penang. For example, M$ 159 for five days in Singapore including hotel and meals. Five days around Lake Toba in Sumatra costs as little as M$ 189 (by boat) or M$

360 (by plane) including hotel and meals. Among other places, try New SIA Tours and Travel, 35 Weld Quay for these bargains.

Further Travel

Domestic Flights
- MAS to *Ipoh*   M$ 41
- *Langkawi*   M$ 42
- *Kota Baru*   M$ 72
- *Kuala Terengganu* M$ 80
- *Kuala Lumpur*   M$ 80

International Flights
There are direct flights to / from:
- *Singapore* – M$ 150 (SIA)
- *Bangkok* – M$ 270 (MAS), M$ 215 (Thai)
- *Phuket* (Thailand) – M$ 112
- *Medan* (Indonesia) – M$ 81 (MAS or Garuda)

Tickets for India (Madras), Europe and Australia are cheaper here than in Bangkok.

Tickets to Hong Kong and the Philippines are cheaper in Bangkok.

Ask around in the discount travel agents, for example, on Lebuh Chulia, where there is a student travel agency, MSL Travel, No. 340, Tel. 616112.
- *MAS*, Komtar, Tel. 620011.
- *Garuda*, Wisma Chocolate Products, Lorong Aboo Sittee, Tel. 365257.
- *SIA*, Wisma Penang Garden, 42 Sultan Ahmad Shah, Tel. 363201.
- *Thai Airways*, Wisma Central, Jalan Macalister, Tel. 64848
- *Cathay Pacific*, AIA Building, 68 Lebuh Bish-op, Tel. 620411.

Trains
You can get tickets and make reservations from Butterworth Railway Station, or from the Railway Booking Office on Weld Quay, next to the ferry landing, Tel. 610290.
Trains go to 2nd class / 3rd class:
- *Ipoh*   M$ 10.20 /   6.30
- *Kuala Lumpur*   M$ 21.90 / 13.50
- *Singapore*   M$ 43.30 / 26.60

●*Hat Yai*   M$ 11.50
●*Bangkok*   M$ 39.00
(add M$ 2.80 express charge
and M$ 9.10 / 6.30 for a sleeper).

Bus

There are many buses that leave from the Butterworth ferry landing. You can usually buy tickets before getting on the bus, but sometimes there is a small surcharge.

●*Alor Setar*   M$ 3.24
●*Kuala Perlis* (Langkawi)M$ 6
●*Taiping*   M$ 3.50
●*Kuala Kangsar*   M$ 4
●*Ipoh*   M$ 6.50
●*Lumut*   M$ 8
●*Kuala Lumpur*   M$ 12.70 / 14.70
●*Malacca*   M$ 17.50 / 21.40
●*Johor Baru*   M$ 29
●*Singapore*   M$ 20
●*Ko Samui (Thailand)*   M$ 35
●*Phuket (Thailand)*   M$ 38

Taxis

From the *Cathay* or the *Eng Aun Hotel*, there are taxis to *Hat Yai (Thailand)* for M$ 20; or from the *Butterworth ferry landing* to:

●*Alor Setar*   M$ 7.80
●*Kuala Perlis*   M$ 12
●*Padang Besar*   M$ 14.50
●*Taiping*   M$ 7.25
●*Kuala Kangsar*   M$ 9.40
●*Ipoh*   M$ 13.50
●*Cameron Highlands*   M$ 30
●*Kuala Lumpur*   M$ 27
●*Johor Baru*   M$ 60
●*Kota Baru*   M$ 36

Ships

●To *Langkawi* (M$ 25).
●To *Belawan (Sumatra, Indonesia)*, the harbor of *Medan* on the *Gadis Langkasuka*. (Mondays and Wednesdays, 18:30, from M$ 55-61, booking agents are located in some hotels, like the *Pin Seng* on Love Lane.) Do not buy a bus or taxi ticket for the stretch from Belawan to Medan. Regular buses run all day and night and are much cheaper. Remember, things are cheaper in Indonesia!

●Want to catch a boat to *Madras (India)*? Two trips per month. Ask at Jumabhoy, 39 Green Hall.
●Sometimes yachts sail to *Phuket (Thailand)*. Ask at *Sri Mutiara Shipping*, room 202, 25 Lebuh Light.

Taiping

Taiping is about 90km southwest of Penang and about 70km northwest of Ipoh. It lies along the Sungei Larut, in a valley bordered on the east side by Gunung Hijau or Green Mountain, at 1500m. It rains more here than in any other city in Malaysia. The afternoon is not complete without a shower.

The city is a few kilometers east of the main Kuala Lumpur to Penang road, and a few kilometers north of the new highway connecting Ipoh and Cangkat Jering. The train station is a little west of the town center.

Taiping has a population of 150,000 and is one of the oldest Malaysian cities. It is one of the very few with a Chinese name which means "eternal peace." This peace was negotiated at Pangkor in 1874. It was the beginning of direct British rule on the peninsula outside of the Straits Settlements. The British invaded ostensibly because of fighting between rival secret societies of Chinese tin miners in Larut, near Taiping. These secret societies, or triads, were founded in Shaolin Monastery in Fujian, China, in the 17th century, as fighting units against the foreign rule of the

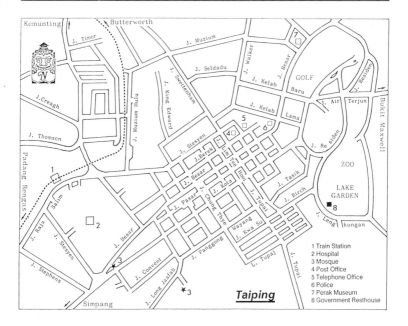

```
Kemunting          Butterworth
        J. Timor              J. Muzium
                                            J. Walker
                                                        J. Besar
                                        J. Seldadu              GOLF
                                                    J. Kelab    Baru
J.Creagh                                                            J. Air  Terjun
                                            J. Kelab                        Bukit Maxwell
                                                    Lama
J. Thomson                                  5
                                            4   6       J. Re siden
                        J. Stesyen                                  ZOO
                            J. Berek                    J. Tasik
                1           J. Besar                            LAKE
                            J. Pasar      J. Kota          J. Birch   GARDEN
Padang Rengas                                                      8
                                        Chung Thye  J. Tupai
                2       J. Besar            J. Kwa Sui  J. Leng  kungan
J. Raja                                 Wayang
J. Salim                            J. Panggong
J. Stesyen                                              L. Tupai        1 Train Station
                        J. Convent                                      2 Hospital
J. Stephens                     J. Long Jaafab    ★3                    3 Mosque
            Simpang                                                     4 Post Office
                                                    Taiping             5 Telephone Office
                                                                        6 Police
                                                                        7 Perak Museum
                                                                        8 Government Resthouse
```

Manchu or Qing Dynasty. This is not to say that the British would not have found some other reason to invade. They were also engaged in tin mining, and they saw the chaos in Perak as a good opportunity to further their interests.

The British attacked with the support of the Sultan, who also saw the triads as a threat. Representatives of all parties met in Pangkor to negotiate a peace treaty under the auspices of Sir Andrew Clarke. This increased the influence of the Sultan, but he was obliged to take on a British adviser. The adviser had final say in all matters other than religion and issues pertaining to Malay customs.

Taiping was the first capital of Perak and remained so until 1935. Today, Ipoh has taken over from Taiping as the most important tin mining center in Malaysia.

Accommodation / Food

There is a surprisingly large assortment of hotels in Taiping, at least 25.
The most expensive are:
●*Meridien*, 2 Simpang Rd, 88 rooms, SR M$ 48-65, DR M$ 58-75. Tel. 05-831133.
●*Panorama Hotel*, 61-79 Jalan Kota, 70 rooms, SR M$ 48-78, DR M$ 58-88, suites M$ 115-122. Tel. 05-834111.

There is quite a good selection of middle-priced hotels:
●*Mirimar*, 30 Jalan Peng Loong, 22 rooms, SR M$ 20-22, DR M$ 24-28. Tel. 05-821077/8.

●*Oriental Hotel*, 14 Barrack Rd, 15 rooms, SR M$ 24, DR M$ 28-42. Tel. 05-825433.

●*Government Resthouse*, located directly on the Lake Garden or Taman Tasik. A bit dirty, but comfortable, with a nice view. Jalan Sultan Mansor, 28 rooms, DR M$ 22-30. Tel. 05-822044 / 571.

At the other end of the range (all without a shower in the rooms):

●*Kung Aun Hotel*, 50 Jalan Eastern, 10 rooms, SR M$ 6, DR M$ 8. Tel. 05-822329.

●*Cheong Onn*, 24 Jalan Iskandar, 11 rooms, SR M$ 7. Tel. 05-822815.

●*Peace Hotel*, 30-32 Jalan Iskandar, SR M$ 8-9, DR M$ 12. Tel. 05-823379.

●*Wah Bee Hotel*, 62-64 Jalan Kota, Tel. 05-822065, 11 rooms, SR M$ 8, DR M$12.

There are some 20 similar hotels located around the center of the city. Try Jalan Kota and the area around the market.

There are all sorts of very cheap *food stands* in the market. Follow your nose and you are sure to find something good.

What to See

There are a few good neoclassical colonial government buildings left over from the time Taiping was the capital of Perak. The *Perak Museum* is the oldest in Malaysia, dating back to 1886. It is on Jalan Muzium, opposite the prison, a bit north of the center of town. There are exhibits on natural history, history, culture, jewelry, weapons with a good *kris* collection, Orang Asli tools, ceremonial objects, a sultan's throne and a lot of old photographs. Not too much information is in English. Open Monday-Sunday from 9:30 to 17:30, Friday from 9:30 to 12:15 and 14:45 to 17:00, admission free. There is also a *Railway Museum*.

The *Lake Garden* is attractive and popular, and a good example of how an old tin mine and its resultant ponds can be converted into something useful. This park was built in 1890. You can rent boats at the lake. It has a golf course, an Allied war cemetery and a small *zoo* (normally open until 18:00, but sometimes it is open at night to allow visitors to view nocturnal animals).

At the northeast corner of the Lake Garden, there is a small road, Jalan Air Terjun which goes 10 km to the oldest hill station in Malaysia, *Maxwell Hill* or *Bukit Larut*. Private vehicles are not allowed on the narrow asphalt road. The only motorized way to get up is with the official Land Rovers that depart every hour from 7:00 to 19:00. The trip takes about 40 minutes and costs M$ 4.00 for a round-trip. Of course, you can also walk along a good path through the jungle. The view in the morning is great, clear to the ocean.

There is a tea house about halfway up, and at the 1100m summit is the *Cottage*. The Bungalows are expensive (M$ 30-100), while the *Larut Resthouse* and the *Speedy Resthouse* are cheaper. Book rooms through the Hill Superintendent, Tel. 05-886241.

On clear mornings, you can see over the Larut plain all the way to the coastline between Pangkor and Penang. You can also go up a little bit higher to the telecommunications station. The view from there is better, as you might expect. There are also some walking paths that go through the jungle.

Maxwell Hill (named for Sir William Maxwell) used to be covered with tea plantations, but they have long since been swallowed up by the forest.

Excursions

To the *Kuala Gula Bird Preserve:*

From Taiping, go 24km in the direction of Penang to Semanggol, and there make a left (or a right, if you are coming from Penang), heading for Kuala Kurau. After about 16km, an unmarked road branches off to the left. From here it is another 4km over a bad road to the fishing village of *Kuala Gula*. If you do not have your own car, you might be able to catch a ride with a plantation truck as far as the last turn-off. Here you can rent a boat for a few hours if you want for around M$ 100.

The village is divided into a Malay part and a Chinese part. As usual, the two halves of the village have only minimal contact with one another. You should stop in at the Ranger office in the Malay section to inform them of your visit. More information can be acquired at the Forestry Wildlife Department, Kuala Lumpur.

In the mangroves you can see rare herons, storks, cranes and eagles scanning the water for their next meals. A visit to a mangrove is a

worthwhile experience. If you come during a flood, you can ride right in on your boat.

On the road to Penang, just before Bagan Serai in *Kampong Tinggi*, there are two mosques on the left side of the road. The newer one was built in 1930 in the Malay-Indian style. The older one from 1877, is made out of wood and is, unfortunately, falling into ruin.

Further Travel

●*Buses:* There are hourly departures for *Penang* and *Ipoh* (M$ 3). You can also go directly from Taiping to *Lumut / Pangkor*.
●*Trains:* Taiping is on the line from *Butterworth* to *Kuala Lumpur*. All trains stop here. Price depends on class and type of train.

Kuala Kangsar

On the Perak River, roughly halfway between Taiping and Ipoh, Kuala Kangsar with a population of 20,000, has been the seat of the Sultan of Perak since 1876.

Hugh Low, a famous British botanist who spent 30 years on Borneo, lived here in the late 19th century. He was the first to try and grow the all-important rubber tree *Hevea brasiliensis* in Malaysia. He achieved this in the garden of his own house, now a government rest house. The first twelve seedlings came from London in 1879, where they were brought three years earlier after being smuggled out of Brazil by Sir Henry Wickham. At that time, whoever wanted to grow rubber was given 40 hectares of land to do so.

One of the first three rubber trees planted in Malaysia can be found today on the grounds of the District Office. Another is planted near the rest house.

The interesting sights are all in the area around the rest house overloo-king the river, slightly outside town. There is the pompous white **Istana Iskandariah Palace**. It has six domes on the roof, and a banquet hall that can seat 700 for dinner or 2000 for a lunch buffet. The palace is usually open. The present Sultan, Azlan Shah, a popular and intelligent man who has been King of Malaysia since 1989, does not actually live here very often.

You can take a look around the fine old wooden palace, **Istana Kanangan**, which now houses the **Royal Perak Museum** or Muzium Diraja Perak. Open Saturday-Wednesday from 9:30 to 17:30, Thursday 9:30 to 12:45, closed Fridays, admission free. This is one of the few remaining Malay palace designs as wooden buildings do not last too long in this hot, wet climate.

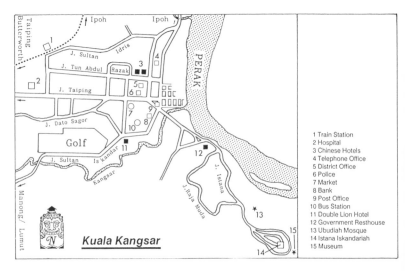

1 Train Station
2 Hospital
3 Chinese Hotels
4 Telephone Office
5 District Office
6 Police
7 Market
8 Bank
9 Post Office
10 Bus Station
11 Double Lion Hotel
12 Government Resthouse
13 Ubudiah Mosque
14 Istana Iskandariah
15 Museum

Kuala Kangsar

The main attraction is the **Ubudiah Mosque** on Chandan Hill. It is one of the most beautiful and most often photographed mosques in Malaysia, though the interior is quite plain.

It was designed by the British and built by an Indian Moslem, Timor Tengah, at the request of the then-Sultan Idris Shah during World War I. Next to the mosque are the new graves of the Sultan's family.

The **royal houseboat**, *balai gambang*, named "Cempaka Sari," might be docked in the river. According to tradition, newly crowned sultans must ride in the boat to the mouth of the Perak River and visit the graves of their predecessors. The trip ends at Beting Bras Basah, where the Sultanate of Perak was established in 1528.

In the city, take a look at **Malay College**, the prestigious school that used to educate only the children of the royal families. Coming from Ipoh, make a right at the clock tower. Coming from the palace, go through the intersection, then take the next right, then go left onto Jalan Tun Abdul Razak. You will see the main building of the college on your right.

From Kuala Kangsar, a worthwhile side-trip is to the nearby **Pottery village of Labu Sayong** where a special kind of black ceramic is made.

Accommodation

The standard inexpensive hotels are:
● **Tin Heong**, 34 Jalan Raja Chulan, 13 rooms, SR M$ 12, DR M$ 15-26. Tel. 05-851255.

● **Double Lion**, 74 Jalan Kangsa, 16 rooms, SR M$ 12, DR M$ 16-25. Tel. 05-851010.
● In addition, there are a few **cheap Chinese hotels** in the center of town. None of these have showers in the rooms.

Arrival / Departure

● You can get to Kuala Kangsar on the **train**. The station is on Jalan Sultan Idris, on the northwestern edge of town.
● You can also ride the **bus**. The bus station is on Jalan Bendahara, southeast of the clock tower.

Kuala Kangsar used to lie on the main road between Penang and Kuala Lumpur. Since the completion of the highway between Ipoh and Changkat Jering, the city has become a bit quieter.

Kuala Kangsar is also the point of departure for trips on the *East-West Highway* through Gerik to Kota Baru and other points on the east coast.

There are regular buses to Ipoh, with connections to Kuala Lumpur, Taiping and Butterworth.

Gerik (Grik)

Gerik is at the intersection of the **East-West Highway** and the road to Thailand via Keroh. The area around Hulu Perak is still largely covered with jungle. As usual, this is being rapidly logged. There are two dammed lakes in the area. The smaller one to the south is **Tasek Chenderoh**. The larger one to the north is **Tasek Temengor**, by which the East-West highway passes. There are many Orang Asli (Senoi and Negritos) living in the area.

For the highway trip you should leave Gerik no later than 16:00. The road is closed during hours of darkness. There are military bases every 5km along until Jeli, the end of the highway.

It is obvious that the highway was not built only to cut 600km off the trip from Penang to Kota Baru, but for military purposes as well. The highway cuts into the territory previously controlled by guerrillas who operated both in Malaysia and Thailand.

Thailand made peace with the guerrillas on the sixtieth birthday of the King in 1987 by granting a general amnesty to them. Malaysia signed a peace treaty with the Malayan Communist Party (MCP) in 1989.

The highway cost several hundred million *ringgit* to cut through the rugged Malaysian interior and took ten years of arduous work. The highway gave the military a big edge in the fight against the guerrillas. It passes some striking scenery and the drive is a pleasant one.

In Gerik there are markets, gas stations and stores.

Accommodation

●There are also several **places to stay**. The cheap Chinese hotels on Jalan Takong Datoh are **Bee Loon** and **Eng Wah**.
●The **Rome** is more expensive, 1 Jalan Tan Saban. Tel. 05-885242.
●For **food**, you can always eat in coffee shops or the hotel restaurants.

Arrival / Departure

Traveling from Penang to Kota Baru, you can take a direct **bus** (*Mara Express*). From Ipoh, you can take a direct *Perak Roadways* bus to Gerik. From here, you can take a share taxi (M$ 16) or a bus to Kota Baru.

Many Malaysians travel north from Perak through Keroh to go shopping in Betong in Thailand. This connection to Thailand is somewhat uncomfortable. The road to the north is poor and not until Yala in Thailand are you again in a fully-settled area. It might be an interesting trip because of this fact. Betong is a popular vacation spot for Malaysians who do not want to go all the way to Hat Yai.

●Coming from Kuala Kangsar, you will pass through **Lenggong**, a town of 30,000, just north of Tasek Chenderoh.

The people here used to make their living from tobacco, and similar to the Burmese, they still smoke cheroots today. (The tobacco from Lenggong can only be used for cigarettes.) Now, the town is known for Lenggong tea. Visitors are welcome in the plantations, 450m above sea level. Some Chinese people come all the way from Kuala Lumpur and Ipoh just to eat at one of the four restaurants here. A specialty is fish dumplings and the innards of the tender *belida fish* with fermented bean paste. Another expensive fresh-water fish specialty is *jelawat*.

Ipoh

With 420,000 people, Ipoh is the second-largest city in Malaysia. Ipoh joined Kuala Lumpur and Penang by being awarded "city status" on May 17, 1988. About halfway between Penang (170km) and Kuala Lumpur (200km), it is on the rail line from Bangkok to Singapore as well as on the north-south road, which will be a full-blown highway in 1992. It is located in the Kinta Valley, which is bounded on the east by the Big

Titiwangsa Range with peaks over 2000m, and on the west by the Little Kledang Range with peaks around 1000m.

The climate here is quite comfortable and not as humid as in the rest of Malaysia. Due to the nearby mountains, it can be quite cool in the mornings or after a rain shower. Especially nice are the green parks which are a result of prosperity and good city planning. Aside from being the capital of Perak and the seat of the Kinta District, Ipoh is also the most important industrial city in the state. Products manufactured here include the following, cement, textiles, plastic and rubber products, tin products like pewter, banknotes and computer chips.

Ipoh owes its prosperity to the tin boom of one hundred years ago. The Kinta Valley is still the world's largest source of *tin* and the city is literally built on tin.

It takes its name from the *Ipoh Tree* or *upas, Antiaris toxicaria*, whose sap is used by the Orang Asli to make poison for their blow guns and spears. There are a few such trees in Ipoh. There is a young fenced one in front of the train station and a big, older one in Seenivasagam Park.

When the city was founded, Chinese settlers came here in great numbers. At the turn of the century, there were 11,000 residents and a dozen years later, the population had more than tripled. The city was very prosperous and for a while, the streets were paved with marble, which is still quarried in the area

today. Some residents at the time decided to mine for tin in the streets! The city was laid out in a grid like Kuala Lumpur, with a large Malay *padang* or plaza. It soon had banks, theaters, a hospital, schools, churches, temples, clubs, and a stop on the rail line from Penang to Kuala Lumpur. Ipoh became a place where money could be spent easily. There were bars, massage parlors, horse races, polo, big game hunting, and of course, good food.

Ipoh is still called the "City of Millionaires," among other superlatives: The cleanest city, home of the prettiest women and the best Chinese food in Malaysia.

Ipoh has the Japanese to thank for naming it the administrative capital of Perak (which was previously Taiping.) Towards the end of the Japanese occupation, paper money was so worthless that it was valued by weight, rather than by the printed value.

During the Emergency, Ipoh was right in the middle of the action. Even today, the Curfew Laws take effect starting at the eastern edge of town.

The fall in the price of tin forced a lot of the mining operations to close down. Perak worked at diversifying its industry, but it was too little, too late. The Klang Valley won the race for modernization. The location of Ipoh is not as well suited to industry. The harbor of Lumut, as well as the airport, need to be expanded significantly if there is to be any further development. The state of

Ipoh

Butterworth

Padang
Bandaran

J. Tun Abdu Razak

J. Panglima Bukit Gantang

KINTA

J. Bandar Raya

J. Pasar

J. Kelab

J. Hill

J. Leech

J. Lahat

J. Datoh

Kuala Lumpur

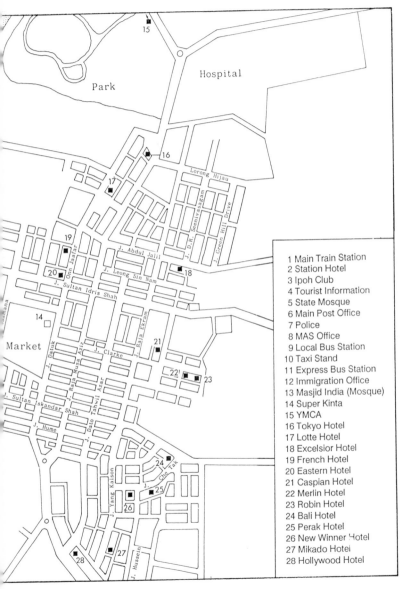

Park

Hospital

Lorong Hijau

J. Abdul Jalil

J. Leong Sin Nam

J. Sultan Idris Shah

Market

J. Clarke

J. Sultan Iskandar Shah

J. Hume

1 Main Train Station
2 Station Hotel
3 Ipoh Club
4 Tourist Information
5 State Mosque
6 Main Post Office
7 Police
8 MAS Office
9 Local Bus Station
10 Taxi Stand
11 Express Bus Station
12 Immigration Office
13 Masjid India (Mosque)
14 Super Kinta
15 YMCA
16 Tokyo Hotel
17 Lotte Hotel
18 Excelsior Hotel
19 French Hotel
20 Eastern Hotel
21 Caspian Hotel
22 Merlin Hotel
23 Robin Hotel
24 Bali Hotel
25 Perak Hotel
26 New Winner Hotel
27 Mikado Hotei
28 Hollywood Hotel

Perak, like the rest of the country, is trying to follow the example of Thailand in expanding its tourism industry.

Accommodation

●If you are looking for colonial atmosphere and comfort, the **Station Hotel**, above the train station is just the place. The official price for the 34 spacious rooms ranges from M$ 70-100 for a single and M$ 100-150 for a double. They have suites for M$ 300. In practice, they discount heavily, usually to around M$ 50-60 a room, although they once offered me a room for as low as M$ 40, Club Road, Tel. 05-512588.

●The one great hotel in Ipoh is **The Royal Casuarina**, located outside of the center of town near the race track. The management prides itself on action and something always seems to be going on here. The food is OK, if not entirely up to the level of the hotel. 200 rooms, M$ 130-1400 (!) Address: 18 Jalan Gopeng, 30250 Ipoh, Tel. 05-505555.

●The next down the list are the **Excelsior**, in the New Town, and the **Tambun Inn** (formerly the King's Hotel), just outside of town. The Excelsior is near some good Chinese restaurants like the Overseas Restaurant. Both have a lot of business.

●**Excelsior**, 125 rooms, M$ 118-280, Clark St, Tel. 05-536666.

●**Tambun Inn**, 91 Jalan Tambun, M$ 78-320, Tel. 05-552211.

Middle-Range Hotels:

●**City Hotel**, 79 Chamberlain Rd, 67 rooms, SR M$ 26-28, DR M4 30-34, all rooms with A / C and bathroom.
Tel. 512911.

●**Fairmont Hotel**, 10 Kampar Rd, 58 rooms, SR M$ 40-44, DR M$ 50-80, all rooms with A / C and bathroom. Tel. 511100.

●**Winner Hotel**, 32-38 Jalan Ali Pitchay, 54 rooms, SR M$ 20.70, A / C 29080, DR 34.55, A / C 34.50, Deluxe M$ 50.40, all rooms with bathroom. Tel. 515177.

●**New Hotel Perak**, Jalan Ali Pitchay, SR M$ 15, A / C 23, DR 17.55, A / C 25.30, all with bathroom. Tel. 515011.

●**Diamond**, 3-9 Jalan Ali Pitchay, 24 rooms, SR M$ 28, DR M$ 32, all rooms with bathroom. Tel. 513644.

●**New Kowloon**, 92 Jalan Yang Kalsom, SR M$ 18.40, A / C 25.30, DR M$ 27.60 with A / C, all rooms with bathroom, friendly atmosphere. Tel. 515264.

●**Hollywood**, 72-76 Chamberlain Rd, 42 rooms, SR M$ 20.70, A / C 25.30, DR A / C 32.20, 44.85 with two big beds and TV. Clean and friendly, all rooms with bathroom. Tel. 515322.

●**Eastern**, 118 Jalan Sultan Idris, 30 rooms, SR M$ 75, DR M$ 85-110, nicely furnished rooms, all with A / C, bathroom, TV. Tel. 543936.

●**French**, 60-62 Jalan Cockman, 40 rooms, SR M$ 69-85, DR M$ 79-85, good rooms with A / C, bathroom, TV. Tel. 513455.

●**Lotte**, 97 Jalan Cockman, 30 rooms, SR M$ 65, Dr M$ 75, well furnished with A / C, bathroom, TV. Tel. 542215-7.

●**Mikado**, 86-88 Jalan Yang Kalsom, 44 rooms, SR M$ 40.25, DR M$ 48.30, good rooms with A / C, bathroom, TV. Tel. 515855.

Cheap Hotels in the area:

Most of these are simple, inexpensive hotels and many of them also double as brothels. Most of the cheap hotels are around Jubilee Street, Jalan Clare, Jalan Raja Ekram and Jalan Raja Musa Aziz.

A word about the bordellos: the situation here is different from in the West or in Thailand. They are simple Chinese hotels. Some prostitutes live in the rooms and rent their services by the hour. If you do not bother them, they will not bother you. The atmosphere is very proper and not much is said about it, nor are there any apparent signs of the business. You can tell the brothel-hotels by the men who sit downstairs playing cards or mahjong. The same applies to cheap hotels in Kuala Lumpur.

Women traveling alone may want to avoid these hotels. At the very least, people will be curious as to why a *kweilo* or Westerner would even want to set foot inside one of these hotels.

●*Cathay*, 92-94 Chamberlain Rd, 26 rooms, SR M$ 14, DR 35.30 (with shower), unfriendly, loud, food in the restaurant is OK. Tel. 513322.
●*New Ipoh Hotel*, 163 Jalan Sultan Idris Shah, 10 rooms, M$ 10-16 with shower. Tel. 548663.
●*Mayflower*, 62 Jalan Faja Ekram (Cowan St.), 18 rooms, SR M$ 12.60, DR M$ 14.70 with fan, no shower.
Tel. 549407. ●*Kum Lock*, 48 Cowan St. SR M$ 10, DR M$ 15 with fan, no bathroom.
●*New Capitol*, opposite above , SR M$ 10, DR M$ 12 (all rooms with fan, no shower), not very attractive.
●*Casplan*, 6 Jalan Jubilee, 9 rooms, SR M$ 27.60 (fan), 34.50 (A / C), DR M$ 32.20 (fan), 39.10 (A / C), a simple middle class hotel. Tel. 542324.
●*Shanghai*, 85 Jalan Clare, 9 rooms, DR M$ 18.40 (fan, shower, double bed), 20.70 (fan, shower, 2 beds), 23.00 (A / C, shower); 3 pers. M$ 30.00; 4 pers. M$ 32.20 (A / C, bathroom), well-organized.
●*Robin*, 106 Jalan Clare, 24 rooms, DR M$ 21.85 (fan, shower, 2 beds), M$ 25.30 (A / C, shower, 2 beds); 4 pers. (2 double beds) M$ 36.80 (A / C, shower), 5 pers. (2 double beds, one twin bed) M$ 41.40 (A / C, shower), quiet location, friendly. Tel. 513408.
●*Merlin*, opposite the Shanghai, 92 Jalan Clare, 35 rooms, DR M$ 39 / 10, with 2 double beds M$ 57.50, all rooms with A / C and bathroom, not very friendly. Tel. 541351.
●*Sun Sun*, Jalan Raja Ekram, SR M$ 11.00, DR 13.65 (fan, no shower).

Around Jalan Raja Musa Aziz (Anderson St.), there are some more cheap hotels, mostly loud like those around Cowan Street:
●*Kong Ah*, No. 37, 10 rooms, 2 twin beds M$ 22.00, 2 double beds 28.30, all rooms with fan and shower, clean. Tel. 548990.
●*South Isles*, opposite above, 1 pers. M$ 10.50, 2 pers. 12.60, all rooms with fan, no shower, friendly and clean.

●*Lee Kong*, 1 bed M$ 10.50, 2 beds M$ 14.50, all rooms with fan, no shower, nice and clean, restaurant downstairs.
●*Federal*, 1 bed M$ 11.00, 2 beds M$ 13.00, all rooms with fan, no shower, clean but a bit loud since it is on the corner.
●*Lok Kheng Loi*, opposite above, SR M$ 8.00, DR 10.00, all rooms with fan, no shower, bath / shower upstairs, toilet downstairs next to the restaurant, relatively clean, very friendly.
●*Say Ney*, next to the *French Hotel*, Jalan Onn Jaafer (Cockman St.), 1 pers. M$ 14.00, 2 Pers. 16.00, fan, no shower.
●The *Tokyo* looks a bit better from the outside, but pretty much the same on the inside, 161 Jalan Anderson, SR M$ 15 (fan, shower), DR M$ 21 (fan, bathroom), M$ 25 (A / C, bathroom).

●*Youth Hostel:* This is another possibility. Near the Seenivasagam Park, on the banks of the Kinta River. It enjoys views of the rock outcroppings with little hill temples and the Subramanniam Temple, the destination of the Thaipusam penitents.
●*YMCA*, 211 Jalan Raja Muda Aziz, 21 rooms, M$ 24-36, dormitory M$ 7 per person. If you do not have too much luggage, there is an attractive path to the YMCA from the Old City by the side of the river.

What to See

The Old and New Towns are compact and it takes no longer than 20-30 minutes to walk through them. You might take a stroll around the *Old Town* west of the Kinta River and look at the old colonial buildings. The Train Station, the Station Hotel (dinner for M$ 8.50.), the courts, the city government building, and the attractive clock tower, without which no Malaysian city is complete.

There is also the **State Mosque**, a little north of the Padang. The Padang has regular soccer and field hockey games. On its north side is the renowned St. Michael School. Just to the east is the Masjid India or Indian Mosque. To the southwest of the Padang is the Ipoh Club, an old British colonial club. Along Jalan Panglima Bukit Gantang to the north, in the direction of Penang, are some banks and state government buildings.

Immigration is located on the ground floor of the left of the two buildings at Bangunan Kerajaan Persekutuan.

The streets of the **New Town** are lined with Chinese shop houses, which create a fine setting. There are also two large shopping centers next to the telecom building, Yik Foong and Super Kinta, and lots of restaurants and hotels. The **Pasar Besar Market** is also worth seeing. The new supermarket that has moved into the building makes an interesting contrast.

To the south, on the Kinta River, on Jalan Masjid is a slightly weather-beaten mosque. Right nearby, on Jalan Datuk, is the best mosque in the city, **Masjid Paloh**, built in 1912 with a richly decorated pulpit.

If you do not want to run around Ipoh, you can ride around in a **trishaw** (decide on the price beforehand!) Mostly women and children ride these in Ipoh.

November is tourism month in Perak state, and there should be special events planned.

Addresses

- **Train Station:** Tel. 05-540481
- **Main Post Office (Pos Besar):** On the south of the square in front of the train station.
- **Police:** There are several stations around the city. The main one is in between the train and bus stations.
- **Tourist Information:** Ground floor of the city government building (not very useful.)
- **Drug Stores:** All over the city.
- **Banks:** Several branches near the clock tower in the Old Town.
- How do you get to the **bus or train station**? Simple: All local buses go to the bus station, and from there it is a five-minute walk to the train station.
- To get to the **airport (Lapangan Terbang / Aerodrome):** Get on a bus that says: Aerodrome via Housing Trust

Public Transportation

The **taxis** are all theoretically run on meters and have been since March 1988. There are also **share taxis**, that go to points outside of the city. There are share taxi stands in the New Town. It is best to ask the drivers where they are going (for example, Batu Gajah or Tanjung Rambutan).

There are **buses** that go all over the city as well. They leave from the local bus station, opposite the express bus station. Local buses are larger than long-distance buses.

There is a simple rule for taking the bus in Ipoh: All local buses go to the bus station. If the sign on the bus says Ipoh, Stesen Bas or Bus Station, then the bus is going towards the city. Sometimes the conductors change the sign over just before the last stop, which might delay you a bit, but the bus will turn around at the last stop and head back into the city. The bus station is also the place to change buses. Fares from the city to the edges of town are usually between 40 and 55 *sen*. Different bus companies have different routes:

●*"Reliance"*: To Kuala Kangsar.
●*"Ipoh Bus"*: Various destinations within the city.
●*"General"*: Batu Gajah, Tanjung Rambutan, Sungai Durian, Bruas.
●*"Kinta"*: Gopeng, Kampar.
●*"Century"*: Tambun, Tanjung Rambutan (Taman Cempaka).

What to See Outside of the City

The most worthwhile sights in Ipoh are actually outside the city. For example, if you follow Jalan Tambun about 1 km out of town (past the traffic circle with a fountain), you will come to the **Japanese Garden** on your right. It was a Japanese gift to the Perak Turf Club.

If you continue for another 3 km (passing a **Thai temple** on the left and a **Chinese cemetery** on the right), the road goes gradually downhill and there is an unpaved road that branches off to the right. Follow the unpaved road for about 1 km crossing a stream to get to the first **prehistoric rock paintings** discovered on the Peninsula. They were discovered by an English soldier fighting the communists in 1958.

A flight of stairs goes up to the rock wall above. Walk about 50 m to the right along the wall and then look up about 10 m. In the middle of the rock face, you can see the iron oxide of the paintings. There must have been more here earlier, 5000 years have faded the paintings somewhat, but they are still clearly recognizable. There are wild boars, cows, deer (one of them obviously pregnant), dolphin-like fish, a tapir, and a few people who look as if they were painted by Joan Miro. It looks as if the site was once a holy place and probably used for a long time.

There is a good view from here of Ipoh and some **limestone outcroppings**. Up above on the rock face many swallows nest, as do bats.

Taking the No. 181 bus from the market, you can go as far as the military base for about 50 *sen*. You will have to walk the rest of the way. Behind the stream is an open iron ore mine. It is worked, like the tin mines, with water cannons. Farther away from the city, past Tambun, on the right (look for the sign) is Om Sai Ram, an Indian cave temple. Past the sign, on the edge of the mountain, is hot spring. Entry is M$ 5.50, sauna M$ 5.00; open daily except Mondays, Sundays and holidays, 15:00-21:00. Farther off in the direction of Tanjung Rambutan (about 13 km) there is an interesting little **Chinese cave temple** on the left. There are a number of palm readers on the way.

The most famous **cave temples** and there are a good dozen all

together, are all outside of the city. One of the best known, *Perak Tong* (*tong* = cave temple), is on Jalan Kuala Kangsar, which is the old road to Penang. It is not far from the entrance to the highway (as you come from the city), about 6 km from the center of town on the right (east) of the road. It is easy to miss, so keep your eyes open.

About 2 km before that on the left is a *Thai temple* (Wat Meh Prasit Sumaki), filled with cement statues of monks paying respect to a large reclining Buddha. The walls are painted with scenes from the life of the Buddha.

Back to Perak Tong. The temple, which has been operating for more than 40 years, has a laughing Buddha in the entrance hall, and a 12 m-tall Buddha in the main chapel. Next to it is an altar for Kuan Yin, (the goddess of mercy), Maitreya, (the future Buddha), Vairochana and others. The walls were painted by various Chinese artists. Inside there is a staircase that is in very bad condition, so be careful on the loose stones. It goes up and out into the daylight and finally reaches a

pavilion and another temple. Unfortunately, it is much in need of renovation. The good view from on top is marred by the Tasek Cement Factory.

As is often the case at well-known cave temples, there is a good, inexpensive *vegetarian restaurant*. You can order what appears to be duck, fish, shrimp or pork, but rest assured, it is all vegetarian.

You can get to the temple on a Reliance bus going in the direction of Kuala Kangsar. If you are interested in further information about the temple, you can contact *Mr. Chong Yin Yat*, the temple manager and the son of the founder. He is also a calligraphy artist (Tel. 05-565387).

The other temple that must be seen, the *Sam Po Tong,* is nearby. It is near the exit for the road to Kuala Lumpur, on the left (look out for Mercedes sign), behind the pomelo stand. These are supposedly the most famous pomelos in all of Malaysia. Next to it, on the left, are two more temples, the *Nam Tien Tong*, which is worth a visit, and the *Lin Sen Tong*, a private temple. Both have vegetarian restaurants nearby.

In Sam Po Tong, you can reach a turtle pool through a tunnel that goes off to the right after the first of two Buddha altars. The turtles, a symbol of longevity, are the main attraction. You can feed the many small and large turtles with greens that you buy outside.

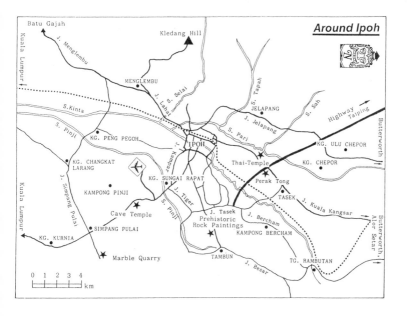

Around Ipoh

If you drive on Tiger Lane coming from Perak Tong or Tambun in the direction of Sam Po Tong, just after you pass through the intersection of Tiger Lane, Tasek Road and Tambun Road, the Geological Institute and **Geological Museum** will be on your right. Another 1 km on your left, a bit beyond the Royal Perak Golf Club, is the **Istana Riswin Palace**, which a former sultan built for his wife. It is a good example of mixed Western and Malay architecture.

If you come off Tiger Lane onto Jalan Gopeng and then make a right onto Jalan Dampar, about 100 m to your right, you will see the **Tai Pee**

Sim Cloister. It houses some beautiful wooden statues. An old monk still lives in the cloister. During the *Festival of 9 Gods* in the fall, many pilgrims stay here. Friendly women around the cloister will answer any questions you might have.

Shopping

Ipoh is not a tourist city – not yet, at least. Oriental Pewter is a local factory that makes **tin souvenirs**. Other than that, the markets and shops are filled with standard Malaysian goods and offer no special luxuries.

Eating

Ipoh is home to some of the best **Chinese food** in Malaysia, and it is cheaper than in Kuala Lumpur.

●*Public Seafood*, good Chinese seafood restaurant. The best place in Pusing (15km along the road to Lumut.)

●*Overseas Restaurant*, opposite the Excelsior Hotel, is one of the best local Chinese restaurants.

●*Up-Up* on Yang Kalsom is known for good fish head curry.

●*Moon Gate*, a Chinese restaurant offering very good value and good food. Grilled shark's fin, lemon chicken, sizzling prawns, deep-fried grouper, and yam cake. Jalan Datoh.

●*Kok Hee* is in a plantation owner's mansion with two towers, one for each wife. A big restaurant with a lot of tables outside and a Chinese-style interior. A lot of clubs and organizations meet here.

●*F.M.S.*, Jalan Laxamana, opposite *Padang*, is a restaurant from the old days. Known for its crab.

●*Szechuan* on Jalan Fair Park near the field hockey stadium. Good roast duck (a half duck is M$ 7), tofu, hot and sour soup, etc. Good value with most of the dishes around M$3.

●*Ipoh Jaya*, Green Lane, good Hokkien mee.

Hawker Food: There is an especially good assortment in *Gourmet Square* in the center of Ipoh Garden. *Wooley Food Center* is a modern style establishment. In *Thum*, they have good steaks (pepper steak for M$ 7), pork chops, fish and chips, etc. for around M$ 3.

There is **vegetarian food** in *Sayur Sayuran* on Jalan Chung Thye Pin.

There is good Indian vegetarian food in the Old Town in *Restoran Krishna Bhawan* where a good portion of Biryani rice costs around M$ 2.50.

You can get very good **Pakistani and North Indian food** served by *Ali* in *Pakeeza*. A / C and thus not cheap, but very good value. Say hello from me if you go there.

Excursions

To Tanjung Rambutan in the upper Kinta Valley.

Take the Century Bus 181 to Ulu Kinta (military base). Then walk another 3 km along the road (cars cannot make it all the way) to the fenced in water intake station. Then go to the left over the bridge that crosses the river. There is a market here used mostly by Orang Asli of the Semai group. To the right the river goes to a picnic area near some rapids. To the left, after about 1 km, it comes to an Orang Asli village. There is another village about 3 km farther on.

If you continue on further, you will come to the beginning of the trail up Gunung Korbu, which at 2182 m is only 4 m lower than the highest mountain on the peninsula, *Gunung Tahan*. Officially, the path falls under curfew restrictions, but it remains open for tourists. Unofficially, you can make the climb in three to four days, hiring an Orang Asli guide from the second village for about M$ 20 a day. You will have to know some Malay if you want to speak with your guide.

If you go about 1 km past Tanjung Rambutan, you will come to the **National Stud Farm** on your right. A veritable must for horse lovers?

Up Kledang Hill (808m).

Take the General bus to Menglembu or better still, the bus for Taman Kledang directly to the start of the asphalt road that ascends the

On the way up Kledang Hill: a view over Ipoh and the Kinta Valley.

locals' favorite hill. There are two television broadcast stations on top (TV 3 and RTM), which are normally closed to visitors. Up high on the mountain, there is some jungle, but the lower parts are all given over to plantations. Every evening, joggers and walkers go at least halfway up. Sunday mornings are popular for picnics on the hill. The view is quite good over Ipoh and the Kinta Valley. To the west are the mountains near Parit where there are still wild elephants, and to the east, the Central Titiwangsa Range.

Natural Caves

There are some interesting natural caves like **Goa Kandu**, past Gopeng on the road to Kuala Lumpur and **Gua Kelawar** near Sungei Siput, about 30 km north of Ipoh on the old road to Kuala Kangsar. You have to go through a plantation, Ladang Sungei Siput to get to the cave. You used to be able to see 1000-year-old cave paintings at the entrance, but they were covered over by new charcoal drawings in 1988, which is a real shame. People from the Malay Nature Society, which sometimes makes Sunday trips here, can fill you in on details.

A trip to see some of the largest flowers in the world, **Rafflesia**, is quite easy, though you may not actually catch them in bloom. 12 km into the valley, past Gopeng, where some power lines cross the road, follow the path to the left. This follows a stream.

Walk for about 30 to 45 minutes, then at the end, go up the slope on your right to the place with all the flower buds. The flowers are only in bloom for four days after nine months of preparation. In three trips, I only managed to see them in bloom once.

Further Excursions

Ipoh can also be used as a departure point for the Cameron Highlands, Teluk Intan, Pangkor Island, Batu Gajah, and Kuala Kangsar.

Hash House Harriers

Every Monday, the Hash House Harriers and every Friday, the Harriettes meet at 18:00. Together they go on runs through the jungle, but you do not have to go fast, and the group divides according to speed. Afterwards, there is beer and soda and a small meal. Guests are welcome (Mondays M$ 7.00 − beer is expensive in Malaysia). Tel. 05-557187.

Further Travel

●There are MAS *flights* to Penang (M$ 41) and Kuala Lumpur (M$ 55). To get to the airport, take the Aerodrome bus from the local bus station.
●*Trains* run in the direction of Butterworth (M$ 10 / 14) and Bangkok (ca. M$ 65) or towards Kuala Lumpur (M$ 13 / 18) and Singapore (M$ 24 / 40). There are six trains daily, including two express trains, in both directions.
●There are **express buses** to Butterworth (M$ 6.50), Hat Yai (ca. M$ 20), Kuala Lumpur (M$ 8.50), and Singapore (ca. M$ 25). Also to Kuala Terengganu, etc. You do not need to reserve seats to get to Butterworth and Kuala Lumpur, as there are several companies operating along these routes. The buses leave from Medan Kidd.
●There are **local buses** to Lumut (M$ 4), Kampar (M$ 1.55), Kuala Kangsar (M$ 2.50), Taiping, etc. Buses to Lumut (Pangkor) leave from opposite the express bus station. Buses to Gerik and Kota Baru leave from the start of the East-West Highway.

Buses leave the local bus station for Taiping, Kuala Kangsar, Kampar, Tapah and Teluk Intan.
●There are **taxis** from Medan Kidd. Fare to Butterworth is M$ 13.50, and to Kuala Lumpur, M$ 15.

Batu Gajah

This is a small town of 12,000 about 20 km south of Ipoh. During the early tin boom days, Batu Gajah was more important than Ipoh. For a while, it was the British administrative center of Perak, and there are a few imposing colonial buildings leftover. Today, Batu Gajah is the seat of the West Kinta district. It is a very quiet town with a lot of schools. The name *batu* means stone and *gajah* means elephant recalling a stone elephant supposedly found in the area. Batu Gajah is also the birthplace of the present Sultan of Perak.

What to See

Kellie's Castle, supposedly a haunted house, is the best known attraction. It was built by a Scottish plantation owner, William Kellie-Smith, who dreamed of building a mansion more splendid than the State Secretariat in Kuala Lumpur. Indian construction crews started work in 1915. In 1926, Kellie went to Britain to buy an elevator for the tower. He never made it back to his castle. He died in Lisbon of pneu-monia after stopping to buy land in Timor, and is buried in the British cemetery in Lisbon. The castle has remained as he left it (except for the horrible graffiti).

Some believe the castle is inhabited by ghosts, and maybe Kellie's ghost has returned. The cellars were supposedly used by the Japanese for torture during the War. Whatever the truth may be, Kellie's Castle is legendary in the area.

If you come on the road from Gopeng to Batu Gajah, you can see the castle clearly on the left. It is 5 km before Batu Gajah. Unfortunately, to reach the castle you need to take a long detour, due to a small river with a strong current in front of

the castle. A little bit upstream is a ford where you can cross. If you come by car you will have to pass the castle and continue for another 2 km towards Batu Gajah. Pass the intersection with the road to Ipoh and Lahat, which is on the right. Turn left at the sign for Ladang Kinta Kellas into a rubber and oil plantation. Here you can ask the guard for permission to use the road through the plantation. He will also be able to give you directions to the castle. You can also take the Perak Roadways bus to the plantation, but they do not go very often.

Coming from Gopeng, about 1 km past the castle, you will see an **Indian temple**, built by Kellie for his plantation workers. Outside, on the right, there is an image of Kellie's face as a tribute to the benefactor.

Continuing on the road from Gopeng, about 1 km before Batu Gajah, you can take a right to get to the amusement park, ***Taman Tasek S.M. Nor***. There are crocodiles, snakes and other animals in addition to the more standard amusement park fare. There is a swimming pool and a pond where you can rent boats. It is quite popular with residents on weekends and holidays.

Food

There are some simple Indian and Malay restaurants. One place worth trying is a Chinese Restaurant called ***Makanan Orang-orang Islam***. It serves Chinese food, prepared according to Islamic purity laws (properly butchered chickens, no pork, etc.) It is opposite the telecommunications building. Everyone knows it, so just ask.

Further Travel

●Batu Gajah has a *rail connection*, but only local trains (RelBas) stop here. If you are taking an express train, you must take a bus to or from Ipoh.
●From Ipoh, there are lots of *buses* to Batu Gajah. From the local bus station, take a "General" bus going to Batu Gajah (M$ 1.10), Tanjung Tualang, Sungai Durian. From the New Town, take a Perak Roadways bus. Or you can take a share taxi from the Sultan Iskandar Shah in the New Town (M$ 1.60).

Lumut

This town on the Dinding River is home to Malaysia's largest naval base. It is also the place to catch the ferry to **Pangkor Island**. Lumut is about 90 km southwest of Ipoh, and south of Taiping. There is nothing particularly interesting to see here for visitors.

There are a few **beaches** on the Dinding Straits that you can reach by taxi (minimum of 7 km from Lumut).

They are Teluk Muruh, Teluk Batik (the main beach) and Teluk Rabiah, and are favored mainly by locals. They are not as good as the Pangkor beaches.

If you are interested in **outdoor adventure**, you might contact the Wilderness Adventure Camp, Teluk Batik, 32200 Lumut (Tel. 05-935559 or their bureau in Kuala Lumpur, 03-9300325). They offer weekend, six, and ten-day courses teaching various skills: canoeing, jungle trekking, climbing, etc. M$ 35 per day (students M$ 30 per day).

The high-point for tourism in Lumut comes during the three-day **Pesta Laut Lumut** in August. There are boat races and other sporting events in a general festival atmosphere. Lumut is being further developed for tourism.

Accommodation

Normally, people only use Lumut as a place to get the ferry to Pangkor, and are not interested in staying here. If you miss the ferry after 19:00, or just want to stick around, here are a few addresses:
●*Government Resthouse*, 7 rooms, M$ 12-15, good. Tel. 05-935938.
●*Phin Lum Hooi Hotel*, 93 Jalan Titi Panjang, 10 rooms, SR MR 9, DR M$ 12, no shower in room, acceptable. Tel. 935641.
●*Lumut Country Resort*, 331 Jalan Titi Panjang, 44 rooms, M$ 70-80. Tel. 05-935009.

Arrival

There are Perak Roadways buses every hour on the hour from **Ipoh** (M$ 3.50) directly to Lumut.

You can also take direct buses from **Taiping** and **Singapore**.

If you miss the direct bus from Ipoh, you can take a regular bus to **Sitiawan** (where there is a small airport) and then take another bus to Lumut from there.

If you have a car, there are a few interesting **detours** along the way:

Bota Kanan, on the Perak River, has a breeding farm for terrapins (turtles). Turn left after you cross the river.

Farther downstream, about halfway to Teluk Intan, with its crooked tower, is **Kampong Gajah**, where James Birch, the first British governor of Perak, was murdered. There are also ten royal graves from the early years of the Sultanate of Perak. Kampong Gajah is known for ceramics and embroidery. You can get here on a bus from the local bus station in Ipoh.

The road from Kampong Gajah to Lumut is very scenic. It passes through an idyllic landscape of wooden houses, durian and other fruit trees, and rice paddies. You can often see *kingfishers* along the way.

Shortly after the turn-off for Kampong Gajah, there is a road to **Bruas**, where there are remains of housing and fortifications from the old Malay kingdoms of Gangga Negara. Do not expect too much. There is a "General" bus that goes to Bruas from the local bus station in Ipoh.

Excursions

Dinding River

On **Pantai Sungai Gelam** beach on the Dinding River near the fishing village of Segari, a little north of Lumut, there is a place where you can observe greenback turtles between March and July. These are smaller than the giant turtles, but they nonetheless grow up to 1 meter long and weigh over 140 kg. Hundreds of turtles used to come here to lay their eggs, but by 1987, there

were only a few dozen. Why? A combination of reasons: tourists and fishermen take the eggs; tourists treat the animals badly, (flashing cameras in their eyes and riding on their backs); the very bright lights on the fishing boats.

Fishing trip to Pulau Sembilan:

This small uninhabited island group lies south of Pangkor (Pulau Sembilan means "Nine Islands.") If you are part of a big group, you can hire a boat and a skipper for around M$ 200. Fishing at night is especially good. You can also camp out on one of the islands, and go snorkeling, or bird watching. In that case, you will have to bring food and water. There is running water on the two main islands. Do not forget mosquito nets or coils.

Ferries to Pangkor

The ferry landing is normally the only part of Lumut that interests visitors at all. You can get there in a few minutes from the terminus of the bus routes. The easiest way is to follow everyone else. Or walk west,

parallel to the river and turn right at the clock tower. Boats leave every 15 minutes if it is crowded, and every 30 minutes otherwise (M$ 1). The trip over the Dinding Straits to the island, at the mouth of the river, takes between 35 and 60 minutes.

Pangkor

According to conventional wisdom, with the exception of the Langkawi Islands, the west coast cannot hold a candle to the east coast in terms of swimming, snorkeling, diving, wind-surfing, etc. Despite all the hype, Penang's beaches are nothing special. Port Dickson near Kuala Lumpur is boring. But in defiance of conventional wisdom, the little island of Pangkor, south of Langkawi, though only 12km long and 4km wide, can certainly hold its own with the east coast.

If you are not expecting too much, you will be genuinely surprised. **Beaches** like Coral Beach or Pantai Puteri Dewi (Beach of the Beautiful Princess), are generally quite good, but not so good for snorkeling. The best place for snorkeling is Emerald Bay, off the smaller island of **Pangkor Laut**, to the west of Pangkor.

There is a new **footpath** around Pangkor Island that goes through the jungle and emerges periodically on different beaches. With time out for swimming, the full circle should take four or five hours.

Taking the path in a clockwise direction, from Khoo's Minicamp,

head for Tortoise Bay, Teluk Nipah, and Thomson Bay. You can camp at the north end of the bay under the trees. Next comes the Malay Kampong Teluk Nipah, Coral Bay, Golden Sand or Pantai Puteri Dewi (with the Pan-Pacific Hotel), Teluk Dalam (or Oyster Bay), and the Malay Kampong Teluk Chempedak.

Along the west coast, the path offers good views of the coast and of the smaller islands offshore.

In the northeast, the path enters the jungle. Monkeys, exotic birds, and with luck, flying lizards, are all visible at times from the path. Finally, the path reaches three Chinese fishing villages: Kampong Sungei Pinang Kecil and Besar, which has a Dutch grave, an Indian temple and a mosque. And then there is Kampong Pangkor with a lighthouse. Interestingly, the rows of houses closest to the river are built on stilts.

You can extend the walk by taking a detour to the ruins of the 17th century Dutch fortification, Kota Belanda, located about 2 km south of Kampong Pangkor, where the ferries land. You will pass through Kampong Teluk Kecil and Teluk Gedung. Behind the fort are the Tiger Rocks.

I once heard of a path that crossed the island from **Coral Bay** to **Sungai Pinang**, over the 300 m hill in the middle of the island. I asked around, and no one knew about it. Maybe you will have more luck.

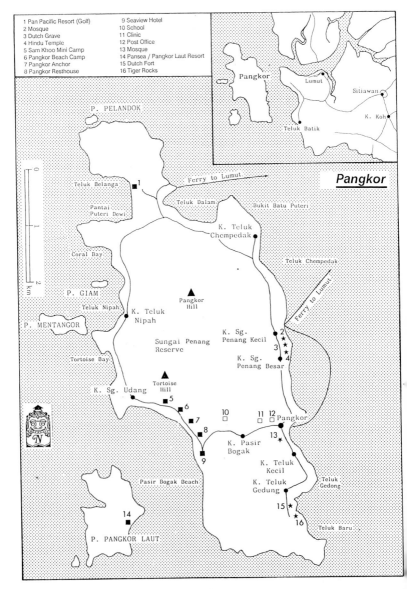

1 Pan Pacific Resort (Golf)
2 Mosque
3 Dutch Grave
4 Hindu Temple
5 Sam Khoo Mini Camp
6 Pangkor Beach Camp
7 Pangkor Anchor
8 Pangkor Resthouse
9 Seaview Hotel
10 School
11 Clinic
12 Post Office
13 Mosque
14 Pansea / Pangkor Laut Resort
15 Dutch Fort
16 Tiger Rocks

Pangkor

Pangkor
Lumut
Sitiawan
K. Koh
Teluk Batik

P. PELANDOK

Teluk Belanga
Ferry to Lumut
Teluk Dalam
Bukit Batu Puteri

Pantai
Puteri Dewi

K. Teluk
Chempedak

Coral Bay

Teluk Chempedak

P. GIAM

Pangkor
Hill

Teluk Nipah

K. Teluk
Nipah

P. MENTANGOR

Sungai Penang
Reserve

K. Sg.
Penang Kecil

Ferry to Lumut

Tortoise Bay

K. Sg.
Penang Besar

Tortoise
Hill

K. Sg. Udang

Pangkor

K. Pasir
Bogak

K. Teluk
Kecil

Teluk
Gedong

Pasir Bogak Beach

K. Teluk
Gedong

Teluk Baru

P. PANGKOR LAUT

Beaches / Accommodation

If, like most people, you want to hit the beach right away, take a bus for 40 *sen* or a taxi for M$ 3.00 to *Pasir Bogak Beach*. It is about 2 to 3 km away on the other side of the island. There are a number of places to stay on this lovely bay:

●In the north, there is the popular *Sam Khoo's Mini Camp*. It consists of little huts that, apart from a mattress, are completely empty. Local students like this place. It can get very crowded on weekends, holidays and school vacations, when it is often completely booked. M$ 4.20-5.20 a night, Tel. 05-951164.

●Just south are the more solid *Pangkor Anchor* and the *Pangkor Paradise*, both M$ 7-8 a night.

●Then the very simple *Mini Longhouse* (from M$ 5.50 per head) and the *Government Resthouse*, from M$ 20, which as usual, promises more than it offers.

●The two hotels at the southeast end of the bay, the *Beach Hut Hotel*, 33 rooms, 5 villas, M$ 30-80, Tel. 05-951159, and the *Sea View Hotel*, 37 rooms, M$ 60-80, Tel. 05-951605, are not as good as they should be, given their prices.

●In a higher price range is the *Pansea* (or Pangkor Laut Resort) on *Pangkor Laut Island*. It has 89 simple rooms, M$ 110-220, Tel. 05-951375, and is on the bay right opposite *Pasir Bogak*. The hotel has its own ferry service. The spectacular Emerald Bay is a just a few minutes away on the other side of the island.

●The best and most expensive hotel is the *Pan Pacific Resort* on *Golden Sands Bay*, 161 rooms, M$ 240-550 (they often give discounts, but the price is always at least M$ 100). Good restaurants. Just spending the day here, eating and swimming, costs M$ 25. The hotel has its own ferry service. There are tennis courts, a 9-hole golf course, a swimming pool, jungle paths in the Northern Pangkor Forest Reserve, windsurfers for M$ 10 per hour and sailboats for M$ 15 per hour. They also have water-skiing for M$ 25 per half hour. For

reservations, call 05-951091 or 03-2913757 in Kuala Lumpur. In Ipoh, you can make reservations at Ipoh Garden, next to Ipoh Garden Plaza, 41 Jalan Tasek or in the Business Center of the Royal Casuarina Hotel.

●There is one hotel in **Kampong Pangkor**, (where the ferry arrives), for those who are interested in life in a fishing village. The **Min Nin**, 1A Jalan Besar, 15 rooms, SR M\$ 18-24, DR 24-32.

Ferry Schedule

Lumut-Pangkor: Every half hour from 7:30 to 19:30.
Pangkor-Lumut: Every half hour from 6:45 to 18:30. The ferry also stops in **Sungai Pinang Kecil** 15 minutes later.
Lumut-Pan Pacific: 8:45, 10:15, 12:30, 14:30, 16:30, 18:30.
Pan Pacific-Lumut: 8:00, 9:30, 11:00, 13:30, 15:30, 17:30.
Lumut-Pansea Pangkor Laut: 8:00, 11:00, 14:00, 18:30.
Pansea Pangkor Laut-Lumut: 9:30, 12:30, 15:30, 19:30 (change on Pangkor).

Cameron Highlands

The Cameron Highlands which are 1500 to 2000 m above sea level, and the largest of the old British hill stations, are in the heart of the Titiwangsa Range. The Highlands were developed by British colonial settlers, who enjoyed the cooler temperatures in the mountains. Today, they are a favorite destination for tourists.

The mountainous area was first measured by the surveyor William Cameron in 1885, and was fully developed by 1931. It was used as a hideout by the communists during

the height of the Emergency. The American silk king, Jim Thompson disappeared here, a mystery yet to be solved. It was rumored to have something to do with the communists, but the official story is that he went on a hunting trip, and never came back. The area was opened to tourists in 1960.

You can get to the highlands from Tapah, 60 km south of Ipoh, and 140 km north of Kuala Lumpur. After passing the usual plantations and a few rice fields, the road leads up into the mountains. The road passes the **Lata Waterfall** on the right, 11 km from Tapah. Nearby is a hot spring and a few Orang Asli villages.

Further up the road are more Orang Asli villages. The road affords some good views of the mountainous jungle. There are giant ferns growing along the road.

The first town, **Ringlet**, some 45 km from Tapah, is uninteresting. It is an agricultural center, just before the border with Pahang. Pahang has no road into the Cameron Highlands.

Another 15 km past Ringlet and you come to **Tanah Rata**, a tourist town, which has a lot of hotels, and offers good hiking. Trails lead to, among other places, **Gunung Beremban** (1841 m). Trails, mountains and waterfalls, followed by evenings around the fire, are not the only attractions in the Cameron Highlands.

The **tea plantations** that fill the entire valley are worth a visit. There is an exceptionally good view from Gunung Brinchang, where the trail forks off after the town of Brinchang (one fork goes up the mountain, the other does not). At this point, the Pallas Tea Estate of the Boh Tea Company is spread out like a lush carpet. The Indian workers pick the leaves with incredible speed.

A bit farther along, there is a plantation workers' settlement on the mountain. (Gunung Brinchang,

2032 m, carries the highest road in Malaysia.) As always, there is a telecommunications station on top. In good weather, you can see over the Kinta Valley to the Straits of Malacca. On the other side, you can see the mountains of Pahang and the terraced vegetable fields around Kampong Tarola.

The vegetables grown around Kampong Tarola are almost all grown for export. They will be familiar to Westerners – potatoes, tomatoes, cauliflower, red and green peppers, asparagus, broccoli, as well as cut flowers, like roses and carnations, most of which cannot grow in the lowlands. *Fruit*, like apples, pears, and Mandarin oranges, are also grown. Almost everything is exported to Singapore.

There are **markets** where produce can be bought, but the people do not seem to want to bargain. One is before the road forks to go up Gunung Brinchang. Go right and then left. Another is near the lake at Tanah Raja.

Accommodation

Expensive:

●*Strawberry Park Hotel*, past Tanah Rata to the left. 172 rooms, M$ 120; too expensive for what it offers. Tel. 05-941166.

●*Merlin Inn Resort*, past Tanah Rata. 64 rooms, SR M$ 80-125, DR M$ 90-135, the best hotel. Tel. 941205.

●*Ye Olde Smoke House*, on the golf course between Tanah Rata and Brinchang, very English (Chinese used not to be admitted, until a Chinese man bought it). 19 rooms, SR M$ 60-210, DR M$ 95-300. Tel. 941214 / 5.

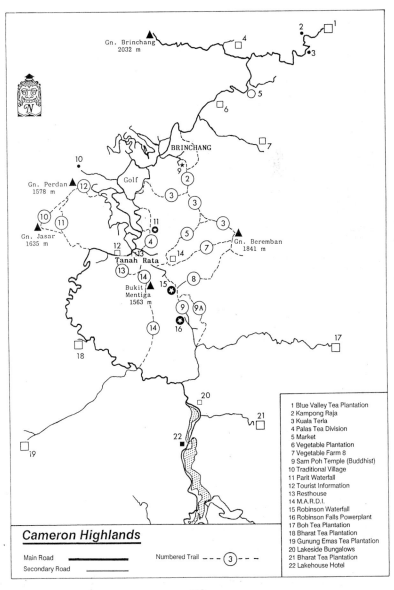

Gn. Brinchang
2032 m

4

2

3

1

5

6

BRINCHANG

7

10

Gn. Perdan
1578 m

Golf

9

2

3

3

3

10

11

Gn. Jasar
1635 m

5

4

14

7

3

Gn. Beremban
1841 m

12

Tanah Rata

13

14

8

Bukit
Mentiga
1563 m

15

9

9∧

16

14

17

18

20

21

22

19

Cameron Highlands

1 Blue Valley Tea Plantation
2 Kampong Raja
3 Kuala Terla
4 Palas Tea Division
5 Market
6 Vegetable Plantation
7 Vegetable Farm 8
9 Sam Poh Temple (Buddhist)
10 Traditional Village
11 Parit Waterfall
12 Tourist Information
13 Resthouse
14 M.A.R.D.I.
15 Robinson Waterfall
16 Robinson Falls Powerplant
17 Boh Tea Plantation
18 Bharat Tea Plantation
19 Gunung Emas Tea Plantation
20 Lakeside Bungalows
21 Bharat Tea Plantation
22 Lakehouse Hotel

Main Road

Secondary Road

Numbered Trail --- 3 ---

The Blowgun

There are still some groups in Malaysia who use the blowgun or *sumpitan* as their primary hunting weapon. On the peninsula, it is primarily the **Senoi** (the **Semang**, who migrated earlier, only later learned to use the blowgun from the Senoi). On Sarawak, it is primarily the **Penan / Punan**, who are the last nomads and whose existence is continually threatened by logging. While the Penan make their blowguns out of hardwood, the Senoi use bamboo, specifically the *"buloh sewoor"* variety. This kind has a good 2 meter distance between knots and is therefore very well suited for the purpose.

This type of bamboo grows only between 1500 and 2000 m, so it is no surprise that blowgun hunting was developed by the *Senoi* who live at high altitudes. Such a blowgun is easy to make.

Lacking the proper bamboo, the lowland Orang Asli in and around Johor must make their blowguns out of hardwood. There are

Blowgun and quiver

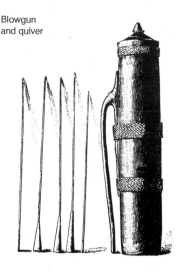

also blowguns made out of shorter straws fitted together. This is more of an emergency measure. The mouth-piece is attached separately.

The blowguns and quivers of the *Senoi* are geometrically designed. The 30 cm darts are made of bamboo. The shaft is made of the soft wood of the sago palm or *"nibong"*. The point is coated with the poisonous juice of the *ipoh or upas tree (Antairis toxicara)*. Darts with bamboo points are used to hunt birds and small monkeys.

For hunting large animals, like wild pigs, the Penan sometimes use metal-tipped darts. Some Orang Asli use only metal darts. You can buy blowgun sets in the Cameron Highlands for around M$ 12-15.

●*Golf Course Inn*, past Tanah Rata. 28 rooms, SR M$ 69-110, DR M$ 80-110. Tel. 941411.

●*Foster's Lake House*, on the lake at Tanah Rata. You can go fishing. 12 rooms, SR M$ 130-180, DR M$ 150-200, also very English. Tel. 996152.

Middle-Priced:
●*Brinchang Hotel*, M$ 55-70.
●*Highland Hotel*, M$ 60-65.
●*Kowloon Hotel*, M$ 55-70.
●*Sri Sentosa Hotel*, M$ 45-60.
All of the above are in Brinchang and have bathrooms and showers in the rooms.

Cheap Hotels:
●*Rest House* in Tanah Rata, M$ 6 / bed with hot shower.
●*Wong's Villa* in Brinchang, M$ 4 / bed.
●*Lido* in Brinchang, 10 rooms, M$ 8-16 with bathroom. Tel. 941271.
●*Orient* in Tanah Rata, 12 rooms, SR M$ 14, DR M$ 25-35 (with shower). Tel. 941633.
●*Hong Kong* in Brinchang, DR M$ 22. Tel. 941722.
●*Seah Meng* and *Town House* in Tanah Rata, SR M$ 12-18, DR M$ 30-35, and 32-48. Tel. 941615 and 941666.
●There are *more hotels* on the Tanah Rata main road.
●There are numerous *chalets* along the road between Brinchang and Tanah Rata.
●There are also two *youth hostels*.

Main vacation times in Malaysia are during the first half of April, the first half of August, and throughout December. It may be very difficult to find a place to stay at these times.

Shopping

Aside from fruit, vegetables and tea, you can also buy mounted butterflies caught by the Orang Asli, though it is probably better not to buy them and thereby lessen the demand for their capture. You can also buy Orang Asli blowguns for around M$ 12-15.

Food

On the main street of Tanah Rata, there is a good assortment of restaurants. The two Indian places have curries, roti canai and roti pisang. There is also good Chinese food at the Hollywood, among other places. The Cameron Highlands are also known for strawberries, with cream(!) and you can also get English specialities in the English-style lodges.

Excursions

As you might expect, there are a number of good hikes and walks from Tanah Rata. For example, there is a trail to the **Robinson Waterfall** and continuing farther along Path 9 or 9A (see map) is the **Boh Tea Plantation**. Or, you can go up **Gunung Beremban** by taking Path 8, just before the waterfall. The path follows the ridge and you should expect to walk about 1.5 hours. Shorter and steeper is the 7 km path to the summit from the MARDI Station (Malaysian Agricultural Research Development Institute). At the MARDI Station you can buy tea grown in the surrounding area.

The **Sam Poh Temple** is worth a visit, and there are some interesting trails leading to the temple.

To the northwest of Tanah Rata, there are trails up **Gunung Jasar** (1635 m) and **Gunung Perdan** (1578 m) Both peaks offer fine views of the mountains in the eastern Cameron Highlands.

There is a steep footpath from Brinchang up **Gunung Brinchang** that comes out by the telecommunications station. It is best to get permission to use this trail from the police in Brinchang. With a ten-speed bicycle, you can ride the road up and down the mountain. This is the highest point in Malaysia accessible by car.

Shortly before the summit, an unmarked, overgrown path splits off to the right. It goes over a ridge to the summit of **Gunung Irau** (2110 m), the highest peak in the area. The whole detour takes about 2 to 3 hours.

Beyond Brinchang is the northeast part of the Highlands. Continuing through Kampong Raja, you get to the **Blue Valley Tea Estate**. Go through the plantation and after about 1 km, take the left fork through the vegetable fields. From here, you can follow the plastic pipes and then a barely recognizable trail to the summit of **Gunung Siku** (1916 m). The trail is exciting, since almost no one ever goes there. Take a *parang* or machete.

If you continue for another 3 km you will reach a gate-post, from here go another 4 km to reach the LLN Hydrology Station, with its waterfall. Follow the main path up from here to the embankment and then go left along the border between Pahang and Kelantan where there are border markers every 100 meters to **Peak 6040** (1841 m).

From here, you can make a four day round trip to **Gunung Chali**

Pondok (1920 m) and **Gunung Yong Blar** (2181 m, the third highest mountain on the peninsula). Only for true enthusiasts.

In addition to half-day hikes and visits to tea plantations, there are **longer hikes** available to those who are interested. The Orang Asli Department arranges interesting, 4-day group trips across all sorts of terrain. Methods of transportation include hiking, river rafting, and driving. You have the option of starting and ending in Kuala Lumpur. The trips are mostly for Malaysians, but foreigners may also go along.

●**Orang Asli Department**, Cameron Highlands Office: 941433

Further Travel

There are hourly **buses** from Tanah Rata to Tapah, as well as taxis. There is also a **direct bus to Kuala Lumpur** for M$ 10.50. Inquire in the *Town House*.

Kuala Selangor

A town at the mouth of the Selangor River. The main attraction here is not the sparse remains of two 17th century Dutch forts on Bukit Melawati, but the **Kuala Selangor Nature Park** or Taman Alam K.S., opened in 1987. It is a project of the very active Selangor chapter of the Malayan Nature Society (Zoology Dept., Universiti Kebangssan Malaysia, Bangi, Selangor, Tel. 03-7753330).

There is a lake in the **mangrove**, with two bird blinds for bird watching and a nature walk with explanations written along the way.

There are 130 different kinds of birds found here. They include migratory birds which rest here on their way south during October and November. There are also cranes and storks.

A visit to the park is a good alternative for those who are not planning on going to **Kuala Gula** between Penang and Taiping. The park is well-known for several varieties of monkeys, including the otherwise rare Silver Leaf Monkey.

Kuala Selangor Hill or Bukit Selangor is a granite hill with a comfortable rest house and a light tower on top. It is largely covered with rain forest and fig trees. There is

also a royal mausoleum and the so-called Seven Springs or Telaga Tujoh.

Kampong Kuantan, 10 km north of Kuala Selangor on the Selangor River, is known for its thousands of glow-worms. If you want to take a boat there, inquire at Encik Jalaluddin's shop at the T-junction. He takes groups of four of five people, leaving between 19:00 and 19:30. Wear shoes and a long sleeved shirt as the mosquitoes can be bloodthirsty.

Accommodation

●The **Resthouse** on top of the hill is a romantic spot. There are, however, cheaper places to stay in town.

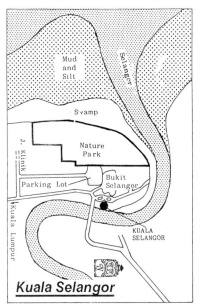

Kuala Selangor

Arrival

You can get to Kuala Selangor from Kuala Lumpur, by passing through either Klang, or, better, through Sungai Buloh. From Kuala Lumpur direct (leave from Jalan Damansara, Taman Tun Dr. Ismail) or through Klang, take the Selangor Bus 141 from the Puduraya Bus Station, or take a taxi (M$ 7 per person).

Coming from the north, you have to take a secondary road from Teluk Intan. Take a public bus to Sabak Bernam on the border between Perak and Selangor, and then directly to Kuala Selangor.

Kuala Lumpur

Kuala Lumpur means, "muddy river mouth." Where the Masjid Jame Mosque now stands, at the meeting of the Klang and Gombek Rivers, was nothing more than a mining settlement 130 years ago. In **1857**, 87 men set off up the Klang River, in search of new tin sources.

Near the present-day Ampang, the *pawang* (Malay mystics who specialized in finding tin sources) announced that a new tin source had been found. The Chinese adventurers (they were all Chinese, except for the mystic) founded a settlement there, but only 18 of them made it through the first month; the rest fell to malaria.

For ten years after the settlement was founded until his death in **1885**, Yap Ah Loy or Kapitan China was the man in charge. In **1880**, he was compelled to take on a British counselor, Frank Swettenham. Working with the British and the

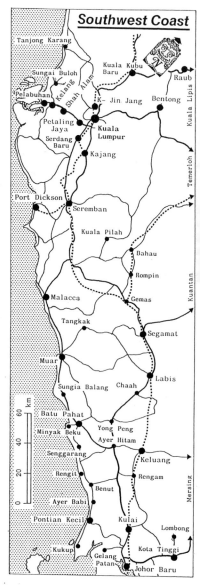

Southwest Coast

178

Port Klang. In *1974*, KL seceded from Selangor and became a newly-designated, federal territory, increasing its area from 93 to 244 km². In *1984*, the population passed the one million mark.

KL, as Kuala Lumpur, is always called, is unmistakably oriented towards Singapore. It is amazing how fast the skyline has shot up over the last ten years. In the mid-70's there were no skyscrapers. The skyline is now dominated by Dayabumi, Malaysian Banking Berhad, MAS and other status symbols of private, semi-private and

Sultan of Selangor, the very wealthy Yap managed to rebuild and restore order to the settlement. It had been completely destroyed by Chinese and Malay factions fighting for control of the mines. When Yap took control, he saw to it that the growing town had brothels, opium dens and a hospital. He also required that new houses be built out of brick, so that the town could not be easily destroyed again. In *1879*, the first brick houses were built (some of the oldest still survive on Jalan Hang Lakui).

In the *1880's*, world tin prices rose and the town grew correspondingly. KL was already taking on the look and feel of a city. In *1886*, it was connected by rail to the harbor at

Modern Kuala Lumpur:
The Tabung Haji Building

Kuala Lumpur, Hauptbahnhof

governmental institutions. In truth, it is only the surface of the city that has changed, the people are still the same. They know that KL is no international metropolis.

But it is the **Capital of Malaysia** with its oversized office towers, brand-new government complexes, and new housing subdivisions expanding out to the edge of the forests and plantations, sometimes reclaiming old mining areas. Traffic can get bad, and the situation does not favor the pedestrian, who is often helpless in the face of an onslaught of cars. There are new shopping centers springing up everywhere. But, in contrast to Singapore, there is little overall planning towards integrating modern shopping centers intelligently into an older urban center.

Nonetheless, there is a lot to see that is unique to KL, like the Train Station, or the Moorish-Western mix of the Sultan Abdul Samad Building. Looking at these architectural treasures in the shadows of the new halls of power is an interesting contrast indeed.

In the **Old City**, the KL of years ago is still alive. The narrow, winding streets are lined with small, old Chinese, Indian and Malay stores and workshops.

Accommodation

Similar to Penang, KL has many **cheap Chinese hotels**, but in KL they are spread over a larger area. They are also not such good value. Some of them are normally only rented by the hour, and while it is possible to stay overnight, women traveling alone might do well to look elsewhere. The city is actually much prouder of its **luxury hotels**. In fact, so many of them have gone up recently that they have to offer considerable discounts to stay in business. A double room of this quality for M$ 60-70, 40-50% under the normal price, would be unthinkable in America or Europe. Nowhere in the world are there as many cheap luxury hotels as in KL and Singapore (which dictates the prices in KL). However, for those on a tight budget, there is still a good assortment of cheaper hotels.

Chinatown is next to the train station, and consists of the area around Jalan Cecil, Sultan, Balai Polis, Petaling, Panggong and Bandar.

●*Wan Kow*, 16 Jalan Sultan, towards Jalan Petaling, 17 rooms, for M$ 18 or four people for M$ 32, Tel. 2382909.

●*Colonial*, 39-45 Jalan Sultan, also good. 36 large clean rooms, without windows for M$ 16-24 (with shower), and sometimes A / C. Not for those with a rat-phobia. Tel. 2380336.

●*Hwa Yik*, 61 Jalan Sultan, 11 rooms, M$ 13-24 (A / C, shower). Tel. 2385208.

●*Lok Ann*, corner of Jalan Sultan and Petaling, more expensive, 21 rooms with A / C and bathroom, M$ 35.50 (2 twin beds), M$ 39.60 (double bed and single bed), M$ 46.80 (2 double beds).

●*Dunla*, 142 Jalan Petaling, 16 rooms, M$ 16-25.

●*Ma Sien*, 156 Jalan Petaling, 12 rooms, M$ 16-25.

●*Sun Kong*, 210 Jalan Bandar, 7 rooms, M$ 24 (2 double beds, bath fan), good for 4 people.

●*Starlight*, near Klang bus station on Jalan Sultan Mohammed, more expensive, 42 rooms, M$ 35-40 with A / C and bath, Tel. 2389811.

●*Meridian International Youth Hostel*, 36 Jalan Hang Kasturi near the Central Market, Tel. 2321428.

The selection of cheap hotels around the central shopping area of Jalan Bukit Bintang and Jalan Imbi has decreased over the years as the area gets continually more expensive:

●*Weng Hua*, 6A Jalan Bukit Bintang, 15 rooms, M$ 25-30.

●*Park Hotel* 80A Jalan Bukit Bintang, 15 rooms, M$ 36-44, with A / C, bath, Tel. 2427288.

●*Tai Ichi*, 78 Jalan Bukit Bintang, 29 rooms, M$ 42-48 with A / C, bath, Tel. 2427669.

●*Imperial*, Jalan Hicks, 90 rooms, M$ 56-110, with A / C, bath and TV. Clean, Tel. 2422377.

●There are a few expensive hotels in the area: *Federal, Prince, Regent*. The Golden Mile starts on Jalan Sultan Ismail with a row of luxury hotels: *Hilton, Equatorial, Shangri-La, Merlin*.

●If you are arriving by train and you do not want to go far, there is the colonial **Station Hotel** by the main entrance. 30 gigantic rooms, for M$ 30 (SR), M$ 40 (DR), extra beds, M$ 10, all with A / C and bathroom. Lots of good restaurants nearby, Tel. 2747433, 2747881.

●If you arrive on the bus, and do not want to go far, the **Puduraya Hotel** is on the fourth floor of the Pudaraya Bus Station on Jalan Pudu. It is not such good value, but it is comfortable. 200 rooms, M$ 55-130, Tel. 2321000.

A little bit further down Jalan Pudu, going away from the city, there are around a dozen **Rumah Tumpangan** (hostels), for M$ 14-20.

●South of the city center in Brickfields, there is a **YMCA**, Jalan Kandang Kerbau and Jalan Brickfields, 60 rooms, M$ 10 (dorm) to M$ 50 (DR with A / C, bathroom), Tel. 2741439. To get there, take the No. 12 minibus and get off at the Lido Cinema.

●Since the YMCA is often full, you might try the nearby *Lido*, 7-9A Jalan Marsh, 29 rooms, M$ 24-36, Tel. 2741258.

●*YWCA*, Jalan Davidson, has rooms for M$ 15-25, takes only women.

●The **youth hostel** is the cheapest place to stay, but it is a long way out of town. Jalan Vethavanam, off Jalan Ipoh. From Pudu Raya, take bus 66, 146, or 147. Beds are M$ 2.50 / 2.00 for members and M$ 4.00 / 3.00 for non-members.

The *area with the most cheap hotels* is around Jalan Tuanku Abdul Rahman (TAR) and Raja Laut north of the Padang. As in Chinatown, a lot of the old small hotels and guest houses are being torn down and replaced. So do not be surprised if you cannot find one or two of the places described here.

●*Teck Sin*, 31A Jalan Tuanku Abdul Rahman, 14 rooms, M$ 17.

●*Coliseum*, 98 Jalan Tuanku Abdul Rahman, usually full, 10 large rooms, M$ 12.60 (SR) and M$ 18.90 (DR), some with fan, some with A / C. Famous "sizzling steaks" in the restaurant downstairs for M$ 13-16. Tel. 2926270.

●*Rex*, 132 Jalan Tuanku Abdul Rahman, 15 rooms, M$ 15.70 (SR), 18.90 (DR), not very friendly, Tel. 2983895.

Kuala Lumpur

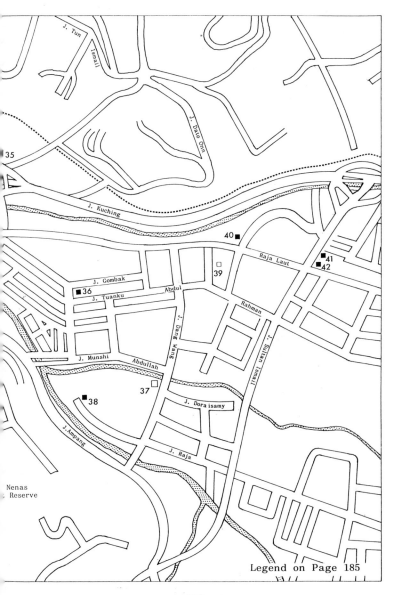

J. Tun
Ismail

J. Dato Onn

35

J. Kuching

40 ■

Raja Laut

■ 41
■ 42

□ 39

J. Gombak

■ 36

J. Tuanku

Abdul

Rahman

J. Dang Wang

J. Sultan Ismail

J. Munshi Abdullah

37 □

■ 38

J. Dora isamy

J. Ampang

J. Raja

Nenas
Reserve

Legend on Page 185

•*Tivoli*, 136 Jalan Tuanku Abdul Rahman, 17 rooms, M$ 16.80 (SR), 19.95 (DR), M$ 25 (A / C, shower).

•*Kowloon*, 142 Jalan Tuanku Abdul Rahman, 28 rooms, M$ 27.5 or 31.90 (double bed), M$ 37.40 (DR, A / C, shower), M$ 41.80 (deluxe). Recently renovated, recommended. Tel. 2926455.

•*Shiraz*, corner of Medan Tuanku, somewhat expensive, 56 rooms, M$ 35-110, with a good Pakistani restaurant downstairs. Tel. 2920159.

•*Dashrun*, 285 Jalan Tuanku Abdul Rahman, 41 rooms, M$ 45-65, modern. Tel. 2929314.

There are also some cheap places on *Jalan Raja Laut*, which runs parallel to TAR:

•*Loyal City*, 16A Jalan Raja Laut, 12 rooms, M$ 15-18, Tel. 2980672.

•*Sin Hua*, 62 Jalan Raja Laut, 10 rooms, M$ 12, Tel. 2924307.

•*New Calinmen*, 110 Jalan Raja Laut, 40 rooms, SR M$ 20-30, DR M$ 34-38, bath. Clean. Tel. 298088.

•*Alisan*, 132 Jalan Raja Laut, 15 rooms, M$ 20-28, average. Tel. 2986905.

•*Kong Ming*, 326E Jalan Raja Laut, 14 rooms, M$ 15-30, Tel. 2922208.

•*Sentosa*, 316 Jalan Raja Laut, 42 rooms, M$ 24-28, 30-45 with A / C, Tel. 2925644.

•*City Hotel*, 366 Jalan Raja Laut, 90 rooms, M$ 38-63, Tel. 2924466.

•There are many more hotels in the area, both cheap and expensive. There is the

Holiday Inn City Center, The Grand Continental, Grand Central, and the luxury **Pan Pacific**. There is also the somewhat cheaper **Grand Pacific**, next to the Putra World Trade Center and opposite the Mall shopping center.

KL has over 10,000 hotel beds and lots of vacancies, as most people only stay for a short while.

What to See

The best place to start is where the city's two rivers merge. Here, surrounded by palm trees is the **Masjid Jame** or Friday Mosque. It was built in 1909 and modeled on the Moti Masjid or Pearl Mosque in Delhi. The red brick, white-detailed building, with its stunning minaret, arcades and domes, is particularly beautiful in the evening. In an area of high office towers, the mosque is a wonderful place to rest and reflect.

The city abounds with similar striking contrasts between the old and the new. The Tudor-style **Selangor Club** (the "*Spotted Dog*") provides another one. Located on the Padang, it was built in 1890 and was the center of British society in KL. Today it is used as a meeting place by the Malay elite.

Across the river from the Friday Mosque is the **Bangunan Sultan Abdul Samad** (formerly the Secretariat), built between 1894-97. With its arcades, domes and 41 m clock tower, it is a fine example of the mixed Western-Islamic style which is characteristic of the old public buildings in KL. Today, the building houses judicial offices.

Legend to Pages 182-183

1 Kuala Lumpur Visitors Center
2 National Museum, Art Gallery
3 National Mosque
4 Main Train Station
5 Station Hotel
6 Taxi Stand
7 Main Post Office
8 Menara Dayabumi Building
9 Weekend Art Market
10 Sultan Abdul Samad Building
11 Central Market
12 Sri Mariamman Temple
13 Bus Station
14 Post Office
15 Chinatown
16 Inexpensive Hotels
17 Malaya Hotel
18 Inexpensive Hotels
19 Lok Ann Hotel
20 Sikh Temple
21 Kongsi Chan See Shu Yuen
23 Chinese Temple
24 Merdeka Stadium
25 Chimwoo Stadium
26 Stadium Negara
27 YMCA
28 Inexpensive Hotels
29 Puduraya Taxi and Bus Station
30 Hindu Temple
31 Sikh Temple
32 Wisma Budiman
33 St. John's Cathedral
34 Masjid Jame (Mosque)
35 Bank Negara
36 Coliseum Hotel, Inexpensive Hotels
37 Wilaya Shopping Complex
38 Eastern Hotel
39 MARA Building
40 Holiday Inn
41 Plaza Hotel
42 Grand Continental Hotel
43 To the National Monument

Other buildings on Jalan Raja are the **High Court** (Mahkamah Tinggi), **City Hall** (Dewan Bandaraya), the **Bureau of Information** (Jabatan Penerangan) to the north, the old **Main Post Office** and the **Agriculture Bank** to the south, all designed by *A.C. Norman.*

Also worth seeing is the impressive **Masjid India**, the mosque of the Indian Moslems. It is on Jalan Masjid, north of the City Hall on the right.

South of the government buildings is one of the most elegant and expensive symbols of the new KL. The Islamic style **Kompleks Dayabumi** was built by a subsidiary of UMNO at a cost of M$ 600 million. It was sold to the state-owned petroleum company, Petronas. You

can go up to the 34th floor on Saturdays at 14:30, but come early to see the fountains in the lobby.

Right next door is the **Pos Besar**, the main post office, where you can receive letters *post restante*.

From here, it is just a short walk to the famous mosque-like **Train Station**, built between 1911 and 1917. The train offices are located opposite the station.

The National Mosque, **Masjid Negara**, is an interesting futuristic building from 1965. It can hold 8000 worshipers. The 18 sides on the roof stand for the 13 states of Malaysia and the 5 pillars of Islam. The minaret is 75 m high. The 48 domes are reminiscent of the mosque at Mecca. You can visit the mosque, Saturday-Thursday· 9:00 to 18:00, Friday 14:45 to 18:00.

On the same side of Jalan Sultan Hishamuddin is the **Kuala Lumpur Visitors' Center**, open Monday-Friday, 8:00 to 16:15, Saturday 8:00 to 12:45. Right next door in the building with the art deco facade, is the **National Art Gallery**. The gallery has a permanent collection of Malaysian art and changing exhibitions of works from all over the world. Open from 10:00-18:00, closed Fridays from 12:15-14:45.

The **Lake Gardens**, Tasek Perdana, are located west of the city. The paths and hills make it a popular place to walk and jog. There is a place where you can rent boats on the lake for M$ 4 / hour – during vacations from 10:30-11:30 and

14:00-17:30, and weekends and holidays from 8:00-17:30.

Overlooking the lake, there are two large colonial villas. They used to be the residences of the Governor or General Resident and the British Ambassador. Actually, Common-wealth countries do not have a British Embassy, but rather a British High Commission. Symbolically, these buildings are owned by the Malaysian government.

The **National Monument**, Tugu Peringat Negara, is on a hill to the north. The monument, by Felix de Weldon, is based on the Iwo Jima Memorial in Washington. The seven figures symbolize, among other things, unity, leadership, strength, bravery and vigilance. It was erected in 1966 to mark the victory over the communists in the Emergency. It is also intended to honor the war dead of Malaysia.

The **Parliament**, built in 1963, is on a more distant hill. There is an 18-floor office tower and a 3-floor main building that contains the House of Representatives (Dewan Rakyat) and the Senate (Dewan Negara). You can visit the Parlia-ment when it is in session, but dress appropriately.

On the east side of the Lake Garden is the **Tun Abdul Razak Memorial**, where the second Prime Minister of Malaysia lived. On the south side is the **National Museum**, Muzium Negara, built in 1963 in a modified Minangkabau style. The mosaic on the exterior is based on modern Malaysian batik patterns.

Temple, built in 1873. The temple contains a six-story pagoda, *gopuram*, which is the starting point for the Thaipusam procession. Nearby, on Jalan Cecil, is the **Night Market**, Pasar Malam.

To the south, near Merdeka Stadium, is the richly decorated **Kongsi Chan See Shu Yuen**, the clan house of the Chan, Chin and Tan families.

North of Chinatown, near Lebuh Pudu is the **Sze Yeoh Temple**, where Sen Sze Ya or Seng Mang Lee, the god of pioneers, is worshiped. His statue was brought to the temple seven years after the founding of KL. The temple was financed largely by Kapitan China, whose picture can be found on one of the minor altars. Other gods honored here include the beloved Guan Yin.

The museum is worth visiting (open daily from 9.30-18.00, closed Fridays from 12.15-14.45), though the collection is small. Downstairs: shadowplay figures, traditional dolls, information on Chinese and Indian dance, a sultan's throne, a Baba house from Malacca and Orang Asli objects. Upstairs: the animal kingdom, tin mining, rubber production and forestry. Outside: a house from Terengganu, megaliths, woodcarvings from Sarawak, a tin excavator, a Rolls Royce and a Proton Saga.

East of the train station, on Jalan Bandar, is the **Maha Sri Mariamman**

The temple is very close to the **Central Market**, which was renovated in 1986. With boutiques, shops, restaurants, artwork and food strands, the market has become a popular meeting place. Almost every day except during Ramadan there is music, dance and other performances. For information call 03-2746542. The schedule is also posted by the information stand. Most performances begin at 19:45, some at 17:00.

If you are specifically interested in the culture of the individual ethnic groups, you might want to visit one of the cultural centers:

National Cultural Complex, Jalan Ismail, northeast of the Lake Garden, has courses in art, dance and drama.

Chin Woo Association Stadium, on Jalan Wesley, near Jalan Hang Jebat, east of Petaline St., is a Chinese sports and cultural center: Tai Chi, Kung Fu, gallery, etc.

Temple of Fine Arts, on Jalan Berhala in Brickfields is an Indian cultural center.

Aman Club, on Jalan Damai 5 / 6, northeast of the intersection of Tun Abdul Razak and Jalan Ampang is a Sikh restaurant and cultural center.

In **Ampang Park**, Jalan Ampang, there is Malay dancing at the **Yasmin Restaurant**.

●You can get more specific information at the Visitors' Center.

The **Merdeka Stadium** is southeast of Chinatown. The interest of this 50,000 spectator arena is historical. On August 31, 1957, Tunku Abdul Rahman, the first prime minister of the country, declared Malaysia's independence or *merdeka* from here. Next to it is the **Stadium Negara**, with its domed roof.

Farther to the south is the **Istana Negara**, the official residence of the elected king, or Yang Di Pertuan Agung. You can visit him on the first day of Hari Raya Puasa, when he has an official open house.

Those interested in the lives of the Chinese tin barons should visit the **Wisma Loke** on Medan Tuanku. There is also an art gallery and an antique shop.

If you are looking for a bit of green in the middle of the city, there are alternatives to the Lake Gardens, like **Bukit Nana**, Nana Hill. You can get there by the road leading to the telecommunications station.

There is also a gondola ride that goes to the top.

City Transportation

You can reach most of the main attractions by foot in one day. There are **no trishaws** in KL.

●Almost all **taxis** run on meters and are very reasonable, costing about M$1-2 for most trips in the city. They are more comfortable than the bus. Non A / C taxis start at 70 *sen* for the first mile and then charge 30 *sen* for each additional half-mile. A / C taxis begin at M$1. You can also rent taxis by the hour, for M$ 6 (non A / C) or M$ 12 (A / C). Fares go up by 50% between midnight and 6:00 A.M. There is a charge of 10 *sen* per person if there are more than two people and a charge of 10 *sen* per bag or package.

●The **buses** are extensive, but the system is complicated. In general, the Len Sen buses serve the north, while the Kenderaan buses serve the south. The Bas Mini cost 50 *sen*, and go all over the city. The best thing to do is ask directions for your destination at the bus stop. You can buy a **Panduan Bas**, Bus Guide, at any news-stand.

Tourist Information

Malaysia is working hard to promote tourism, the nation's fourth-largest source of income.

●The official government organization is the **TDC**, or the **Tourist Development Corporation of Malaysia**.

●The main office is located in the Putro World Trade Center which belongs to UMNO, the ruling party, at Menara Data

Onn, 25th floor, Jalan Tun Ismail, 50480, Kuala Lumpur. Open Monday-Friday, 8:00 to 16:15, Saturday 8:00 to 12:45. Tel. 03-2935188.

● In the same building, on Level 2, you can visit the **TDC Information Center**, Tel. 03-2914247.

● There is an information counter in the **Train Station**.

● There is a Tourist Information Center in **Subang International Airport**, open daily from 10:00 to 21:00. Tel. 7465707.

● **K.L. Visitors' Center**, 3 Jalan Sultan Hishamuddin, open Monday-Friday, 8:00 to 16:15, Saturday until 12:45. Tel. 2301369.

Food

KL, like the rest of Malaysia, has some great places to eat. Many can be found in parking lots that become night markets. These markets can be located in China Town, in and around the Central Market on Jalan Bukit Bintang and Imbi. Others can be found on Jalan Munshi Abdullah near the corner of Dang Wangi, in the Chow Kitt Market, in the **Sunday Market**, on Jalan Brickfields, and in the Puduraya Bus Station. There is a good selection of Malaysian, Western and Japanese food in the basement of *Yaohan* in the Mall. Upstairs is a good **Food Center**, in the style of a miniature city.

Malay food is available in *Satay Anika* or *Rasa Utara* on Bukit Bintang Plaza. Also try *Sate Ria* at 9 Jalan Tuanku Abdul Rahman, in the *Kampung Restoran* on Jalan Tun Perak and in *Warong Rasa Sayang* on Jalan Raja Muda Musa.

Indian and Pakistani cuisines are well represented in KL. The selection includes *Bilal* and *Simla* at 33 and 95 Jalan Ampang. *Ceylon* on Jalan Melayu is near Jalan T.A.R. At 600 Medan T.A.R. is *Bangles*.

Nearby is *Shiraz*, in the hotel of the same name. Opposite is the *Akbar*. Cheaper alternatives include the *Taj Mahal* on Lebuh Ampang and there are of course many options on Jalan Brickfields, where many Indians live.

Chinese food is available throughout the city. Interesting places include *Fook Woh Yuen* at the end of Jalan Petaling. It closes at 9:00 PM. *Fatt Woh Yuen* on the neighboring Jalan Balai Polis is another good choice. There is good food at *Pines*, 297 Jalan Brickfields, near the police station. Many hotels also have good Chinese food.

As in most capitals, there is a good assortment of foreign food. For instance, **Thai food** is available at *Sri Chiengmai* on Jalan Perak, or at *Sri Pattaya*, 93 Jalan Maharajalela.

Korean food is available at *Airirang*, 144 Jalan Bukit Bintang, or at *Koryo-Won* in Kompleks Antarabangsa on Jalan Sultan Ismail.

There is **Japanese food** in *Yaohan*, The Mall, and *Fima Rantei*, Jalan Damansara.

Such restaurants are expensive, as are the better **Western Restaurants**. *Le Coq d'Or* in a turn of the century villa at 121 Jalan Ampang. *The Ship* at 40 Jalan Sultan Ismail has good steaks as does the *Coliseum*. *L'Espresso* in Wisma Stephens on Jalan Raja Chulan. *Esquire Kitchen* in Sungei Wang Plaza. The *Bullock Cart Restaurant* is

on nearby Jalan Hicks. Somewhat cheaper is the *Happy Corner* on Jalan Ampang, but it closes early. A local favorite for cakes and pizzas is *English Hotbreads* at 60 Jalan Sultan. There is also *Angel Cake House*. Those interested in pubs can try the *Brass Rail* on Medan T.A.R. or the *Vatican*, opposite the main post office.

There are also many **Fast Food Restaurants** all over KL.

Nightlife

Obviously, the nightlife of Islamic Malaysia is nothing like that of Bangkok. Nonetheless, you can find almost anything if you know where to go and whom to ask. Here are a few **bars** that offer a pleasant place to sit and listen to music.

●*Cotton Club*, Plaza Yow Chuan, Jazz performers like Wah Idris and Lukis II.

●*California*, KL Plaza, relaxed atmosphere, M$ 2.50 for a beer between 17:00 and 21:00.

●*Colonel's Place*, Jalan Padang Walter Grenier, light music.

●*Hop Sack*, KL Plaza, an English-style pub with live music.

●*Dinty's*, Jalan Tun Sambathan, blues, rock'n'roll, country.

●*Coffee Terrace, Hotel Fortuna*, a quiet place after dinner.

●*The Rogue's Gallery*, 19 Jalan 52 /1 Petaling Jaya, jazz, blues, reggae, good food.

Shopping

There are many new **shopping centers** around KL and by Malaysian standards, they offer a wide variety of goods at decent prices. There are many around Jalan Bukit Bintang and Jalan Imbi. The largest **book stores** in the city are nearby, MPH and the Berita Book Center. They have a good selection of Malaysian literature. **Computers**, software, and accessories are available on the ground and second floors of the Imbi Plaza.

A good place to buy cheap **textiles** is in the Globe Silk Store on Jalan T.A.R. (Jalan Batu). There are other good stores around there as well. The **Chow Kitt Market**, in the western part of town, is one of the main Malay markets.

Handicrafts are sold in the new Aked Ibu Kota (Monday-Saturday 9:00 to 18:00) on Jalan T.A.R., in the Central Market. Also in the Sunday Market or Pasar Minggu, which is at its busiest on Saturday evenings, and the Karyaneka Handicraft Center on Jalan Raja Chulan near the Bukit Bintang shopping centers. The latter has 14 wooden houses, representing the 13 states of Malaysia and the Federal Territory of KL with a good assortment of handicrafts at fixed prices (open daily from 9:30 to 18:00, Mondays until 17:00). They often have exhibits

about Malaysian culture. You can take a look at some higher quality handicrafts at *Infokraf* (open 10:00 to 18:00, near Padang).

The **Night Market**, Pasar Malam, on Jalan Cecil has a good selection of t-shirts, jeans and cassette tapes, but listen to them first!

The **supermarkets** are the best source of Western groceries. For example, shop in Yaohan, The Mall, Fairtrade (Jalan Raja Chulan), Jaya, and Yow Chuan Plaza at the corner of Jalan Tun Razak and Jalan Ampang.

Addresses

●*Immigration:* Jalan Pantai Bharu. Open Monday-Friday 8:00 to 16:15, Saturday until 12:45 (closed Fridays from 12:00 to 14:30). Tel. 2555077.

●*Emergency:* Call 999 for fire, police and ambu-lance.

●*KL Taxi Drivers' Association:* Tel. 2215252. There are other organizations.

●*Money Changers:* All over the center of the city. They take travelers' checks.

●*Banks:* Open Monday-Friday from 10:00 to 15:00, Saturdays from 9:30 to 11:30.

●*American Express:* In the Bangunan MAS building, 5th floor, Jalan Sultan Ismail, Tel. 03-2613000.

●*Post Offices:* Open 8:00 to 17:00. The main office is open till 19:00. If you are receiving mail, make sure to inquire under your first name since mail in Malaysia, as in Thailand, is often sorted that way. In general, it is better to send parcels and cartons from Singapore.

●*Telephones:* Use 10 *sen* coins. International calls can be made from the **Central Telephone Office**, Bukit Mahkamah, Jalan Raja Chulan, open 24 hours, or from the airport from 7:30 to 23:30. The cheapest time to make long distance calls inside Malaysia is from 18:00 to 7:00. Singapore is a domestic call, area code 02-.

●*Hospital:* The *University of Malaya Hospital* on Jalan Universiti in Petaling Jaya has a good reputation.

●*City Swimming Pool* or Kolam Renang Bandaraya: Jalan Raja Chulan, opposite Jalan Perak. Open from 9:30 to 12:30, 14:00 to 16:30, 19:30 to 21:00.

●*Airlines:* See below under "Further Travel."

Embassies

Australia:	Tel. 2423122
Austria:	Tel. 2484277
Bangladesh:	Tel. 2423271
Belgium:	Tel. 2485733
Brunei:	Tel. 2612800
Burma:	Tel. 2424085
Canada:	Tel. 2612000
China:	Tel. 2428495
Czechoslovakia:	Tel. 2427185
Denmark:	Tel. 2416088
Finland:	Tel. 2611088
France:	Tel. 2484122
Germany:	Tel. 2429666
India:	Tel. 2617000
Indonesia:	Tel. 9842011
Ireland:	Tel. 2985111
Italy:	Tel. 4565122
Japan:	Tel. 2427044
Netherlands:	Tel. 2426544
New Zealand:	Tel. 2486422
Norway:	Tel. 2430144
Pakistan:	Tel. 2418877
Philippines:	Tel. 2484233
Poland:	Tel. 4560940
Singapore:	Tel. 2616277
South Korea:	Tel. 9842177
Spain:	Tel. 2484868
Sri Lanka:	Tel. 2423154
Sweden:	Tel. 2485981
Switzerland:	Tel. 2480622
Thailand:	Tel. 2488222
U.K.:	Tel. 2482122
U.S.A.:	Tel. 2489011
Vietnam:	Tel. 2484036

Holidays / Festivals

Federal Territory Day (February 1): Parades, culture shows, sports events, etc.

Thaipusam (February): Procession from the Mariamman Temple in Chinatown to the Batu Caves; over 100,000 spectators.

Selangor Festival (March-July).

Merdeka Month (August): In the Central Market. Parades on the 31st, Merdeka Night, the national holiday.

Malaysia Festival (late September): Two weeks of culture shows, dance, drama and exhibitions.

Deepavali (November): In the Central Market.

Christmas (December): In the Central Market.

Regular Exhibitions: In the Central Market and the Karyaneka Handicraft Center.

Excursions

Factory Visits:

Known throughout the world, Selangor Pewter is made at the largest pewter factory in the world. Pewter is an alloy of 97% fine tin and 3% antimony and copper. They also have information on batik and silverworking. It is located at 4 Jalan Usahawan 6, in the Setapak Industrial Park, Tel. 03-4221000. Open Monday-Saturday 8:30 to 16:45, Sundays and holidays from 9:00 to 16:00. You can combine a trip here with a trip to the *National Zoo* and *Aquarium*. Open daily from 9:00 to 17:00. Admission is M$ 7.00, M$ 1.00 for a camera. The entire animal kingdom of Malaysia is represented at the zoo, but there is little background information. From Jalan Ampang, take the Len Chee Bus 177 or the Len Seng Bus 170. From Lebuh Ampang, take the Minibus 17.

The *Genting Highlands*

are 55 km from Kuala Lumpur. The best way to get there is to take a bus (M$ 4.50) or a taxi (M$ 7.00) from Puduraya. The resort is 1711 m high and offers walks, golf, squash, bowling and other sports as well as a 1460 m high Chinese cave temple. There is a casino which Malays may not enter. Also a big hotel which costs M$ 125-2000 per night. There is a cheaper one though, with rooms from M$ 27 to M$ 80.

On the way to the Highlands you pass *Mimaland*, a private park with swimming, fishing (you can rent rods), and hiking. Admission is M$ 2.00, or M$ 6.00 including transportation. To get there, take the Len Seng Bus 174 from Lebuh Ampang for M$ 1.00, or from ENE Plaza, Jalan Pudu, take the Mimaland Bus.

If you take the 174 bus a bit farther to the 12th mile of Jalan Gombak, you come to the grounds of the

Orang Asli Department.

There is an administration building, a hospital and a small, but very interesting *Orang Asli Museum*. It is open only on weekends from 9:00-17:00. On display are clothing, weapons, tools, carvings, masks, and information on house construction, hunting and fishing. There is a small shop that has a few things for sale. At the time of my last visit, there was not much there, and what they had got was overpriced. The products did not have much to do

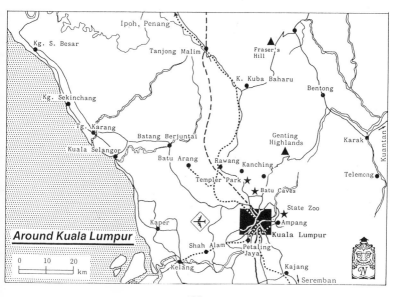

Around Kuala Lumpur

with the Orang Asli, other than that they made them. The blowguns in the Cameron Highlands are much cheaper.

Batu Caves

A must for anyone visiting Kuala Lumpur are the Batu Caves, 13 km outside of the city. To get there, take the Len Bus 70 from Lebuh Pudu or the Mini Bus 11 from the Bangkok Bank. The Hindu shrine, devoted to Shiva and his son, Lord Subramaniam, has been here since 1892. The caves are up to 400 m long and 120 m high. During the Thaipusam Festival, over 100,000 watch as the

devoted climb the 250 steps to the shrine at the top. The impressive caves occupy the southernmost large limestone hill on the Asian mainland.

Templer Park

You can combine a visit to the caves with one to Templer Park. It is only 10 km from the caves and 22 km from Kuala Lumpur on the road to Ipoh and Penang. You can go directly there from Puduraya for M$ 1.50 with the Len Buses 66, 78, 81, and 83. It has a waterfall, a stream to swim in, a fishing pond and paths through the jungle. There is a great view of the surrounding area from the 350 m high *Bukit Takun*, which is crowded on Sundays with climbers from Kuala Lumpur. There are both hard and easy paths up, and the easier ones do not require rope or any kind of equipment, though the tough ones certainly do. Botanists love the park, as it has over 204 species of plants. Every now and then, you can see monkeys and other animals up in the trees. In the neighboring, smaller hill, *Anak Takun*, there are some cave paths. The park is being further developed – for example, a bird preserve is in the works.

West of Kuala Lumpur

is *PJ (Petaling Jaya)*, a commuter city and an industrial suburb of KL, with over 200,000 residents. PJ is a city in its own right with good restaurants, galleries, shopping centers, etc. The campus of the

Universiti Malaya is pleasant. Also worth seeing are the Thai temple, *Wat Chetawan*, with its large reclining Buddha and the Hindu *Sivan Temple* on Bukit Gasing. There is still some jungle on the hill and it also provides a good view. Mini Bus 46 goes near here.

As you leave the Federal Territory, you will see the M$ 6 million *Triumphal Arch* over the highway, a gift from the grandiose Sultan of Selangor.

Shah Alam

24 km from Kuala Lumpur is the new capital of Selangor, Shah Alam. When KL became a national possession, Selangor had to build a new capital, but it receives M$ 300 million per year compensation.) Shah Alam was planned to have a population of 200,000, but has only about 20% of that at present, but it is growing all the time. It is a slightly sterile place.

Next to the palace is the spectacular new *Selangor State Mosque*

(Masjic Negeri Selangor Darul Ehsan or Masjid Sultan Salahuddin Abdul Aziz Shah), named after the present sultan. He came up with the M$ 160 million needed for its construction. It is a wonderful example of modern Islamic architecture that is deeply rooted in local tradition. Unfortunately, non-believers may not enter the main chapel with its giant dome of English construction and crystal lantern from Germany.

There are boat trips on the large lake near Shah Alam. The city is also the birthplace of the Proton Saga, the Malaysian luxury car.

Kelang

Another 32 km brings you to Kelang with a population of over 200,000, the traditional, sultans' city. The *Gedung Raja Abdullah Museum* (Saturday-Thursday 10:00 to 18:00, M$ 1.00) and the *Sultans' Mausoleum* are located here.

It is another 8 km to **Port Klang** or Pelabuhan Kelang, formerly Port Swettenham, the principal deep sea port of the Klang Valley. There are, of course, good seafood restaurants here. A trip to **Carey Island** is interesting, particularly if you are interested in the sea-faring Orang Asli group, the Mah Meri. They are known for their wood carvings, which are finer than those of the Jah Hut Orang Asli. Their specialty is grotesque masks. There is a new bridge over the Sungai Langat, a little south of Port Klang. From here, it's about 13 km through oil palm plantations to Kampong Sungai Bumbun. If you go to Belon Kasim, people will be glad to see you, as they do not get too many visitors.

There are also nice **beaches** in Selangor, near Port Klang. There is fine sand, clear water and (hopefully still) clean beaches on **Pulau Babi** and at **Pantai Bagan Lalang** in Sepang.

Kuala Selangor

(see separate section) is a worthwhile excursion from Kuala Lumpur. To get there, take the Selangor Bus 141 from Puduraya, or a taxi for M$ 7.00 per person. Information about the nature park is available from the Malayan Nature Society, Sektion Selangor. Tel. 03-7753330.

You can even go **white water rafting**. Asia Overland, at 35M, Jalan Dewan Sultan near Jalan T.A.R., Tel. 2925622 / 37, organizes tours for M$ 60.00 per person. They also occasionally organize expensive Orang Asli trips from the Cameron Highlands (see separate section) to Gua Musang.

Kajang

Should the road to Seremban take you to Kajang station, save your appetite for the most famous **Satay** in Malaysia. Try the Satay Terkenal Sejak 1917 which simply means, "famous since 1917" or the Tasmin Satay.

Amusement parks

Many amusement parks will be built in the next few years.

•*Kelab Desa Kancing / Templer Park*: M$ 6 million project, with a roller coaster and water rides.

•*Mimaland Expansion*: New water park.

•*Marine World*: M$ 25 million project, with wave pools (2 m waves for surfing!), water sports and a giant aquarium that you walk though via an acrylic tunnel – an Australian model.

•*Sungei Besi*: M$ 500 million huge amusement park with two race tracks.

•*Bandar Sunway Center*: A large, M$ 300 million water park.

Although interesting projects, they are often products of the competition between Selangor and the Federal Territory. They are certainly competing for the favors of the people. Critics warn that the owners risk taking a bath, but the truth remains to be seen.

Further Travel

Flights

The cheapest way to reach the *International Airport* in Subang is with the Kenderaan Bus 47 from the Klang Bus Station on Jalan Sultan Mohammed (diagonally opposite the train station) for M$ 1.20. The trip takes about 45 minutes and the first bus leaves at 6:00 A.M. Be prepared to pay a hefty fare in a taxi. City taxis do not like to travel that far out. From the airport to the city, they use a coupon system that costs M$ 15 a trip. It usually costs more going the other way, as taxi drivers usually have to wait a long time to pick up a fare at the airport.

Airport Tax
•Domestic Flights: M$ 3.00
•Singapore / Brunei: M$ 5.00
•International Flights: M$ 15.00

Domestic Flights with MAS:
•*Langkawi* – M$ 112
•*Alor Setar* – M$ 94
•*Penang* – M$ 80
•*Ipoh* – M$ 55
•*Kota Baru* – M$ 86
•*Kuala Terengganu* – M$ 80
•*Kuantan* – M$ 61
•*Johor Baru* – M$ 77
•*Singapore* – M$ 130 (note the difference from Johor Baru)
•*Kuching* – M$ 211 (from there to *Brunei* costs M$ 192 and to *Kota Kinabalu* costs M$ 198)

Pelangi Air (Tel. 03-7454555, ext. 2020 / 2021), flies minor domestic routes:
•Penang - Kuala Terengganu
•Kuala Terengganu-Kerteh / Kuantan
•Kuala Lumpur - Kerteh and Tioman
•Kerteh - Tioman
•Kuantan - Johor Baru
•Singapore - Tioman

International flights (round-trip)
•*Bangkok* with MAS or Thai International for M$ 400.
•*Jakarta* for M$ 400.
•*Hong Kong* for M$ 800.
•*Manila* for M$ 600.
•*Tokyo* for M$ 1300.
Also Europe, North America, Australia, etc. **Student tickets** are available through AUSST c / o MSL Associates, Southeast Asia Hotel, 69 Jalan Haji Hussein, Tel. 2984132.

Airlines
•*Aeroflot,* Wisma Tong Ah, 1 Jalan Perak, Tel. 2613331.
•*Air India,* Bangunan Angkasa Raya, 123 Jalan Ampang, Tel. 2420166.
•*Air Lanka,* Bgn. Perangsang Segemal, Jalan Kg. Attap, Tel. 2740211.

●**Biman,** same address as above, Tel. 2483765.
●**Cathay Pacific,** UBN Tower, Jalan P. Ramlee, Tel. 2383377.
●**China Airlines,** 22 Jalan Imbi, Tel. 2427344.
●**Garuda Indonesia,** same address as Air India, Tel. 2484072.
●**Japan Air Lines,** Pernas Int. Bldg., Jalan Sultan Ismail, Tel. 2611722.
●**Korean Air,** MUI Plaza, Jalan P. Ramlee, Tel. 2428311.
●**Lufthansa**, same address as JAL, Tel. 2614666.
●**Malaysia (MAS),** Bgn MAS, Jalan Sultan Ismail, Tel. 2610555.
●**Philippine Airlines,** Wisma Stephens, Jalan Raja Chulan, Tel. 2429040.
●**Qantas,** same address as Cathay Pacific, Tel. 2381769.
●**Royal Brunei,** Wisma Merlin, Jalan Sultan Ismail, Tel. 2426550.
●**Singapore Airlines,** Wisma SIA, Jalan Dang Wangi, Tel. 2923122.
●**Swissair**, same address as Royal Brunei, Tel. 2426744.
●**Thai,** Bgn Kuwasa, Jalan Raja Laut, Tel. 2937100.

Taxis

Long distance taxis from Puduraya Bus Station (2nd floor, Tel. 2320821 / 2325082), prices are per person:
●**Padang Besar** – M$ 47
●**Alor Setar** – M$ 36
●**Butterworth** – M$ 30
●**Taiping** – M$ 21
●**Kuala Kangsar** – M$ 18.50
●**Ipoh** – M$ 15
●**Cameron Highlands** – M$ 21
●**Kelang** – M$ 3
●**Seremban** – M$ 6
●**Malacca** – M$ 13
●**Johor Baru** – M$ 31
●**Kuantan** – M$ 20
●**Kuala Terengganu** – M$ 35
●**Kota Baru** – M$ 45
●**Kuala Lipis** – M$ 15
●**Jerantut** – M$ 16

Buses

You can go almost anywhere from **Puduraya**. *Ekspres Nasional* runs good buses. Their office is in the terminal. At night, when Puduraya is closed, you can wait for buses on the south side of terminal. When the buses have free seats, they always stop here.
●**Alor Setar** – M$ 19.50, A / C M$ 20.00.
●**Butterworth** – M$ 12.70, A / C M$ 14.70
●**Gerik** – M$ 11.50, A / C M$ 14.00.
●**Ipoh** – M$ 7.20, A / C M$ 8.50
●**Cameron Highlands / Tanah Rata** – M$ 7.75, leaves at 8:30 AM
●**Seremban** – M$ 3.00
●**Port Dickson** – M$ 3.30
●**Malacca** – M$ 5.50, A / C M$ 6.50
●**Johor Baru** – M$ 15.50
●**Singapore** – M$ 15.50, A / C M$ 17.50, book in advance if possible.
●**Raub** – M$ 7.00
●**Temerloh** – M$ 4.90
●**Kuantan** – M$ 12.10
●**Kuala Terengganu** – M$ 17.00
●**Kota Baru** – M$ 19.00, A / C M$ 24
There are also a few smaller bus terminals scattered around with buses going only to certain destinations.

●*Klang Bus Terminal*, south of Chinatown on Jalan Sultan Mohammed. Buses to the airport, Petaling Jaya, and Klang.
●*Central Pahang Omnibus*, at Kompleks Damai J. Tun Razak on Jalan Pahang opposite the General Hospital. Buses to Bentong and Raub.
●*MARA* goes from Jalan Medan Tuanku, near the Hotel Shiraz. Buses to Kuantan.
●*Budaya Espres* from Lorong Medan Tuanku, near the Hotel Dashrun. Buses to Kota Baru.
●*Putra Bus Terminal*, Putra World Trade Center. Buses to Temerloh and other places.

Car Rental
●*Mayflower / Acme*, Tel. 2486739.
●*Avis*, Tel. 2743057.
●*Sintat*, Tel. 2743028.
●*National*, Tel. 2489188.
●*Hertz*, Tel. 2329125.
●*Budget*, Tel. 2611122.

Train
For prices, see the chart in the appendix. If you are traveling at night, you would do well to reserve a sleeper well in advance (one month is the maximum). Without advance booking you will be unlikely to get one.

Ship
Cruise Muhibah sails from *Port Klang* to Singapore, Sarawak and Sabah. For more information, contact Feri Malaysia, Menara Utama, UMBC, Jalan Sultan Sulaiman, Tel. 2388899.

Hitchhiking
To Ipoh and Penang, take the Len Bus 70 to the turnoff for the Batu Caves. To the south, go to the Ceras / Peel roundabout. From Seremban, the road divides. One goes through Segamat, and the other goes through Malacca, Muar, and Batu Pahat. The two join up again in Ayer Hitam and continue on to Johor Baru and Singapore.

Seremban

Seremban is the capital of the state of Negeri Sembilan or Nine States. The state was originally composed of nine smaller states and is now divided into seven administrative districts. The original states were unified at the end of the 19th century and Seremban was chosen as the capital. It was also the seat of the British Resident for the state, who arrived in 1895. The state was originally settled by the Minangkabau from Sumatra. The people of Negeri Sembilan are still very aware of their distinct cultural identity. Many public buildings are built in a style derived from traditional Minangkabau architecture.

The city (pop. 150,000) has no particular sights, though the mountainous setting is very attractive. There are quite a few interesting *excursions in the surrounding area*, and Seremban can be used as a starting point for them. The city lies along the North-South highway, 64 km south of Kuala Lumpur, and less than an hour away.

Seremban is also on the train line from Kuala Lumpur to Singapore.

Accommodation
●*Hotel Tasik,* Jalan Tetamu (on the Lake Garden), the best place in town, 41 rooms, M$ 80-100, Tel. 06-730994 / 5.
●*Carlton,* 47 Jalan Tuan Sheikh, 38 rooms, SR M$ 20-26, DR M$ 26-50 (A / C, shower), Tel. 725336 / 7.
●*International New Hotel,* 126 Jalan Veloo, 22 rooms, SR M$ 14-25 (some with shower), Tel. 714957.

There are a few cheap hotels in the area around Tuanku Munawir, Tuan Sheikh, Tunku Hassan (near the bus station).
- *Golden Hill, Mee Lee, Merry, Oriental, Wado,* etc. SR M$ 8-12, DR M$ 10-20, all with shower.
- *Century*, 25-29 Jalan Tuanku Munawir, 18 rooms, SR M$ 28, DR M$ 37 (A / C, shower), Tel. 76261 / 3.

The area is a veritable paradise for lovers of *Government Resthouses* (M$ 20-80), as there are five nearby. They are listed here,

but coordinate your stay with the section on excursions, as they are out of town:
- Kuala Pilah District: *Kuala Pilah,* Jalan Seremban (near Sri Menanti).
- Jempol District: Bahau, *Lake Garden* (near Tasek Bera).
- Jelebu District: *Kuala Klawang,* Jalan Simpang Pertang (near Gunung Telpa Burok).
- Tampin District: *Tampin,* Jalan Seremban, (near Gunung Tampin Nature Park).
- Rembau District: *Rembau,* Jalan Kampong Mulia (near Pedas Hotspring).

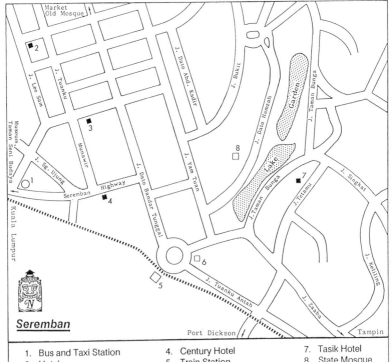

1. Bus and Taxi Station	4. Century Hotel	7. Tasik Hotel
2. Hotel	5. Train Station	8. State Mosque
3. Carlton Hotel	6. Main Post Office	

You can make **reservations** through the State Economic Development Corporation, on Jalan Yam Tuan, Seremban, Tel. 06-723251.

What to See

The city's main attraction is the **Lake Garden** in the middle of town. It is an attractive park and there are pools for swimming. The modern state mosque sits at the edge of the Garden, and is supposed to represent the nine original states of Negeri Sembilan. Near the park is the **State Secretariat**, a fine example of colonial architecture.

Out of town beyond the bus station is **Taman Seni Budaya**, a handicraft center. There is also a small **museum** here and part of an old palace.

All three houses are in the Minangkabau style.

Food

There are, as always, the **food centers**. Seremban also has a few good restaurants.

If you like Malay food, try some **Minangkabau food**, which tends to be spicy. For example, *masak lemak cili api* which is rice in coconut milk with "fire chilies" – the name says it all, *rendang minang*, or *lemang*, sticky rice in bamboo.

Malay food: Try the *Jempol* or *Anira* restaurants, both in Kompleks Negeri, Fatimah, Jalan Tuanku Munawir. *Bilal* is also good on Jalan Dato' Bandar Tunggal, Seremban's main shopping street.

Indian food: For good banana leaf cuisine, try *Samy*, 120 Jalan Yam Tuan, or *Anura*, 97 Jalan Tuanku Antar.

Chinese food: Try the *Happy Restaurant*, on the main street. There are plenty of other good places.

Excursions

Port Dickson, 32 km southwest of Seremban is the main beach resort of Negeri Sembilan. There are many hotels, bungalows, water sports, etc. (see separate section below). There are regular bus (M$ 1.30) and taxi connections.

Sri Menati, 32 km east of Seremban, is the residence of the state's rulers. The main attraction is the palace of the Yang di-Pertuan Besar, Sultan Tuanku Mohammad, built in 1902 and used until 1931. The **Istana Lama** is a good example of traditional Minangkabau architecture, though without the curved roof. The old palace can be visited, but not the new one, which was built in 1931 in a big park. To get there, take a bus to Kuala Pilah. Buses leave from there every 45 minutes to Sri Menati. On the way there, you will pass **Hulu Bendol**, a protected woods area, with lakes and a waterfall. It's a favorite spot for picnics.

23 to 32 km past Seremban, you can see groups of **prehistoric stones**. They are in groups of about 40, some higher than 3 m. There are also some near Alor Gajah and Tampin, 25 km south of Port Dickson (see separate section).

If you want to do some hiking, climb **Gunung Angsi** (826 m) The path starts 16 km past Seremban, 21 km before Kuala Pilah, on the right side, near a sloping curve by a stream.

Take the path for half an hour until you reach a clearing, then follow the red markers up the steep path to the summit. There is a good view over the Seremban Valley. Wear long pants and a long-sleeved shirt, as the path is overgrown in parts. Take food and water and plan on a 3-4 hour trek. Gunung Angsi is in a protected forest area.

To the northeast, there are other ***protected forest areas:***

●16 km north of Seremban, 5 km from the beginning of the Pantai-Lenggeng road, is a good picnic area. It's near a stream and there are various nature trails.

●22 km from Seremban on the road to Kuala Klawang and Bukit Tangga Pass, there is a small road that leads

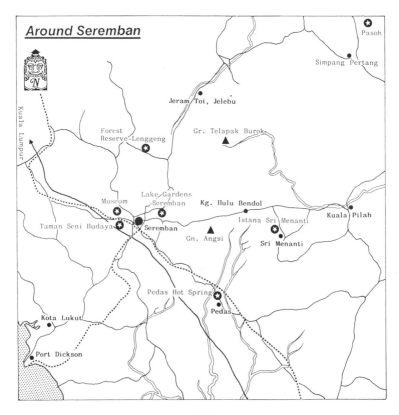

Around Seremban

off to the right. It goes to a telecommunications station at the summit of **Gunung Telapak Burok** (1195 m). You can follow the road to the summit.

There is a *hot spring* in Pedas, just west of the road to Malacca. Get there with the Southern Omnibus. You can also stop by on the way from Malacca.

Towards Pasoh

If you want to visit an area of undisturbed deep jungle with all sorts of wildlife, including White Hand Gibbons and Mouse Deer, stop by the Forest Research Institute Kepong in Selangor. They can arrange a visit to the **Pasoh Forest Reserve** in Negeri Sembilan. You can reserve a place in the cheap hostel there too where you can cook for yourself if you bring your own food.

There are paths throughout the forest. A 35 m observation tower (temporarily closed at the time of this writing), offers an excellent view and also an insight into the structure of the rain forest.

You can reach Pasoh from the road from Kuala Pilah to Simpang Pertang. Just before you get there, you must turn right at the sign marked "FELDA Pasoh" opposite the gas station. Follow the yellow posts through the oil palm plantation for about 3 km to the research center and office.

If you do not have a car, take a bus or taxi to the turn off and do the rest on foot.

Further Travel

The *bus and taxi station* is on Jalan Sungai Ujong.

Taxis to:
- *Tampin* – M$ 3
- *Port Dickson* – M$ 2
- *Kuala Lumpur* – M$ 5
- *Malacca* – M$ 6
- *Gemas* – M$ 7
- *Baahau, Jempol* – M$ 4
- *Kuala Pilah* – M$ 3
- *Kuala Klawang, Jelebu* – M$ 3
- *Rembau* – M$ 2

Buses to:
- *Rendau* – M$1.10.
- *Tampin* – M$ 2.40 with Southern (every 30 minutes), and M$ 3 with Mara.
- *Kuala Pilah* – M$ 2.
- *Bahau* – M$ 3 with United Bus (every 30 minutes).
- *Port Dickson* – M$ 1.10 with Restu Bus Express (every 2 hours), and M$ 1.10 with Bus Utam Singh (every 30 minutes).
- *Kuala Klawang* – M$ 1.80 with Lim Omnibus (every 30 minutes).
- *Kuala Lumpur* – M$ 2.20 with Cekap Express (every 20 minutes); M$ 2.20, non A / C, 2.60 with A / C with Syarikat Bus SKS (every 10 minutes).
- *Johor Baru* – M$ 12.50 with Mara (daily at 12:00 noon).
- *Kota Baru* – M$ 26 with A / C or 22 without A / C with Bumi Express.
- *Kuala Terengganu* – M$ 20 with A / C or 16.50 without A / C with Bumi Express.
- *Malacca* – M$ 2.86 with Mara Labu Sendayan (every 30 minutes).

Trains to:
- *Singapore* – M$ 25 with A / C or M$ 22 without A / C.
- *Kuala Lumpur* – M$ 11 with A / C or M$ 8 without A / C.

Port Dickson

Port Dickson (pop. 30,000), is the biggest and most popular beach resort of the Klang Valley. There is an 18 km long beach south of the harbor. Here you can find many weekend cottages, bungalows and hotels, all in the shade of casuarina and banyan trees.

As with the entire west coast south of Langkawi, the water here is not clear enough for good snorkeling. There is wind-surfing, sailing, waterskiing, and, of course, swimming, or just do as the locals do every weekend and have a big picnic in a peaceful spot.

Tourists are welcome at the Port Dickson Club on a temporary basis. The main resort area is not near the center of town.

Accommodation

- **Lido**, 8th Mile, Teluk Kemang, 22 rooms, M$ 22-30, Tel. 06-405273.
- **Milo**, 22-24 Wilkinson St., 25 rooms, M$ 19-24 (shower), Tel. 723451.
- **Pantai Motel**, 9th Mile, 22 rooms, M$ 20-35 (A / C, shower), Tel. 405265.
- **Sea View**, 841 Batu (Mile) 1, 20 rooms, M$ 25-35 (shower), Tel. 471818.
- **Happy City**, 26 Jalan Raja Aman Shah, 12 rooms, M$ 16-28 (shower), Tel. 473103.
- **Kong Ming**, Batu 8, Teluk Kemang, 13 rooms, M$ 22 (no shower), Tel. 405239.
- **Merlin**, 218 / 9 Jalan Pantai, 10 rooms, M$ 15-30 (some with A / C, showers), Tel. 473544.
- **Youth Hostel**, a good 5 km out of Port Dickson.
- **Methodist Center Hostel**, 17 km south of Port Dickson, dormitory, bungalows, Tel. 405229.

There are the following **government bungalows**, which cost M$ 20 to 100 per night, in Port Dickson:
- **Taman Seri**, 1, 2, 3, and 4 A / B, 5A / B, 3 km along Jalan Pantai (Beach Road).
- **Purnama**, 12.8 km, Jalan Pantai.
- **Mawar**, 16 km, Jalan Pantai.
Make reservations at the Port Dickson District Office, Tel. 06-471555.

More expensive places include:
- **Ming Court**, 11 km, Jalan Pantai, 165 rooms, M$ 140-350.
- **Pantai Dickson Resort**, 200 bungalows, M$ 180-210, Tel. 06-405473 or 03-2304945 in Kuala Lumpur.
- **Si Rusa Inn**, 160 rooms, M$ 120-350.

Excursions

In clear weather, you can go to the **old lighthouse** on Cape Rachido, built by the Portuguese in the 16th century. It is about 180 m above Blue Lagoon Village. Theoretically, you can see Sumatra about 40 km away or at least, the island of Pulau Rubat (Riau). Check on the weather before you go. West of the cape, there is an Outward Bound School at Pasir Panjang (long sand).

There is an hourly bus that goes 25 km south to **Pengkalan Kempas**. Here you can visit the Grave of Sheikh Ahmad Manjun, who died in 1467 fighting Sultan Mansur Shah. The big attractions here are the **prehistoric stones**, three of which are decorated with reliefs. They are the only decorated megaliths in the entire Malaysia / Indonesia region. People of all religions come here to pray for good harvests.

The Minangkabau in Negeri Sembilan

The **Minangkabau** are a matrilineal people from central Sumatra who were in contact with the Malay Peninsula as early as the 12th century. In the 14th century, a large group settled in the area around Malacca. As opposed to the Acehnese from northern Sumatra or the Bugis from Sulawesi, the Minangkabau never came as conquerors. They were interested only in peacefully growing rice. However, they were ready to defend their land. In order to do this, they unified their many small states into a union which was later called Negeri Sembilan and elected a leader or Yang di-Pertuan Besar.

As in Sumatra, the Islamic Minangkabau maintain many of their pre-Islamic customs and organizations, known as the Adat Perpateh. The most important of these is matrilineality or Suku. All possessions pass from mother to daughter, but remain family, rather than individual, property. Names are also passed on from mother to daughter.

When a man gets married, he lives in the home of his wife's family as a guest, while still remaining a member of his own family. He is then obligated to work for both his mother and his wife!

Women and men discuss decisions separately from one another, though the results are meant to please everyone. The head of a family group is the older brother of the mother or "mamak". The system worked, and still works, very well. Today, the Minangkabau are an intact, dynamic and economically successful people.

It is interesting that the Minangkabau are Muslim, but nonetheless maintain a very non-Islamic social hierarchy. At the time of their conversion, the Muslim missionaries were more tolerant than today's Dakhwah. Perhaps they had to let the Minangkabau maintain their own social order in order for them to agree to accept Islam.

A classic Minangkabau house in Bukittinggi, Sumatra.

205

Formerly, one could identify the areas where the Minangkabau lived by their distinctive houses. This is still true to some extent, and you can find Minangkabau houses in other parts of Malaysia outside of Negeri Sembilan. I have seen modern stylized Minangkabau houses in Ipoh and elsewhere. Typically, they have a saddle-roof with high pointed gables. The roofs can have any number of gables, which might seem irregularly placed.

In fact, each gable represents one family that lives in the house. When each daughter gets married, a new gable is added. Like most Malaysian houses, Minangkabau houses are typically on stilts. The roof provides good ventilation and protects the inhabitants from cold air. This is not a problem in Malaysia, but it is in their homeland, Bukittinggi, Sumatra. The women's head-dresses are reminiscent of the gabled roofs of the houses.

There is a legend about a buffalo calf whose horns were sharpened and tipped with poison. The calf was left to go hungry before a fight with a Javanese buffalo cow of the Majapahit Kingdom. When the calf saw the buffalo, it ran to drink its milk, but wound up poisoning the calf with its sharpened horns. This clever stunt gave the Minangkabau victory as well as their name (*minang* = conqueror, and *kabau* = buffalo).

Further Travel

Buses leave for **Seremban** every 30 minutes. There are four daily buses to **Port Klang** at M$ 3.50 and to **Kuala Lumpur** for M$ 3.30. Also four a day to **Malacca**, between 8:30 and 16:00, with Barat Express.

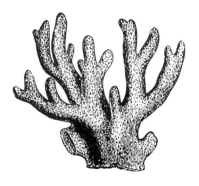

Malacca / Melaka

This is the oldest city in Malaysia, with a population of around 100,000. The city's name invokes one of the most poignant chapters of Malaysian history – the rise of a Malaysian city-state to a regional power and its eventual suppression by European colonial powers. There has been no Sultan of Malacca since the Portuguese forced him out in 1511. The ruling family fled to Johor, Perak and the east coast. Today, the tiny state is ruled by a governor. Incidentally, Malacca takes its name from the indigenous *melaka* tree.

The history of Malacca is described in detail in the chapter on history at the beginning of the book. In contrast to its golden age, the city is in a slump today. A lot of faith is being put in tourism to revive the economy.

The center of the city, particularly the area around the Malacca River, where Chinese merchants once traded goods from all over the world, still retains a lot of its old character. Outside the historic center, the big new tourist hotels wait silently for the boom.

Malacca is 150 km southeast of Kuala Lumpur and 250 km northwest of Singapore on the aptly-named Straits of Malacca. It can be reached from Kuala Lumpur by bus for M$ 6.50 or taxi, M$ 16.00, or from Singapore by a regular bus which is S$ 11.00. It is not on any railway line. At the time of writing, plans were underway to reinstate an air service to Malacca.

Accommodation

Since quite a number of tourists visit Malacca, there is a large selection of cheap hotels. There are at least as many on the beach as in the city proper. Despite relatively unattractive beaches and murky water, the town of **Kampung Tanjung Kling**, 15 km northwest of the city, has become something of a travelers' center. Here you can find an assortment of cheap places to stay, including bungalows and dormitory rooms. Many restaurants offer typical traveler food – banana omelets, muesli, etc.

●**S.H.M., Hawaii, Sunset,** and **Raya Sayang** (M$ 2-6 per bed) all have restaurants. Each has its own charm.

●One luxury place in the area is **Shah's Beach Resort**, with bungalows for M$ 70-85, or around M$ 25 per person. Sunday brunch is M$ 6.50, lunch is M$ 3.00. Tel. 06-226202.

To get to Tanjung Kling, take the No. 51 bus from the bus station for 85 *sen*.

●The big travelers' meeting place in Malacca is the **Trilogy**. It's at 218A Jalan Parameswara, somewhat east of the center of town, on the road to the Portuguese quarter. Good atmosphere. Free coffee and tea, beds are M$ 5, rooms M$ 8-14, bicycles for rent. Take bus No. 17 from the bus station, and get out at the Chinese temple. There is also a guest house of the same name in the center of town trying to capitalize on the name.

●Right nearby is the **Cowboy Lim Travelers' House**, which makes a good alternative with similar prices, 165A Jalan Melaka Jaya.

You can find lots of *cheap hotels* on Jalan Munshi Abdullah, Bunga Raya and Bendahara, all of which are in the center of town.

●*Malacca*, 27A Jalan Munshi Abdullah, 20 rooms, M$ 14-20 (shower, some with A / C, good rooms), Tel. 222499.

●*Ang Kee*, 22 Jalan Munshi Abdullah, 14 rooms, M$ 28-40 (A / C, shower), quiet, Tel. 249122.

●*Cathay*, 100 Jalan Munshi Abdullah, 26 rooms, M$ 12-26, quiet and comfortable, Tel. 223337.

●*Central*, 31-41 Jalan Bendahara, one of the cheapest, M$ 9-11, Tel. 222984.

●*Eastern Lodging*, 85 Jalan Bendahara, 12 rooms, M$ 8-14, relatively quiet, Tel. 223483.

●*Suan Kee*, 105-7 Jalan Bunga Raya, 11 rooms, M$ 8-13, Tel. 223040.

●*New Chin Nam*, 151 Jalan Bunga Raya, 12 rooms, M$ 12-30, Tel. 224962.

●*Ng Fook*, 154 Jalan Bunga Raya, 35 rooms, M$ 15-27 (some with A / C, shower), Tel. 228206.

●*Majestic*, 188 Jalan Bunga Raya, an old hotel, 20 rooms, M$ 16-32, with A / C and shower, Tel. 222367.

●*Tong Ah*, 16 Jalan Kee Ann, 10 rooms, M$ 6-8, Tel. 224813.

●*New London*, 54 Jalan Pasar Baru by the market, 13 rooms, M$ 11-15 (shower).

●*Chong Hoe*, 26 Jalan Tukang Emas, 10 rooms, M$ 9-20 (shower), clean, Tel. 226102.

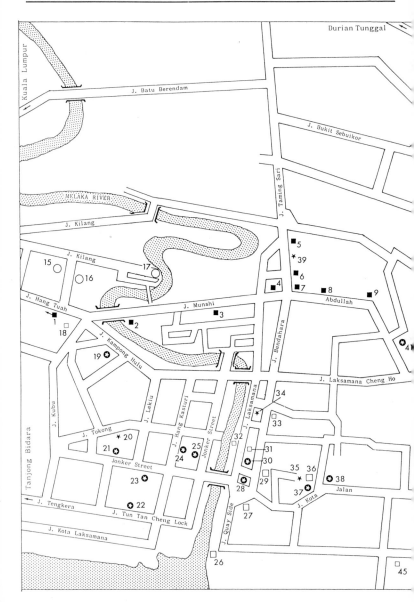

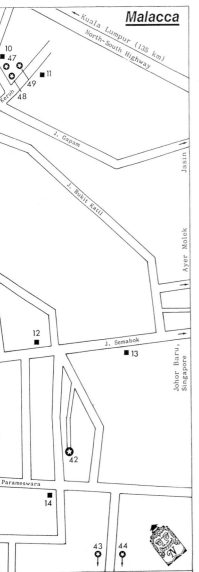

Malacca

1 to the Sentosa Hotel
2 Plaza Inn
3 Regal Hotel
4 Ramada Renaissance
5 Midtown
6 City Bayview
7 Wisma Hotel
8 Merlin Melaka
9 Palace Hotel
10 Air Keroh Country Resort
11 Malacca Village Resort
12 Tan Kim Hock Hotel
13 Lotus Inn
14 Trilogy
15 Malacca Bus Terminal
16 Taxi Station
17 Express Bus Terminal
18 Immigration Office
19 Kampong Hulu Mosque
20 Cheng Hoon Teng Temple
21 Hang Kasturi's Mausoleum
22 Baba Nyonya Heritage
23 Antique Shops
24 Kampong Kling Mosque
25 Sri Poyyatha V. Moorthi Temple
26 Customs
27 Tourist Information and Tourist Police
28 Queen Victoria Fountain
29 Stadthuys (Museum)
30 Christ Church
31 Main Post Office
32 Telephone Office
33 Police
34 Francis Xavier Church
35 St. Paul's Church
36 Dutch Cemetery
37 A Famosa / Santiago Gate
38 Memorial Hall
39 St. Peter's Church
40 Bukit China
41 Sultan Fountain
42 St. John's Fortification
43 Portuguese Place 44 Portuguese Quarter
45 MAS Office
46 Ayer Keroh Recreation Center
47 Mini-Malaysia
48 Malacca Zoo
49 Ayer Keroh Lake
50 Ayer Keroh Exhibit
51 Cowboy Lim Traveler House

•*Kane's Place*, 136A Jalan Laksamana Cheng Ho, a private house with a dorm room and rooms, M$ 10-12, Tel. 315124.

Mid-priced hotels in the same area:
•*Palace*, 201 Jalan Munshi Abdullah, 48 rooms, M$ 37-40, Tel. 225329.
Wisma, 114A Jalan Bendahara, 39 rooms, M$ 30-70, Tel. 228311.

More expensive hotels
•*Merlin Inn*, 243 rooms, M$ 85-400, Tel. 240777.
•*Plaza Inn*, Jalan Munshi Abdullah, 142 rooms, M$ 100-140.
•*Ramada Renaissance*, Jalan Bendahara, 295 rooms, M$ 95-160.
•*City Bayview*, on the same street, 182 rooms, M$ 80-200, Tel. 239888.

Near the *Ayer Keroh* leisure center:
•*Ayer Keroh Country Resort*, with 50 motel rooms, for M$ 46 and 15 chalets for M$ 70.
•*Malacca Village Resort*, with 147 rooms, for M$ 140-800.

What to See

The center of historic Malacca is *St. Paul's Hill*. Near here, next to the bridge over the Malacca River, you will find the *Tourist Information Center*, Tel. 225895. Not far away is the *Tourist Police*, a new organization in Malaysia, Tel. 222222, ext. 148.

Opposite the Tourist Information Center is the Dutch *Stadthuys*, the old seat of the Dutch governor, finished in 1650. Today, it houses the *Malacca Historical Museum*, with relics from the times of Dutch and Portuguese rule and also traditional Chinese and Malay wedding clothes and other interesting objects. One room is set up

with the original furniture and contents from the 17th century.

Next to the Stadthuys is the Dutch *Christ Church*, from 1753. The wooden ceiling beams are all carved from one tree. Over the altar is the Lord's Supper in colored tiles. Other artifacts include a brass Bible from 1773 and Armenian gravestones on the floor.

In front of the church are two characteristic signs of the British presence. The obligatory *Clock Tower* which is actually a gift from the Chinese at the end of the 19th century and the *Victoria Fountain*.

The neo-Gothic *Francis Xavier Church* dates from 1849 and honors the French father known as the Apostle of the East.

On Paul's Hill, next to the old lighthouse, are the *ruins of St. Paul's Church*. It was originally known as Duarte Coelho, and built by the Portuguese in 1521. The Dutch buried their nobility here. It was formerly the resting place of Francis Xavier until his remains were taken to Goa, India. Today you can see the empty grave. The inscriptions on the large gravestones are interesting, too.

If you descend the hill to the east, you come to **Santiago Gate**, the symbol of the city and the only remains of the A Famosa fortifications. They were built by d'Albuquerque in 1511, and severely damaged by the Dutch during their attack in 1641. They were repaired in 1670. The gate survives today thanks to Sir Stamford Raffles, the founder of Singapore. The coat of arms and the inscription, VOC, are Dutch. A restoration of the fortifications is planned.

Right nearby, in front of the large *padang* is a reproduction of the old **Sultan's Palace**. It is built entirely of wood, as was typical for the Malays (which is why there are no surviving old palaces).

The palace houses the **State Cultural Museum** or Muzium Budaya, which contains a reproduction of a royal audience, pictures of court life, clothing, weapons, musical instruments and models of old houses, among other things.

Near that, on Padang Bandar Hilir, is a **Light and Sound Show**, put together at a cost of over M$ 8 million. The palace of the governor used to be on the hill. There is a Dutch cemetery nearby.

In front of you, on Jalan Kota is **Memorial Hall**, formerly the Malacca

All in red: Stadthuys, church and clocktower.

211

Club. The Malaysian struggle for independence is documented here in papers, contracts, videos, and other forms.

On Padang Pahalwan, you can take a ride in a typical Malaccan *Ox-Cart*. It's M$ 1.00 for a ten-minute ride (weekends and holidays from 10:00 to 19:00). There are actually only ten of these carts left in Malacca, and they are not allowed in the city.

The street that leads off to the east, Jalan Parameswara, goes to Bukit St. John. This hill has an 18th century Dutch fortification on top with a chapel dedicated to John the Baptist. The cannon are aimed at the land behind Malacca, where the danger of attack was greatest in the past.

A bit further down and Jalan d'Albuquerque turns off to the right. Follow it down to the *Portuguese Quarter*, home of the Eurasian community that even today continues to speak Cristao, a dialect of Portuguese from the 16 and 17th centuries. Many of the people here look no different from Malays. Another racially-mixed group are the

Chinese-Malay, or Straits-Born Chinese, also known as Baba Nyona. They have lived here for many generations, in contrast to most of the Chinese who immigrated either in this or the previous century.)

At the end of the street is the Portuguese Square / Medan Portugis, where there are some very expensive Portuguese restaurants. Saturday evenings there is a changing program of Portuguese and other folk dancing for M$ 2.00.

Behind the square is a path that runs down to the ocean. It's a nice walk on a moonlit night.

The end of June marks the arrival of *St. Peter's Festival*, in which multi-colored, highly decorated boats are blessed. There are also many other events going on. If you are around, try to make it.

On the other side of the river, straight ahead on Jonker St., there are a lot of *Antique Shops*, which are quite reasonably priced. On the street that runs parallel to the left, Jalan Tun Tan Cheng Lok (nice houses here), is the private *Baba Nyonya Heritage Museum*. There is

quite a lot of information about this interesting group of mixed Chinese and Malay background who are also known as Peranakan. Magnificent wedding costumes.

At the intersection of Hang Jebat and Tokong is the **Grave of Hang Kasturi**, a friend of Hang Tuah, whose history is familiar to all Malaysians. Four friends in the service of Sultan Shah saved the life of his prime minister, or Bendahara. Betraying the sultan, one day Hang Tuah killed Hang Jebat, whose grave is nearby on Jalan Kampong Kuli.

Next to the grave is the oldest Chinese temple in Malaysia, the **Cheng Hoon Teng Temple**, built in 1646. The main altar is dedicated to the goddess of mercy and the one to the left is dedicated to the goddess of the sky, the guardian of fishermen and sea travelers.

Magnificent wood carvings on the inside, and glass and porcelain on the outside, represent different mythological figures. In the courtyard the three teachings are represented; Buddhism, Confucianism and Taoism. All of the building materials for the temple were brought from China.

Kampong Kling Mosque is on Jalan Tukang Emas. Like the two other old mosques in Malacca, it is built in Sumatran style, with a three-tiered pyramidic roof and good carvings.

About 100 meters further, on Jalan Kampong Hulu is what might be the oldest mosque in Malaysia the

Kampong Hulu Mosque, built in 1728. There is also one in Kuala Terengganu that is roughly the same age.

The third old mosque, **Tranquerah Mosque**, is on Jalan Tengkera, somewhat outside of the city. It houses the grave of Sultan Hussain, who gave Singapore to Sir Stamford Raffles.

Next to the Kampong Kling Mosque is the oldest Indian temple in Malaysia, the **Sri Poyyatha Vinayagar Moorthi Temple**, which dates back to the beginning of the 19th century.

Back on the east bank of the river are a few more things to see, on and around **Bukit China**. The hill is the largest cemetery outside of China (106 acres, with 12,000 graves, some of which go back to the Ming Dynasty.) In the 15th century, it was home to Princess Hang Li Poh and 500 court ladies, sent here in 1459 by the Emperor of China to Sultan Mansur Shah as proof of friendship. In 1629, the Portuguese built a Franciscan cloister here, which was destroyed by the Acehnese.

At the foot of the hill, at the end of Jalan Munshi Abdullah, is **Hang Li Poh's Fountain**. The thick walls were built by the Dutch. At one time, it was one of Malacca's most important sources of water. Today, tourists throw coins in the fountain to insure they will return to Malacca one day.

Also worth seeing is **St. Peter's Church**, to the west on Jalan Tun Sri Lanang. It was built in 1710 in a composite of European and Asian styles. Inside, there is an Iberian alabaster statue of Jesus before the Resurrection.

● **Immigration**, Jalan Hang Tuah, Tel. 224895.

● **Police**, Jalan Banda Kaba, Tel. 222222.

● **Main Post Office**, Jalan Laksamana, Tel. 233846.

Shopping

Antiques and exotic Chinese products are available. You can still find tiny shoes for Chinese women who had their feet bound as tiny feet were once thought of as sexy in China. Mr. Yeo's shoe shop on Jalan Hang Jebat specializes in them and he still has some 80 and 90 year old women from Malacca and Penang as customers. He makes them to order at M$ 100-150 a pair. Mostly, though, he sells them to tourists as souvenirs for M$ 50-60.

Food

Starting on Jalan Munshi Abdullah by the bridge over the river:

● *Restoran Banana Leaf* offers **Tamil food** – rice, vegetables, curries, all eaten with the right hand from a banana leaf.

● *Vazhai Elai*, at No. 42, has **North Indian food**.

● *Siang Chiang* on the same street has the best *yong tau foo* in town.

● Jalan Bendahara is filled with **coffee shops** and **grocery stores**. Kim Hock and Tong Seng have dried shrimp, palm sugar *gula melaka, sambal belacan, dodol* and other local foods.

● Jalan Bunga Raya, with the cheap hotels, is also the place for **ice cream**. *Min Chon Hygienic Ice Cafe* has good *pak poh* or eight treasures, a variant of *ais kacang*. The *Tai Chong Ice Cafe* is also good. This is also the location of the **Pasar Malam** or night market.

● There is good **hawker food** all over this district at night. Try *sup kambing* which is Indian goat or mutton soup, or curry *laksa*.

● *Glutton's Corner* is next to the Padang on the waterfront. It is a good place for oyster omelets, *mee Siam, sate celup* and *kangkung*.

● **Nyonya food** is from Malacca and you should try *taman melaka jaya* in *ole sayang* or *Nyonya makko*. The colorful deserts are the best-known aspect of Nyonya cuisine.

Excursions

Ayer Keroh

is an area about 10 to 15 km outside the city that has been developed into a recreation area in order to attract more tourists. The **Melaka Zoo** has indigenous animals in relatively natural settings. The **Mini Malaysia Cultural Center** has houses from the various states of Malaysia, including Sabah and Sarawak. Inside there are dioramas arranged to depict real-life events like weddings, circumcisions, Hari Raya Open House, and food preparation. There are cultural shows on weekends. Food and souvenirs are on sale every day.

Open weekdays from 10:00-18:00 and weekends and holidays from 9:00-19:00.

The park is currently being expanded into an **ASEAN Mini Park**, with houses from each of the ASEAN nations, Malaysia, Thailand, Indonesia, Singapore, the Philippines and Brunei.

The compound also includes the **Hutan Rekreasi**, or Recreational Woods. There are camping and picnic areas, walking and bicycle paths, a jogging and fitness course and a wooden observation tower. For further information, contact the tourist office (Tel. 225895), Hutan Rekreasi (Tel. 328401) or Pejabat Hutan Melaka.

"Rubber Forest": Rubber trees in rows and columns.

215

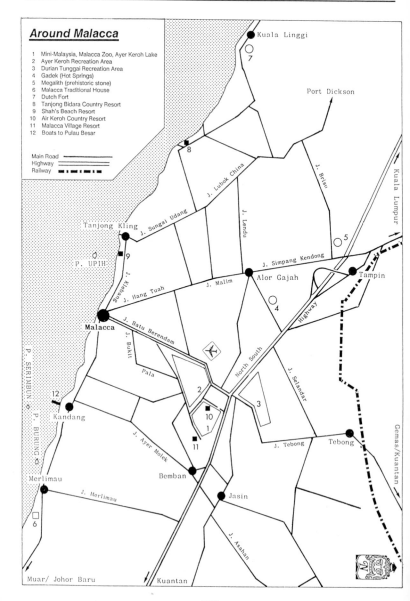

Around Malacca

1 Mini-Malaysia, Malacca Zoo, Ayer Keroh Lake
2 Ayer Keroh Recreation Area
3 Durian Tunggai Recreation Area
4 Gadek (Hot Springs)
5 Megalith (prehistoric stone)
6 Malacca Traditional House
7 Dutch Fort
8 Tanjong Bidara Country Resort
9 Shah's Beach Resort
10 Air Keroh Country Resort
11 Malacca Village Resort
12 Boats to Pulau Besar

Main Road
Highway
Railway

Kuala Linggi
Port Dickson
Kuala Lumpur
J. Brisu
J. Lubok China
J. Landu
J. Sungai Udang
Tanjong Kling
P. UPIH
J. Simpang Kendong
Alor Gajah
Tampin
J. Malim
J. Hang Tuah
J. Sungai Kling
Highway
Malacca
J. Batu Berendam
P. SERIMBUN
J. Bukit
Pala
North South
J. Selandar
P. BURUNG
Kandang
J. Ayer Molek
Tebong
J. Tebong
Merlimau
J. Merlimau
Bemban
Jasin
J. Asahan
Muar/ Johor Baru
Kuantan
Gemas/Kuantan

There is also a **crocodile farm** here, Taman Buaya, with 110 crocodiles, all in pretty miserable shape. It is not recommended.

At **Ayer Keroh Lake**, you can rent boats. There is a golf course at the country club and a few good, but expensive, hotels.

Durian Tunggal Recreational Lake,

north of Ayer Keroh, is 16 km out of the city on the road to Kuantan. There are boats for rent, fishing, wind surfing, camping, jogging trails and playgrounds. A **deer park** is being built here and a **bird park** is being built in Alor Gajah, just a bit to the northeast on the road to Seremban.

Gadek Hot Springs

25 km outside the city on the road to Tampin is the Gadek Hot Spring. There are also some **megaliths** nearby.

Southeast

10 km outside of the city, to the southeast, there is delicious grilled fish in **Pernu** and **Serkam**. 5 km from **Merlimau** on the way to Muar is an outstanding, traditional **Malacca House**, built in the 19th century.

Pulau Besar

Since Malacca is not home to any good beaches, the tourism experts decided to develop a nearby quiet island, **Pulau Besar**. Take a boat from Umbai Jetty. There are 87 bungalows, a 35-room motel, 2 hotels, a swimming pool, all sorts of water sports and conference facilities.

Muar

(Bandar Panggaram / Bandar Maharani) is known for its good and affordable food. Like Segamat, it is a departure point for a hike up **Gunung Ledang**. Muar has a lot in common with Malacca, only 38 km away. Farther south, between Muar and Batu Pahat, there is a **Thermal Bath** in Sungai Balang. **Resthouses** in **Muar:**

● **Tanjung Mas**, Jalan Sultana, M\$ 18.90 (no A / C), M\$ 27.30 to 50.40 (A / C), Tel. 06-922306.

● **Batu Pahat:** 870 Jalan Tasek, M\$ 32 (no A / C), M\$ 38 (A / C), Tel. 441181.

● **Kluang:** Jalan Government Office, M\$ 33.60 (A / C), Tel. 07-721567.

Gunung Ledang, 1276 m (Mount Ophir)

This mountain, rising out of the plains, is the highest in Johor. As the southernmost mountain in Malaysia, it is very popular with Singaporeans.

The mountain was supposedly the home of a beautiful princess, Putri or Princess Gunung Ledang, in the 15th century, the love of Sultan Mansur Shah of Malacca. The famous British naturalist, Wallace, was the first foreigner to climb the mountain in 1854.

There are two routes to the summit. The first route starts at either Tangkak or Sagil in Johor. The best way to get there is from Muar or from Segamat, which lies on the rail line. The other route begins in Asahan in the State of Malacca. Get there via Jasin.

Starting point: **Lembaga Penapis Air**, the first town along the river. In case you come at night, it is about 1.5 km down an irrigation canal in the forest. At 914 meters, there is a camping area, Padang Batu. The area around the summit is rocky, so watch your step. If you want to take it easy, there is a road that goes up to a telecommunications station near the summit. It starts near **Tangkak** and you can drive to within 200 or so meters of the summit and then walk the rest.

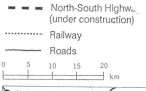

- - - North-South Highw.
(under construction)

.... Railway

———— Roads

```
0    5    10   15   20
|----|----|----|----| km
```

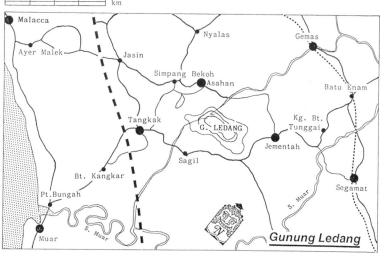

Festivals

In addition to the nationwide festivals, Malacca has a few of its own. Ask at the tourist office for specific dates.
- *Masimagam Festival*, similar to Thaipusam in Cheng (late February / early March).
- *Palm Sunday* in St. Peter's, a procession of some 15,000 Christians (the Sunday before Easter).
- *Mariamman Festival* in temples (early May).
- *Merbuk* or Malay barred ground-dove (bird) singing contests (mid-June).
- *Festival of San Juang* or St. John (late June).
- *St. Anna Festival* with a procession (late July).
- *Malacca City Carnival* (July and August).
- In the Subramaniam Temple, of Gajah Beran, *Hindus walk over hot coals* (mid-August).
- *Gasing Contests*, Padang Pahlawan, competitions in Malay, Chinese and Indian martial arts (August).
- *Ocean Carnival, Dragonfly Contests* on Klebang Besar Beach with boat races (August).
- *Santa Cruz Festival* with light procession (mid-September).
- *Francis Xavier Festival* (early December).

Further Travel

Taxis:
The taxi stand is on the side street between Jalan Kilang and Hang Tuah (Tel. 223630).
- *Kuala Lumpur* – M$ 13.00.
- *Muar* – M$ 3.50.
- *Tampin* – M$ 2.80 (rail connection).
- *Johor Baru* – M$ 17.00.
- *Alor Gajah* – M$ 2.00.

Buses:
The bus station is on Jalan Kilang. The local bus terminal is between Jalan Kilang and Hang Tuah. There are buses to:

- *Kuala Lumpur* – M$ 5.50 / M$ 6.25 A / C with Jebat Express. Tel. 222503.
- *Seremban* – M$ 2.85 / M$ 3.40 A / C with Skt. Labu Sendayan Express. Tel. 220687.
- *Port Dickson / Klang* – M$ 3.20 / M$ 7.20 with Klang Barat Express. Tel. 249937.
- *Ipoh / Butterworth* – M$ 13.00 / M$ 17.50 with Ekspres Nasional.
- *Taiping* – M$ 21.40. Tel. 220687.
- *Kuala Terengganu / Kota Baru*: M$ 19 / M$ 23 A / C to Kuala Terengganu and M$ 25 / M$ 29 A / C to Kota Baru with Bumi Express. Tel. 248959.
- *Ipoh / Lumut* – M$ 14.50 to Ipoh and M$ 18.50 to Lumut with Murni Express. Tel. 249126.
- *Kuantan / Temerloh* – M$ 11.00 to Kuantan and M$ 5.00 to Segamat with Cepat Express. Tel. 220687. M$ 10.95 to Kuantan and M$ 6.50 to Temerloh with Tanjong Keramat Express.
- *Johor Baru / Singapore* – M$ 8 / M$ 10 A / C to Johor Baru and M$ 8.50 / M$ 11 to Singapore with Melaka-Singapore Express.
- *Tampin / Muar* – M$ 1.60 / M$ 2.10 A / C to Tampin, M$ 1.80 / M$ 2.80 to Muar with MCW Express.

Ferries
to Dumai in *Sumatra*, leave Malacca harbor on Thursdays at 10:00 and return on Tuesdays, Thursdays and Saturdays at 14:00. For reservations and information contact: *Madai Shipping*, 320 Jalan Kilang, Tel. 06-240671. It costs around M$ 100 for the five-hour trip.

Flights:
From the small *Batu Berendam Airport*, 10 km from the city, there is a flight to Pekanbaru on Sumatra every Friday at 13:50 for M$ 140.00 one-way. For information and reservation, contact Malacca Oriental Travel, Tel. 224877 or Atlas Travel (MAS-tel.: 235722). The private *Pelingi Airways* has flights to various cities within Malaysia. You might want to ask about that. There are also plans to expand the airport.

Johor Baru (JB)

Johor Baru is the third largest city in Malaysia, with a population of over 300,000, and is the capital of Johor, the southernmost state in Peninsular Malaysia.

Baru means new and *lama* means old. Since there is a new Johor, it follows that there must be an old one as well. There is indeed a Johor Lama, the old capital on the Johor River, but not much is there. New Johor owes much of its prosperity to Singapore. Since Singaporean independence, Johor Baru's population has tripled.

Johor Baru was known as Ujung Tanah (Land's End) or Iskandar Perti before it was declared the capital of Johor in 1866. It is on the rail line between Kuala Lumpur and Singapore. Johor Baru also forms one of the endpoints of the North-South Highway that runs along the entire west coast of the Peninsula. The city is a point of departure, primarily for Singaporeans, to the east coast destinations of Desaru and Mersing, including various islands.

Johor Baru is connected to Singapore by the Causeway, which is heavily trafficked by cars, trucks, trains and pedestrians.

The newly-expanded Senai Airport, the new name of which is Sultan Ismail International Airport, offers good competition on some routes (e.g. to Sabah or Sarawak) to Singapore's Changi Airport.

Johor has a strong agricultural industry. Rubber trees, oil palms, pineapples and pepper are all grown here. The state is also an important industrial and trading center. The expansion since 1972 of Pasir Guadang from a fishing village to a 3000 hectare super harbor with freeport status is typical of Johor's development.

Accommodation

Some people like to stay in Johor Baru when visiting Singapore. Apart from the sometimes run-down guest houses in the Island Republic, there are not many cheap hotel rooms there. If you do not mind the bus trip, which costs only 70 *sen*, it makes sense to stay in Johor Baru. Altogether there are more than 50 hotels. Constantly going through the border crossing can be a bit of a pain, however.

Hotels near the train station:
●**First Hotel**, Jalan Station, 42 rooms, M$ 18-80, Tel. 222888.
●**Lido**, 37D-1, 33D-2 Jalan Ah Fook, 11 rooms, M$ 17 (shower), Tel. 234752.
●**Tong Fong**, 5A Jalan Ah Fook, 12 rooms, M$ 14-16 (shower), Tel. 221165.
●**Tong Hong**, 39 Jalan Meldrum, 18 rooms, M$ 12-14, Tel. 222074.
●**Pelangi**, 49R Jalan Lumba Kuda.

Mid-priced hotels in the Center:
●**Rasa Sayang Baru**, 10 Jalan Dato Dalam, 110 rooms, M$ 37-60, Tel. 224744.
●**Top**, 12 Jalan Meldrum, 37 rooms, M$ 28-56, Tel. 224755.
●**Hawaii**, 21 Jalan Meldrum, 36 rooms, from M$ 33.
●**J.B.**, 80A Jalan Ah Fook, 32 rooms, M$ 23-32, Tel. 224989.
●**Wato Inn**, 15R Jalan Bukit Meldrum, 22 rooms, M$ 31-47, Tel. 221328.

Expensive:

● *Merlin Tower*, Jalan Meldrum, 104 rooms, M$ 100-180, Tel. 225811.

● *Tropical Inn*, 15 Jalan Gereja, 160 rooms, M$ 110-450, Tel. 221888.

● *Merlin Inn*, 10 Bukit Meldrum, 104 rooms, M$ 65-180.

What to See

The Causeway, finished in 1924, is a granite bridge. It is 1056 meters long and up to 23 meters deep. At the end of the 70's, it was widened from 8 m to 21 m, which still seems too narrow. Heavy traffic is the rule.

The *Istana Besar* or Great Palace is the sultan's palace. It was built in 1866 under Abu Bakar, and faces the Straits of Johor. The present Sultan lives in a modern palace, Bukit Serene, on the edge of town, which cannot be visited. It is next to

1 Istana Bukit Serene	8 Sultan Abu Bakar College	15 Bus Station
2 Chinese Temple	9 Resthouse	16 Main Post Office
3 Hospital	10 Royal Mausoleum	17 Tourist Information
4 Holiday Plaza	11 Tropical Inn	18 Merlin Tower Hotel
5 Holiday Inn	12 Sultan Abu Bakar Mosque	19 Customs / Immigration
6 Wisma Daiman	13 Zoo	20 Train Station
7 Jaro Handicraft Center	14 Istana Besar	21 Merlin Inn

the **Taman Tasek** nature park, where there are places to stay. The old palace is still used for formal occasions like audiences and coronations. It houses a *museum* with displays of jewelry, clothing and weapons belonging to the ruling family. There is an attractive park here with jogging paths, picnic spots, a Japanese garden, orchids and a fern garden.

The **Masjid Sultan Abu Bakar Mosque** was finished in 1900 to honor the Father of Modern Johor, who himself laid the cornerstone in 1892. The vaguely European-style mosque has room for some 2000 worshipers. It is one of the most beautiful mosques in Malaysia. The main altar is a masterpiece of traditional woodworking.

The **Royal Mausoleum** is near the intersection of Jalan Petri and Jalan Mahmoodiah and is the final resting place of the royal family. Entry is not permitted, but there are some graves outside.

The **State Secretariat** or Bangunan Sultan Ibrahim, finished in 1940, may be visited. Its square tower is the symbol of the city, and there are good mosaics in the Great Hall.

Shopping

Holiday Plaza on Jalan Dato Sulaiman, Century Garden, offer Malay handicrafts.
JARO has a shop on Jalan Waterworks with artwork and handicrafts done by the handicapped.

There are more crafts in **Johor Craftown Center**, 36 Jalan Skudai including batik, mats, and other items.

Food

There are lots of **food stalls** on Jalan Skudai.
●Try the *Tepian Tebrau Stalls* and those next to the Central Market.
●Johor is famous for **seafood** including oysters, shrimp, grilled squid, crabs, *laksa Johor*, and *lontong* which is rice in spicy coconut sauce.
●*Malay food* can be found at *Medina*, 12 Jalan Meldrum, and *Medan Selera Food Court* in Tun Abdul Razak Complex, among others.
●For **Indian food** try *Granee's Banana Leaf and Pub*, 27 Jalan Segget, and *Kerala*, 33 Jalan Ibrahim. There are others.
●Good **Chinese restaurants** include *Ming Dragon*, Holiday Plaza; *Tong Ah*, 14 Jalan Ibrahim; *New Hong Kong*, 69A Jalan Sultan Ibrahim; *Stulang Laut*, on the beach of Johor Baru; and *Moon Place*, Johor Tower, Jalan Gereja.
●There is good **seafood** at *Jaws Seafood Restaurant*, Jalan Skudai; *Prawn House*, 22 Jalan Kancil; and *Century Garden*, Midland Garden. This place is 5 km west of the city with a view of Singapore over the Straits of Johor. They specialize in "Drunken Prawns".

Excursions

Ulu Tiram Estate

is a working plantation open to visitors. You can see the processing of rubber and palm oil. It is 26 km northeast of Johor Baru on the road to Mersing. There are regular bus connections.

Kota Tinggi:

The 32 m high **Lombong Waterfalls** near Kota Tinggi are billed as one of the biggest attractions in the state of Johor. If you go beyond Tiram on the road to Mersing, you will reach Kota Tinggi after 56 km. Take a taxi from Johor Baru for M$ 3.00, no A / C, or Bus No. 41 for M$ 2.00. From Kota Tinggi it is 80 *sen* for the 15 km ride to the waterfalls.

There are bungalows here for around M$ 30, a restaurant, food stands and a camping area. For information call Tel. 07-231132-5. Admission is M$ 1.00 for adults, 20-40 *sen* for children. Cemetery fans will want to see the **old graves** in Kampong Kelantan. **Makam Tun**

Habib features 15 graves of the royal family, 1.5 km south of Kota Tinggi.

●There are at least 5 hotels in Kota Tinggi, should you decide to stay here: **Koko, Kolee, Kota HK, Bunga Raya,** SR M$ 11-16, DR M$ 18-34.

Johor Lama

A sleepy fishing village that was the capital of the Sultanate of Johor for 40 years (1528-64 and 1570-87), from the fall of Malacca until the Portuguese seized the town with 500 men at the end of their three year war in Malaya. Part of the old fortifications have been restored.

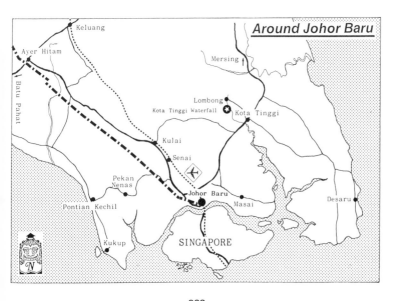

Around Johor Baru

The best way to get here is by boat along the Johor River from Kota Tinggi, but you can also drive.

Desaru

or Casuarina Village: A very nice, but expensive beach resort patronized primarily by wealthy Singaporeans. From Singapore, you can take a ferry from Changi Point to Kampong Penggerang for M$ / S$ 5.00 and then take a taxi for M$ 30 to Desaru. There is a bus from Kota Tinggi that covers the 94 km for M$ 5.20. Along the way, the bus passes through plantation after plantation, part of a state-sponsored development project. It all used to be jungle.

The **beach** is 25 km long. Parts of it have pretty good surf. There is wind-surfing, sailing, snorkeling, canoeing, volleyball, tennis, and horseback and bicycle riding. There is also an 18-hole golf course surrounded by jungle with views out to the ocean.

The resort is currently being developed and there is no telling what it will look like in a couple of years. It is still pretty quiet though, as there are only a few expensive places to stay:
- **Desaru View Hotel**, 134 rooms, M$ 150-650, Tel. 07-838221.
- **Merlin Inn**, 100 rooms, M$ 115-280, Tel. 838101.
- **Holiday Resort**, with 35 rustic Minangkabau bungalows for M$ 70-200.
- There is a cheaper **camping area** with huts and dormitories for around M$ 10 per bed.
- **Food** is available in the restaurant of the Holiday Resort, but it is expensive (e.g. breakfast from M$ 4-7). There are hawkers here on weekends.

Mersing

A bustling fishing town and the place to get a boat for a number of outlying islands, the best-known being Pulau Tioman and Pulau Rawa. Detailed information is in the section on the east coast.

Kukup,

20 km south of Pontian Kecil, is a big destination for Johor Baru residents in search of good **seafood**. There are many restaurants in houses on stilts over the water that serve all kinds of fresh fish, shrimp, crabs, etc. There are buses from Johor Baru to Pontian and then to Kukup.

Kong Kong,

near Masai, 48 km east of Johor Baru, is another fishing village that people visit for the food. Take the bus from Johor Baru. Kong Kong is also a good place to get a boat to visit Johor Lama.

Ayer Hitam

at the intersection of the North-South Highway and the road from Batu Pahat to Kluang, has a big market. It is a good place to buy vases and pottery, among other things. Singapore buses often stop here. You can visit *Aw-Pottery* in Kampong Macam, about 1 km southeast of Ayer Hitam. They have a 48 m kiln in which they can fire some 2000 pieces simultaneously.

Further Travel

Flights with MAS:
You can leave your bags free of charge in the MAS office, open daily except Sundays from 9:00-17:00.
- **Kuala Lumpur** – M$ 77.
- **Kuantan** – M$ 77.
- **Kuala Terengganu** – M$ 163.

Taxis:
- **Airport** – M$ 20.
- **Malacca** – M$ 17.
- **Kuala Lumpur** – M$ 31 / M$ 36 A / C.
- **Kuantan** – M$ 30 A / C.
- **Seremban** – M$ 25 / M$ 30.
- **Pontian** – M$ 4.
- **Segamat** – M$ 14.
- **Ayer Hitam** – M$ 7.
- **Kluang** – M$ 8.

Buses:
There are buses to locations all over the country. The terminal is in the center of town. Sample prices:
- **Malacca** – M$ 10.
- **Singapore** – M$ 0.70.

Trains:
- **Singapore** – M$ 8.00, A / C.
- **Kuala Lumpur** – M$ 27, A / C.

Car Rentals:
- *Avis*, Tel. 07-237970.
- *Sintat*, Tel. 227110.
- *Hertz*, Tel. 229552.
- *Calio*, Tel. 233325.
- *Halaju Selatan*, Tel. 234234.

The East Coast

From North to South

The east coast consists largely of hundreds of kilometers of beaches dotted with Malay fishing villages and *kampongs*. There are few big towns here and not very many plantations, either. Malays make up an overwhelming 90% of the population. In general, life is quieter than on the more developed west coast. Offshore there are many beautiful islands with good snorkeling and diving. The main travelers' stops are **Marang, Rantau Abang** and **Cherating**.

Tourist Information

Kelantan
Kelantan Tourist Information Center, Jalan Ibrahim, Kota Baru, Tel. 097-21155.
Terengganu
TDC Regional Office, 2243 Tingkat Bawah, Wisma MCIS, Jalan Sultan Zainal Abidin, Kuala Terengganu, Tel. 096-21433.
Pahang
Pahang State Economic Development (Tourism Division), Bang. Lembaga Kemajuan Negeri Pahang, Jalan Haji Abdul Aziz, Kuantan, Tel. 095-22166.
Johor
TDC Regional Office, Lots 1,2 and 3, COM.T.A.R., Jalan Ah Fook, Johor Baru, Tel. 07-223590 / 1.

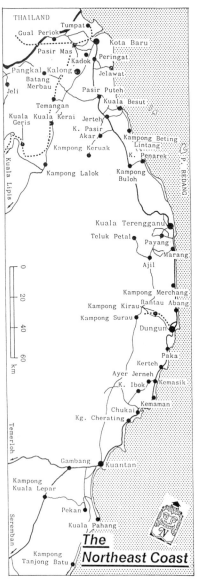

Kota Baru

Kota Baru is the capital of Kelantan and has a population of 200,000. The name means simply "New City", but Kota Baru is no longer new, in fact, it is over 200 years old now. Like all Malay capitals, it used to be at the mouth of a river. Over the past 200 years however, the Kelantan River has meandered some 12 km to the north. Since only small ships can reach it, Kota Baru is no longer a port city.

Kelantan is billed as the center of Malay culture and Kota Baru is supposed to be the primary cultural destination within the state. In fact, the city has little to offer in that respect. Malay culture is very much part of the *kampongs* and not an aspect of the big cities.

The city is very active and has been a travelers' center since the construction of the East-West Highway. The highway connects it with Penang and the road to Kuala Lumpur via Gua Musang and Kuala Lipis.

The nearby border crossing between Rantau Panjang and Sungai Golok is a favorite destination for locals shopping for goods from Hat Yai. It is also a convenient place for travelers to cross over into Thailand. There is a railway connection from Sungai Golok onto Hat Yai and Bangkok. The famous east coast beaches begin south of Kota Baru.

Accommodation

There are more than 2 dozen hotels in the city, but most of the *travelers' places* are outside the center of town, on Jalan Pengkalan Chepa, towards the airport on bus No.4 or 9:

●*Mummy's Hitec Hostel*, 4398 Jalan Pengkalan Chepa. Mummy gives this place its atmosphere. Dormitory beds for M$ 3, rooms for M$ 8. Breakfast, city tours, bike rentals, and women's haircuts are all available.

●*Rainbow Inn*, 4423 Jalan Pengkalan Chepa, is right next to the Thai Consulate. They offer free coffee and tea and you can even cook for yourself in their kitchen.

●*Traveller's House*, 2881 Jalan Pengkalan Chepa, has double rooms for M$ 8. Closer to town.

●There is a new *Hitec* on the site where the original stood on Jalan Suara Muda near the market. Dormitory beds for M$ 5, rooms for M$ 10 / 12.

●*Friendly Guest House*, 2899 Jalan Pintu Pong, not far from the Istana Balai Besar, just a few minutes from the bus station, has rooms for M$ 10, dormitory beds for M$ 4.

●*Town Guest House*, 2921 Jalan Pintu Pong, hasDR for M$ 10 and dormitory beds for M$ 5, free coffee and tea.

●Those looking for somewhere a bit better and quieter should try the *Rebana House*. It's near the Istana Kota Lama in a side street off Jalan Sultanah Zainab. Nearby are some silverwork shops for which Kelantan is famous.

There are a few hotels around the corner from the bus station:

●*Maryland*, 2726 Jalan Tok Hakim, 14 rooms, M$ 16-31, shower, not bad, but loud. Tel. 782811.

●*New Bali*, 3655 Jalan Tok Hakim, 13 rooms, M$ 13-22, shower, clean and quiet. Tel. 722686.

●*New Tokyo*, 3945 Jalan Tok Hakim, 22 rooms, SR from M$ 20, DR M$ 30, A / C, shower, friendly atmosphere. Tel. 749488.

●*North Malaya*, 3856 Jalan Tok Hakim, 21 rooms, M$ 12-14, 16-20, shower, Tel. 22171.

●*Ah Chiew* and *Mee Ching*, opposite the New Tokyo, are very simple.

●*Kelantan*, right near the bus station, DR M$ 14, M$ 16 (3 beds), M$ 18 (4 beds), good, but loud.

●*Rex*, Jalan Temenggong, 24 rooms, M$ 6 / 15, with shower, Tel. 21419.

●*Prince*, 1953 Jalan Temenggong, 12 rooms, M$ 10 / 20.

●*Berling*, 826 Jalan Temenggong, 37 rooms, M$ 14-50, Tel. 785255.

●*Hoover*, 1653 Jalan Dato Pati, 11 rooms M$ 12 / 20-24, with shower, Tel. 21439.

More expensive hotels:

●*Munri*, Jalan Dato Pati, 38 rooms, M$ 52-150, Tel. 782399.

●*Kobaru*, Jalan Doktor, 35 rooms, M$ 60-200.

●Closer to the Istana, at Merkada Place is the *Aman*, 236C Jalan Tengku, 20 rooms, M$ 18-20, large DR 26-49 with shower, Tel. 743049.

●Next door is the expensive *Indah*, 44 rooms M$ 48-80, Tel. 785081.

●The best place in town is the *Perdana*, Jalan Mahmud, 136 rooms, M$ 65-400, Tel. 785000.

There are a few places on the *"Beach of Passionate Love"* or *Pantai Cinta Berahi*, famous for its name, but nothing special really.

●*Long House Beach Motel*, 19 rooms, M$ 20-40, Tel. 740090.

●*Pantai Cinta Berahi Resort*, 21 rooms, M$ 55-60, Tel. 781307.

What to See

Malaysians who died in the First World War are honored in **Merdeka Square**, in the center of town. The nationalist, Tok Jangut was hanged here by the British. To the north is the **State Mosque**, finished in 1926 after ten years of construction.

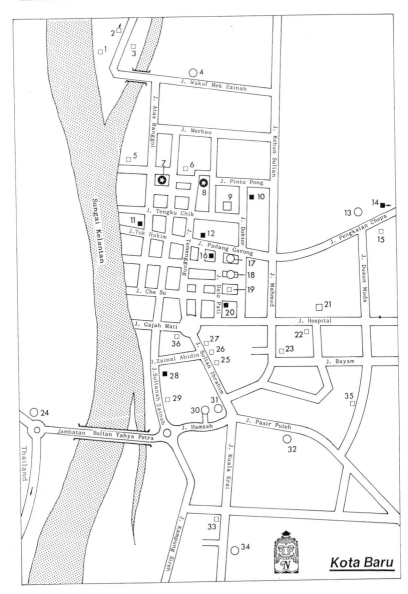

Kota Baru

1   Kite Maker
2   to Cinta Berahi Beach
3   Batik and Songket Center
4   Buses to the Beach (nos. 10, 28)
5   Handicraft Center
6   Museum
7   Merdeka Square
8   Istana Balai Besar
9   Central Market
10 Town Guest House
11 New Bali Hotel
12 New Tokyo Hotel
13 Buses to the Airport (nos. 4, 8)
14 Mummy's Hitec Hostel,
    Rainbow House,
    Traveler's Hostel,
    Thai Consulate
15 Traditional Woodworking
16 Ah Chiew Hotel
    Mee Ching Hotel
17 City Bus Terminal
18 Taxi Stand
19 Kobaru Hotel
20 Murni Hotel
21 Hospital
22 Stadium
23 Food Stalls
24 Buses to Train Station (no. 19),
    Wat Photivihan, Wakaf Baru.
25 Post Office
26 Police
27 Tourist Information
28 Rebana House
29 Silversmiths
30 Long Distance Bus Station
31 Long Distance Bus Station
32 MARA Bus Station
33 Batik Factory
34 No. 5 bus to Kuala Kerai
35 Immigration

To the east is the *Istana Balai Besar Palace*, built in 1844. It is still used during important occasions. You can visit the throne room and audience halls, which have attractive wood carvings. In front of the palace are some food stalls offering satay, noodles, and *ayaam percik* spicy grilled chicken, among other dishes.

The *State Museum* in the Istana Jahar is worth visiting. The collection includes archaeological finds, drums, gongs, silverwork, shadow puppets, furniture and kites. Open daily, from 10:;00-18:00, except Wednesdays.

A bit further to the east is the *market*, where handicrafts are sold along with fruit and vegetables. Along the river, southeast of Merdeka Square, are some *floating bamboo houses*.

You can catch a glimpse of Malay culture in the Gelanggang Seni, the *Kelantan Cultural Center*. There are . demonstrations here every Wednesday and Saturday from March to October (except during Ramadan) from 15:30-17:30. There is kite flying *wau* (only Saturdays), self-defense *silat*, drumming *rebana ubi* (Saturdays) or *kertok* (Wednesdays) and top spinning *gasing*. Wednesday evening from 21:00-24:00, there are dances *tarian tradisi* and shadow puppet *wayang kulit* shows. Sometimes, they do the two-hour dance drama, the Mak Yong. The evening programs vary.

There are also a number of festivals here promoting traditional activities like kite flying, drumming, top spinning and bird calling contests.

●For information contact the *Tourist Information Center*, Jalan Ibrahim (Saturday-Wednesday: 8:30-16:30; Thursday: 8:30-13:15; closed Fridays).

Shopping

Kota Baru is renowned as a center for Malay handicrafts and there are a number of **work shops** within the city. Here are a few things to look for when shopping:

•**Silver:** Look either for filigree jewelry or hammered silver bowls, plates, etc. A good place to start is Jalan Sultanah Zainab in Kampong Sireh. Also try Kampong Morak 9 km outside of Kota Baru, and Kampong Badang in the Handicraft Center, 10 km from Kota Baru on the way to Pantai Cinta Berahi.

•**Batik:** Kubor Kuda in Kota Baru west of the cultural center; Semasa Batik in Kampong Puteh 3 km from Kota Baru; Kampong Penambang 3.2 km from Kota Baru on the road to the beach; Kampong Badang (see the sectionon Silver).

•**Songket:** Kampong Penambang, (see the section on Batik).

•**Bamboo Goods:** The main market, Pasar Besar.

Food

There are plenty of **food stalls** in Merdeka Square as well as in the square between the bus station and the market. Try *nasi dagang* or curry and rice, *ayam percik*, grilled chikken, *laksa*, noodles in spicy soup, and *shish kebab*.

Beaches

•**Pantai Cinta Berahi** is the beach resort of Kota Baru. It's nothing special, but worth the trip for the handicrafts sold here. Take bus 10 for 60 *sen*. For accommodation, see above.

•**Pantai Dasar Sabak**, 10 km from Kota Baru, offers a beach and a fishing village with beautifully painted boats. The Japanese landed here in 1941 with bicycles. Take bus 9.

•**Pantai Irama** is typical of east coast beaches. 25 km from Kota Baru, it is a favorite for camping and picnics.

•**Pantai Bisikan Bayu**, 58 km from Kota Baru in Dalam Ru, is good for swimming, snorkeling and fishing.

•**Pantai Kuda** is 25 km to the northwest, near the Thai border.

Excursions

Kuala Besar is a fishing village at the mouth of Kelantan River.

Wat Photivihan, a Thai temple opened in 1980, has the largest reclining Buddha image in Southeast Asia at 40 m-long and 11 m-high. It is in Kampong Jambu. Take bus 19 or 27 going to Tumpat and get off at Cabang Empat Took Mengah, a little over 2 km from the temple.

In **Tumpat**, the endpoint of the railway, you can rent a boat for a trip up the Kelantan River for M$ 30 per hour. On **Pulau Jong**, in the river delta, there is a traditional boat-building industry. They have boat races in honor of the Sultan's birthday (March 30-April 1).

Masjid Kampong Laut is the oldest mosque in Malaysia built out of wood. It is 300 years old. It has been moved from its original location on the riverbank to Kampong Nilam Puri, 10 km south of Kota Baru, for fear it would be destroyed by flooding. It is a replica of the Javanese mosque in Demak.

On the way to the *Thai border* at Rantau Panjang / Sungai Golok you can check out the *market* at Pasir Mas. It is just past the Sultan Yahya Bridge, the longest bridge on the east coast. Take bus 6 for M$ 1.00 . If you are crossing the border, check out the active river traffic. There are lots of shops and hotels welcoming Malaysian tourists on the other side.

There is also the *Jeram Pasu Waterfall* in the area 39 km south of

Kota Baru, a bit southwest of the road to Kuala Terengganu, in Distrikt Pair Puteh.

If you have your own car, you can drive through the jungle on the new road to *Gua Musang*. Then drive further south to *Merapoh*, where there are dramatic limestone outcroppings. For information on driving, call Mars Kelantan International Travel, Tel. 744737. There is a hotel in Gua Mesang:
●*Kesedar Inn*, 21 rooms, M$ 25-42.

The Tourist Office offers *three interesting excursions*, unfortunately in conjunction with the Hotel Perdana, and therefore needlessly expensive:

a) *Be a Villager or a Dancer:* Live for three days and two nights with a Malay family of artists or craftsmen. For example, kite makers, puppet makers, silversmiths, top makers, potters, batik makers, or dance teachers. 8 families participated in 1988. For a minimum of 2 persons it is M$ 160 a person, and children under 12 are free.

b) ›*River Safari & Jungle Trekking:* A day-long boat trip, including jungle walking, a visit to a waterfall and a pottery workshop, for M$ 60 including lunch, and children under 12 free.

c) *African Queen Tours:* A day-long boat trip for M$ 80 including lunch, with children under 12 free, for a minimum of 6 persons.

●For *information and bookings*, contact: Tourist Information Center,

Jalan Sultan Ibrahim, Tel. 09-785534 / 783543 or Hotel Perdana, Tel. 785000.

Further Travel

Flights with MAS:
Sultan Ismail Petr Airport is 10 km east of the city. The MAS Office is on Jalan Padang Garong at the Hotel Kesina Baru, Tel. 743144.
●*Kuala Lumpur* – M$ 86
●*Penang* – M$ 72
●*Alor Setar* – M$ 59; all daily connections.

Taxis:
●*Kuala Lumpur* – M$ 40.
●*Kuala Terengganu* – M$ 10.
●*Kuantan* – M$ 25.
●*Johor Baru* – M$ 46.
    For further information contact the Malay Drivers' Association, Jalan Dato Pati, Tel. 785624.

Buses:
●*Kuala Lumpur* – M$ 26.
●*Kuala Terengganu* – M$ 5.70.
●*Kuantan* – M$ 15.
●*Johor Baru* – M$ 28.
●*Malacca* – M$ 25.
●*Butterworth* – M$ 18.
Bus Stations: *Jalan Hamzah* for long distance buses. *Langgar Bus Station*, Jalan Pasir Puteh (SKMK) and Jalan Pendek (Local).

Trains from Wakaf Baru:
    to **Kuala Lipis** leaves at 6:42, to **Gemas** leaves at 10:58, to **Gua Musang** leaves at 13:57

Kuala Terengganu

This is the capital of the Sultanate of Terengganu. In contrast to Kuantan and Kota Baru, it is much smaller and has an almost village-like character. The state population of 200,000 contains the highest percentage of Malays of any state.

    The oil boom has been responsible for the construction of some modern buildings and a few big supermarkets which seem oddly out of place. Most of the land speculation has taken place to the south of the city though, and hasn't affected it too much.

    Of the three state capitals on the east coast, I find Kuala Terengganu the most interesting. There are rows of houses on stilts over the wide, sandy Terengganu River. There is a nearby island, Pulau Duyong and some attractive hills on the western edge of town. A *kampong*, Kampong Dalam Kota, in the middle of the city and a big market. There are also some old stately villas in a mixed European and Asian style.

    Kuala Terengganu is 170 km south of Kota Baru and 209 km north of Kuantan. Until the 1930's, there were no roads at all in the state. The oil boom necessitated the construction of a highway running the length of the east coast. It goes inland north of Kuala Terengganu and is thus not particularly interesting. To the south, it runs right along the coast, offering great views of the ocean and coconut-shaded kampongs.

Accommodation

Near the bus station there are some cheap, but pretty seedy hotels. Look carefully before you decide on one.

●*Rex*, Jalan Masjid Abidin, has relatively clean double rooms with a fan and a bathroom for M$ 15. There is a restaurant next door.

●*Sea View*, 18 rooms, M$ 16-26, Tel. 09-621911.

On the other side of the bus station, there are more hotels on Jalan Banggol:

●*Mali*, 78 Jalan Banggol, 15 rooms, M$ 10 / 18 (no shower), very simple. Tel. 623278.

●*City*, 97 / 99 Jalan Banggol, 33 rooms, M$ 12, 20, 30, with shower, Tel. 621481.

●*Golden City*, 101 / 103 Jalan Banggol, 18 rooms, M$ 12-20, with shower, Tel. 621777;

●*Bunga Raya*, 105 / 111 Jalan Banggol, 38 rooms, M$ 16-30, with shower, Tel. 621166.

There are some better hotels on Jalan Paya Bunga / Sultan Ismail:

●*Sri Hoover*, 49 Jalan Paya Bunga, 60 rooms, SR M$ 32-54, DR M$ 35-62, Suites M$ 80, all rooms with A / C, bathroom, clean and well-cared for. Tel. 633833.

●*Warisan*, 55 Jalan Paya Bunga, 36 rooms, M$ 33-58, A / C, shower, almost as good as Sri Hoover. Tel. 622688.

●*Meriah*, 67 Jalan Paya Bunga, 41 rooms, M$ 18-32, A / C, shower, the outside could use some renovation, but it offers a lot for the money.

●*Sri Terengganu*, 120A / B Jalan Paya Bunga, 20 rooms, M$ 20-48, A / C, shower, Tel. 634622.

●There is a *hostel* at 35 Jalan Sultan Zainal Abidin. Rooms are M$ 12, dorm beds, M$ 7, Tel. 635766.

●On Bukit Pak Apil, there is a luxurious motel with a good view, the *Motel Desa*, 20 rooms, M$ 90-100, Tel. 623033.

●The best place in town is on Batu Buruk Beach, the *Pantai Primula*, 173 rooms, M$ 115-800, offering watersports, tennis, and squash. Tel. 622100.

Pulau Duyong Besar

Some travelers completely forgo Kuala Terengganu proper and head off for the island *Pulau Duyong Besar*. To get there, take a ferry from the pier at the end of Jalan Sultan Ismail for 30 *sen*. There is a village there renowned for its boatmaking. A few travelers have settled here semi-permanently to study the art.

From the boats, take a left on the street to get to *Awi's Rumah Kuning* or Yellow House. Awi has 14-20 beds for M$ 5.00. The house is right on the river, next to a boat-maker. Coffee and tea are free, but no food is served.

The island is only 1.7 km long and less than 700 m wide. It's a pleasant walk around the island. Awi organizes boat trips up the river and to other islands.

Even if you are not going to stay here, I found the island very interesting, though the *kampong* itself was very dirty.

What to See

Aside from the trip to the island, there are a few things in the city that are worth seeing. There are some hundred year-old *Chinese shop houses* on Jalan Bandar, which are on stilts above the water. They are even more picturesque when viewed from the water.

You can take a boat to *Seberang Takir*, on the other side of the river mouth, for a view of the city and the ocean. Dried fish and *krupuk* are made here.

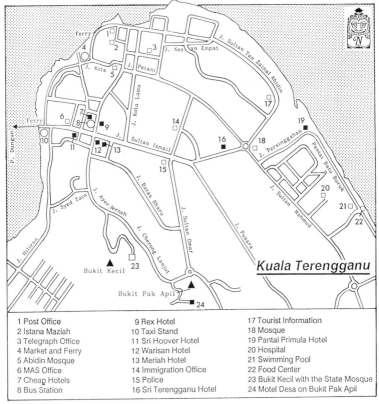

Kuala Terengganu

1 Post Office	9 Rex Hotel	17 Tourist Information
2 Istana Maziah	10 Taxi Stand	18 Mosque
3 Telegraph Office	11 Sri Hoover Hotel	19 Pantai Primula Hotel
4 Market and Ferry	12 Warisan Hotel	20 Hospital
5 Abidin Mosque	13 Meriah Hotel	21 Swimming Pool
6 MAS Office	14 Immigration Office	22 Food Center
7 Cheap Hotels	15 Police	23 Bukit Kecil with the State Mosque
8 Bus Station	16 Sri Terengganu Hotel	24 Motel Desa on Bukit Pak Apil

A little further along Jalan Bandar is the fresh market, **Pasar Besar**, where you can also buy local handicrafts.

Further still and you come to the **Istana Maziah**, built in 1894, a palace used for official receptions. It is a nice combination of European and Malay architecture. The old palace was burned to the ground along with 1500 houses in a great fire in 1882.

The sultan resides in a modern palace, the **Istana Badariah**, outside of the city, left on the way to Dungun. It has a private golf course. Interestingly almost all sultans are avid golfers.

The state mosque, **Masjid Abidin**, is right around the corner from the old palace on Jalan Masjid Abidin. It is modeled on the national mosque in Kuala Lumpur.

Kampong Dalam Kota, the village-in-the-city, lies somewhat to the east. There are a lot of attractive Malay houses here.

The government offices, including *immigration*, are located in Wisma Darul Iman on Jalan Sultan Omar.

There is a *Swimming Pool Complex* on the beach at Pantai Batu Buruk, open daily from 9:00 to 19:30, admission M$ 1 during the week and M$ 1.50 on weekends, Tel. 09-621044. It's next to the Taman Selera Food Center.

The *State Museum* is on Bukit Kecil, south of the center of town. Jalan Ayer Jerneh goes up the hill. There is a collection of historical relics, including bicycles that the Japanese used with great success in their invasion of the Peninsula.

Further to the south is the unmistakable *Bukit Besar* with a telecommunications station on top. There is a fantastic view from on top. You can see all the way to Kapas Island over the Terengganu River. There is a small road that leads to the top. It is a long walk from the center of the city.

●*Information:* TDC, East Coast Region Office, 2243 Wisma MCIS, Jalan Sultan Zainal Abidin, Tel. 09-621433 / 893.

Shopping

East Coast Specialties: Batik, brocade or *songket*, mats, baskets, and other souvenirs are sold in Pasar Besar and in the Handicraft Center in Rusila, some 10 km outside of Kuala Terengganu on the road to Marang. The Handicraft Center has demonstrations of techniques.

In Chendering, 6 km out of town before the Handicraft Center, you can watch *silk weaving* in the Suterasemai Center.

Some 5 km upstream in Kampong Pulau Rusa, you can see *songket* and *batik* being made.

There is a good handicraft shop, Usaha Desa, on Jalan Sultan Ismail.

Food

There are a couple of supermarkets at the beginning of Jalan Sultan Ismail. The main *hawker centers* are parallel to Jalan Bandar and opposite the bus station.

There is a *Malay food center* opposite the old Istana. The Taman Selera Food Center is very popular, open from 19:00 to midnight. Good restaurants are as follows:
Malay:
●*Buyong*, Jalan Kota Lama.
●*Zainuddin*, Jalan Tok Lam.
●*Nara*, Jalan Kamaruddin.
●*Istiqlal* and *Mali*, Jalan Banggol.
●*Rumah Cik Wan*, Jalan Sultan Zainal Abidin.
Chinese:
●*Good Luck*, Jalan Engku Sar.
●*Lee Kee* and *Kui Ping*, Jalan Engku Sar.
Indian:
●*Taufik*, Jalan Masjid.
●*Dewi*, Jalan Kampong Dalam.

Island Excursions

Kuala Terengganu is a good starting point for trips to *Pulau Redang* and *Pulau Perhentian*. The second can be reached faster from Besut.

Pulau Redang

Take a boat from the K.T.Jetty or from the Chendering Fisheries Complex for the 50 km trip (2 1 / 2 hours) to the island. For M$ 200, you can rent your own boat for up to 12 passengers.

The boat comes into Kampong Pulau Redang, the main settlement

on the archipelago, which, aside from Redang, includes Pinang, Ling, Ekor Tebu, Paku Besar, Paku Kecil, Kerengga Besar, Kerengga Kecil and Lima Islands.

The town consists of about 200 houses on stilts. There is a school, a clinic, a post office, a mosque and a police station. There are also stores and restaurants. 81% of the population is involved with fishing. A handful, unfortunately, collect giant turtles and birds' nests from hills along the ocean. There is also some agriculture, and goats and sheep are raised.

You can see coral formations underneath the boardwalk here. Redang is a protected marine area.

The island is a great place for snorkeling and diving. The coral reef, which has both hard and soft coral, begins right off the shore. There are sea anemones, barracudas, manta rays, marlins, and various other sea life.

The best place to swim is Teluk Dalam Bay, which has crystal-clear water and fine sand.

For a change of pace, you can take some good jungle walks. There are sea eagles, monkeys, birds of prey, etc. Giant turtles lay their eggs on the beach.

The best place to sleep is in tents. There are a number of public tent sites, which usually have fresh water. But they are often overrun with day tourists and large groups. It is better to find a private site at one of the many *kampongs* around the island.

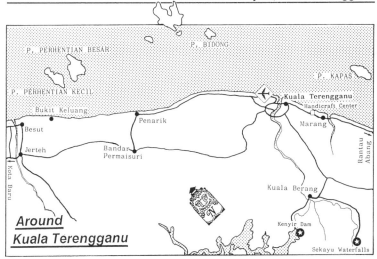

Around Kuala Terengganu

Pulau Bidong

If you were wondering why this 500 acre island, between Pulau Redang and Kuala Terengganu, has not been developed for tourism, here is the answer. Since 1978, it has been the holding center for all **Vietnamese Boat People** who have come to Malaysia. Aside from a transit camp for 5000 people in Sungei Besi, near Kuala Lumpur, this island is the only place in the country where refugees are permitted to live.

The camp is administered by the United Nations High Commission for Refugees (UNHCR). Its population of around 45,000 is waiting for permission to emigrate to a third country, usually the U.S., France, Canada or Australia. Almost 220,000 people have gone through this camp. But it is becoming more difficult for Boat People to be accepted. Some 1000-2000 refugees, mostly older, uneducated and / or handicapped people, have been waiting seven years or more. There are educational programs in languages, carpentry, auto mechanics, laboring, and typing. These programs are responsible for the very high rate of resettlement out of Bidong, but there is constant talk of closing the camp.

Malaysia has expressed concern that keeping the campopen has attracted people who would not otherwise have left Vietnam or who could have left through the Orderly Departure Program. Other countries in the area, most notably Thailand and Hong Kong, have been grappling with similar problems.

Pulau Perhentian

There is a little island, Perhentian Kecil, and a big one, Perhentian

Besar. The islands are 21 km from Besut. There are many walking trails on the larger island. The boat from Besut costs M$ 15 per passenger, or M$ 10 per passenger if there are more than 10. You can also rent boats by the day. The trip takes 2 hours from Besut's Fisheries Complex. You can also get there from Kuala Terengganu.

Unlike Redang, there is real accommodation on Perhentian: bungalows and a **Rest House** for M$ 12.00. For reservations, contact the District Office, Kampong Raja / Besut, Tel. 09-976328. There is also a man named Hashem who rents private bungalows for around M$ 5.00.

Like Redang, Perhentian is a protected marine area. There is a lot of attractive coral and all kinds of interesting underwater life, including giant turtles and sharks. There is food available in the *kampong* on Perhentian Kecil.

Other Excursions

Dendong Beach Park,

the main resort of Besut is to the south, at the base of Bukit Kluang. You can reach the beach with a car. At low tide, you can walk to two more beaches. There are changing rooms, and food and drinks are available.

There are another couple of **good beaches** between Besut and the Sultan Mahmut Airport in Kuala Terengganu. Penarik Ru Sepuluh Beach and Merang Beach (not to be confused with Marang to the south). You can see **Bidong Island** from the beach.

Kenyir Dam

is the largest dam and dammed lake in Malaysia. First go to Kuala Brang, by bus it is M$ 1.90, and by taxi, M$ 3.00, then turn right to the 155 m-high dam. Four turbines generate 400 megawatts and it took

9 years to build. Tourism is just being added as an afterthought. Boat rides, fishing, waterskiing, visits to Orang Asli villages, and lakeside accommodation are all being planned.

From Kuala Brang, there are buses that go the 16 km to the **Sekayu Waterfall**, a fine set of cascades. Nearby are about 8 km of jungle paths. There are bungalows for M$ 35 and dormitory beds available here. The last bus leaves to go back to Kuala Terengganu at 19:00. Park admission is M$ 1.00.

Further Travel

Flights:
MAS flies from the Sultan Mahmut Airport, 18 km away, to:
- **Johor Baru** – M$ 163.
- **Kuala Lumpur** – M$ 86.
- **Penang** – M$ 80.
- **Kerteh** – M$ 40.

Contact the **MAS Office**, Wisma Maju, Jalan Bunga Raya, Tel. 09-622266 / 621415.

Taxis:
To the airport is M$ 15 from hotels and M$ 12 from the taxi stand. It is M$ 20 to Sekayu. Tours around the city are M$ 5, Tel. 621581.

Buses:
- **Kuala Lumpur** – M$ 17, M$ 20 with A / C.
- **Butterworth** – M$ 21, M$ 23 A / C.
- **Kota Baru** – M$ 6, M$ 7 A / C.
- **Kuantan** – M$ 7, M$ 8 A / C.
- **Johor Baru** – M$ 18, M$ 22 A / C.
- **Singapore** – M$ 23, A / C only.

Buses leave from the bus station on Jalan Masjid Abidin. To get to **Besut**, take a bus from Kuala Terengganu to Jerteh for M$ 2.70, then a bus or taxi to Besut. There is a rest house in Kampong Raja on the Besut River.

Marang

An idyllic fishing village at the mouth of the Marang River, slowly waking up to tourism. It is located 20 km south of Kuala Terengganu, 40 km north of Rantau Abang or 60 km north of Dungun.

Marang has good beaches, and offers snorkeling off **Kapas Island** and the chance to experience life in a Malay *kampong*.

Getting around is easy. Just wait at the nearest bus stop for the next bus going the direction you want to go.

Accommodation

● Coming from Kuala Terengganu, the first travelers' place you get to is **Ibi's Guesthouse**. If you come on a bus, you can get off at the Caltex station to your left. If the bus is only going as far as Marang, get off behind the market. Everyone knows Karmal Ibi, the proprietor. The guest house, in Kampong Paya, has three bungalows for M$ 13, and 4 rooms for M$ 10; dorm beds cost M$ 4. Coffee and tea are free. There is a boat you can rent to go to Kapas Island. The palm lined beach is accessible by way of a wooden bridge.

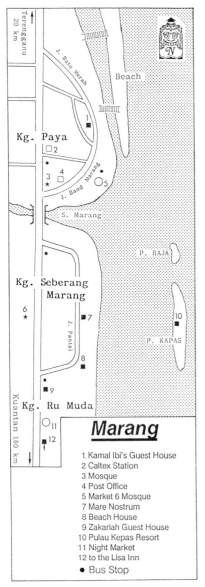

Kg. Paya

Kg. Seberang
Marang

Kg. Ru Muda

Marang

1. Kamal Ibi's Guest House
2. Caltex Station
3. Mosque
4. Post Office
5. Market 6 Mosque
7. Mare Nostrum
8. Beach House
9. Zakariah Guest House
10. Pulau Kepas Resort
11. Night Market
12. to the Lisa Inn
● Bus Stop

This side of the river, known as **Seberang Marang**, offers a good view of the fishing boats on the other bank.

●A few hundred meters to the south, over the bridge, Jalan Pantai turns off to the left. Here there is a sign that points to **Mare Nostrum**, a guest house run by a Swiss, Willy Schaer. It is a nice place, but somewhat more expensive than budget travelers might be prepared for. There are huts, M$ 10 with a single bed and M$ 20 with a double bed. Single rooms are M$ 20, double rooms are M$ 40. The best place to stay is in the main house, which he will rent out entirely for M$ 150 or M$ 40-50 a room. There are good views from here. Food is available with new dishes every day, fresh juices, shakes, and beer. There is also a well-stocked library (not just books that have been left behind).

Boat fare to Kapas Island 6 km away is M$ 15.00. Willy also has snorkeling gear for his guests. 313 Jalan Pantai, Seberang Marang, 21600 Marang, Tel. 09-682417.

●The **Beach House** is next door. It is officially part of Kampong Ru Muda, Tel. 682403. The price of the rooms varies, but the cheapest is M$ 10 for a single room. There are also bungalows for 2 people for M$ 40, no A / C and larger ones for M$ 120 for a five-person bungalow, with A / C. The price is a little high for what you get. Dinner is served here, but is also quite expensive. Haji Sulaiman's Beach House is a favorite with Singaporean tourists.

●On the main road, 2 km south of the bridge, in Kampong Ru Mada, is **Zakaria Guest House**, Tel. 692329. It is on the inexpensive side. The cost is M$ 5 a person, for shared bathrooms, M$ 2 for breakfast, M$ 3 for other dishes. The place is a bit grimy and the location is noisy. But the travelers I met here all seemed to like it. To get there from Kuala Terengganu, take a bus going to Ru Muda or Dungun for M$ 1.00. Get off at the sign for Zakaria Guest House. They have some good boat trips here to various islands, upriver on the Marang, and to Rantau Abang.

●Further south, in the next municipality,

240

Pulau Kerengga, is the **Liza Inn**, Tel. 632989, with rooms for M$ 10-60, and a restaurant. A good place.

Excursions

Kampong Ru Muda,

as you can tell by looking around the shops lining the main street, is well known for *krupuk*, a kind of gray shrimp toast, and dried fish.

The people of Marang tend to support the Islamic PAS, the opposition party to UMNO, as they are strict, orthodox Muslims. Unbelievers (meaning tourists and westerners) are viewed with some suspicion, but you willnot run into any real problems. Make sure you follow accepted codes of behavior.

There is a **night market** on weekends.

Trip to Kapas Island

Boats to Kapas are almost all M$ 15.00. If you are so inclined, you can arrange to have the boat show you around other islands as well, like **Rajah Island**, which belongs to the Sultan of Terengganu, and boasts remarkable coral formations. The underwater life here is spectacular, some say better than Tioman.

Pulau Kapas Resort , has rooms for M$ 20, M$ 28 with bathroom, breakfast for M$ 2.80 and lunch or dinner for M$ 6. It has tough supply problems. Tel. Liza Inn 632989.

Further Travel

Flights with MAS:
- **Kuala Lumpur** – M$ 80
- **Penang** – M$ 80
- **Johor Baru** – M$ 132

Taxis:
- **Kota Baru** – M$ 10
- **Kuantan** – M$ 17

Buses:
- **Kota Baru** – M$ 5.70
- **Kuantan** – M$ 7.00
- **Kuala Lumpur** – M$ 20

Rantau Abang

20 km north of Dungun and 60 km south of Kuala Terengganu, Rantau Abang is a *kampong* stretched out along the road. Its fame is due to the hundreds of **leatherback turtles** that come to lay their eggs here each year. The 19 km stretch of beach is home to these giants between February and October, but especially between June and August.

Usually, it is pretty easy to find these unusual sea creatures, but there are fewer than there used to be, primarily a result of tourism.

Accommodation

You can take a bus from Kuala Terengganu or Dungun directly to Rantau Abang or to either the Merantau Inn or the Tanjung Jara Beach Hotel for M$ 3.60 from Kuala Terengganu, and for around M$ 1.00 from Kuala Dungun.
- There is one very successful, though overpriced, place to stay in town, the **Tanjung Jara**. It has an annex right near the Rantau Abang Visitor Center, with 10 simple, clean and ridiculously overpriced bungalows (M$ 103.50 each). It is less than 700 meters north of the Visitor Center, where you can find out more about the giant turtles.

241

•The rest of the places to stay are all very simple, even primitive, without much atmosphere, very like the bungalows at Cherating. Most people only come for one night, hoping to see the turtles, so the bungalow operations do not have to compete against each other too much.

People sit out on the beach during the evening, eating, drinking, swimming perhaps, and waiting....

•*Ismail's Beach Resort*, rooms for M$ 10 (double bed, no shower), M$ 30 (twin beds and a bathroom), M$ 50 (twin bed, double bed, fan, bathroom) and M$ 60 (two double beds). Dorm beds are M$ 4-5. There is a restaurant with good food and music. The huts are a bit shabby on the outside, but OK inside.

•*Awang's* has rooms for M$ 10 / 16 / 30, 5 bungalows (M$ 50, two or three beds, bathroom) and a restaurant (Nasi Goreng M$ 1.60; juices M$ 1.00).

•*Sany* is very similar.

•Up one price category: **Merantau Inn**, between Rantau Abang and Tanjung Jara. Bungalows cost M$ 35 and M$ 38.50 for 2 beds and a bathroom (extra beds are M$ 10), or M$ 60 and M$ 71 for larger beds in a better room. Nice atmosphere, good service. The quality of the food in the restaurant was inconsistent. Tel. 09-841131).

Food

There are a few places on the main street where the road turns off towards the beach-front.

No. 1 has toast, cheese omelettes, fried eggs, French fries, and juices.

No. 3 has *roti canai* (with or without an egg), good *roti canai pisang* (with banana), and *nasi goreng*.

No. 5 has *nasi* or *sayur* (vegetable) *goreng*, and other dishes.

400 meters north of the information center, on the left, is the **Umu Restaurant** with grilled fish, and fish and chips.

Our turtle experience

was somewhat atypical. The guides promised they would come and get us if any turtles were spotted, no matter what time it was. The bungalow operators have a kind of alarm system worked out using spotters and motorcycles so that they can keep each other informed about turtle sightings. This greatly increases the chance of seeing one. When one first comes onto land and starts to lay its eggs, undisturbed by noise or flashlights, the spotters run and tell the other bungalow operators who then bring their guests.

I did not want to go to sleep. Around 3:00 a.m., I looked at my watch and wondered if they had they forgotten us. I decided it was time for my daily jog, and set off for Rantau Abang. I met another disappointed traveler in a restaurant there and he confirmed that no turtles had been seen all night. Discouraged, I jogged back and went to bed. I stirred briefly around 6:00. It was light out, so there was no hope now. At 7:00 there was a knock on the door: "Turtle!"

We quickly got dressed and into the van which took us the 1 kilometer to the site. By the time we got there, the eggs had already been lain (a few were already put aside by the spotters) and the turtle was on its way back to the water. Some spotters tried to hold onto the turtle, to give us more of a chance to look, but they were dragged in along with it. There were only a dozen or so spectators instead of the hundreds that are sometimes present, so things worked out well for us.

Hawksbill

Leatherback Turtles

(Dermochelys coriacea),
Penyu Belimbing in Malay.

In this species, the largest of the sea turtles, the legs of the leatherback have developed into fins. They cover enormous distances under water. Marked turtles that have been sighted in Rantau Abang have also been sighted as far away as Borneo, the Philippines, and southern Japan.

Leatherbacks are an average of 1.55 meters long and 350 kg. The largest ever measured was almost 1.80 meters long and weighed 590 kg. As their name implies, they have an elastic, leather-like shell with seven lengthwise ribs. Their fins have no claws.

There are only a few places in the world where the females come on land. They favor beaches in French Guyana, Surinam, Costa Rica, Mexico, Irian Jaya and Tonga. No one is really sure why they like coming to Rantau Abang – or liked coming, to be more precise; in the 1950's, more than 10,000 came every year, now the figure is around 600. They seem to like the coarse sand here and there is not much of a slope.

Between February and October, but especially during July and August, female turtles come ashore on the 19 km stretch of beach to **lay their eggs**. They do this 5 to 9 times a season at intervals of 9 to 14 days, each time laying from 50-140, 50 to 55 mm soft-shelled eggs.

When the turtle is not disturbed by noise, lights oranything else, she will start to dig a nest with all four fins. Then she digs a deeper, up to 60 cm, trench with her hind fins, to lay the eggs into. Once the turtle begins laying her eggs, she will not stop, even if she is killed. But if she is disturbed, she may never come back to Rantau Abang. After a few hours, the whole thing is over, and the turtle covers her tracks and returns to the sea.

Egg collectors, licensed by the State Fisheries Department and identified by their badges, take the eggs and place them in fenced-in breeding areas. They carefully note the number of eggs and their age. Traditionally the eggs were eaten by local people. They are also sought after for their power as an aphrodisiac. Today, trading in sea turtle eggs is illegal, at least, officially.

After about 56 days, the eggs hatch, and out come grayish baby turtles with white stripes on their backs. When hatched, they are only around 5 or 6 cm long. As soon as they can move, they go to the ocean as quickly as possible. They are in great danger from the start and have to avoid both air and water-borne predators. Only one out of every thousand eggs is thought to produce a mature sea turtle. Now, they are brought to the water's edge, to save them from at least the initial dangers.

The official egg collectors / beach watchers and guides are allowed to collect a M$ 2.00 fee from turtle observers in their area of the beach. Watching is free near the breeding areas. Observers are only allowed in the area once the turtle has started laying her eggs.

Other Sea Turtles

The **Green Turtles** *(Chelonia mydas)*, or **Penyu Agar** in Malay at 1.05 m and 140 kg, come to Pulau Redang, Perhentian and other places along the east coast, including Chendah Beach, near Club Med at Cherating.

The **Pacific Ridley Turtle** *(Lepidochelys olivacea)*, or **Penyu Lipis** at 65 cm and 35 kg, come ashore mostly at Penarik in the north and Dungun in the south.

The **Hawksbill Turtle** *(Callagur borneonsis)*, or **Penyu Sisik** at 80 cm and 60 kg, is the first to come to Pulau Redang.

The **Visitor Center** is worth looking at. It is open from June-August, Fridays 8:00-12:00, Saturdays 10:00-22:00, Sundays 8:00-16:00, Mondays 8:00-18:00, closed Tuesdays, Wednesdays 8:00-16:00, Thursdays 10:00-22:00 (the weekend is on Thursday and Friday in Terengganu). During the rest of the year, it is open on Sundays, Mondays and Wednesdays 8:00-16:00, Thursdays 8:00-12:45, and closed Fridays and Tuesdays.

There are life-sized models of giant turtles andsome good explanations of their behavior. There is a video of the entire egg laying process. You can also buy models of freshly hatched turtles.

Behavior

Though the following rules are often broken by official watchers, observers must follow them:
● No campfires (light disturbs the turtles).
● Do not shine flashlights on the beach.
● No music or loud noise.
● Do not stand near turtles laying eggs.
● Do not shine lights in their eyes.
● Do not touch the turtles for any reason.
● Do not throw any plastic bags on the beach (the turtles mistake them for jelly-fish, eat them and later die of asphyxiation. In short, do not do anything to disturb the turtles coming on land to lay their eggs and returning to the water.

As mentioned, sometimes local residents and even officials have very insensitive attitudes towards the turtles. It makes one wonder if the entire beach should be closed to all visitors and declared a protected marine area.

Some tourists are incensed at the treatment of the animals and have mentioned that they would not have come to Rantau Abang at all had they known what to expect.

We were lucky, as no one molested "our" turtle. At least not too much. The guide grabbed its fins and tried to get it to slow it down on its return to the water so the tourists could get in a last look.

This is a typical conflict between environmental and tourism concerns. On one hand, the turtles might be a lot better off if they had the whole beach to themselves; there also might be a lot more of them. On the other hand, seeing one of them can be a truly meaningful experience, and without that attraction, Rantau Abang would lose all of its income from tourism.

What is really needed is better training for beach watchers and guides.

Kuala Dungun — Kemaman

The 80 km beach between these two cities, the main towns in southern Terengganu, is just as good as those to the north.

Aside from a few hotels in Telok Senanjang near Kemaman, this part of the coast is completely undeveloped for tourism.

That is not to say that this is 80 km of virgin beach. On the contrary, this is the center of the big offshore oil industry which produces 200,000 barrels per day. The landscape here is being quickly destroyed. Luckily, about 40 km of the coast has been spared this development, so you can still go to the village of **Kemasik**, for example, to see something of the traditional east coast life.

Kemaman / Chukai

The two towns are usually thought of together. **Kemaman** is the capital of the district of the same name and **Chukai** is the business center.

Accommodation

●**Kintowa**, 275 Jalan Masjid, 14 rooms, M$ 11 / 25, Tel. 09-591303.
●**Terang Bulan**, 283 Jalan Masjid, 12 rooms, M$ 12-28.

●**Tong Juan**, 117 Jalan Sulaiman, 10 rooms, the cheapest place at M$ 7, Tel. 591346.
●**Furinmen** on the same street is a step up.
●**Muni Hotel**, 312 Jalan Che Teh, M$ 70-120, expensive.
●There are many more hotels to choose from.

Buses leave Kemaman regularly in all directions including Kuantan, Cherating, Kuala Dungun and Kuala Terengganu.

Kuala Dungun

80 km to the north, on the mouth of the Dungun River, is the interesting fishing town of **Kuala Dungun**.

Ore from the mines on Bukit Besi used to be shipped out of here, after it had come 28 km on the train, but those days are gone. There is very good, inexpensive **seafood** available here and there is also a big **market** at the port every morning.

Accommodation

●**Sri Dungun**, 135 Jalan Tambun, 27 rooms, M$ 16-35, Tel. 09-841881.
●**Kasanya**, 225 Jalan Tambun, 44 rooms, M$ 18-26, 30-50, Tel. 841704.
●**Mali**, 229 Jalan Tambun, 16 rooms, M$ 10-12, 18-21, Tel. 842826.
●**Sin Chew**, Jalan Besar, 14 rooms, M$ 10, 12-20, Tel. 841412.

Long-distance taxis which cost M$ 6 to KualaTerengganu, and M$ 9.50 to Kuantan park at the market.

Long-distance buses leave from out of town and there are local buses that go to the bus stop. The new East Coast Highway runs along the ocean between Kuantan and

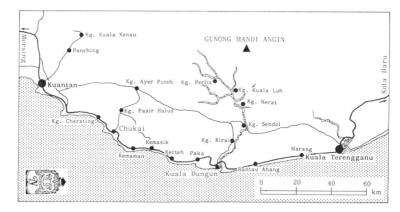

Kuala Terengganu and is a positive by-product of the oil boom. Since the construction of the highway, the old road, which runs parallel to the new one, but inland, is not used very much. It is still quite important for agriculture, however.

Excursions

Pulau Tenggol: This uninhabited island can be reached by boat in about two hours from Dungun. There are campsites with well-water.

The main beach is Teluk Air Tawar, which has clean white sand and crystal clear water, which is good for snorkeling. Around the bend to the south, there is quite a lot of under-water life 4 to 6 meters down.

Nyireh Island, 30 minutes further away, is also worth a visit.

Trips to the islands are organized by the good, but overpriced *Tanjung Jara Beach Hotel*, 13 km north of Dungun. It costs M$ 140-350, Tel. 09-841801. See the section on Rantau Abang.

Sungai Dungun: The Tanjung Jara Beach Hotel also organizes boat trips up the river. There are all sorts of possibilities with most boats leaving from Dungun or Kampong Kuala Loh.

Adventurous souls can go with a guide from the upper reaches of the Loh River over the watershed on Gunung Mandi Angin to a tributary, finally arriving in Kuala Tahan, the main town in Taman Negara. This is just one possible trip. It is expensive and takes a lot of time.

● For more information, ask Abi in the *Tanjung Jara Beach Hotel*.

Cherating

47 km north of Kuantan, in a lovely bay, is the travelers' center of Cherating. It is a good place for swimming and wind-surfing, especially in November and December during the rainy season, but sometimes it can be too rough.

246

You can get a bus here from either Kuantan or Kemaman.

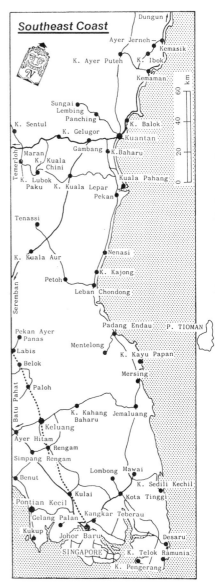

Southeast Coast

Accommodation

There are quite a few guest houses and bungalow operations:

●*Coconut Inn*, 6 fancy bungalows M$ 14, 6 huts M$ 12, 6 A-Frames M$ 5 / 10, extra beds M$ 2; BBQ from time to time. Tel. 09-503299. ●*Kampong Inn*, 15 bungalows, SR M$ 4, DR M$ 10 / 20, M$ 28 per family, very simple, graying bed linens, decent food in restaurant.

●*Mak Long Teh Guest House*, 16 rooms M$ 5, 5 bungalows M$ 10 / 15. Tel. 09-503290.

●*Mak De'Guest House*, 13 rooms M$ 5 or M$ 10 with meals, 5 bungalows M$ 10 or M$ 15 with meals, good atmosphere. Tel. 09-511316.

●*Maznah's Guest House*, 20 rooms M$ 12 or M$ 30 with meals.

●*Blue Lagoon*, 3 rooms M$ 10, 2 bungalows M$ 5.

●*Sri Cherating*, 5 rooms M$ 10, 2 bungalows M$ 15.

●*Grand Pa*, 9 bungalows M$ 10 / 15.

●*Hussain Bungalow*, 5 bungalows, 6 rooms M$ 6, very seedy.

●*Cherating Beach Village*, 6 bungalows M$ 10.

●*Cherating Mini Motel*, 12 bungalows M$ 25, with fan and mosquito net, 10 rooms M$ 20, extra person M$ 5, with bathroom and shower. All prices include breakfast. The best place on the beach, but also the most expensive.

●The other places are all very simple. Some have restaurants and most of them offer very good value for the money.

●Just to the north on *Chendor Beach* is the extensive, state-operated *Club Med*. It costs US$ 128 peak season per person, including meals and sports facilities.

For over M$ 150 a day, you can go and use the facilities during the day (8 days for M$ 1050). Of course you can walk down the beach for free and take a look at the place. At the end of the bay, near the rooms, there is a path to the club's sailboats. The path goes up a hill which offers a good view of the coastline. There is also a beach in front of the Club where turtles, though not giant ones come to lay their eggs. There is also a small, fenced-off area for the eggs.

There is another motel on the beach, which is not as attractive, but a good deal cheaper than Le Club.

Kuantan

Kuantan is both the capital of Pahang Darul Makmur and the economic center of the east coast, due to its central location. There is an airport and major roads leading to Singapore, Kuala Lumpur and Kota Baru. The sultans have traditionally lived in Pekan, 45 km to the south.

The city does not have much to offer in the way of sights or attractions. It is a clean and partly modern, but by no means hectic town, located right on the Kuantan River near the ocean. Kuantan is a good place from which to explore the surrounding area. There are a lot of cheap places to stay and plenty of places to eat including the food market near the main market on the river, near the bus station.

Accommodation

There are three streets of **cheap hotels**: Jalan Besar, Teluk Sisek and Bukit Ubi:
- **Tong Nam Ah**, 98 Jalan Besar, 12 rooms, M$ 10-15, Tel. 09-521204.
- **Ting Ah**, 126 Jalan Besar, 10 rooms, M$ 10-20, Tel. 521350.
- **Baru Raya**, 134 Jalan Besar, 26 rooms, M$ 22-37, Tel. 524953.

- **New Embassy**, 50 / 2 Jalan Teluk Sisek, 18 rooms, M$ 12-26, Tel. 524277.
- **Meriah**, 144 Jalan Teluk Sisek, 12 rooms, M$ 25-35, Tel. 525433.
- **Ping Rock**, 236 Jalan Teluk Sisek, 14 rooms, SR M$ 5, DR M$ 30.
- **Annexe Resthouse**, Jalan Teluk Sisek at the end of the street, 17 rooms, M$ 17-22, Tel. 526917.
- **Kheng Heng**, 46 Jalan Bukit Ubi, 20 rooms, SR M$ 12, DR M$ 16-28.
- **New Capitol**, 55 Jalan Bukit Ubi, 12 rooms, M$ 19-26, Tel. 524222.
- **New Weng Yuen**, 63-65 Jalan Bukit Ubi, 20 rooms, SR M$ 13-15, DR M$ 22-29, Tel. 501543.
- **Ming Hen**, 22-24 Jalan Mahkota, 10 rooms, M$ 9-13, Tel. 524885.
- **Malaysia**, 25-27 Jalan Hj. Abdul Aziz, 18 rooms, M$ 14-16.
- I can also recommend the old **Asram Bendahara**, in Telok Chempedak. Under new management since 1988, it is nice and clean. Rooms are M$ 18 upstairs and M$ 14 downstairs. There is also a dormitory. It is between the Hyatt and the Merlin, about 100 meters from the beach. The full address is : Mike Foo, Asrama Bendahara, Telok Chempedak, 25-50 Kuantan, Pahang, Darulmakmur.

There are also a lot of **mid-priced** and **expensive hotels:**
- **Samudra**: M$ 70-90.
- **Champagne Emas**: M$ 40-50.
- **Suraya**: M$ 58-73.
- **Yenmita**: M$ 61-95.
- **Pacific**, 60-62 Jalan Bukit Ubi, 48 rooms, SR M$ 55-80, DR M$ 60-90, recommended.

The most expensive hotels are nearby, at the beach resort of Telok Chempedak, just north of the city:
- **Hyatt Kuantan**, 185 rooms, M$ 130-200, Tel. 525211.
- **Merlin Inn Resort**, 106 rooms, M$ 100-170, Tel. 522388.
- **Samudra Beach Motel**, 20 rooms from M$ 52.
- **Kuantan Hotel**, 22 rooms from M$ 30.

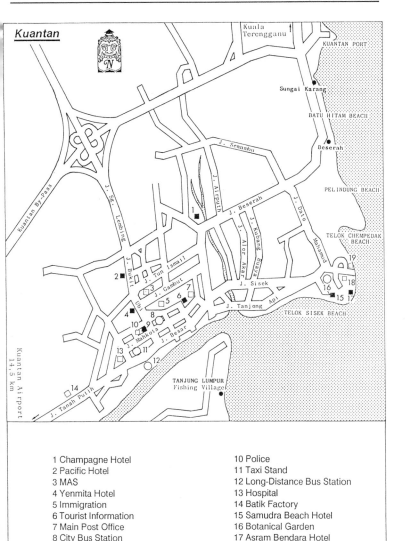

1 Champagne Hotel
2 Pacific Hotel
3 MAS
4 Yenmita Hotel
5 Immigration
6 Tourist Information
7 Main Post Office
8 City Bus Station
9 Kheng Heng Hotel

10 Police
11 Taxi Stand
12 Long-Distance Bus Station
13 Hospital
14 Batik Factory
15 Samudra Beach Hotel
16 Botanical Garden
17 Asram Bendara Hotel
18 Karyaneka Pahang

Information

●*Tourist Information Center*, Bangunan LKNP, Jalan Hj. Abdul Aziz, Kuantan, Tel. 09-512960, open Monday-Friday from 8:00-16:15, Saturday from 8:00-12:45.
●*Tourist Information Counter* in the Karyaneka Shop, Telok Chempedak, open Sundays.

Excursions / Beaches

Teluk Chempedak,

a beach 5 km away offers swimming, wind surfing, sailing, water skiing, and golf. To get there, take the 39 bus for 50 *sen*. There is also a walk through the jungle to *Pelinding Beach* and a mini zoo.

Beserah

A fishing village, 10 km north of Kuantan, which is rapidly becoming a suburb. Local handicrafts, like batik and wood carvings, are produced in the village. The main industry, like much of the east coast, is the production of *krupuk*, dried fish, *belacan* or shrimp paste and preserved fish. And of course, there is fishing. When the animal-headed fishing boats *bangau* come in, the catch is unloaded into ox-carts on the beach.

●You can stay at **Yaffar**, where they have five double rooms for M\$ 10. Look for the sign on your left as you come from Kuantan.

Pantai Pelindung, to the south, is being developed for tourism. There is a new 30 room wooden hotel being built here, powered by solar energy, with fishing, rowing and sailing facilities.

North of Beserah is *Pantai Batu Hitam* or Black Stone Beach, a good place to picnic and swim. Often, big fish swim into the shallow water and die here, thus the nickname, Suicide Beach.

Sungai Karang

Just to the north is the village of *Sungai Karang*, where products are made out of sea shells. These and other handicrafts are made in the shop, Kijang Emas. As on the rest of the east coast, there might be people spinning tops, flying kites, etc. Also interesting is the trained, coconut-picking monkey that hangs in the trees.

Tasek Chini

is 60 km west of Kuantan. It is known as the home of the Malaysian equivalent of the Loch Ness Monster, who supposedly inhabits a sunken Khmer-style city.

To get here, take a car, bus or taxi from Kuantan toMaran on the road to Kuala Lumpur, then go left to Kampong Lubok Paku or Kampong Belimbing. You can take a boat to the lake from there. It is a lot easier as part of an organized tour.

Every March, the big Panguni Uthiram Festival takes place in the *Marathandhavar Temple* on the Maran Jerantut Road toward Kuala Lipis. Ask about the exact dates in the Tourist Office.

Gunung Tapis Park

is a small jungle park with campsites, trails, rafting and fishing. Make arrangements through the Tourist Office or the Outward Bound Society. The park, which is still being developed, is 12 km north of the largest underground tin-mine in the world, Sungai Lembing, now closed. The last part of the road requires a four-wheel drive vehicle.

There are buses for M$ 1.60 and taxis that go as far as Sungai Lembing. The mine was closed in 1988. Before that, it could be visited by tourists. The Tourist Office should have information as to whether or not it may be visited now that it is closed.

The Charah Caves

are in a limestone hill, 25 km west of Kuantan. The caves contain a 10 m-long reclining Buddha built and cared for by a Thai monk. Entry is M$ 1.00. You can see the hill, Gunung Tapis on the trip to Sungai Lembing.

Pekan,

the Royal Town, has traditionally been the residence of the sultans of Pahang. It is at the mouth of the longest river on the Peninsula, the Sungai Pahang. Despite its historical importance, Pekan, 45 km south of Kuantan, is still a small town with a *kampong*-like atmosphere. However, there are a few imposing buildings. The modern palace, Istana Abu Bakar has its own polo field. There are two other palaces, Istana Permai

and Istana Leban Tunggal. There are also two mosques, Abdullah and Abu Bakar, and the Abu Bakar Museum (open daily, 9:30-17:00, except Fridays; there is information on tin mining, forestry, weapons, textiles, ceramics, and shadow puppet plays). There is also a royal gallery, Balai Rong, with objects from the rule of the sultans.

●There is a comfortable, but hidden away **Resthouse** in town, Tel. 09-421240. There is also the **Pekan Hotel**.

Further Travel

Flights with MAS:
●**Kuala Lumpur** – M$ 61
●**Johor Baru** – M$ 77
●lights a week are planned to **Tioman** with Pelangi Air – ask at the Tourist Office.
 MAS Office, Wisma Persatuan Bolasepak Pahang, 7 Jalan Gambut, Tel. 09-521218.

Taxis:
●**Kuala Dungun** – M$ 10.
●**Kuala Terengganu** – M$ 17.
●**Kota Baru** – M$ 25.
●**Kuala Lumpur** – M$ 23.
●**Temerloh** – M$ 9.
●**Jerantut** – M$ 15.
●**Kuala Lipis** – M$ 25.
●**Bentong** – M$ 14.
●**Pekan** – M$ 4.
●**Rompin** – M$ 10.
●**Mersing** – M$ 14.
●**Segamat** – M$ 15.
●Prices are per person and could vary.

Buses:
●**Kuala Terengganu** – M$ 7.
●**Kota Baru** – M$ 13.
●**Pekan** – M$ 2.20.
●**Rompin** – M$ 7.
●**Endau** – M$ 7.
●**Mersing** – M$ 10.25.

- *Johor Baru* – M$ 12 / 15 with A / C.
- *Singapore* – M$ 17 / 22 with A / C.
- *Temerloh* – M$ 4.30.
- *Jerantut* – M$ 6.40.
- *Kuala Lipis* – M$ 10.40.
- *Kuala Lumpur* – M$ 9.
- *Malacca* – M$ 10.80.
- *Butterworth/Penang* – M$ 21/25 with A/C.

Ships:
- Mini cruises on the *Mujibah* leave on Saturdays at 14:30, **to Kuching**, on to **Kota Kinabalu**, and back to Kuantan. The ship arrives back Tuesday at 12:00. At 18:00 it leaves for Singapore, arriving back in Kuantan on Saturday at 9:00.
- *Prices from Kuantan* (one-way, round trip prices are double):
- *Kuching* – M$ 160 / 235 / 350.
- *Kota Kinabalu* – M$ 265 / 380 / 550.
- *Singapore* – M$ 99 / 140 / 210.

- *Information: Feri Malaysia*, Menara Utama UMBC, Jalan Sultan Sulaiman, Kuala Lumpur, Tel. 03-2388899.

Mersing

Mersing is a bustling fishing port and a starting point for boats to many outlying islands. The best-known islands are **Pulau Tioman** and **Pulau Rawa**, both of which are regularly served by hydrofoil.

The Mersing Boat Hire Association runs the ferry operation and fishing trips.

Mersing is 134 km from Johor Baru, which costs M$ 10.00 in a taxi or M$ 5.50 on a bus.

There are also **beaches** in the area, as you might expect. There is a good one 10 km north at Kampong Kayu Papan near the island Pulau Sentindan.

From Mersing, it takes an hour by boat for M$ 15 to travel the 10 km to **Pulau Rawa**. You can stay and eat at the bungalows run by Rawa Safaris (see below). There are fine beaches with good snorkeling. The island is the private property of one of the Sultan's nephews.

All the islands around Mersing have been designated as protected marine parks including Chebeh, Tulai, Tioman, Sembilang, Seri Buat, Rawa, Babi Hujung, Babi Tengah, Babi Besar, Tinggi, Mentinggi, and Sibu. You can count on good snorkeling and diving wherever you are, except perhaps for Tioman, much of which has unfortunately been damaged or destroyed.

Accommodation

- *Tong Ah Lodging House* is the cheapest, 53 Jalan Abu Bakar.
- *Golden City*, 23 Jalan Abu Bakar.
- *Embassy*, 2 Jalan Ismail, M$ 20-30, Tel. 07-791302.
- *Mersing*, 1 Jalan Dato Timor, Tel. 791004.
- *Resthouse*, 490 Jalan Ismail, M$ 35.00, convenient, but expensive. Tel. 791101.
- *Rawa Safaris* on Rawa Island, c / o Tourist Center, M$ 30-56, Tel. 791204.

Excursions

Pulau Tioman
is the largest island in the archipelago and the most famous (see below).

Endau Rompin Park
is the largest jungle area in the southern part of the Peninsula, on the border between Johor and

252

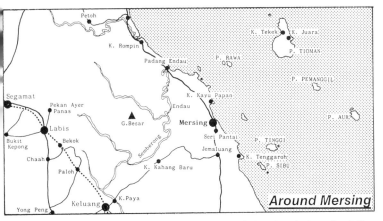

Around Mersing

Pahang. The national government has plans to make this into a second national park, but the two states would rather see the area opened up to logging. For information contact the Tourist Information Center in Mersing or Johor Baru.

●*Authorization to enter the park* is available from the State Security Council, Bangunan Sultan Ibrahim, Bukit Timbalan, Johor Baru. A boat trip up the Endau River is worthwhile, it costs M$ 120 per boat for an 8 hour trip. Boat trips with trekking are organized by Giamso Safari, 27A Jalan Abu Bakar in Mersing, Tel. 09-791636. The park is home to the 50-70 remaining Sumatran Rhinos in Malaysia.
●There is a *Resthouse* in Kuala Rompin, 12 rooms, M$ 12-25, simple rooms and good food, Tel. 09-455234.
●*Buses* to the park go from:
Endau – M$ 1.60, Nenasi – M$ 2.00, Mersing – M$ 5.00, buses also from other towns.
●*With a car*, it is possible to take off on your own route. Taking the road from Kluang to Mersing, turn off near the Kahang Police Station (about 40 km from Kluang), onto an unmarked plantation road. The road

goes north (follow the telephone lines). You will eventually come to an oil mill and to a Wildlife Department Ranger Station. Keep going and you will come to a river and the nearby Orang Asli settlement, Kampong Peta. Take note, the last stretch of road requires a four-wheel drive vehicle.

There is a good camping spot east of Gunung Janing and west of Sungai Endau around 60 km or 2 to 3 hours from Kahang.

Gunung Besar

The highest mountain in the area is *Gunung Besar* at 1036 m. You can hike up from Labis which is on the Segamat-Kluang road. For *authorization*, including a map and other information, contact the Department of Wildlife in Segamat. It takes 1-2 days for processing.

Segamat

is on the railway between Kuala Lumpur and Singapore and on the main north-south road. There are some hotels here, including some in the M$ 10-30 range. To get here, take a train, bus, or taxi for M$ 14 from Johor Baru. Segamat is also a good place to start a trip up *Gunung Ledang*.

Tioman

It is the best known island off the east coast of Malaysia, thanks to some clever marketing – "One of the ten most beautiful islands in the world" and so forth. It is also well-known as the location for the popular film version of "South Pacific".

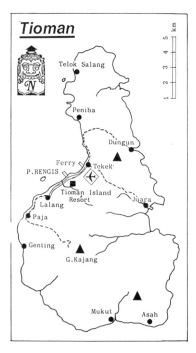

Tioman

Telok Salang
Peniba
Dungun
Ferry Tekek
P.RENGIS
Tioman Island
Resort Juara
Lalang
Paja
Genting
G.Kajang
Mukut Asah

The island has been known to sailors for around 2000 years. There is a legend that a dragon princess was on her way from China to Singapore. She stopped to rest in the calm water, and stayed there to become the island.

The island has definitely felt the strain of tourism and there are other islands with better beaches and diving. The landscape of Tioman is still beautiful though, topped by the 1038 m high Gunung Kajang.

If you get bored of swimming, snorkeling, wind-surfing and lying on the beach, there is some good hiking on the island especially over the island to Juara or the three-hour hike to Kampong Dungun.

The best places for **snorkeling** and **diving** are near Salang, where the water is calm, and off the two nearby islands, Renggis and Tulai.

Getting There

You can reach the 39 km long by 19 km wide island from Mersing with either the expensive, but fast **Merlin Hydrofoil** (M$ 30, one hour trip, departing at 12:00) or with a *local boat* for about half the money (3 to 5 hour trip).

●The **Merlin Hydrofoil** lands at the *Tioman Island Resort*, Tel. 009-445444 / 03-2305266.

●The **regular boat** lands in Kampong Tekek, on the west side of the island. There will probably be guest house agents there ready to entice you to their simple huts. Huts go for M$ 4-8 or M$ 10, including food in Tekek, Salang, Genting, Lalang, and Juara on the east side of the island. Some of the more remote bungalow operations might have boats waiting to take you out to them.

•You can *fly* directly to the island from Kuala Lumpur (MAS has daily flights) or from Singapore's Seletar Airport with Tradewinds Charter Service. **Charter flight** can be arranged from Mersing.

The best way to get to Kampong Dungun is to take a boat. This costs M$ 80 a day, which is pretty good, if you can get a dozen people together.

Fishing trips are also a possibility.

Accommodation

•*Tioman Island Resort*, rooms for M$ 75 a night or bungalows for M$ 130 a night. The hotel has restaurants and a swimming pool.
In *Kampong Tekik:*
•*Razali Guest House*, 4 rooms, M$ 6.
•*Samudra Swiss Cottage*, 6 rooms, M$ 4-10.
•*Tekik Chalet*, 15 rooms, M$ 7-17.
•*Tekik Inn*, 9 rooms, M$ 7.
•*Wan Endut Guest House*, 3 rooms, M$ 7.
•*Jumat Guest House*, 2 rooms, M$ 6-16.
•*Yahya Chalet*, 2 rooms, M$ 5.
•*Aris Chalet*, 14 rooms, M$ 6.
•*Manap Chalet*, 13 rooms, M$ 16.

In *Ayer Batang:*
•*Nazri's Place*, 13 bungalows, M$ 4-5.
•*Mokhtar Chalet*, 6 bungalows, M$ 5.
•*Hamidon Chalet*, 4 rooms, 4 bungalows, M$ 4-5.
•*Aziz House*, 4 rooms, 3 bungalows, M$ 4-5.
•*Osman Chalets*, 3 bungalows, M$ 5.
•*Zul Chalets*, 14 bungalows, M$ 5.
•*Zaid Chalets*, 5 bungalows, M$ 5.

In *Kampong Salong:*
•*Bidin Guest House*, 11 rooms, M$ 6-16.

In *Kampong Juara:*
•*Au Awang Chalet*, 3 bungalows, M$ 3-4.
•*Sunny Hussain Chalet*, 4 bungalows, M$ 5-18.

Central Malaysia

Not too long ago, this was all jungle. It is being cleared away at an alarming rate and being transformed into rubber and palm oil plantations. Most tourists take the trip across the center of the Peninsula, either to go from the west coast to the east coast or to visit Taman Negara. The destinations are described from Kuala Lumpur to the east and northeast.
•**Gerik** is listed under "West Coast."
•**Maran** is listed under "East Coast, Kuantan."

Fraser's Hill

In comparison to the Cameron Highlands, Fraser's Hill is quieter and less developed. The area was named after Louis James Fraser, an English adventurer who lived in a hut on the hill at the beginning of this century. He made his name trading tin and opium, which was legal at the time. He also ran a network of mule wagons used to transport tin.

His compatriot, Bishop Ferguson-Davie, who first ascended the hill in 1910, went up again in 1919 to search for Fraser. He had suddenly disappeared, never to be heard from again. In the same year, the area was fully explored.

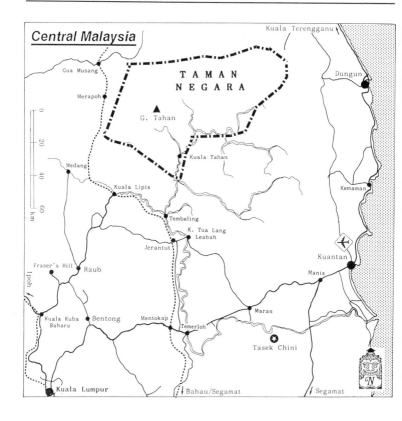

Today, next to the bungalows, chalets and a hotel, there is a golf course run by a tin-mine owner who has discovered a more profitable business. The course is a favorite of Kuala Lumpur residents on weekends. A sports center with squash courts, tennis courts, a heated swimming pool and a sauna is planned.

The main agricultural product here is not vegetables, but flowers. There is a mini zoo for children, with horseback riding, and a camping area. There are some good walks in the area as well.

One popular trip is to Jeriau Waterfall. It is around 1500 m above sea level and the temperature varies between 14° and 18°C.

Information: 09-382201, daily from 8:00 to 16:15.

Arrival

You can get to Fraser's Hill *from Kuala Lumpur* in 2 hours or Ipoh in 3 hours with the "gap route," which turns off the main road at Kota Kubu Baru. The road continues past Fraser' Hill to Raub and Kuala Lipis, mostly through the forest. At the "gap," which is on your left as you come from Kuala Lumpur there is a turn-off for Fraser's Hill – 8 km up a bad road. The road is open from 6:30 to 19:00. Traffic is only allowed to go in one direction at a time, so you might have to wait to go up.

You can get a bus here *from Kota Kubu Baru*. The buses leave daily at 8:00 and 12:00 and return at 10:00 and 14:00.

There are direct buses . *from Kuala Lumpur* Tuesday to Friday and Sunday at 15:00, Saturday at 11:00 and 17:00, for M$ 16.50.

Accommodation

● *Merlin Hotel Fraser's Hill*, Jalan Lady Guillemand, 109 rooms, M$ 80-300, Tel. 09-382274 / 9.
● *Fraser's Hill Bungalows*, M$ 25-55 (extra beds, M$ 10), Tel. 382201.
● *Puncak Inn* offers the best value.
● There is a *Government Resthouse* in the "gap." It is a nice old, English-style house in the jungle where you can observe monkeys, birds, etc.

Raub

Raub is a town on the Kuala Lumpur - Kuala Lipis - Kota Baru road with a population of around 25,000.

Accommodation

● *Lucky*, 36 Jalan Manson, 5 rooms, M$ 10-12, Tel. 09-351864.
● *Sin Heng*, 37 Jalan Manson, 5 rooms, M$ 12-14, Tel. 351029.

● *Kim Seng*, 39 Jalan Manson, 7 rooms, M$ 13-15.40, Tel. 351226.
● *Dragon*, 18 rooms, M$ 20, Tel. 351321.
● *Raub*, 57-58 Jalan Lipis, 21 rooms, M$ 28.
● *Tong Nam Bee*, 55 Jalan Bibby, 10 rooms, M$ 8-10.
● *Rest House Raub*, 22 rooms, M$ 16-24, Tel. 351455.

Further Travel

There are *buses* and *taxis* to Kuala Lumpur, Kuala Lipis, Bentong, Kuala Kubu Baru which is on the way to Fraser's Hill, and other places.

Bentong

This is a town on the Kuala Lumpur - Jerantut - Taman Negara road with a population of around 25,000.

Accommodation

● *Cheong Aik*, 49 Jalan Ah Peng, 15 rooms, M$ 7-11.
● *Union*, 50 Jalan Ah Peng, 26 rooms, M$ 7-10, Tel. 721088.
● *Panggong Wayang Lyceum*, 10 rooms, M$ 7-10, Tel. 221351.
● *Sentosa Rumah Tumpangan*, 56 Jalan Besar, Triang, 15 rooms, M$ 7-10.

Further Travel

There are *buses* and *taxis* to Raub, Kuala Lumpur, and Temerloh, among other places.

Kuala Lipis

A town of 12,000 in the middle of the Peninsula in the state of Pahang. Kuala Lipis is in a pleasant spot on the banks of the Sungai Jelai, which joins the Sungai Tembeling in Kuala Tembeling to become the Sungai Pahang.

There are a few attractive colonial buildings in town. For a time, Kuala Lipis was the capital of Malaya. The resthouse on the hill overlooking the city is particularly fine.

Kuala Lipis is on the rail line from Gemas to Kota Baru and on the new road from Kuala Lumpur to Kota Baru. It is possible to go on jungle excursions in the area. One organizer is Johnny Ton Ban Tok, Tel. 311313 / 135, 16 Jalan Jelai.

Accommodation

- *Resthouse*, Tel. 09-311267.
- *Sri Lipis*, Tel. 262369, both around M$ 30 for a double room.
- There are cheaper places to stay on the main street like *Paris* and *Sang Sang* at M$ 12-15 for a double room.

Temerloh

A small town with a population of 12,000 on the Sungai Pahang, on the road between Kuala Lumpur (153 km) and Kuantan (128 km). Temerloh is at the intersection of theroad to Jerantut in the north and Bahau in the south. Its location makes Temerloh an important transport center. There is a big *market* on Saturdays.

You can get here by bus or taxi from Kuala Lumpur, Bentong, Jerantut or Kuantan. Mentakab, 10 km to the west, is on the railway from Gemas to Kota Baru.

Accommodation

- *Government Resthouse*, Jalan Dato Hamzah, 10 rooms, SR M$ 25, DR M$ 30-60, well situated with a view of the Pahang River. Tel. 09-51254.
- *Center Point*, C308-311 Jalan Kuantan, 41 rooms, SR M$ 38, DR M$ 48 with A / C, Tel. 51788.
- *Tropicana*, A73 Jalan Sultan Ahmad, 45 rooms, SR M$ 14-18, DR M$ 18-24.
- *Temerloh Hotel*, 29-30 Jalan Kuantan, 22 rooms, SR M$ 9, DR M$ 21-27 (A / C), Tel. 51499.
- *Ban Hin Hotel*, 40 Jalan Tengku Besar (bus station), 17 rooms, SR M$ 8-18, DR M$ 20-26, Tel. 291250.
- *Fudo Hotel*, 132 Jalan Mentakab, 11 rooms, SR M$ 9, DR M$ 10-12.
- *Isis Hotel*, 12 Jalan Tengku Besar (bus station), 15 rooms, SR M$ 13, DR M$ 15-18, Tel. 51324.
- *Kam San* and *Kwai Pan*, C67 / 66 Jalan Dato Ngau Ken Lock, each with 14 rooms, SR M$ 10-11, DR M$ 12-20, Tel. 291294 / 51431.

Excursions

Taman Negara,

via Jerantut or try a visit to the *Jah Hut* (Orang Asli who have mixed with the Semai) in the Sungai Krau valley. They are known from the book, "Tales of a Shaman, Jah Hut Myths" as told by Batin Long bin Hok, Times Books International, Singapore.

Tasek Bera.

Get a permit at the Jabatan Hal Ehwal Orang Asli, Jalan Dato Ngau Ken Lock near the Temerloh Hotel. It used to be a good ride through the jungle to get to the reed-filled lake. Now it is mostly a ride past plantations. There used to be a lot of Semelai (Proto-Malays) settlements on the banks of the lake, but now they are concentrated mostly around Fort Iskander, a former communist stronghold.

From Temerloh, Seremban or Malacca, go to Bahau, and either take a taxi from there (expensive, M$ 50), or take a bus to Ladang Geddes. Then take a motorcycle taxi to Fort Iskander / Skanda for M$ 1.80 + 15. You can rent boats for M$ 20. This is a trip only for those who feel they must get to every corner of Malaysia.

Tasek Chini,

a legendary lotus-filled lake is the "Loch Ness" of Malaysia. It is halfway between Temerloh and Kuantan.

Ulu Lepar,

is a jungle reserve some 72 km from Temerloh, near the road to Kuantan (56 km). Make a left at Kampong Sri Jaya. Get **permission** to visit here from the Department of Wildlife and National Parks in Kuala Lumpur. Since most of the surrounding jungle has been destroyed, there are quite a few animals here including elephants and tapirs.

Jerantut

This is a small town on the way to Taman Negara. You can get here by bus from Kuantan for M$ 6.40 or Kuala Lumpur for M$ 12 and by taxi from just about anywhere. Taxis are M$ 16 from Kuala Lumpur. Trains arrive from Gemas or Kota Baru (Kuala Krai).

Buses leave Jerantut for Kuala Tembeling (starting point for boats into the national park) at 11:30 or 12:30 and cost M$ 2. They arrive in time to catch the boat at 14:00.

Accommodation

•**Government Resthouse**. They also sell carvings by the Jah Hut Orang Asli for good prices. For example, M$ 30-40 for a 30 cm high statue. Tel. 09-62214.

•**Jerantut Hotel**, Jalan Besar.

Taman Negara

Taman Negara means simply, National Park. There are dozens in Thailand, but there is only this one in Peninsular Malaysia. However, it is quite big, 4343 km^2. It has a maximum dimension of 120 km from east to west and 60 km from north to south. It is just about in the geographical center of the Peninsula, and is composed of land from three states, Pahang, Kelantan and Terengganu. Pahang has the lion's share. As early as 1925, 1300 km^2 of Pahang were designated as the Gunung Tahan Animal Reserve. It was combined with parts of Kelantan and Terengganu into the present National Park in 1939.

During British rule, the park was known as the King George V National Park. The name was changed at Independence.

The goal of the park is to preserve and protect the flora and fauna for posterity. The Malaysian jungle is the oldest primary rain forest in the world, about 130 million years old. This national park might very well be the most important thing for visitors to see in all of Malaysia.

Geologically, the park is mostly sedimentary stone, sandstone in particular. The eastern part is largely granite. There are also limestone outcrops throughout the park, including Gua Peningat, the highest in Malaysia at 723 m. Quartzite dominates in the mountainous region around Gunung Tahan, the highest peak in Peninsular Malaysia (2187 m), where the vegetation is temperate.

There is an incredible variety of *vegetation*. The lowland forest (60 m above sea level) is marked by

giant *tualang* trees, the low mountains by oaks and laurel, and the mountainousregions by dwarf or rain forest vegetation.

The variety of *fauna* is just as impressive, but it is sometimes harder to locate. There are over 250 species of birds in the park.

The park area was originally the home of the *Orang Asli*. Some of them work as guides in the park, though there are more Malays. You might stumble upon one of their huts in the park. They have sloping roofs made of leaves that protect the cooking fire from the rain, outside the house. Opposite Kuala Tahan, on the other side of the river, there is a settlement of 700 Batek people, a sub-group of Negritos.

In Kuala Atok and Sungai Tiang, just outside the park, there are *Negrito settlements* on land that the government is trying to develop. Negritos are primarily nomadic, living from hunting and gathering. Their houses in the park are therefore never built with an eye towards permanence.

I find it disappointing that so few Orang Asli are employed as guides. They obviously know a lot more about the park than the Malay guides who are trained in Kuala Tahan. I have no idea what the Batek themselves think about this.

When To Visit

Taman Negara is closed during the northeast monsoon season, from the middle of November to the

middle of January. The dry season follows next, and runs through March, when there are only 5 to 6 cm of rain. You have a better chance of seeing wild animals during the beginning of the park season, just after the park reopens, than at the end.

April through August, 15 to 17 cm of rain, is drier than September through December, with 20 to 25 cm. The wettest month is October, with 30 cm of rain.

As always in Malaysia, rain comes in sudden, heavy showers which make the rivers swell. Do not camp too close to water when it might rain! You can expect high humidity in the jungle all year around, but not too much sunlight if you stay under tree cover. If you pass through a cleared area or hike up Gunung Tahan past the tree-line, the sun can be very bright. Average midday temperatures go up to 32°C.

Registration

If you want to visit the park, you must register with the Park Bookings Officer, Department of Wildlife and National Parks (Perhilitan), Jalan Ceras, Kuala Lumpur. Or, you can register by telephone: 03-9052872, from 8:00-16:15.

Theoretically, you could go straight to Kuala Tembeling and hope for a place in the boat and in the hostel.

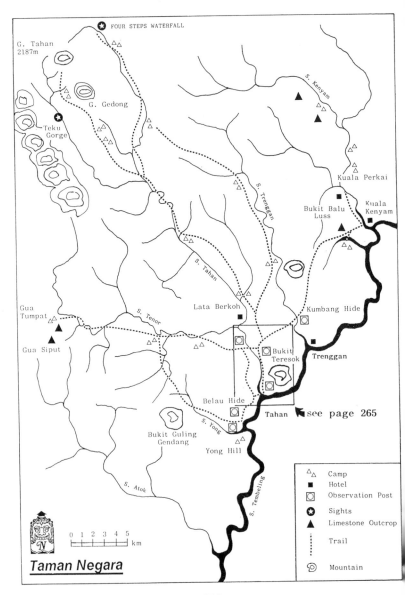

FOUR STEPS WATERFALL

G. Tahan
2187m

G. Gedong

S. Kenyam

Teku
Gorge

Kuala Perkai

Bukit Balu
Luss

Kuala
Kenyam

S. Trenggan

S. Tahan

Gua
Tumpat

S. Tenor

Lata Berkoh

Kumbang Hide

Gua Siput

Bukit
Teresok

Trenggan

Belau Hide

Tahan ⟨ see page 265

S. Yong

Bukit Guling
Gendang

Yong Hill

S. Atok

S. Tembeling

△△	Camp
■	Hotel
▣	Observation Post
✪	Sights
▲	Limestone Outcrop
⋯	Trail
◎	Mountain

0 1 2 3 4 5
km

Taman Negara

But it is much better to at least call first. If you regis-ter in person in Kuala Lumpur (the office is 10 km out of town), you will have to pay a M$ 30 deposit which covers the boat ride and a M$ 1 entry fee.

Be sure to get a copy of the **excellent brochure**, *Taman Negara Malaysia, Information and Trail Guides*. It costs only M$ 1. You can find it at the office in Kuala Lumpur and now probably in Kuala Tahan.

After a brief experiment with privatisation in 1987, which brought higher prices, poor service and fewer visitors (10,000 instead of 12,000), the contract with the River Park Sdn. Bhd. was renewed.

Costs

The prices now are higher than they were before the privatisation, as there are many recent capital improvements. Prices keep going up. For example, a long-boat costs M$ 2000 today instead of the M$ 500 it cost a few years ago. The same goes for a 40-PS outboard motor, which has shot up from M$ 2000 to twice that today. Here is a list of prices:

• **Boat Trip:** M$ 30 round-trip from Kuala Tembeling to Kuala Tahan.
• **Rest House:** M$ 38 a night for a single room.
• **Chalet:** M$ 30 a night / room.
• **Visitors' Lodge:** M$ 8.50 a person / night.
• **Hostel:** M$ 10 a person / night.
• **Blinds / Hides** (observation tents): M$ 5 / tent.
• **Three-Person Boats** from Kuala Tahan to:
Lata Berkoh – M$ 52
Kuala Terengganu – M$ 55
Kuala Atok – M$ 60
Bumbun Belau – M$ 45.50
Sungai Tiang – M$ 52
Kuala Kenyam – M$ 90
Kuala Perkai – M$ 100

Kenyam Kecil – M$ 115
Kuala Kelapor – M$ 130
Kuala Aur – M$ 165
Kampung Bantal – M$ 140

The most drastic increase in price comes from the decision to make guides manda-tory when hiking **Gunung Tahan**.

30 new guides have been hired, and they must be hired for M$ 50 a day! They are also responsible for keeping the trails clean. They must also be fit enough to run all the way back to Kuala Tahan non-stop in case of an emergency.

Getting to the Park

The only way to get to the park is to take a boat from **Kuala Tembeling** right before the Sungai Tembeling joins the Jelai to form the Pahang. The long-boats have sun roofs and comfortable seats for around 10 people. The relaxing 60 km trip up the Sungai Tembeling takes from 3 to 4 hours and the boats leave around 14:00.

Make boat **reservations** when you register. Another park entrance, in the west near Merapoh is being planned. There is also talk of building a jeep road to the "Padang," a flat area 2 to 3 hours below the summit of Gunung Tahan. It would be nothing short of an outrage:
presently, there are no roads at all in the park, and it should remain that way. But civilization is very close to Kuala Tahan. In the village nearby, where most of the park employees live, there are cars, loud music, etc. Kuala Tahan is not exactly a quiet place. But then again it is only the entrance to the park.

Getting to Kuala Tembeling

Train:
• From Kuala Lumpur or Singapore, take the night train which leaves at 22:00, through Gemas to Tembeling station. Make sure you tell them you are getting off; the train stops only on demand! The train gets in at 7:57. From here, it is about half an hour's walk to the boat landing.

●From Kota Baru, there is a train that leaves at 10:00 and arrives in Jerantut at 19:30, where you will have to spend the night.

Bus or Share-Taxi:
●From the second floor of Kuala Lumpur's Puduraya Bus Station or Perhentian Bas Pudu Raya or from the taxi stand, go to either Temerloh or Jerantut which is the best choice. You can also get buses to Temerloh from the Pahang Bus Station, Jalan Tun Razak, Kuala Lumpur. There are regular buses and taxis between Temerloh and Jerantut, and between Jerantut and Kuala Tembeling. From Kuala Lumpur, the whole trip should cost M$ 15 on the bus or M$ 20 in a taxi.

Private Car:
●From Kota Baru, take the new road through Gua Musang, and Kuala Lipis to Jerantut.
*From Kuala Lumpur, there are a number of possibilities. Either take the "Gap" route near Fraser's Hill through Raub to Jerantut, or go through Bentong to Raub, or through Mentokap Temerloh to Jerantut. From there, there is a steep, narrow road to Kuala Tembeling. The parking area is a bit past the boat landing. Both are marked.

Pelangi Air:
●From Kuala Lumpur Subang Airport to Sungai Tiang the round-trip is M$ 160.
From there, it is only 45 minutes to Kuala Tahan for M$ 10. So, from Kuala Lumpur, you can actually get to the park in about an hour and a half. There are flights on the following days:
Sunday: 10:35, back at 11:35
Tuesday / Wednesday: 11:20, back at 12:20;
Thursday: 11:40, back at 12:40
It is best to call Pelangi Air at Tel. 03-2610555.

Jungle Trekking

There is a network (not always good) of marked trails throughout the park. All official trails are marked with yellow pieces of metal on trees, but where trails lead is only noted at junctions.

It is best to start with the **trek around Kuala Tahan — Bukit Teresek** which is 344 m:

It takes about an hour to get to the summit. The best time to go is in the early morning. There are 22 kinds of trees marked, plus birds, gibbons, and other animals. There are also fabulous views from the summit
● over the Sungai Tembeling to the hills on the other side (outside of the park).
● over the park to Gunung Tahan.
● of the area between the Sungai Tahan, Sungai Trenggan and Ulu Kenyam (with the Gua Besar limestone outcroppings).

Then, you can either take the steep path that follows the Tahan River or take a look into Tabing Hide (blind). Look out for barking deer, wild boars and tapirs. Then back-track a bit to Muda Salt Lick where you can expect to see animal tracks, and then to the Tahan River. Both paths meet up at Lubuk Simpon, a swimming hole on the Tahan River.

Another **short hike** goes up Teresek Hill to **Teresek Spring** which supplies the drinking water for Kuala Tahan and then further to Bukit Indah (122 m), a quartzite hill. It takes about 20 minutes to reach the top. You can do it in a half or full day, ending with a swim in the Tembeling River.

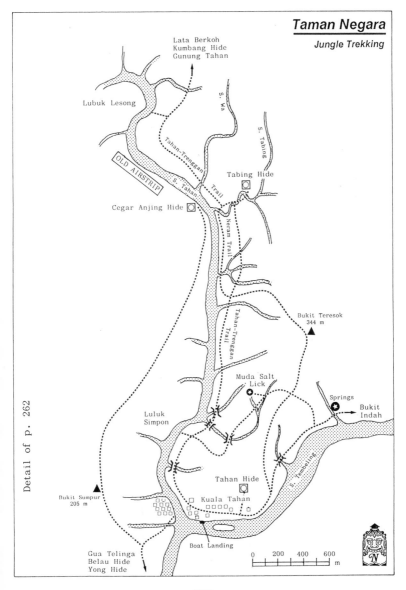

Taman Negara

Jungle Trekking

Lata Berkoh
Kumbang Hide
Gunung Tahan

Lubuk Lesong

S. Wa

S. Tabing

Tahan-Trenggan Trail

OLD AIRSTRIP

S. Tahan

Tabing Hide

Cegar Anjing Hide

Neram Trail

Bukit Teresok
344 m

Tahan-Trenggan Trail

Muda Salt Lick

Springs

Bukit Indah

Luluk Simpon

S. Tembeling

Tahan Hide

Bukit Sumpur
205 m

Kuala Tahan

Detail of p. 262

Gua Telinga
Belau Hide
Yong Hide

Boat Landing

0   200   400   600
m

N

265

Shorter hikes on this side of the Tahan River include the walk to **Kubang Hide** (blind) which takes 3 to 6 hours from Kuala Tahan, depending on your speed, or 45 minutes by boat to Kuala Trenggan and then another 45 minutes to the hut. You can continue in the same direction and go to **Kuala Kenyam** and **Kuala Perkal**, which you can also reach by boat – faster, but a lot more expensive. Before you reach Kuala Kenyam, you will get to **Bukit Batu Luas**. There is an easy, marked path to the summit (130 m). Plan on 2 to 3 days for the whole trip, depending on how fast you walk, how much you want to stop, etc. This is the best hike to get acquainted with the tropical rainforest.

On the other side of Tahan River (you might have to pay someone to take you over), there is a good, short hike to **Belau Hide** (blind) with a side-trip to the **Gua Telinga Caves**. It is a half day's undertaking, and parts of the caves are ankle-deep in guano and bat droppings. Just follow the rope the whole way. You can also reach Belau and Yong Hide with a boat in a 10 minute ride up the Tembeling.

If you want to make a long hike of it, you can continue on from Belau Hide along the **Rentis-Tenor Trail** to **Bukit Guling Gendang** at 569 m. It is a one-hour hike up the hill, with a nice view from the top of Gunung Tahan and some of the large limestone outcroppings. Go further to **Renuis Camp** (the Sungai Tenor is good for fishing) and past Lameh Camp to **Sungai Tahan**. Either stay on the right bank or wade across the Tahan and take the **Neram Path** back to Kuala Tahan. Plan on 2-3 days in total.

You can hike to the four-tiered **waterfall** near the source of the Tahan in 4 days. The round trip takes 8 days and is seldom attempted.

The high-point is still the **ascent of Gunung Tahan**, the highest mountain on the Peninsula. The trip is estimated to take nine days. The usual campsites on the way are the following:

1. Sungai Melantai (3-5 hours from Kuala Tahan).
2. Kuala Puteh (4-8 hours, 27 hills up to 576 m).
3. Kuala Teku (168 m, 7 rivers to wade through).
4. Wray's Camp (1100 m), Gunung Pankin (1463 m), Gunung Tangga Lima Belas (1539 m), Gunung Reskit (1666 m) (3-8 hours, last three campsites are along a ridge with a good view, but no water source).
5. Padang (1500 m), 300 m lower than Gunung Gedong Shoulder (1830 m), 4-6 hours from Wray's Camp. 2-3 hours to the summit of Gunung Tahan.
6. Kuala Teku.
7. Kuala Puteh.

8. Sungai Melantai or Kuala Tahan. That is the official hiking plan. Since you have to hire a guide from the park at M$ 50 a day, they would prefer you to spend as much time as possible. It is possible to go much faster. I was assured in Kuala Lumpur that you need not follow their plan, and that you can change the trip however you want.

It is a long trip a total of 50 km through jungle and mountains. There are many ups and downs between Wray's Camp and Gunung Gedong Shoulder, at times the trail is washed away to the roots. There are 14 river crossings (7 times across the Tahan, each way) and there is mud everywhere. More than just a casual stroll, there is a total gain of over 3800 m including all the ups and downs.

Nonetheless, the trail is very rewarding. If you take more time, you can enjoy the campsites by fishing, swimming, and relaxing. On the Padang, it can get as cold as 4° C. All camps above Wray's Camp will be either cool or cold. The change in vegetation between Kuala Teku and the summit is truly striking. On the Gunung Gedong Shoulder (further up on the ridge is the wreck of an airplane) there is only undergrowth, and the view is spectacular.

Boat and Fishing Trips

If you have no desire to hike all over the country, you can always rent a boat and ride to where ever you want to go.

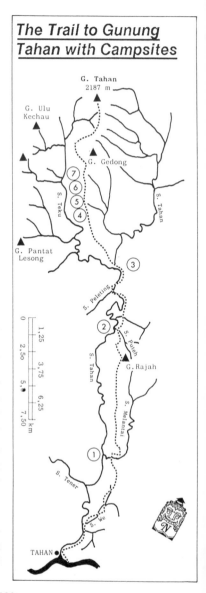

The Trail to Gunung Tahan with Campsites

Lata Berkoh and *Kuala Perkai* are popular fishing spots. Do not expect too much here, though.

The best seasons are during February and March and from June to August. It is best to use a rod up to 2m long, and a 3.5 to 6 kg line, and silver, red or copper flies, 2.5 to 4 cm long are recommended. Use Abu Killers for big fish. Locals use certain fruits such as *buah maris, ara, ubi kayu* for bait. The main **fish** are: *sebarau, kelah, kejor, ikan daun* and *toman* Serpent-Head Fish.

There is better fishing in **Endau Rompin** and in some other parts of the park that you can onlyreach by boat. Fishing in Malaysia is free.

You could follow the Tembeling further upstream, leaving the park and arriving in **Ulu Tembeling**. Just outside the park, there are a few *kampongs* where people build the long narrow boats called *jalor* which are used in the park. These cost M$ 3000 per boat.

In one of these *kampongs*, **Bantal**, archaeologists have discovered the remains of some old settlements. They date from the stone-age to the time of the Ming Dynasty, proving that the river valley has been inhabited for quite some time.

It is forbidden to:
- Hunt, or bring firearms into the park.
- Disturb any animal or plant life.
- Pick any flowers or other plants.
- Write on trees or rocks.
- Bring pets into the park.

Jungle Gear

The first time I was in Malaysia, I bought a pair of jungle pants – green, of course – and a matching shirt.

At about the same time, I bought my jungle boots, made of canvas and rubber. I still have them. After more than 20 trips into the jungle (some for as long as 5 days and nights), and years of hash-runs every Monday (1 or 1 ½ hours running cross-country in the jungle), they have served me well.

In the forest, I wear running shorts, t-shirt, and sneakers with socks. I also carry a backpack. My Kelabit guide on Murud, the highest mountain in Sarawak, was a hunter from Pa Lungan who wore only a pair of primitive jungle boots made of plastic, with no socks. We cannot follow this example. I just want to make the point that jungle gear does not have to be expensive, only comfortable enough to protect your feet and to let your body breathe.

Of course everyone is afraid of *leeches*, but long trousers and boots are no guarantee against them. Many people end up wondering, as they strip off their clothes, how so many leeches could find their way through long trousers, two pairs of socks and high jungle boots. I wasn't bitten at all in shorts.

If you walk quickly, the leeches do not take the trouble to keep up with you. So you are in danger only when resting or in water. You are well protected with knee-socks specially made out of linen. On top of that, use insect repellent on your socks and shoes – not on the skin! If you want to avoid harsh chemicals, keep plenty of salt handy or try rubbing soap into your shoes and socks. Tincture of tobacco is also good. If you discover leeches on your skin, you can pick them off with your hands. Malaysian leeches let go when you pull on them. Salt or a lighted cigarette will definitely get rid of them. Normally, you will not notice leeches. You will, however, notice

the striped tiger leeches immediately. They create a burning sensation, so you react to them right away.

Make sure you take warm clothes if you are planning on spending the night at a high altitude.

If you will be wading through rivers as in the hike up Gunung Tahan, take a pair of rubber sandals or flip-flops (thongs). An extra pair of shoes might also be a good idea. On the way up Gunung Tahan, you sometimes see old, worn-out shoes.

A hammock is very useful in the jungle. If you don't have one, you can use a mat. For cover, you can use a small tarpaulin or a tent tied to a tree.

Equipment List

●*Shoes:* Comfort is the most important thing. Running shoes are usually good for a long trek. Take an extra pair. Trekking shoes are even better, if you have them. The locally made ones cost around M$ 20 and are very good. Make sure you break in your shoes before you use them in the jungle. Take rubber sandals for crossing rivers as the stones can be very slippery.

●*Socks:* Cotton is best. Some people like 2 thin pairs, again comfort is the most important thing. Just make sure your feet can breathe, as your feet will be wet most of the time. Always bring extra socks. Anti-leech socks made of linen are good if you can find them (try the Malayan Nature Society in Selangor).

●*Clothes:* Cotton is again the best thing. Clothes should be light, comfortable and airy. Take a sweater, anorak or warm-up suit for high altitudes. Remember to take extra clothes so you will have something dry to change into. If you will be gone for a long time, count on having to wash your clothes. A cap might be good for nights at high altitudes and a waterproof hat might also be useful.

●*Backpacks:* Wear a waterproof one, if possible. Make sure it is comfortable, and practice walking with it full before you go into the jungle.

●*Sleeping Items:* You'll need a mat or a hammock, a tarpaulin sheet to protect against rain, and a sleeping bag for high altitudes. A light tent is useful if you will be out for a long time.

●*Food:* Locals like to bring rice, instant noodles, vegetables, and canned curries. There is a wide selection in the shops, but you should stock up in Jerantut, because in Kuala Tembeling, where you get the boat for the park, there is little to choose from. In Kuala Tahan, the park headquarters, there is a small shop suited only for emergencies. I prefer to travel light and forego hot food. For 4 days, I take only muesli, powdered milk, Milo or Ovaltine and powdered sports drinks like Gatorade, all packed in plastic bags. You can, of course, take as much as you like, but be careful about the weight! Also remember that glass containers are not allowed in the park, and are far too heavy, anyway.

●*Parang / Machete:* Only necessary if you are going cross-country, not needed on the trails.

●*Pocketknife*

●*Eating Utensils:* A spoon or chopsticks, at the least.

●*Water Bottles:* Plastic canteens, bags and / or cups.

●*Stove:* If you want warm meals. You can also make camp-fires to cook – there is enough firewood, but bring whatever else you need.

●*First Aid Kit:* Including bandages, disinfectant, etc.

●*Insect Repellent:* Baygon or Off are good against leeches.

●*Miscellaneous:* Flashlight (torch), binoculars, powdered sports drinks, reading material, camera, small towel, and a toothbrush.

Sarawak and Sabah

N (Indonesia)

Getting to Sabah and Sarawak

Sabah and Sarawak are accessible only from Southeast Asia. Travelers from outside the area must first fly to either Peninsular Malaysia or Singapore, and from there onto Sabah and Sarawak.

It is possible to book a flight all the way through to East Malaysia from Europe, Australia or North America,

but this is not recommended as it is usually more expensive and might have other conditions attached.

There are three possibilities for getting to Sabah and / or Sarawak from Southeast Asia: Peninsular Malaysia, Singapore, and Indonesia (Java and Kalimantan).

Since it's an international flight, flying from Singapore is generally more expensive than from Johor Baru. Johor Baru is just over the bridge from Singapore and you can

Prices for Transportation to East Malaysia (Cheapest Class, One-Way):

		Airplane	Ship
Kuala Lumpur	- Kuching	162 M$	160 M$
	- Kota Kinabalu	266 M$	265M$
Singapur	- Kuching	170 S$	200 S$
	- Kota Kinabalu	346 S$	310 S$
Johor Baru	- Kuching	125 M$	—
	- Kota Kinabalu	256 M$	—
Kuching	- Kota Kinabalu	198 M$	140 M$
Pontianak	- Kuching (Merpati)	148 M$	—
Jakarta	- Pontianak (Merpati)	80.000 Rp.	—

get to the airport in just 40 minutes on the bus from Singapore, a trip well worth taking.

You can only enter East Malaysia **overland** from **Brunei to Sarawak**. There is no problem passing between Sarawak and Sabah.

The border point between Sabah and Sarawak is called Sindumin in Sabah and Merapok in Sarawak. Both states have immigration posts at the border. If you are coming from Sabah, go directly to the office to get an exit stamp. The official will hand you a new card and take the old one. Then you have to write exactly the same information that was on the old card on the new one. Then you will get a new entry stamp, which does not extend your old visa, only ratifies it.

The border between Sarawak / Sabah and Kalimantan is closed to land travel. Crossing is illegal and if you do so, you will not have the proper stamps in your passport and will have to deal with some very angry immigration officials later on.

You can fly from Kalimantan into Malaysia, either from Tarakan to Tawau, Sabah or from Pontianak to Kuching, Sarawak.

If you have enough time, you can **take a ship** from Kuantan, Port Klang or Singapore to Kuching or Kota Kinabalu. Traveling by ship is comfortable, and there are many things on the boat to keep you entertained, like a swimming pool and a movie theater.

The schedule is as follows: from Kuantan (Saturday) to Kota Kinabalu (Monday), Kuching (Tuesday), Singapore (Thursday), and finally Port Klang (Friday). On the way back, the boat sails from Port Klang (Saturday) to Singapore (Sunday), Kuching (Monday), Kota Kinabalu (Wednesday), Singapore (Friday) and finally to Kuantan (Saturday).

Unfortunately, the price is somewhat high. It varies, depending on the type of cabin, from M$ 160-350 (Kuantan-Kuching), M$ 265-550 (Kuantan-Kota Kinabalu) one-way, or between M$ 320-700 (to Kuching) and M$ 530-1100 (to Kota Kinabalu) round-trip.

The trip from Singapore to Kuching costs between S$ 200-355 (to Kota Kinabalu: S$ 310-620) one-way, or S$ 400-710 (to Kota Kinabalu: S$ 620-1240) round-trip.

For information and reservations, contact Feri Malaysia, Ground Floor, Menara Utama UMBC, Jalan Sultan Sulaiman, 50000 Kuala Lumpur, Tel. 03-2388899.

Traveling Between Sabah and Sarawak

If you want to visit both East Malaysian states, you will either have to go through Brunei or around it. The only real way to do the latter is to fly over it. For example, from Lawas to Miri, or from Lawas to Limbang and then to Miri.

The **best route**, in our opinion, is to fly from Lawas to Miri or vice-versa. It's a fairly painless trip from

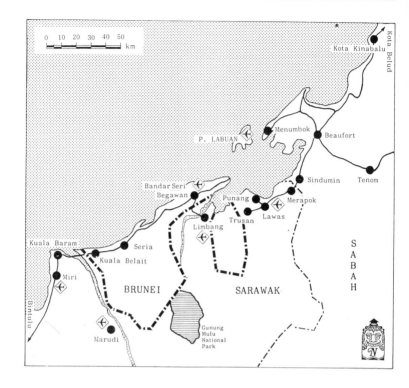

Kota Kinabalu to Lawas, and there are some beautiful, virtually untouched areas along the way. By taking the cheap flight to Miri for M$ 59, you can save yourself both time and money that expensive Brunei would otherwise consume.

Through Brunei

If you want to go through Brunei, you can take a bus from Miri to the border. The trip to the border crossing at Kuala Belait costs around M$ 8. This requires first taking a bus from Miri to Kuala Baram, followed by a motorboat over the river, and then another bus on the other side, which takes you to the border crossing.

Finally a Brunei bus will take you the rest of the way to Kuala Belait. The next town along is Seria and there are 30 daily buses for this short trip costing B$ 1.

From Seria, it is another hour and a half bus ride to Bandar Seri Begawan, costing B$ 4.

If you leave Miri early enough, and the first bus is at 9:00, you can reach Bandar Seri Begawan in one day. Here, you must stay in one of the expensive hotels.

Accommodation in
Bandar Seri Begawan

●*Pusat Bella* (Youth Hostel), Jalan Sungei Kianggeh, B$ 10 / person for the first three nights, then B$ 5 / person thereafter, dormitory beds; not very clean.
Tel. 23926.
●*Capitol Hotel*, Jalan Tasek Lama, Tel. 23561, behind the youth hostel, double rooms are B$ 85; all rooms with A / C, TV and refrigerator.
●*National Inn*, Jalan Tutong, Tel. 21128, double rooms B$ 70-115.

From Bandar Seri Begawan
to Sarawak or Sabah

The next day, you can take a speedboat for B$ 10 to Limbang in Sarawak. Then another boat to Punang and finally, a taxi to Lawas. Altogether this costs about M$ 14.

If you don't want to go through Limbang, you can take a boat directly from Bandar Seri Begawan to Lawas for M$ 16. There are buses from Lawas that go into Sabah (see section on Sindumin / Merapok).

The third possibility is a boat directly from Bandar Seri Begawan to Labuan Island for B$ 15-20. Then take a ferry to Menumbok in Sabah for M$ 7. There are bus connections to Beaufort and Kota Kinabalu from there.

Special Customs Regulations for Sarawak

There are special regulations that apply to anyone taking items out of Sarawak. If you are taking any **handicrafts** or **art objects** out, you must take care that they are not categorically considered antiques.

If they are, you must have written permission from the curator of the Sarawak Museum to remove them. Anything made before 1850 falls into this restricted category.

You can avoid problems with this regulation by purchasing souvenirs in authorized shops. These shops are recommended either by the Sarawak Tourist Association or by the Tourist Development Corporation. An example of one of these shops is in the Sarawak Museum.

Another strict regulation prohibits moving or removing **protected plants** and **animals**. This ordinance, enacted in 1958, forbids the hunting, killing or capture of any protected animal species as well as the collection of protected plants. This law also prohibits the export of anything made from a protected species, for example skins, tortoise shell products, and crocodile skin products. without special permission. Address your questions to the National Park and Wildlife Office, Jalan Gartek, Kuching, Tel. 24474.

This is a good time to mention the question of whether or not one should buy the butterflies that are mounted and offered for sale everywhere. To get an idea of how rare they are, think about how often you personally have seen such butterflies. And the argument, "I just wanted to buy an example," is ridiculous. Consider how many tourists come through and then think about each one "just buying an example."

At present, it is also forbidden to bring **meat products** from Sarawak to Peninsular Malaysia, as there have been cases of foot-and-mouth disease on Sarawak.

The transport of **tobacco** and **cocoa plants** to Peninsular Malaysia is also prohibited. There is a chance that these products could bring new pests from Borneo to the mainland.

The Climate and when to Travel

There is very little variation in the tropical climate of Sabah and Sarawak. Temperatures vary from 22°C to 32°C, throughout the year. Normally it gets a little cooler after it rains. The humidity is fairly constant at around 80%. In the mountains, especially in Kinabalu Park, the temperature can get much lower. At night on Mount Kinabalu, it can get down to freezing.

There are no seasons as there are in North America or Europe. However, there are times with more and less rain. In **Sarawak**, the northeast monsoon arrives between October and February, and it rains more than

usual. Annual rainfall varies between 300 and 500 cm. **Sabah** has different rainy seasons, a situation caused by the mountains, depending on where you are. In the **north**, the dry season begins in December and runs through May. The month with the greatest rainfall is October. In the **south** (Sandakan, Lahad Datu, Tawau), the dry season runs from March to September. The rain is heaviest in January. It also regularly rains during the dry season.

There are two rainy seasons in Sabah, and thispresents something of a problem deciding on the best time to travel. Since a visit to Sabah almost always involves a trip up Mount Kinabalu, we would recommend the months **February through April**. The weather in northern Sabah, where Mount Kinabalu is located, is relatively dry in these months. At the end of the dry season, you can move south, where it will just be drying up.

There are similar problems in planning a trip to Sarawak. On one hand, the excessive rain during the monsoon can make many activities impossible. On the other hand, much inland transportation is dependent on rivers, many of which become impassable during the dry season. Probably the best time to travel is at the end of the rainy season or the beginning of the dry season, from March to June. This is a particularly good time if you plan to go far inland.

Do remember that it is not always dry during the dry season and it does not always rain during the rainy season. The seasons are named for the prevailing weather.

The weather can be an important consideration if you plan on touring both Sabah and Sarawak, but are not sure in which order. If you want to visit both states of East Malaysia, the best time to travel would probably be in February and March, going to Sabah in February and, towards the middle of March, heading down to Sarawak. This is the best way to stay fairly dry in both places.

Another advantage of this route is that you don't have to carry all the gear you need for the mountains in Sabah. You can simply ship the sweaters, jackets, hiking boots, etc., back home.

Equipment

For a trip to Sabah or Sarawak, you will need a few things in addition to what you might take on a more routine trip. As a rough guideline, consult the section on equipment under Taman Negara, in Peninsular Malaysia.

In addition, we strongly recommend taking some large **plastic bags** (trash bags or the like). These are very useful for keeping things dry within your backpack. They can also be used as rain covers for non-waterproof packs.

Transportation

Transportation in Sabah and Sarawak is very similar to that in Peninsular Malaysia. Possibilities include **buses, taxis, rental cars** and flying with **MAS**. You can also **hitchhike** along certain routes, such as the road between Miri and Sibu in Sarawak and between Kota Kinabalu and Kota Belud, Ranau and Beaufort in Sabah. To do this, you will, of course, need more time.

In comparison to Peninsular Malaysia, most of the buses in Sabah look quite different. So do not be surprised when you arrive at a bus station to find a collection of Jeeps and other four-wheel drive vehicles posing as "buses". There are a lot of roads that are often impassable without a four-wheel drive and a high chassis. There are not as many seats on these buses as on their mainland counterparts, but usually there are more customers, so book your tickets early!

In Sarawak, and also in Sabah, **airplanes** are a far more important means of transportation than they are on the mainland. Many small towns in Sarawak like Long Pa Sia and Long Seridan are only accessible by air or foot, which might take many days. It is also far quicker and more comfortable to fly between, for example, Kota Kinabalu and Sandakan, than to sit on a crowded bus for 10 or 12 hours. The price of flying is usually not prohibitively expensive. For example, the bus to Sandakan costs M$ 35, the plane M$ 69.

There is an airport tax of M$ 3 per flight.

Almost all flights within Sabah and Sarawak are on **Twin Otter** planes. These little machines, which carry a maximum of 19 passengers are unbelievably agile, and can even be outfitted to take off and land on water. Since they are so small, there is a fairly strict **luggage limit**. Only 10kg (22 lbs.) per person is free. The charge for each additional kilo varies depending upon the route, from 40 *sen* to M$ 1.45.

Not only are Twin Otter flights worthwhile because they save so much time, but they are a travel experience unto themselves. It is a completely different experience to fly over a jungle just above the treetops than to soar above the earth in a jumbo jet. The experience can be a bit unsettling for those prone to motion sickness or during bad weather. Think about taking some medicine beforehand if this is the case.

In Sarawak, **ships** and **boats** are important means of transportation. In the interior, the rivers are the primary avenues of transportation. Every kind of boat is used, some of them downright adventurous. Along the coast to Sibu there are ferries and freighters which take passengers. Express boats are the most comfortable means of transportation, offering air-conditioning and videos. If you find it too cold or too loud below, you can ride on the deck, where the view is better, but the price is the same. If you do so, be careful not to get sunburned: the wind cools you off fast, but the sun's rays are as strong as ever. Every town has a harbor with an express boat terminal. Travel up the smaller rivers requires an outboard motor or a dugout canoe, which you can usually rent in the towns.

During the dry season, June through August, the level of water in the rivers drops so severely that the express boats cannot follow their normal routes. Sometimes there is no transportation at all, but usually you can count on irregular river boats. These boats have steel plates mounted on their undersides to prevent them from being destroyed when they run aground. Even so, they do not always reach their destinations. Be sure to get your tickets especially early during the dry season.

Accommodation

As in Peninsular Malaysia, there is a variety of accommodation to choose from in Sabah and Sarawak. The selection of luxury hotels, however, is rather limited outside of the main towns, though there are lesser hotels that charge luxury hotel prices. A cheaper alternative are the Chinese hotels, when they are available. Some towns also have mission stations, which usually have rooms available for traveling missionaries. They might rent these to tourists when not otherwise in use.

The average price for a double room in Sarawak is around M$ 20-25 and around M$ 25-30 in Sabah.

During long jungle treks, you can normally stay in a long-house or a private house. Often, you will find that you do not have to pay money for such accommodation, although you might be asked, but gifts are expected by the hosts. Naturally, you are expected to bring your own food.

Costs

Unfortunately, Sabah and Sarawak are as expensive as they are interesting. Traveling here costs quite a bit more than in Peninsular Malaysia.

Plan on spending around M$ 25 per night for a double room as well as more for food. A cola costs M$ 1, a *nasi* or *mee goreng* is M$ 2.50-3.50 in cheap restaurants, and a cup of coffee is M$ 0.80-1.00.

Transportation is also more expensive. For example, the route from Johor Baru, on to Kuching, Sibu, Miri, Lawas, Kota Kinabalu, Sandakan, Kota Kinabalu, and back to Johor Baru costs around M$ 600 per person. This includes transportation by bus, boat and plane, assuming you fly from Johor Baru to Kuching, Miri to Lawas, and Kota Kinabalu to Johor Baru. If you make an additional trip to the interior of Sarawak, it will cost around M$ 100 more, by boat and bus.

In addition, there are the costs for multi-day boat tours with a guide. For 2-3 people, it costs between M$ 150 and 250 a person for three days.

Visiting national parks is also quite expensive. For Kinabalu Park, count on around M$ 60 per person including a permit, accommodation and a guide for two people climbing the mountain for three days.

For a three-week tour of Sarawak and Sabah, with some jungle trekking, visits to national parks and other remote places, you have to figure on around US$ 800 per person.

Note that the expected rate of inflation for 1991 will be between 5 and 7%.

Gifts

If you are on your own in Sabah or Sarawak, you will certainly be invited into someone's home. Whether it is an urban household or an Iban long-house, it is always a good idea to bring a few small gifts. They do not necessarily have to be digital watches. Much better are pictures of you and your family, postcards or coins from your home country, small bottles of perfume, lighters, and in the interior, cigarettes and candy are always welcome. In our experience, balloons have always proved a big hit for the children in long-houses.

Flora and Fauna

Even today, the name Borneo calls to mind an image of impenetrable jungle. Scientifically, this vegetation is known as a **tropical rain forest**. This type of forest is distinguished by lots of precipitation, high humidity, a constant yearly temperature of between 24°C and 28°C, and a great variety of flora and fauna.

The original vegetation of Borneo was overwhelmingly tropical rain forest. Unfortunately, in the last few years, much of this has been destroyed, either falling prey to loggers or cut down to make way for urban expansion. There are also many plantations in Sabah and Sarawak including rubber, palm oil, banana, cocoa and pepper farms.

In 1986, the road from Sibu to Bintulu was entirely surrounded by jungle. In 1988, there were stretches where no trees were visible at all. It has been estimated that if the destruction continues at its current rate, there will be no more rain forest in this area by the year 2000.

Those who want to experience the real jungle must either go deep into the interior or be content with the national parks. In the parks you can view undisturbed jungle with a wide variety of plants such as *Rafflesia* which is a parasite with huge blossoms up to 1 meter across, giant trees, strangling figs, carnivorous plants and mangroves.

As the rain forest is being cut down, it is not surprising that the variety of animal life is beginning to diminish also. There are many animals that are now only found in the parks. But viewing animals in the wild is nothing like visiting a zoo. Above all, patience is required, since the animals must come to you. A few lessons in the art of observation would also be helpful.

Sabah and Sarawak are also home to a number of endangered species. Many well-known primates, like the **orang-utan** or **proboscis monkey** are only seen in reserves these days, for example Sepilok in Sabah or Bako Park in Sarawak.

Varanus bengalensis

284

Sarawak

Sarawak, the largest Malaysian state, with an area of 124,449 square kilometers, lies along the northwest coast of Borneo, one of the world's largest islands. It borders the Sultanate of Brunei along the northeast coast, the Malaysian state of Sabah to the east and the Indonesian province of Kalimantan to the south.

Topographically, Sarawak is divided into three regions: the mangrove swamps along the coast which turn into tropical rainforest further inland; and the forest mountain range along the Malaysian-Indonesian border. This last region contains the highest mountain in Sarawak, Mount Murud (2423 m).

Although there has been a road connecting Kuching and Miri since 1984, it is at times nothing more than a dusty, pot-hole-ridden path. The major rivers still remain the main arteries of transportation. These include the Sungei Sarawak at 217 km, the Batang Lupar at 228 km, the Batang Rajang at 564 km and the Sungei Baram at 402 km. The Rajang is the longest river in Sarawak, and the first 242 km to Kapit are accessible with a coastal steamer. Express boats go further inland.

There is also a national air transport system, which operates out of small airstrips all over the state.

About the State

The state of Sarawak has its own constitution in addition to the national constitution of Malaysia, which also functions here.

The governor, or Yang di-Pertuan Negeri, is the nominal head of the state. The parliament, Majilis Mesyuarat Kerajaan Negeri, is made up of the president and between 4 and 8 members of the senate, Dewan Undangan Negeri. The senate and the parliament have legislative and executive power, so long as they do not contradict the constitution of Malaysia. The government of the state is responsible for maintaining and administering the land, the raw material sources and the forests.

Sarawak is known as the "Land of the Rhinoceros Bird" and the coat of arms portrays a Rhinoceros Bird with outstretched wings. The thirteen feathers on each wing and on the tail represent the thirteen states of Malaysia. The hibiscus blossom is the national flower of Malaysia. The motto of the state is "Hidup Selalu Berkhidmat," which translates roughly as, "Live to Serve."

History

From the 15th century to the beginning of the 19th century, Sarawak was part of the Sultanate of Brunei. The *Dayak Revolt*, supported by Malays and Chinese, came in 1839, in opposition to the rule of the Sultan of Brunei, Raja Madu Hassim. This gave the English adventurer *James Brooke* the perfect opportunity to intervene. With the might of the cannons on his ship, "The Royalist," he was able to pacify the rebellion. As thanks for his quick action, the Sultan gave Brooke the land that is now Sarawak.

According to one story, the name Sarawak comes from the Sultan's speech as he gave the land to Brooke, "Serah kapada awak" or "I give it to you."

Brooke became the Sultan of Sarawak in 1841, the date which marks the beginning of the reign of the White Rajas, and the era of the Brooke Family. When James Brooke died in 1868, his nephew, *Charles Brooke* took over. In 1888, Sarawak was made a British protectorate. Under Charles Brooke, the state developed rapidly. Before he took over, he spent months in the jungle with the Dayaks and became familiar with their concerns. As he personally took an interest in all affairs of the state, Sarawak flourished, economically and culturally, and peace reigned. His personal interest in the culture of Sarawak is still visible today in some of Kuching's buildings like the Istana (the government palace) and the Sarawak Museum. The museum was partially developed by Alfred Russel Wallace, one of the founders of the theory of evolution.

After the death of Charles Brooke in 1917, his son *Charles Vynar Brooke* took over. He ruled until the Japanese occupation. That marked the beginning of a period of economic exploitation by the Japanese. In *1945*, the allies recaptured Borneo and Charles Vynar Brooke took over once again. In July of that year, he handed Sarawak over to Great Britain, which ruled Sarawak as a colony until 1963. During this time, British troops had frequent skirmishes with communist rebels.

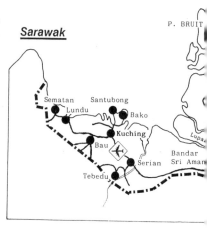

Sarawak

On *July 16, 1963*, Sarawak became independent of Great Britain and joined the Federation of Malaysian States.

The history of Sarawak in the last hundred years was very much influenced by the Brooke Family. One of their most glorified accomplishments was the elimination of head-hunting, which was practiced as late as the 1930s.

coastline of Sarawak and Sabah plays a major role in the economy of the two states. Due to its high quality (low sulfur content), oil has become a major export commodity. Indeed, the off-shore oil industry has done much to establish many large towns in Sarawak, like Miri.

Economy

As part of Malaysia, the economy of Sarawak is very closely linked with that of the rest of the country. The *oil-rich*

In addition to oil, **natural gas** from around Bintalu is also a major product of Sarawak. It is mostly exported to Japan.

Malaysia is one of the world's major **pepper** producers. It produces around 27,550 U.S. tons of pepper a year, about 90% of which comes from Sarawak. Another important export is **timber** from the huge jungles of Borneo where originally, there were around 13.4 million hectares of primary rain forest. American and Japanese concerns consume about 100,000 hectares yearly. Other exports include **rubber** and **palm oil**.

Religion

In Sarawak, Islam is not very widespread and is limited mostly to the large towns. In the interior, many of the people are Christians and there are still practicing missionaries there. The Anglican church is particularly active. Although officially Christian, many native people in Sarawak are actually animists.

Iban (Sea Dayak)	*302,794*
Chinese	*293,755*
Malays	*182,709*
Bidayuh (Land Dayak)	*83,709*
Melanau	*53,232*
Other Groups (Kenyah, Kayan, Punan, Murut)	*49,939*
Non-native Groups (e.g. Europeans)	*10,208*

People

In 1980, the total population of Sarawak was approximately 1.3 million. That means a density of approximately 10 people per square kilometer. But one should keep in mind that around 40% of the population lives in the three big cities: Kuching with a population of 350,000; Sibu whose population is 135,000 and Miri with a population of 100,000.

The remainder of the population lives in the countryside or in the forest. The population is ethnically divided as follows:

The Dayak

A variety of ethnic groups, living in the interior of Sarawak, are collectively known as the **Dayak**. They include the Iban or Lake Dayak, the Kayan, the Kenyah, the Murut and the Nhadju or Land Dayak. Hunters and gatherers, such as the **Punan** are not counted among the Dayak.

The name Dayak comes from the Dutch, and is a misappropriation of the Malay word *daya* meaning, interior land. The Dutch used this word to refer to all groups that lived in the interior of Borneo. In contrast to the Europeans, the people named themselves after the rivers along which they lived. The people who lived on the Kahajan River called themselves Oloh Kahajan or "People from the Kahajan." The people who lived in the north of the island called themselves Kami Benua, or "We of this Land." The Kajan

Festivals: In a long-house in Sarawak (above); Chinese New Year.

(Ho)

(Ho)

The Call of the Wild: Mount Kinabalu, the highest peak in Southeast Asia, offers an

exciting challenge.

Adventures: Trekking through the jungle in Sabah, Sarawak or Taman Negara is a

(PR)

(Ho)

once-in-a-lifetime experience... You never know who might be watching.

(ML)

Life in a Long-house in Sarawak: In other civilizations, balloons can be a big attraction.

(GU)

Taking a Break: Top spinners, cabinet makers.

called them *ivan* or *hiwan*, meaning wanderers. In time, they took the name for themselves, and were known as the Kami Ivan or "We Wanderers." This later became Kami Iban and finally Iban, a name which was also used by the Europeans.

Even today, it is not entirely clear in what order the different groups of Dayak came to settle in Borneo.

A plausible theory is that the Punan are the oldest inhabitants of the island. They were very likely there when the island was still a part of the mainland. After Borneo broke off from the mainland, no new migrants came for a long time. Eventually, a new group of mongoloid people came from south China over the Malay Peninsula and Sumatra to Borneo. They were the ancestors of the Kayan, who originally landed on the south of the island and then traveled up the rivers to Sarawak. Next to arrive were the Murut who live in what is now Sabah, who came either directly from Assam (they share some common cultural traits with the people there) or from Assam via the Philippines.

The last "indigenous" group to arrive was the **Iban**. They came from near Palembang on Sumatra to what is now Sarawak some 300 years ago. At the end of the 16th century, Malay nobles from Sumatra came to administer the southern part of Sarawak at the request of the Sultan of Brunei. These aristocrats were pirates, and they planned to recruit the people in Sarawak for their ships. The plan backfired, however, as the people were not very warlike and proved to be poor seamen. For this reason, the pirates sent for their families from Sumatra. The Iban are descended from this group. After that, the pirates lived only on the rivers near the coast. Due to internecine feuds and rivalries, some of them moved inland along the rivers. Their ongoing competition led to the creation of the **long-house**, still used today. These houses, built on stilts, were fortified to provide protection from enemies. One long-house housed an entire extended family group and there was a loose association from long-house to long-house.

The cultures of the different groups of Dayak are quite similar, though there are

interesting differences between the Iban and the Kayan. While the Kayan are clearly divided into three social classes, nobles, freemen and slaves, there is not as clear a difference among the Iban. Their social status is documented by their physical location within the long-house: the further outside the main room they live, the lower their social status.

The leader of the long-house acts as the leader, according to the unwritten traditions known as *adat*. In making decisions, the leader usually consults with the oldest men in the long-house and the village in order to reach some kind of consensus.

Among the Iban, the *title of leader* is not hereditary. The next leader is chosen from the most able men in the long-house. The Kayan, on the other hand, do have hereditary leadership and the current leader may choose his successor from among his children. However, the one chosen does not necessarily have to be the eldest son; the successor is chosen on the basis of merit. In some cases, a daughter may be designated as the next leader, but usually a man is chosen.

In addition to the leader, the *medicine man* (*manang*) has an important position within the community. He has the ability to contact and appease the spirit world of the Iban. The Iban believe that the course of their lives is greatly influenced by nature spirits which are in turn under a higher divine authority. The spirits are constantly searching for new human souls to prey upon and the people can only protect themselves through an elaborate series of rituals. For the Iban, the highest god is the god of war because only he has the power to subordinate all the other gods. The medicine men have the ability to read the will of the gods in the innards of animals and may thus advise their people on how to avoid the gods' ill will. Peoples' dreams are particularly meaningful to the Dayak and they see them as a compliment to the real world. Sometimes when the spirits descend upon a fresh human soul, which can happen easily during sleep, it can lead to an entire long-house being cleared out. The Dayak often believe this to be happening during a bad illness.

At one time, all the Dayak were **head-hunters**, a practice which was founded in religious belief. Collecting heads was seen as a way of gaining the power of other people. It was also a way for people to get closer to the gods. The **tattoos** sported by both male and female Dayak are linked to the practice of head-hunting. Such tattoos are still common today. If you ask the Dayak about the procedures for tattooing or the meaning of the designs, the answer will more than likely be a non-answer such as, "It is just a design." But don't be too quick to assume that the Dayak have lost yet another aspect of their culture. On the contrary, the tattoos have great spiritual significance and are thought to be instilled with magic powers; more often than not, the Dayak will not want to discuss this with outsiders.

Among some groups, the traditional animist beliefs have been weakened by exposure to Christianity or Islam. Nonetheless, people continue to get tattoos, partially as protection, and partially as a way of maintaining their own traditions in the face of change.

The Dayak have **monogamous marriages**. If possible, the couple comes from the same level of society. Originally, there was little intermarriage between different extended family groups. Within each family there are strict incest taboos. A marriage represents an official binding of two family groups. Since a marriage means a change in living for both partners, certain religious rituals must be performed to avert misfortune. The Dayak also have the institution of divorce, and it is often a public affair, since the entire community might be affected by the loss of a worker. *Adat* has clear guidelines concerning when a marriage may be terminated. Reasons are either "of the inner world," like adultery, or "of the outer world," like a bad dream, which the Dayak see as reality. A divorce can sometimes result in someone being banished from a family or a part of society.

The extent to which the traditional meaning of marriage is retained, is dependent upon the amount of missionary activity in an area. Many groups use a combination of *adat* and missionary-taught values,

The **economy** of the Dayak is almost entirely centered on the production of rice. This is grown in dry fields, which are cut out of and burned away from the jungle. Hunting and gathering plants play a smaller role. More and more Dayak are getting involved with the lumber industry, as the relatively high salaries are attractive to them.

Manners in a Long-house

Before entering a long-house, one must have permission; friends never enter without it. Usually, the leader of a group approaches the long-house to request permission to enter.

It is quite improper to wear shoes or sandals in a long-house, and especially not on the mats that are used for sitting and sleeping. After entering the long-house, it is proper to give gifts to the chief, the *tuai rumah*, of the house. Sweets, cigarettes, alcohol and small things like lighters and balloons are greatly appreciated. Be careful in choosing your gifts, however.

Once, we visited a long-house and brought balloons. At first, everyone loved them, though they couldn't seem to blow them up by themselves, we had to do that for about 50 people. Everyone was happy until someone touched a balloon with a lit cigarette and it exploded. Suddenly, everyone was silent. They thought we were playing a trick on them. Fortunately, the situation was saved by our guide who explained the proper way to handle balloons.

Along with the gifts, give the *tuai rumah* the food you have brought along with you (rice and canned food, usually.) Make sure you have at least enough to eat for the length of your stay. It will be cooked for you by the residents.

When a guest in a long-house, you should always keep in mind that the people there are just as proud of their way of life as we are of ours. Upon entering a long-house, one is traditionally greeted with a drink, usually coffee during the day and *tuak* or rice wine during the evening. It is improper to refuse this drink. If for any reason, you really do not want to drink it, take it anyway, thank your hosts, and try and take at least a sip, but do not refuse to accept the container, at least.

It is also considered impolite to refuse food that is offered. If you do not want to eat, take some anyway, move it around a bit with your fingers, bring some to your lips and thank your hosts. Food and drinks are consumed with **both hands**.

Ask permission before you take any photographs, and do not ask again if it is refused.

Animals that belong to the long-house should not be mistreated in any way. Do not, for example, throw stones at them or kick them, as the people believe that mistreating animals brings misfortune in the future.

If a long-house is taboo or *pantang*, it may not be entered by strangers. You will know this because either someone will inform you or a white flag will be hanging at the entrance. After a death or some similar misfortune, a long-house is usually taboo.

If you have trouble sleeping, you might want to take some ear-plugs, as a long-house is anything but quiet. The walls are very thin and are only around 2.5 meters high. The roof is a couple of meters above the walls. This promotes good air circulation as well as good smoke circulation.

By paying attention to a few simple rules of behavior, a visit to a long-house can be an unforgettable experience. When you arrive, you should state how long you plan to stay. The guide will also probably want to know this, so he can plan on getting home at a certain time. It is usually enough to simply bring gifts and enough food for one's own consumption. Sometimes, however, you might be asked for money at the end of your stay; the people are well aware of what they can get for money.

You will have to judge for yourself whether or not to pay, but after a few days in a long-house, it is very apparent how poor the people usually are.

If you spend a long time in a long-house, you will certainly want to take part in the activities of everyday life. This is usually allowed, but be sure to ask your hosts' permission before you do anything.

The Punan

The Punan, or Penan, are descended from the first inhabitants of Borneo. These people are traditionally jungle nomads, hunters and gatherers. In 1982, there were approximately 4000 of them counted in Sarawak and Brunei. The Malaysian government is making an effort to permanently settle the Punan, but it has not been entirely

successful. The Punan are not one distinct group, but are spread out all over the island. Different groups have different cultures and languages.

As hunters and gatherers, the Punan are experts at living in and off the jungle. They are excellent hunters with blowguns and poisoned darts. They hunt everything from small rodents and monkeys to wild pigs and deer. For big game, the blowgun darts are fitted with a spear tip, as the poisoned darts alone are often not enough to kill an animal. Though they also trap animals, hunting with a blowgun is a more prestigious way to land game.

The most important food sources for these people are jungle plants. The Punan are familiar with an incredible diversity of edible plants that grow in the areas where they live. These plants include sago, a good source of carbohydrates, and fruits like durian, mangosteen, and rambutan. In addition to these well-known plants, there are many others about which little is known in Western circles. Apart from hunting and gathering, the Punan sometimes grow their own crops like manioc, rice and sweet potatoes. They choose the location for their settlements based on its proximity to edible plants.

When the supply is depleted, they pick up their few possessions and move elsewhere. The Punan hardly ever build permanent housing. Sometimes they live in caves. If no natural shelter is available, they will build simple huts or lean-tos, usually without four walls. For a floor, they use a kind of mat made from branches. The roofs are usually made from rattan or palm fronds.

A settlement might also be moved for mystical reasons, like a death, or a bad dream.

It is interesting to observe the groups of Punan that have become sedentary. They build their main, permanent settlement in the center of an area, and then usually live in small hunting camps surrounding it, moving frequently from camp to camp. More and more people are establishing semi-permanent settlements, and the nomadic way of life is dying.

For the people who remain nomadic, the range of options is shrinking as logging and other economic interests infringe on their ancestral lands. Now the only possibilities are either to settle permanently in one place or to allow the government to set them up on a reservation, where they can lead a semblance of their traditional life.

Bruno Manser

This 34 year-old Swiss is a living example of the classic explorer-adventurer. After graduating from high school, he worked as a shepherd in the Alps, a job which gave him plenty of time to pursue his main hobby, reading. He read books about "primitive" peoples and was especially impressed with the Punan of Borneo, who were at the time, still entirely nomadic. Eventually, he decided he wanted to visit and live with these people.

Manser went to Borneo in 1984 and began to look for the Punan. Finally, in the Limbang district of Sarawak, he found a group. He lived with them for several months and began to learn their ways. During this time, he observed that the areas where the Punan lived were continuously shrinking, due to logging operations, one of the mainstays of the Malaysian economy. With the Punan, Manser began to plan protests, including petitions to the government and blockades of logging roads. There were no clear results of his actions, except for Manser being declared a criminal. Logging has remained the same exploitative industry. He was arrested and his passport, as well as his notes on the life of the Punan, were confiscated. As a result of his activities, the entire Limbang area is closed to foreigners.

There are two important concerns involved here: Timber is one of the most important exports of Southeast Asia; in order to reduce the destruction of the tropical rainforests, it is illogical to try to disrupt the supply from source countries. A more effective method would be to reduce the demand for tropical timber in the industrialized countries that are its chief consumers. The second concern is for the protection of the traditional way of life of the Punan. Such apparently primitive peoples seem very exotic to the West. But do we really have the right to place them in protected areas like animals?

Surely much more should be done to prepare these people for a life in our world, a world which is going to reach them eventually.

The international controversy caused by Manser focused attention on the need to preserve the world's tropical rain forests and on the plight of aboriginal peoples. For this reason, many international organizations have supported Manser's actions.

National Parks

There are three national parks in Sarawak, the Bako, the Niah and the Gunung Mulu National Parks. All three are worth visiting. The only real disadvantage is the very high cost of getting to the Gunung Mulu Park. Since each park is in a very different topographical zone, they provide a good overall view of Sarawak in its natural state.

Sarawak's national parks are very well maintained and are home to a wide variety of native flora and fauna. Hopefully, they will be with us for a very long time as good examples of tropical rainforests. Unfortunately, the parks have become a kind of Noah's Ark, and are home to species that are no longer found anywhere else. Perhaps in the future, such species might be reintroduced outside the parks.

Time and time again it has been saddening for us to see tourists marveling at the wonders of nature, and at the same time littering the jungle with everything from cola cans to film canisters. Along with the garbage, graffiti is constantly being carved into trees and written on rocks, spoiling the beauty of nature. Some people also find it necessary to test their strength on plants or stones, especially stalactites, that may have been thousands of years in the making. At the risk of sounding repetitive, we would like to ask you again, please treat nature inside and outside the parks with the utmost respect. The Forestry Department has two slogans that are worth quoting here:

*"**Nature does not belong to you. You belong to it.**"*

*"**Take nothing but pictures, leave nothing but footprints.**"*

Permits

If you are planning to visit one or more national parks, you will need to register in advance. There is usually no limit on how long you may stay, so plan on getting a permit for several days in case your plans change. You can get permits for all three parks in Sarawak in Kuching. Go to the Sarawak Tourist Info Centre, Jl. Main Bazaar, Tel. 248088. You can get a permit to visit Niah and Gunung Mulu Parks at the regional office in Miri. The address there is:

- Officer in Charge,
  National Parks and Wildlife Section,
  Forest Office,
  Miri.
  Tel. 36637.

When you register, you can also make room reservations.

We would recommend registering in Kuching, as the office there has very good information on all three parks. They also have maps with marked trails. For Bako Park, there are two small books with information on animal and bird life in the park. They make it quite simple to identify animals and their habitats, which might in turn make it easier to find some. In Miri, there is rarely good information available.

Kuching

According to legend, the city got its name through an unfortunate misunderstanding. When James Brooke's ship first approached the city, he pointed to it and asked his Malay interpreter what it was called. The interpreter thought he was pointing to a passing cat and responded with the Malay word for cat, *"kuching."*

Today, Kuching is the capital of Sarawak and the administrative seat of the first district. It has a population of around 305,000.

The city is located some 32 km inland along the Sarawak River. The center of town is on the southern bank. This is where the main activities of the city take place, but there is little worth seeing from the time of the Rajas. The unmistakable monuments from that period, the Istana and Fort Margherita, are located on the north bank. Since Kuching has the only international airport in Sarawak, a visit to the state will most likely begin here.

Though the other cities of Sarawak have little to offer the tourist except as starting points for journeys inland, there is a lot to see in Kuching. It is worth spending a few days here.

What to See

The **Sarawak Museum** is the biggest attraction. It was built in 1888 by Charles Brooke and Alfred Russel Wallace. Wallace was a co-founder of the theory of evolution, named the Wallace Line, a link between the Asian and the Australian-Melanesian animal worlds. This line runs between Bali and Lombok and between Borneo and Sulawesi or Celebes.

The museum, on Jalan Tun Haji Openg, is in the style of a French town hall. It has excellent information about the animal life of Borneo. From snails, mussels and insects, to amphibians, reptiles and mammals. On display are individual specimens and collections of plants and animals that live together.

They have some proboscis monkeys *(Nasalis larvatus)*, which only live on Borneo, on display (interesting for those who missed them in Bako Park).

Opposite the old museum is the newly-built (1984) **Dewan Tun Abdul Razak Museum**. It has information about the ethnological backgrounds of the indigenous peoples of Sarawak. In the foyer are wax figures of some of the peoples and to the right is a small pond with a house on stilts.

There are also many objects collected from archaeological sites,

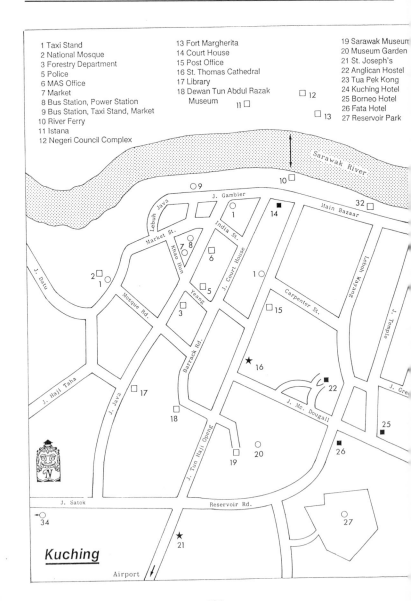

1 Taxi Stand
2 National Mosque
3 Forestry Department
5 Police
6 MAS Office
7 Market
8 Bus Station, Power Station
9 Bus Station, Taxi Stand, Market
10 River Ferry
11 Istana
12 Negeri Council Complex

13 Fort Margherita
14 Court House
15 Post Office
16 St. Thomas Cathedral
17 Library
18 Dewan Tun Abdul Razak
   Museum

19 Sarawak Museum
20 Museum Garden
21 St. Joseph's
22 Anglican Hostel
23 Tua Pek Kong
24 Kuching Hotel
25 Borneo Hotel
26 Fata Hotel
27 Reservoir Park

Kuching

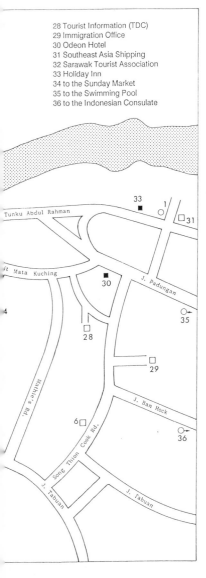

28 Tourist Information (TDC)
29 Immigration Office
30 Odeon Hotel
31 Southeast Asia Shipping
32 Sarawak Tourist Association
33 Holiday Inn
34 to the Sunday Market
35 to the Swimming Pool
36 to the Indonesian Consulate

and a replica of a long-house, which you can enter. Among other things, the decorations include real skulls from the time when headhunting was accepted. The display is real enough to make you forget you are in a museum. There is a lot more in the museum, including good information about Sarawak today.

Open Monday-Thursday, from 9:15 to 17:15; Saturday-Sunday, from 9:15 to 18:00; closed Fridays and holidays. Admission is free.

Fort Margherita, originally intended to protect Kuching from invasion, was built in 1841 and named after the wife of the second Raja, Rana Margaret.

Today, the fort is a police museum, where weapons are on display. Among them are some cannon which were successfully employed against the rebel leader Rentap.

There are also life-sized dioramas of figures from important military conflicts, like the fight against the communists in the 1960s. Relics from the Japanese occupation are also included.

From the 1980's, there are maps showing where crocodiles have been sighted in Sarawak. The locations where people have been attacked are also indicated along with some statistics. One very large stuffed reptile makes it very clear that Sarawak's inland rivers are not the safest swimming holes available.

The Istana or government palace is, like Fort Margherita, on the north bank of the river. It was built by

Charles Brooke in 1870. It houses portraits of the former rulers of Sarawak. Today it is the official residence of the governor of Sarawak and it is not open to visitors. The only chance to see it from up close is to take a boat from Pangkalan Batu. The graves of the Brooke family are located between Fort Margherita and the Istana and the state parliament is housed nearby in the modern (1976) *Counsil Negeri Komplex*.

On the south side of the river, and therefore within the city proper, is the *Court House*, built in 1871, with its *bell tower*. The main entrance

In front of the Dewan Tun Abdul Razak Museum: A Dayak tomb.

seems a bit out of place, with its thick columns and ornate Victorian decoration. The decoration explains the "legitimacy" of the white rajas. The bell tower was added to the building in 1883.

In 1924, the *Brooke Memorial* was erected in front of the Court House. This massive stone column was built to honor Charles Brooke. It contains bronze reliefs representing the four main ethnic groups of Sarawak – Dayaks, Malays, Chinese and Kayan.

Masjid Negeri Sarawak or the National Mosque was begun in 1952 and not finished until 1968. It is the most expensive building in Sarawak. Its golden cupola overlooks the entire city. The mosque may be visited during the day, but be sure to dress conservatively and to leave your shoes at the door. Women should ask permission before entering.

Tua Pek Kong Temple is the oldest Chinese temple in Kuching, built in 1876. It is located on a hill at the intersection of Jalan Tunku Abdul Rahman and Temple Street and is one of the most richly-decorated temples in the city.

Public parks are available for those seeking a bit of a rest from the city. Try the garden of the Sarawak Museum or the *Reservoir Park* on Reservoir Rd. They are both very clean and pleasant and are favorite picnic grounds for locals.

Sunday Market is held every Sunday from 6:00-12:00 and is the biggest and best market in town. In addition to food and other staples, there is a good selection of local artwork by indigenous peoples.

At the intersection of Padungang Rd. and Pending Rd. is the public swimming pool, open daily. The water doesn't always look very inviting – a bit dirty.

Accommodation

Depending on your means, Kuching has hotel rooms from M$ 15 to 200 a night, ranging from simple Chinese hotels to the international class Holiday Inn. If you arrive by plane from the mainland, you should get into Kuching between 1:00 and 2:00 in the morning. Almost all travelers then go straight to the **Kuching Hotel**, which is open all night. This is a good idea for your first night, but if you plan on staying for a few nights, try to change hotels in the morning, since the plane comes in every night at the same time and there will be another noisy crowd the next night.

●**Kuching Hotel**, 6 Temple St., M$ 17.
●**Khiaw Hin**, 52 Temple St., the same simple standards as the Kuching Hotel, but quieter. Tel. 23708.
●**Ah Chew**, 3 Java St., good, from M$ 14.
●**Ng Chew**, 16 Court House Rd., cheap but a bit dirty, near the bus terminal, M$ 15.
●**Syn Ah Hotel**, 16 Market St., very close to the bus terminal as well as the national mosque, M$ 24. Tel. 21459.
●**Anglican Hostel**, on church grounds on Jalan McDougall. Rooms for rent when not otherwise occupied. All rooms are big and clean, a bit stuffy on the second floor. Very friendly and good information. M$ 20-25.
●**Fata Hotel**, McDougall Rd., higher prices, but not much better, from M$ 58. Tel. 248111.
●**Aurora Hotel**, McDougall Rd., a mid-range hotel, from M$ 55. Tel. 240281.
●**Odeon Hotel**, Jalan Padungan, too far from the center of town, M$ 35. Tel. 24200.

●**Borneo Hotel**, Jalan Tabuan, nice, but also too far out of town, from M$ 65. Tel. 244121.
●**Long House Hotel**, Abell Rd., group tours inland are organized here, from M$ 65. Tel. 249333.
●**Mayfair Hotel**, 45 Palm Rd., far from the center, but good, M$ 32. Tel. 416380.
●**Holiday Inn**, Jalan Tunku Abdul Rahman, Kuching's luxury hotel, from M$ 135 (single rooms from M$ 85). Tel. 423111.

Food

Kuching offers all kinds of food. There are good vendors on Market St., India St. and Istoh Rd. There are Indian restaurants along Carpenter St. and Leboh Wayang. Western food is available in the shopping centers like theone in the Holiday Inn. The India St. stalls are particularly good.

Public Transportation

The **airport** is 11 km outside of town. The no. 12 A bus runs there for 65 *sen*, every 25 minutes from 6:25 to 23:30. It runs between the airport and the bus station in Kuching.

Pending, the **harbor** of Kuching, is 12 km out of town. Get there with the No. 1 or No. 17 bus for 70 *sen*.

Taxis:

There are four taxi stands inside the city: at the intersection of Gambier Rd. and Power St.; at the intersection of Jalan Masjid and Gartak St. (in front of the National Mosque); at the intersection of Jalan Tun Haji Openg and Carpenter St; and at the Holiday Inn. Taxis are also available at the airport.

Taxis cost M$ 1.40 for the first kilometer and M$ 0.50 for each additional kilometer. If there is no meter, be sure to set a price beforehand. A taxi from the airport to the city costs around M$ 12.

Buses:

There are 4 bus companies that operate within the city:

●*Bau Transport Company:* Station on Jalan Masjid, red and cream buses, Tel. 63160, 65392.
●*Chin Lian Long Motor Vehicle Co.* Bhd.: Station at the Bus Terminal, Tel. 22767, 32766.
●*Matang Transport Company:* Station on Power St., cream buses, Tel. 22814.
The Sarawak Transport Company: Station on Java St., green and cream buses, Tel. 22679, 22967, 20039.

Boats:

There are boats across the Sungei Sarawak from Pangalan Beta. They leave when they are full and the crossing costs 20 *sen*.

Addresses

●*American Express:* Represented by Sarawak Travel Agencies, 52 India St., Tel. 23708, and 4 Shopping Arcade in the Holiday Inn, Tel. 21779.
●*Books:* The Public Library is on Jalan Java. Nature and ethnology books are available in the Sarawak Museum shop. The Rex Bookstore, which has good maps, is near the market on Khoo Hun Yeang St.
●*Currency Exchange:* There are some large banks in Kuching. If you are changing travelers' checks, askabout the bank's handling fees, which range from 50 *sen* to M$ 2.50 per check. There are money changers around India St. and Power St. that might offer better rates.
●*Immigration:* On Jalan Simpang Tiga in the Federal Government Office Complex, Tel. 25661 / 20894. This is the place to extend your visa.
●*Tourist Information:* Available from the offices of the Sarawak Tourist Association (STA). These are situated at the airport,

Tel. 72576 and on Main Bazaar Rd., Tel. 248088, near the ferry landing. The latter is the main office and has the best information. The TDC has an office on Jalan Satok, on the fourth floor of the Bank Negara Building, room 403, Tel. 56575, 56775.
●*Hospital:* The General Hospital is on Jalan Tun Haji Openg, outside town, Tel. 57555.
●*Indonesian Consulate:* 19 Deshon St., Tel. 20551. There are no other consulates in Kuching.
●*MAS:* Located, in addition to the airport, at Jl. Song Thian Cheok, Tel. 246622. If you have anything to ask, plan on it taking a long time.
●*Post Office:* The main one is at the intersection of Jalan Tun Haji Openg and Carpenter St., Tel. 2131 i. They have a Poste Restante desk.

Important Telephone Numbers

●Airport: 72244
Airlines:
●Hornbill Skyways, Sdn, Bhd: 53388, 72611.
●Merpati Airlines: 23276.
●Singapore Airlines: 20266.
●Royal Brunei Airlines: 21082.
Police: 21222 (Yeang St. / Court House Rd.)
●Telephone Information: 103
●Customs: 33133

Outside of Kuching

There are *a few beaches* close to Kuching.

Between 7:00 and 8:00 in the morning, boats leave for *Santubong*, 32 km from Kuching at the mouth of the Sungei Sarawak. The boats leave from the ferry landing on Jalan Gambier. Santubong is a picturesque Malay village, and the beach is very popular. The boats return around 13:30. There is a government resthousethere, but it must be booked in advance through the District Office in Kuching, Tel. 22533.

Santubong can also be reached by bus from Gartak St. The trip goes over a brand new bridge to the Santubong Peninsula. This costs M$ 1.30.

If you want to stay in the **Government Bungalows**, inquire with the police. You can either rent an entire bungalow for M$ 40 or a single room for M$ 10. There is also a so-called Senior Bungalow, which costs M$ 15 for a room or M$ 60 for the whole thing. It is a great big old house with big rooms, each with a bathroom. It also has a big terrace, a nice balcony and a comfortable sitting room. Highly recommended.

The only problem here is the beach, which is in fact very small. Since the town is at the mouth of a river, the water is also very muddy.

There is **a better beach**, 4 km away at the luxury **Damai Beach Hotel**, which you can use for M$ 20 a day.

There are also buses to **Lundu** and **Sematan**, both of which have good beaches. There are buses from Kuching to Lundu from 7:00 to 14:00. It is a 100 km trip. From there, you can go on to Sematan, which is around 30 km, from 6:20 to 16:40. Both towns have places to stay for around M$ 25.

The town of **Bau** was a gold boom-town in the late 19th century.

There is now a fresh-water lake which is good for swimming where the main mine used to be. It is 35 km from Kuching and buses leave from 6:00 to 18:00, leaving roughly every 40 minutes from the Kuching bus terminal.

Another attraction in the area is the **Bako National Park**.

Various travel agencies in Kuching organize **long-house tours**. Those without much time, but who wish to see a long-house by themselves, can go the 30 km from Kuching to the long-house at **Kampong Sega Benuh**. This is where many of the tours go. Take the No. 6 bus, which leaves Kuching around 11:00.

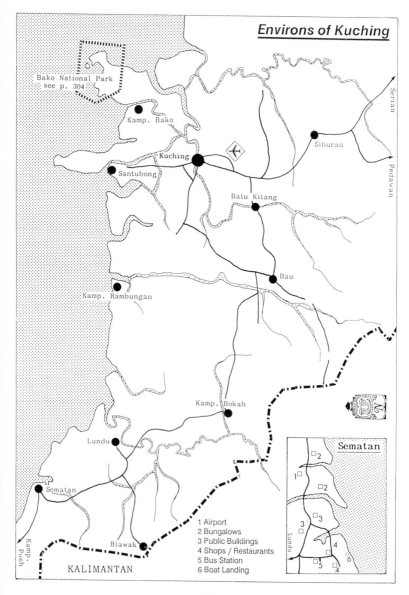

Environs of Kuching

Bako National Park
see p. 304

Kamp. Bako

Siburan

Kuching

Santubong

Batu Kitang

Bau

Kamp. Rambungan

Kamp. Bokah

Serian

Pedawan

Lundu

Sematan

Biawak

Kamp. Pueh

KALIMANTAN

Sematan

Lundu

1 Airport
2 Bungalows
3 Public Buildings
4 Shops / Restaurants
5 Bus Station
6 Boat Landing

Further Travel

Taxis:

At the above-named taxi stands, there are long-distance taxis, which run between the major towns.

Buses:

Express buses leave from the Power St. bus station all over Sarawak:
- *Bau* – M$ 1.35.
- *Bandar Sri Aman*: M$ 11.
- *Batu Kawa* – M$ 0.70.
- *Batu Kitang* – M$ 1.
- *Betong* – M$ 12.60.
- *Kampong Bako* – M$ 1.
- *Lundu* – M$ 5.
- *Muara Tuang* – M$ 2.10.
- *Saratok* – M$ 15.40.
- *Serian* – M$ 3.25.
- *Pedawan* – M$ 4.30.

Ships:

Along with express buses, ships are the most important transportation in Sarawak. The ship traffic runs the whole length of the state to Sabah. The following companies operate regularly out of Kuching:
- To *Sarikei*: daily at 8:00, a 6 hour trip, with MV Mas Jaya 1 and 2 and with MV Concord. Buy tickets at the Boon Tien Shell station on Jalan Tunku Abdul Rahman, Tel. 54601.
- To *Sarikei* and *Sibu*: Tuesday and Saturday at 18:00, an 18 hour trip, with MV Soon Bee. Tickets at the Southern Navigation Terminal Sdn. Bhd. at 21 Green Hill Rd., Tel. 22613, 52267.
- MV Rajah Mas goes to *Sarikei, Binatang* and *Sibu*: Monday and Tuesday at 18:00, between 5 and 15 hours. The agent is the Southeast Asia Shipping Bhd. at 155 Jalan Chan Chin Ann, Tel. 22966.
- The Siam Company at 28 Main Bazaar, Tel. 22832, sells tickets to *Bintulu, Miri, Marudi, Limbang* and *Lawas*. These places are reached by cargo ships and there is no fixed schedule or price list.
- It is also possible to travel around on cargo ships that are not normally for passengers. You can sleep on deck so be

sure to bring a padded mat. There is usually no place to sit and not all ships have food and drinks available. Be sure to ask first. Sample prices:
- *Bintulu* – M$ 30.
- *Kampong Bako* – M$ 2.
- *Lawas* – M$ 150.
- *Limbang* – M$ 120.
- *Marudi* – M$ 100.
- *Miri* – M$ 80.
- *Santubong* – M$ 2.50.
- *Sarikei* – M$ 8 or 20.
- *Sibu* – M$ 10 or 33.

Planes

There are regular *flights* from Kuching Airport, 11 km south of the city, to points in Sarawak, Sabah, Brunei, Peninsular Malaysia, Singapore and Indonesia:
- *Bintulu* – M$ 97.
- *Miri* – M$ 136.
- *Sibu* – M$ 60.
- *Brunei* – M$ 192.
- *Kota Kinabalu* – M$ 198.
- *Johor Baru* – M$ 147 / 125.
- *Kuala Lumpur* – M$ 231 / 162.
- *Singapore* – M$ 170.
- *Pontianak* – M$ 84.
- *Jakarta* – M$ 184.

Bako Park

The Bako Park, about 27 square kilometers, is on a peninsula with a rugged coastline. Because of its accessibility and variety, I rate it as the most interesting National Park in Sarawak.

Getting There

When you register, you will have to decide when you will arrive in the park and when you will leave. Since the park is very close to Kuching, it is a favorite destination for weekend getaways. If at all possible, try to get there during the week. From Kuching, you can get there either by bus or by ship. The MV Juno sails there daily at 8:00 and the MV Sri Belaga leaves at 14:00. The boats leave from Long Wharf, Jalan Gambier, and cost M$ 2 per person. It is a two hour trip to Kampong Bako. From there, you have to rent a motorboat which takes 20-30 minutes to get to Telok Assam and the park office. This boat costs M$ 25 for up to five people. Ask about the specific departure times, as they can change due to varying water levels.

If the day is even the least bit stormy, be sure to protect your belongings by wrapping them completely in plastic. The boats can get very wet!

Bus line 6 goes to Kampong Bako. They leave about every hour from 6:30 to 17:00 from the terminal on

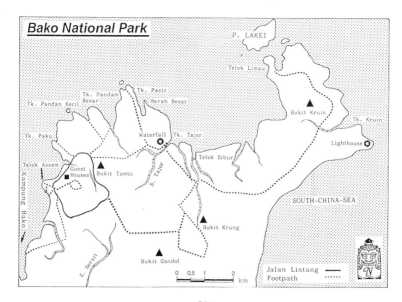

Bako National Park

304

Mosque Rd. The one-hour trip costs about M$ 1.50. You must also rent a motorboat from Kampong Bako. We recommend the bus trip, which is not quite as comfortable, but is far more interesting. The bus has to cross several rivers along the way. At times, this can be exciting as the bus makes its way across on little bridges and ferries.

Accommodation / Food

● There are two old **resthouses** (M$ 30 / day / house), 4 old **hostels**, 2 **deluxe resthouses** (M$ 60 / day / house) and 4 **standard resthouses** (M$ 40 / day / house). There are also four-room buildings (each with 4 beds) with a common kitchen and bathroom (M$ 14 / day / person). Other accommodation is under construction.

● There is a small **canteen** in the park with average prices. If you are cooking for yourself, it is best to bring food from Kuching, though the canteen sells small items like salt, oil and drinks. There is very little fruit available, so try to bring your own.

The Park

In front of the camp office, there is a big map of the park which shows all the trails and gives times and distances. There is also a photo-exhibition about interesting animal and plant life in the park showing what you might discover on each of the trails.

The **trails** are of varying lengths and the time necessary to walk them ranges from 30 minutes to 8 hours. The most time-consuming ones are not so long, but they lead over difficult terrain like steep hills and muddy lowlands. The Lintang Trail, which takes 3 hours, is recommended. This trail covers all the types of vegetation in the park including mangroves, rain forest, and bush growth on the plateau. About halfway through, there is a detour passing a waterfall you can take to lengthen the walk.

Bako Park contains five different types of **vegetation:** Beach vegetation (excellent beaches, too); a mangrove belt; swamp forest; tropical rain forest; and bush growth on the plateau. The most interesting plant in the park must be the **pitcher plant** *(Nepenthes)* which grows on the high plateau. This carnivorous plant has leaves that grow into a "pitcher", which contains digestive juices. The edge of the pitcher is very colorful, in order to attract

insects, but it is covered with a slippery layer so that the insects can never get a grip on it. Over the top of the pitcher, there is a small lid that prevents rain from getting in and diluting the digestive juices. The pitcher itself grows up to 25 cm long. The larger specimens are usually found in the branches of other trees. Around Telok Assam, there are many **Long-tailed Macaque** *(Macaca fascicularis)* which are very forward and will grab anything left in their reach. Another more interesting variety of simian is the **proboscis monkey** *(Nasalis larvatus)*. It lives only on Borneo in coastal mangroves and along the river banks. This endangered species and there are only about 1000 left in all of Sarawak, gets its name from its long nose. Since they live around water, they are also very good swimmers.

Proboscis
Monkey

The Malays call these monkeys orang belanda (Dutchman), since a long nose and a white face were the symbols of Europeans in the colonial era. The best times to see them are just after dawn or just before dusk.

Bako Park used to be a kind of foster home for **orang-utans** *(Pongo pygmaeus)*. Orang-utans that were in captivity were set free here to live a protected life in the wild. That does not happen any more, as the park is too small to support very many of them. There have been no wild orang-utans in Bako Park for some years now.

The park is also home to many varieties of bird life. If you want to see anything, be sure to bring a pair of binoculars.

Bandar Sri Aman

Bandar Sri Aman has a population of around 68,000 and is about 195 km from Kuching and about 85 km from the coast. It is on the Batang Lupar River, and is the administrative seat of the Second Division. The town's original name, Simanggang, was changed in 1978. The purpose of that was to commemorate the surrender of the communist rebels in Rumah Sri Aman in 1973.

There is really nothing special in the town. It is often used as a starting point for **long-house tours**.

An **express boat** from Kuching to Bandar Sri Aman takes about 4-5 hours.

Accommodation

The town's three hotels are all close together and are all very expensive:
● *Alishan*, 4 Council Rd., very clean, good food, from M$ 34. Tel. 2578.
● *Taiwan* 1 Council Rd., clean, from M$ 35. Tel. 2494.
● *Hoover*, 123 Club Rd., the best place in town, from M$ 44. Tel. 2672.

Around Bandar Sri Aman

Skrang River Safari:

Most of these safaris begin in Bandar Sri Aman, though they can also be organized through travel agencies in Kuching.

They consist of visits to Iban long-houses, paired with a long, adventurous boat ride. Going upriver from Bandar Sri Aman, the banks are inhabited, but then fade into jungle after a time as the river begins to get rough. Finally, you reach the Iban long-houses, which are made to look primitive (for example, they do not have corrugated metal roofs). In other words, they are not the present-day versions, but merely living dioramas of the past, and for that reason, they are very disappointing.

These tours, which usually include an overnight stay in the long-houses, are for people who are afraid of going into the jungle by themselves. They are not recommended. Even if you do not have much time, and you would like to visit a long-house, you can visit the towns of **Selepong** and **Gua**, which are not far from the main road.

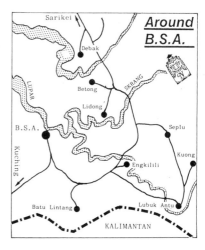

Lubuk Antu

An interesting detour from Bandar Sri Aman is to Lubuk Antu, 80 km by bus. It is a border crossing with Indonesia and has the typical big market and exciting international flavor of a border town.

Further Travel

There are daily **buses** from the bus station to Kuching and Sarikei.
● *Batu Lintang*: M$ 2.30.
● *Betong*: M$ 4.80.
● *Enkilili*: M$ 2.30.
● *Kuching*: M$ 11.
● *Lubuk Antu*: M$ 5.20.
● *Saratok*: M$ 8.30.
● *Sarikei*: M$ 11.20.

Sarikei

Sarikei is on the Batang Rajang River, some 180 km from Bandar Sri Aman. It is at the intersection of the road to Sibu and you can get there with an express boat.

Sarikei is a small town which is important to tourism because of its location. It is the place where you change from bus to express boat or vice-versa. The town is composed of blocks of terraced houses gathered along the river. On the way from the bus to the boat you will pass many food stores where you can renew your supplies.

Accommodation

It is not necessary or desirable to stay overnight in Sarikei unless you have missed a connection to Sibu. There are two hotels near the bus station:
●*Southern Hotel*, 21 Repok Rd., upstairs, good but a little noisy, M$ 32. Tel. 55291.

●*Sarikei Hotel*, 11 Wharf Rd, better than the Southern, not as loud, clean rooms, M$ 36.
●*Ambassador Hotel*, 54 Repok Rd., from M$ 26. Tel. 5264.
●*Payang Puri Hotel*, 1 Jalan Merdeka, from M$ 45. Tel. 5216.

Further Travel

●The *bus station* is right next to the river. There are express buses to Bandar Sri Aman for M$ 11.20 and Saratok for M$ 3.80.
●Between 7:00 and 16:00, there are hourly *express boats* up the Rajang to Sibu. The trip takes about 2-3 hours and costs M$ 5. Express boats to Kuching cost M$ 20 and leave daily at 8:30 am. Cargo boats to Kuching cost M$ 8.

Sibu

Sibu, the second largest city in Sarawak with 135,000 residents, is the administrative seat of the Third Division. Although the city is 129 km from the coast, it is an important harbor, since the wide river is navigable by coastal steamers. Sibu is situated on the right bank of the Rajang,

Due to its location, a lot of Sarawak's economy is centered on Sibu. Rubber, pepper and wood all come through here. Nearby are many sawmills and plantations.

The *night market* is very interesting. It takes place in the early evening on Market Rd. between Cross and Lembangan Roads.

Souvenir hunters should look at the small shops near the harbor and on Channel Rd.

Sibu is also a common starting point for *jungle tours* to the interior. These tours go either up the Rajang towards Kapit or Belaga, or by plane in the same direction. From there, long-house tours can be arranged.

Accommodation / Food

Since Sibu is a busy center of commerce, there are quite a few hotels:

●*Hotel Malaysia*, 8 Kampong Nyabor Rd., clean and quiet, but a bit far out, M$ 45-50. Tel. 332299.

●*Rex Hotel*, 32 Cross Rd., rooms on the third floor are the best and have their own showers and toilets. The ones facing the interior are the best. Good location, M$ 38. Tel. 330625.

●*Today Hotel*, 40 Kampong Nyabor Rd., good rooms, far from the center of town, M$ 28. Tel. 36499.

●*Diman Hotel*, 27 Kampong Nyabor Rd., M$ 15-36.
Tel. 337887.

●*King Hua*, Song Nai Slong Rd., over the movie theater, from M$ 45.

●*Sarawak Hotel*, 34 Cross Rd., centrally located with some cheap rooms. The rooms on the main road are very expensive, M$ 26-77. Tel. 333455.

●*Rest House*, Island Rd. / Hospital Rd., belongs to the Anglican church and rents rooms to travelers when not otherwise in use. Pleasant and very clean, M$ 20.

●*Capitol Hotel*, 19 Wong Nai Slong Rd., near the taxi stand, M$ 40-75. Tel. 336444.

●*Premier Hotel*, Kampong Nyabor Rd., luxury hotel, M$ 80-240. Tel. 323222.

Food: There are a number of Chinese restaurants near the harbor and on Central and Lembangan Roads. The night market also offers an assortment of foods.

Further Travel

●*Taxis* leave from the taxi stand on Cross Rd. / Wong Nai Siong Rd. There are city taxis as well as long-distance taxis that go to *Sarikei* and *Bintulu*.

●*Local buses* leave from the station on Cross Rd. / Market Rd. There is another bus terminal on Channel Rd. From there, buses leave daily for *Bintulu* for M$ 15. To get to *Miri* you have to go to Bintulu first and then change. Altogether the trip takes about 10 hours and costs M$ 30.

●*Express boats* leave daily for *Sarikei* for M$ 5 or direct for *Kuching* for M$ 29. Express boats go up river along the Rajang, to *Kapit* for M$ 15, every hour from 7:00-12:00. The five-hour journey takes you past long-houses, logging camps, mission stations and lots and lots of jungle. The largest town on the river is Kanowit.

●*Coastal ships* leave Sibu regularly for *Kuching* for M$ 10. Sibu is also a stop for ships going from Kuching to Brunei or Sabah, as well as for those coming the other

Sibu

1 Sarawak House, Premiere Hotel
2 MAS Office
3 Post Office
4 Taxi Stand
5 Sarawak Hotel
6 Rex Hotel
7 Guest House
8 Market
9 Night Market
10 Bus Station
11 Stadium
12 Express Boats
13 Docks
14 Police

way. To get a place on one of them, inquire either with the company or directly on board.

● Sibu also has an airport, with *flights* within Sarawak and Sabah. The No. 1 bus goes from Cross Road Bus Station to the airport for 60 *sen*.

● *Belaga*: M$ 76.
● *Bintulu*: M$ 53.
● *Kapit*: M$ 48.
● *Kuching*: M$ 60.
● *Miri*: M$ 75.
● *Kota Kinabalu*: M$ 156.
● *Labuan*: M$ 130.

If you are planning to travel by yourself into the interior, you will need a good deal of cash on hand. It makes sense to change money in Sibu, since the rates are usually better there than in Kapit. Also bear in mind that you will arrive in Kapit after a long boat ride when the banks are already closed. Boats stopping there on their way to Belaga leave in the early morning, so you will lose a whole day by changing money in Kapit. If you are planning a long trip, you should go shopping in the big supermarkets in Sibu. The selection is greater and the prices are better than in places where all the goods must be brought in on small boats.

Kapit

Kapit, the seat of the Seventh District, is 242 km from the coast up the Rajang River. There used to be no road at all coming here. Kapit is pretty much the last boundary between civilization and the wilderness. The town seems like something out of the Wild West. In the shops and restaurants, you will see people in western clothing alongside tattooed Iban, who have come into town for the day on their canoes to sell their game and handiwork.

You can organize individual longhouse tours here. There are some advertisements around town for them, or you can just ask around the harbor. It used to be that almost all tourists went on to Belaga and then arranged trips from there, but this is no longer necessarily the case.

Officially, you need a **permit for tours** that go past Kapit. You can get one from the government office near the boat landing. Further travel inland without a permit is illegal. Sometimes the police check ships going that way, and if you do not have a permit you will be sent back.

Accommodation

●**Guest House**, part of the Mission Station, on the square in front of the church, often booked, M$ 15.
●**Rajang Hotel**, 28 New Basar, rooms with A / C and bath, M$ 26-39. Tel. 796709.
●**Kapit Longhouse**, Berjaya Rd., big rooms, good view of the river from the upper story, M$ 25. Tel. 96415.

Further Travel

●**Express boats** travel daily between Kapit and Sibu. There are also boats to **Belaga** for M$ 24 twice a week. Boat traffic is often erratic during the dry season from June to September, due to the level of the river. Usually, boats traveling during the dry season require around 12 hours to make the trip to Belaga. Sometimes only a maximum of one boat a day makes the trip, but sometimes there might only be one boat a week.

And then there is always the possibility that boats leaving Kapit may not make it all the way to Belaga if the water level is too low. The trip is through a fascinating jungle landscape that is interrupted now and again by an occasional long-house. The most interesting part of the trip is through the **Pelagus Rapids**. Outside of the rainy season, these rapids are navigable only by unladen boats. For the passengers, that means a two-hour walk along a logging road that goes past the rapids.

Currently, there are development projects underway that will make the Pelagus Rapids and other rivers in Sarawak into a giant dammed lake which should be big enough to meet all of Malaysia's energy needs.

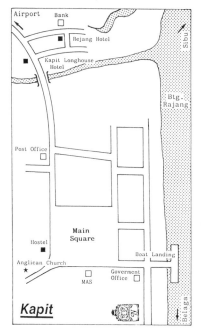

Kapit

One stop along the way to Belaga is the trading post of *Merit* for M$ 15, an ideal starting point for jungle tours. Other boats go daily to *Entawau* for M$ 8 and *Sibu* for M$ 15.

●Those who wish to avoid the long, and in the dryseason, uncomfortable, boat trip, can *fly* from Kapit to *Sibu* for M$ 48 or *Belaga* for M$ 47. There are two flights a week. Get tickets at the MAS Office near the boat landing or at the airport, 2 km away.

Treks

If you do not want to go all the way to Belaga, it is quite possible to trek further downstream on the Rajang.

One possibility is to take a boat from *Kapit* to Belaga, but to get off at *Merit*, about halfway. From there, the daring can

trek to *Tatau* on the coast in about five or six days. This costs about M$ 800, including the boat and the guide, who must also get back home.

There are many other possibilities for treks, but you will have to use your own initiative and make yourself understood in Malay (and maybe learn a few words of Iban). Just be prepared for anything. On one hand, you might stumble across a group of Iban who appear to be living in a previous century. On the other hand, you might meet aboriginal people who play their traditional music for guests on a battery operated cassette recorder, and then only when the guests themselves bring the batteries. And you will notice that most long-houses have corrugated metal roofs, better protection against the rain than the traditional thatch.

●*Hint:* If you are trekking with a guide, determine in advance the exact price for the entire trip. You might be asked to pay the entire sum at once, but as insurance against being left somewhere, it is best that you pay no more than half the total fee up front. If the guide asks too high a price, try and look elsewhere, or at least say you will. Some guides respond very quickly to threats of competition.

Belaga

Belaga is another starting point for jungle treks. This is just about the last place to find a guide and porters. Those not planning a long tour can either take a boat to *Kapit* for M$ 24, or M$ 9 to *Merit*, or one of the twice weekly flights to *Kapit* for M$ 47 or *Sibu* for M$ 76.

Accommodation

●*Belaga Hotel*, near the market, well-run, but the beds in some rooms have seen better days. Good information, M$ 24.

•*Resthouse*, often completely booked, good information, M$ 20.

The Trek from Belaga to Bintulu:

This trek has changed recently and is no longer as interesting as it once was. Apparently, the forest has been completely logged out and there are logging roads through the forest wherever it still exists. It is possible to take these roads with a boat connection all the way to Bintulu, if you need to get there in a hurry. The whole trip can be done in as little as 10 hours. It is a shame that what was once a beautiful stretch of jungle is now a barren wasteland.

Bario

It is possible to trek in the area around *Bario*, in the highlands of Sarawak near the border with Kalimantan. You can get there by plane from *Miri* or *Marudi*. There is

about one flight a week from both places. The flight costs M$ 70 from Miri and M$ 55 from Marudi. It's a Twin Otter plane with a limit of only 10 kg of luggage per person. Overweight luggage costs more.

From Bario, it is possible, with luck, to visit the Punan. Whether or not you will actually be able to depends greatly on the current political situation in the area (government – Punan – Bruno Manser – logging). At times, it is forbidden for foreigners to live with or visit the Punan. Check with the District Office in Miri or Marudi.

If there are no bureaucratic problems, you can get to *Kubaan* from Bario by foot in eight hours. From there, it is about four more hours to *Pa'tik*, a one-time Kelabit settlement where sedentary Punan now live. From time to time, you might also come across nomads.

From Pa'tik, you can either go back to Bario or, when the situation permits, continue further on to *Long Seridan* or *Long Lellang*. From either place, you can fly back to Marudi or Miri. From Long Seridan, it costs M$ 42 to get to Marudi or M$ 57 to Miri; from Long Lellang, it is M$ 46 to Marudi, and M$ 66 to Miri.

Another possibility is to trek from Bario to *Gunung Murud* at 2438 m, the highest mountain in Sarawak. First, go to *Pa'Ukat*, a Kelabit long-house which is about one hour by foot. Another 2.5-3 hours takes you to *Pa'Longan*, another Kelabit long-house, where you can spend the night. There are people there who know the way to the summit of the mountain. They charge about M$ 30 per day. The entire trek takes 3-4 days. It is possible to do it in two days, but that means walking 12 hours a day.

Leaving Pa'Longan in the morning, you walk 3.5 hours towards Kalimantan. You will then come to a shelter near the Dapur River. From the shelter there is a rather unclear path off to the left. Follow this path, crossing two streams, until you get to another collapsed shelter. Turn right here, and again the path is very hard to discern, and you will eventually get to the Dapur. Follow the river for about an hour until you get to a hunting shack in the middle of the forest. The following part is more complicated. You have to follow the river for another hour and a half, wading across three times where the river is met by tributaries. This allows you take a shortcut around some bends in the river. The only problem is that it is difficult to find the path again on the other side.

Once you have crossed the second of the two tributaries, the path goes up steeply for about two hours. Finally, you will come to another shelter, in the Punan style. You should spend the night here, since it is the last water source on the way up.

Next morning everything continues to go up. After half an hour, you come out of the thick forest and the vegetation becomes a lot thinner. Just keep going up and up for about three hours until you reach the summit. How do you know you're there? Simple – all the garbage from an old military camp is still there! There is a helicopter landing pad and lots of Biblical quotes from an old church. There is a good view from the top of Kalimantan and the Mulu mountains.

You can make it all the way back to Pa'Longan, the next day if you leave around 6:00 am.

Trekking Permission: If you are planning a jungle trip out of **Bario**, you must first get permission and register in Miri, in the office of the Fourth Division. Contact the Resident in the district office.

Bintulu

Bintulu is about 200 km from Sibu along the coast. What was a quiet fishing village at the beginning of the 80s is now a city of 60,000 and is still growing. While Bintulu used to be known as a place to get good fish, it is now better known as a center of the natural gas industry. There is now a plant for developing liquid gas and construction of a deep water port for tankers is underway.

There is a popular beach at **Tanjong Batu**.

Outside of town, there are several Kayan and Kenyah long-houses along the **Sungei Kemana**.

Similajau National Park is 16 km east of Bintulu. It consists of nothing more than some protected beaches and forest. It is a popular place for

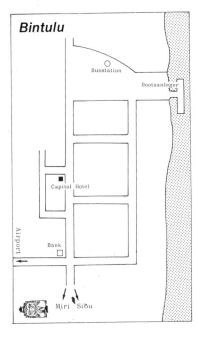

Bintulu

Busstation

Bootsanleger

Capitol Hotel

Bank

Airport

Miri Sibu

●*Police:* 31121
●*Taxi:* 32009

Further Travel

Bintulu is a stop on the route from Sibu to Miri or Batu Niah.

Taxis and *buses* travel this road daily.
●*Niah*: M$ 12 (at 7:00, 11:00, 12:00).
●*Miri*: M$ 17
●*Sibu*: M$ 15.
There are daily *flights* to:
●*Kuching*: M$ 97.
●*Sibu*: M$ 53.
●*Miri*: M$ 57.
●*Kota Kinabalu*: M$ 100.

From Bintulu, there are several daily *boats* to Tubau a trip which takes 3 hours, and costs M$ 14. There is a cheap hotel in Tubau. The next day, you can try and catch a lift with one of the trucks going to logging stations along the Rajang River. This is usually free. The road intersects the river above Belaga. From Belaga, you can get an express boat to Kapit for M$ 20 and from there, go on to Sibu for M$ 15.

locals on weekends and can get very full. It is only recommended for those who are really longing to get to a beach.

Accommodation

Bintulu's various hotels are all geared to business people with a lot of money.
●*Capitol*, from M$ 75.
●*Hoover*, M$ 80-200.
●*New Capitol Hotel*, from M$ 85.
●*Lodging House*, cheap, but good, M$ 38.

Important Phone Numbers

●*Airport:* 31073
●*MAS Office:* 32541 / 31554, in New Commercial Center, 26 Jalan Abang Galau

Batu Niah

A town between Bintulu and Miri and the gateway to the *Niah National Park*, which contains the Niah Caves.

Batu Niah itself is a very small, unremarkable town. There are a few stores where you can buy just about anything and some good and inexpensive Chinese and Malay restaurants.

From Batu Niah, there are *buses* to *Miri* leaving every day at 6:45, 8:00 10:45 and 14:45 for M$ 8.50.

Buses to Bintulu: 6:00, 7:00, 12:00, 15:00.

Accommodation

- *Niah Cave Hotel*, in the building complex on the right as you enter town. Clean rooms and friendly people, M$ 36.
- *Kim Hoe Hotel*, across the street from the above, M$ 38.

Niah Park

Niah National Park occupies about 30 square kilometers of the area around Gunung Subis. In the interior of this 400 m mountain is a giant cave system. It was declared a national monument in 1958 under the administration of the Sarawak Museum. In 1974, the area was designated as a national park.

Arrival

You will need a *permit* for the park to stay in the Government Hostel, unless you live in Batu Niah. You can get to the park by bus or taxi from Miri or Bintulu.

Niah National Park:

0	0,5 1	2 km

Footpath ....
Road ————
Park Boundary —..—
Mountain

Park Hostel
Long-house Rumah Chang
Pangkalan Lubang
Great Cave
Painted Cave
Batu Niah
Bintulu, Miri
Gunung Subis 394 m
Sungei Niah

Batu Niah:

Niah Caves, Footpath
Bintulu, Miri
Post Office
Church Mission
Bus
Police
Hotel
Sungei Niah

•From Miri there are **buses** to Batu Niah at 7:00 and 14:00 for M$ 8.50. The trip takes just under three hours.

•**Taxis** are much faster, but cost around M$ 15 to 20. From Bintulu, there are buses to Batu Niah at 8:00 and 13:00 for M$ 12. Taxis cost more than M$ 25. From Batu Niah, there are park boats to Pangkalan Lubang. They take 30 minutes and cost M$ 5 per person. You can also rent private boats for M$ 25-30 per boat for 3 or 4 people.

•You can also **walk** from Batu Niah to Pangkalan Lubang in about an hour.

Accommodation

•In Pangkalan Lubang, there is a **hostel** that has a total of 30 beds in three dormitory rooms. One night costs M$ 3. Aside from that, there are **three hotels** for M$ 30 in Batu Niah, all of which are quite reasonable.

What to See

The most interesting part of Niah Park is the winding system of caves.

To get to the famous limestone caves, you have to walk about 2.5 miles for 50 minutes from Pangkalan Lubang along a planked walkway. The path goes through the rain forest, past impressive giant trees growing at the base of the mountain. You will need good shoes, as the planks can get slippery, especially after a rainfall. At the end of the path is the entrance to the **Great Cave**, which seems like a gigantic hall. From floor to ceiling, it is almost 60 m high. The Great Cave and the caves behind it can be explored easily on your own, if you have a good flashlight. The **Painted Cave** can be explored with a guide. For groups of up to 20 people, the guide costs M$ 25-30. The money is well-spent as the guide is quite knowledgeable. In the 1950's, 40,000 year old wall paintings, as

well as a human skull from that period, were discovered in the Painted Cave.

The caves were discovered by accident in 1948, by someone collecting birds' nests, for use in Chinese **Birds' Nest soup**. The soup is considered such a delicacy that the nests sell for over M$ 600 per kg. Nest collectors are licensed so as to regulate the number of nests taken. Around 4 million **swiftlets** and several million **bats** live in the caves.

This large animal population produces enough dung to cover large parts of the cave floor. The dung, which is much softer than the stone, is collected to use as guano fertilizer. The nests are collected in April and May and September and October. The nest collectors climb up the smooth walls all the way to the top of the cave and use a hooked rod to pull the nests from their perches. Since the rods have lights on them to help the collector you can watch the process from the ground.

After visiting the caves, it is also possible to go on some **jungle walks**. You will however need a guide who charges around M$ 5 an hour. Supposedly, there are still some orang-utans in the park.

Miri

Miri is the administrative seat of the Fourth Division. The city's population of 100,000 is supported primari-

Swiftlets

ly by the off-shore oil industry. Sailors and oil workers contribute to the character of the town, particularly the night-life. Oil was first discovered in 1900, and since then, Miri has grown into the oil center of Sarawak. The city was almost completely destroyed in World War II, but has since been completely rebuilt.

There are some very popular **beaches** near Miri, like Brighton Beach, Luak Bay and Kampong Beray. Because of their enormous popularity, they are not always as clean as they should be.

You can see the site of the first oil well in Miri, dating from 1910, on **Canada Hill**.

If you are planning a **jungle trek** in the area around **Bario**, you must register and get permission in Miri at the Fourth Division office. The flat office complex is on Kingsway, opposite the multi-story building. Register with the Resident.

Should permission to trek be denied and this might have something to do with Bruno Manser, you can try to get permission to visit Marudi instead, perhaps with the intention of visiting Gunung Mulu Park. Then, in Marudi, you can again ask for permission to go to Bario. This might work. It is necessary to have a permit, since this is checked at the airport. For other possibilities, see the section on Belaga.

Accommodation

The hotels are very expensive as a rule, and the cheapest (from about M$ 35) are very dirty.

●**Lovers' Bay Lodging House**, 7 High St., a dive with dirty rooms, most with their own shower, M$ 25.

●**Thai Foh**, 18 China St., in the center of town, dirty rooms and expensive, M$ 34, or dormitory for M$ 8 / person.

●**Tai Tong**, 28 China St., centrally located, no dormitory, M$ 32.

●**Yeo Lee Lodging House**, 12 China St., same as the others, but more expensive, M$ 38.

●**Fatimah Hotel**, 15 Brooke Rd., a bit out of town. Comfortable and worth the high price, M$ 80-225. Tel. 32255.

●**Hotel Gloria**, 27 Brooke Rd., expensive, but good, M$ 92-120. Tel. 36499.

●**Park Hotel**, Kingsway, in the center of town, standard mid-range hotel, M$ 88-250. Tel. 32355.

Around Miri

Lutong

The industrial town of Lutong is near Miri. If you are interested, you can visit **refineries and plants** there. Contact the Trade Relations Department of Sarawak Shell.

Lambir Hill National Park

19 km away, is a popular getaway with the people of Miri. The very small park has waterfalls, and typical forest vegetation. Unfortunately, it is too small to really sustain all the visitors it gets. If you can get to another park, go elsewhere.

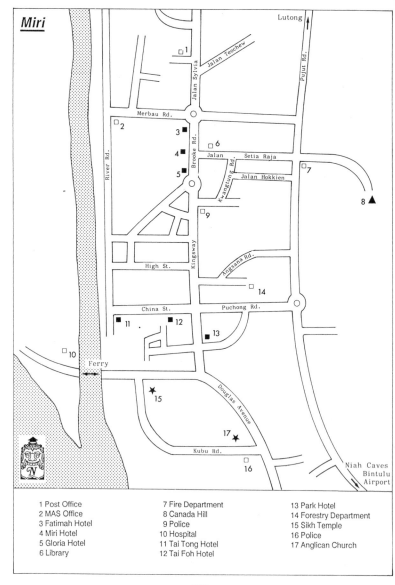

Miri

Lutong

Jalan Sylvia

Jalan Teochew

Pujut Rd.

Merbau Rd.

River Rd.

Brooke Rd.

1

2

3

6

Jalan Setia Raja

4

Kwangtung Rd.

Jalan Hokkien

7

5

8 ▲

9

Kingsway

High St.

Angsana Rd.

14

China St.

Puchong Rd.

11

12

13

10

Ferry

15

Douglas Avenue

17

Kubu Rd.

16

Niah Caves
Bintulu
Airport

1 Post Office	7 Fire Department	13 Park Hotel
2 MAS Office	8 Canada Hill	14 Forestry Department
3 Fatimah Hotel	9 Police	15 Sikh Temple
4 Miri Hotel	10 Hospital	16 Police
5 Gloria Hotel	11 Tai Tong Hotel	17 Anglican Church
6 Library	12 Tai Foh Hotel	

Further Travel

Taxis and **buses** leave daily for:
- **Batu Niah**: M$ 8.50 (at 7:00, 10:30, 12:00, 14:00)
- **Bintulu**: M$ 17
- **Sibu**: M$ 30
- **Kuala Belait / Brunei**: M$ 9.50

Ships go to:
- **Kuching**
- **Bintulu Marudi**
- **Baram Limbang**
- **Lawas**

MAS flies daily to:
- **Kuching**: M$ 136
- **Sibu**: M$ 43
- **Bintulu**: M$ 57
- **Bario**: M$ 70
- **Lawas**: M$ 59
- **Limbang**: M$ 45
- **Marudi**: M$ 29.
- **Kota Kinabalu**: M$ 82

To Brunei

Since 1988, Miri has been the point of departure for Brunei. From 1985 to 1988, a visa, only available in Kuala Lumpur, was needed, but this is no longer the case. Most nationals get permission for a 14 day stay upon arrival.

From Miri, there are three buses daily to **Kuala Belait** in Brunei. From there, you can get a ship to **Labuan** in Sabah. If you want to avoid Brunei's ridiculously high prices, the best thing to do is fly directly from Miri to Kota Kinabalu.

Gunung Mulu Park

Gunung Mulu Park is the largest national park in Sarawak, with an area of 544 square kilometers. Situated around the state's second highest mountain, Gunung Mulu at 2376 m, the park has all kinds of inland vegetation. The area was designated a national park in 1974. The park was closed between 1977 and 1984, as a study of the area's natural history was undertaken. The geological structure of the park is over 30 million years old.

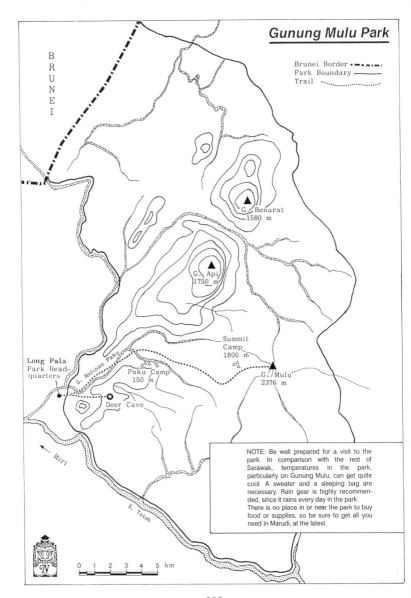

Gunung Mulu Park

Brunei Border ▪━▪━▪━
Park Boundary ————
Trail ·················

B
R
U
N
E
I

G. Benarat
1580 m

G. Api
1750 m

Summit
Camp
1800 m

Long Pala
Park Head-
quarters

S. Melinau Paku

Paku Camp
150 m

G. Mulu
2376 m

Deer Cave

Miri

S. Tutoh

NOTE: Be well prepared for a visit to the
park. In comparison with the rest of
Sarawak, temperatures in the park,
particularly on Gunung Mulu, can get quite
cool. A sweater and a sleeping bag are
necessary. Rain gear is highly recommended, since it rains every day in the park.
There is no place in or near the park to buy
food or supplies, so be sure to get all you
need in Marudi, at the latest.

0 1 2 3 4 5 km

N

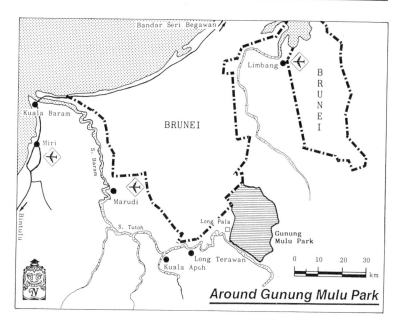

Around Gunung Mulu Park

Arrival

The difficult and expensive trip is a definite minus point for the Gunung Mulu Park. There are several ways to get there from Miri:

1.) **From Miri**, go first to Kuala Baram on the Sungei Baram for M$ 2 by bus. From there, there are express boats every hour to Marudi. The three hour trip costs M$ 12. Spend the night in Marudi. A good, cheap place is the Grand Hotel where double rooms are M$ 25. From Marudi, rent a boat to the park headquarters at Long Pala. The boat costs M$ 800 (!) for 10 people, round-trip.

2.) A cheaper alternative is to get **an express boat directly from Marudi** to Kuala Apoh for M$ 10. The trip takes three hours. The boat travels upstream Mondays, Wednesdays and Fridays and down-stream Tuesdays, Thursdays and Saturdays. From Kuala Apoh, you can then rent a boat for M$ 200-250, round-trip, to make the 4-5 hour trip to Long Pala.

3.) The other possibility is to take an **express boat from Kuala Apoh** to Long Terawan for M$ 5 and rent a boat there for M$ 150-200.

What to See

In the park, there are 1500 varieties of flowering plants, including 170 types of orchids and 10 types of pitcher plants. There are thousands of varieties of mushrooms, mosses and ferns. The animal world is also very rich. There are 67 species of mammals, including many kinds of

primates, 262 species of birds, 74 species of frogs, 47 species of fish, 281 species of butterflies and 458 species of ants.

There are various trails that go throughout the park, many within a short distance of the park headquarters. Other trails take several days, like the one up Gunung Mulu, which takes 3-5 days. There are guides available in the headquarters who charge M$ 20 for day tours and M$ 30 per day for longer trips.

Accommodation

At the moment there is *only one bungalow* in the park, which sleeps 10 people in two rooms. It must be booked in advance at the National Parks and Wildlife Office, Forest Department, in Miri, Tel. 33361 / 36637. The cost is M$ 20 per group. The maximum group size is 10 people. If you have booked far in advance, the booking must be reconfirmed 5 days before the date of arrival. The bungalow has cooking facilities, water and electricity.

Limbang

The administrative seat of the Fifth Division, Limbang, with a population of 26,000 lies between Brunei and Sabah, 13 km inland along the Sungei Limbang. In comparison to Brunei, the city is worth stopping in for those traveling overland to Sabah, if only for the much lower hotel prices.

Accommodation

There are a number of cheap places to stay in Limbang. They are all close to each other:
●*Southeast Asia Hotel*, 27 Market St, big clean rooms, M$ 24. Tel. 21013.
●*Nak*, Bank St., a bit seedy and very loud, M$ 20.
●*Australia*, 63 Bank St., recommended, clean and quiet rooms, friendly people, M$ 26. Tel. 21860.

Further Travel

●Limbang is only accessible by *plane* from Miri. MAS flies from here daily to Miri for M$ 45, Lawas for M$ 25, Labuan for M$ 30 and Kota Kinabalu for M$ 60.
●*Express boats* go daily between Limbang, Bandar Sri Begawan, the capital of Brunei, and Lawas, for M$ 10.

Lawas

See p. 261

Sabah

To the seafarers of the nineteenth century, Sabah was known as the "Land under the Wind." While the Philippines to the north are subject to typhoons all year round, Sabah is just below the typhoon belt, and thus, under the wind.

Despite the safety it offered from storms, this land brought other dangers to sailors. It was known as a haven for fierce pirates, and indeed, there are some places along the coast today where the waters are known to be unsafe.

Sabah is among the most expensive places in Southeast Asia. Coming from Sarawak, the prices will seem noticeably higher, and those coming directly from peninsular Malaysia will be in for a huge shock. But the land does have a lot to offer: the unique Mount Kinabalu; a variety of jungle treks and outstanding beaches with wonderful coral reefs.

Geography

Sabah, the second Malaysian state on Borneo, occupies 76,115 square kilometers on the northeast part of the island. It is bordered on the west by Sarawak and in the south by Kalimantan, the Indonesian part of Borneo. The first islands of the Philippines are just a few kilometers off the coast, to the north, east and southeast. The coastal island of Labuan is part of Sabah.

Topographically, Sabah is primarily mountainous. The mountains run from south to west, near the coast and also in the northeast. The jagged peak of *Mount Kinabalu*, the highest point in Southeast Asia at 4101 m is just over 50 km from the coast. The only flatlands are in the far eastern part of the state, in the area north and south of Sandakan.

Just a few years ago, most of the state was covered with virgin forest. In the past few years, however, with the intensification of the logging and agricultural industries, massive tracts of rainforest have been destroyed. Large continuous rainforests can now only be found in **Kinabalu Park** and inland, near the Kalimantan border. Mangroves flourish along the rivers near Sandakan.

History

In the **14th century**, north Borneo was occupied by the Mongols under Kublai Khan. The first Chinese settlements along the coast were founded in **1424**, under the rule of General Cheng Ho.

In **1521**, the first Europeans, under Magellan, arrived in north Borneo which belonged at the time to the Sultan of Brunei.

In **1763**, the British East India Company established a trading post in North Borneo, on land they purchased from the Sultan of Sulu, who ruled the area around Sandakan.

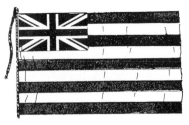

In **1865**, the Consul General of Hong Kong, Baron von Overbeck and the British brothers, Edward and Alfred Dent, purchased north Borneo, now Sabah, from the Sultans of Brunei and Sulu.

Overbeck, who tried in vain to arouse European interest in the territory, sold his shares to the Dent brothers in **1881**. Shortly thereafter, with the help of the British government, they established the North Borneo Company. This enabled Britain to enforce its colonial domination on Sabah. The company was based on profit and profit alone. It worked closely with the British administration of the Straits Settlements and counted on British marines to maintain order and brutally suppress any resistance. Along with Brunei and Sarawak, Sabah was made a British protectorate in **1888**.

1895 marked the start of the rebellion by the chief Mat Salleh, which was not put down until 1900. Mat Salleh was wanted for the murder of two merchants, but eluded the authorities for some time. Later, he made an appeal for the rights of the indigenous people of Sabah, but the British refused to meet him. In 1897, the situation became an open, armed rebellion. The rebels burned trading posts and towns and fought against British troops, mainly Dayaks from Sarawak. Finally, in 1900, he was betrayed by some villagers in Tambunan, where he was staying in his underground hide-out. The hide-out had a complicated system of bamboo pipes to bring water from a river 6 kilometers away. The soldiers who came to arrest Mat Salleh merely cut the water supply and waited for him to come out and surrender. Mat Selleh and his troops tried to fight their way out, but all of them were killed in the attempt.

It was not until the 1920s that an administrative committee was formed that included not only government officials and plantation owners, but chiefs as well.

Until **1912**, the law makers were chosen from among merchants and plantation owners.

In **1942**, the Japanese occupied Sabah. In **1945**, Sabah reverted back to British control.

In **1963**, Sabah became independent and united with Malaya, Sarawak and later Singapore in the Malaysian Federation. Indonesia and the Philippines both had claims to Sabah and refused to recognize the new state. The Indonesian presi-

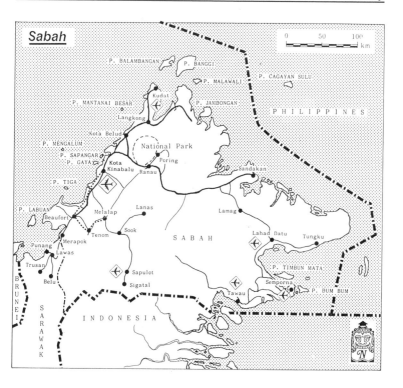

dent, Sukarno, went as far as to try and occupy Sabah, resulting in a jungle war along the border with Kalimantan.

With the overthrow of Sukarno in *1966*, the border confrontation ended and both countries recognized the Malaysian Federation. In *1985*, there was fighting between Christians and Muslims after Christian election victories.

Economy

Oil makes Sabah an important player in the Malaysian economy. In addition, Sabah also has large *mineral resources* including gold, silver, magnesium and chromium.

Another important economic product is *wood* from the jungles. Huge tracts of forest are regularly torn down so that timber can be shipped overseas, mainly to Japan, Korea and Taiwan. Some of the stripped areas are used for agriculture. Important products are *cocoa*, near Tawau, *palm oil*, in the area near Sandakan, *rice* and *coconuts* on the Kudat Peninsula.

Religion

As in Sarawak, there are many religions practiced in Sabah. *Islam* is the state religion, practiced by Malays and Bajau. Christianity is more widespread here, and its adherents include the Kadazan and the Murut. There are also practitioners of Chinese religions and **Hindus**. **Animism** is practiced by the nomadic **Punan**.

Language

The official language is Malay or Bahasa Malaysia. Like in the rest of Malaysia, English is an important language for communicating with foreigners. Some groups still speak Mandarin, other Chinese dialects, or Tamil. The indigenous peoples of Sabah have their own various languages. To get by, English should be enough; but if you really want to get off the beaten path, you should learn a bit of Malay or Indonesian.

The People

The total population of Sabah is approximately 1 million. Here, the Malays are a real minority with only 8% of the population. 63% are from various indigenous ethnic groups. The remainder are from other groups, primarily Indians and Chinese (mainly Hakkas).

The various indigenous groups all live in different parts of the state. The strongest group is the **Kadazan** or **Dusun**. They live primarily along the west coast and in the interior near Ranau and Tambunan.

The "Cowboys" of Sabah, the **Bajau**, live on the west coast between Papar and Kudat. Sometimes you see them in the area around Lahad Datu. The **Murut** live in the southwest, near the border with Kalimantan. The nomadic hunters and gatherers of Sarawak, the **Punan**, sometimes live in Sabah as well, in the area around Tawau.

The traditional way of life for the indigenous peoples of Sabah is very similar to that of their counterparts in Sarawak. For example, they live in **long-houses**. But in contrast to Sarawak, this form of settlement is rarely found anymore. Only in the area around Kudat are there still many long-houses. These belong to the **Rungus**, a sub-group of the Kadazan. The Murut in the interior have also maintained their traditional way of life to some extent.

The Bajau

The Muslim Bajau live along the west coast between Kudat and Papar. According to ethnologists, they migrated here in the 18th and 19th centuries from Mindanao in the southern Philippines.

The Bajau themselves believe, however, that they are descended from Malays in the area around Johor. In their legends, the first Bajau sailed to Borneo with a fleet of ships guiding a princess, the daughter of the Sultan of Johor, to her groom, a Sulu prince. In a surprise attack, the princess was carried off by the Sultan of Brunei. The men in her escort, now without the princess, could neither go back home, nor continue on to where they were going. They were homeless and became a navy without a port. Eventually, they settled on the coast of what is now Sabah and became known as the Bajau.

In the past century, they were known as fearsome pirates who made the coast of Sabah particularly unsafe. They also took their aggressiveness to the land and fought the peaceful Kadazan, forcing them beyond Mount Kinabalu.

Today, the Bajau are more peaceful. They practice farming and raise livestock, perhaps as a relic of earlier days, when they were known as very skillful water buffalo thieves. In the area around Kota Belud, they are known as adroit horse breeders and riders. This is what earned them the nickname "Cowboys of Sabah", at least in the minds of the Tourist Development Corporation (TDC).

The Kadazan (Dusun)

The largest group of people in Sabah is the Kadazan who are also known as the Dusun. These indigenous farmers live in the area from the flatlands of the west coast to the area around Ranau, in the interior. Now, only the Rungus, a sub-group on the Kudat Peninsula still live in long-houses. Most Kadazan farms are only around 2 hectares. They grow primarily wet rice. Due to missionary activity, they have a high standard of education. This enables them to hold some high positions in the government and in commerce.

The Murut

The Murut or "Mountain People," as they were named by the Bajau, were originally nomadic hunters, but most have become sedentary farmers. They live today in the southwest of Sabah and in the jungle area along the border with Kalimantan. They have been continually pushed further back into the jungle, first by migratory Kadazan and then later by Western civilization. The

government has settlement projects designed to get the remaining nomads to live in one place. They are primarily rice farmers. Sometimes they work as laborers for Western civilization; for example, they cleared a path through the jungle for the rail line from Beaufort to Tenom.

Headhunting is also part of the Murut tradition. Cutting off and collecting heads showed the power of a warrior. This was so important that at one time a man could not get married until he had cut off at least one head.

Originally, the mythology of the Murut made a sedentary life impossible. They grew rice and manioc, but believed that the spirits of the earth would only support such agriculture for a short time, so they either plowed new fields or moved every seven years.

The Tamu

Tamu originally meant "visitor" in Malay. In Sabah, this word has a very different, though somehow related meaning. It refers to a type of market that only exists in Sabah, and previously only in Kadazan-settled areas.

The Tamu is a meeting, in which groups of people agree to meet each other at a set time and place, to trade peacefully with one another. This institution goes back to the efforts of agents of the North Borneo Trading Company, who organized these events in order to trade with many chiefs at the same time.

The most important condition of the Tamu is the suspension of fighting and enmity, at least for the day of the market. For this reason, the market was usually located outside of a town like Kota Belud and was declared neutral ground. The various chiefs all swore to keep the peace on a special stone the *batu sumpah*. Then, in a special ceremony, the stone was covered with buffalo blood. According to one legend, a stone in a Tamu near Kota Kinabalu was covered with human blood.

Tamus are more than just big markets, they are real fairs that bring friends and families together. They are also places where people can exchange news from all over. There are always buffalo races (and horse races in Bajau areas) and cockfights to complete the day.

All Tamus are overseen literally, usually from a wooden tower, by an official from the local district, who is on hand to prevent the outbreak of violence.

In recent times, the Tamus have adapted well to the tremendous changes in the culture of Sabah. No longer are just local products sold, now you see plastic and porcelain kitchenware and even cassette tapes for sale. There are groups of Chinese, Indian and Filipino merchants who travel from Tamu to Tamu, and they continually bring new products and ideas with them.

Kota Kinabalu (KK)

The capital of Sabah has been known by various names throughout the history of the state. On old maps, it is called by its old Malay name, Api Api (fire). Later, at the time of the British North Borneo Company, it was known as Jesselton. Charles Jessel was the vice director of the North Borneo Company who was honored by his firm.

In the Second World War, the city, which was known as an important trading center, was completely destroyed by bombs. The only remnant of the colonial era is the main post office building, which was in use until recently, when it was closed due to structural weaknesses.

In 1968, Sabah became a state of the Malaysian Federation. The young government wanted to make a clear break from colonialism and many city names were changed as a result. In honor of Mount Kinabalu, a national symbol of unity, the city was renamed Kota Kinabalu, but it is always simply called **KK**.

Kota Kinabalu is a city undergoing tremendous growth. In 1980, the population was 42,000. By 1986, that number had almost tripled to 120,000. The latest estimates maintain that the population is now over 250,000. This enormous growth has caused some problems in a city without too much room. KK is wedged on a narrow strip between the foothills of the coastal mountains and the sea. To alleviate the crush, there have been projects to build landfills in the ocean.

The rapid growth of the city is due in large part to the influx of Filipinos, who make up a considerable percentage of the population. The night market has many Filipino vendors. They are also commonly held to blame for the city's rising crime rate.

What to See

Unfortunately, Kota Kinabalu lacks the colonial flavor that makes a visit to Kuching so worthwhile. The city nonetheless offers a "fascinating" look at straight, parallel housing blocks built in the 50's and 60's. After the city was completely destroyed in World War II, there was no other way to rebuild it quickly.

The **Sabah State Museum** is certainly worth a visit. Though it cannot compare with the Sarawak Museum in Kuching, it does provide an interesting insight into the natural and cultural history of the state. The building was built in 1982 and 83 on a hill overlooking the city. The intention was to combine the traditional long-house with modern building technology. The result is certainly worth checking out.

The most interesting exhibit here is a piece of the largest tree ever to be felled in Sabah. It was a Kapuar tree *(Dryobalanops lancelota)*. The volume of the tree was 108.15 cubic meters. The diameter of the piece of wood, to the right of the entrance, is 2.45 meters. The tree was worth M$ 20,677.20.

There is also a diorama of a cave containing swiftlets nests, which are used to make Birds' Nest soup.

Also interesting is the Bangkavan Exhibit. Bangkavan is a collection of human skulls which was assembled by the Kadazan. This relic of the headhunting days was given to the old museum in 1972. It is from Kampong Dakata, near Penampang. It had been in a family for four generations. Sometimes mussels and animal bones are also added to the collection. Originally, the owners believed that hanging human skulls from their house would bring good luck. Every five years, they celebrated the Magang Festival to honor the spirits of the skulls. Priestesses or *bobohizans* conducted a seven day ceremony to ward off evil spirits.

You can see the **Masjid Negara** from the museum. In terms of materials and building style, it is the most modern mosque in Malaysia. The structure is made of large concrete slabs with giant columns. On the outside, all the slabs are covered with blue mosaic.

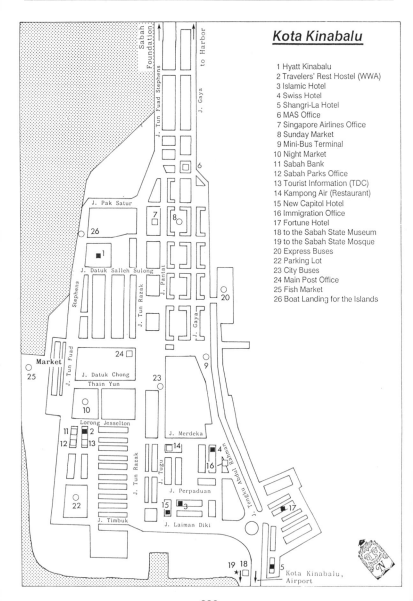

Kota Kinabalu

1 Hyatt Kinabalu
2 Travelers' Rest Hostel (WWA)
3 Islamic Hotel
4 Swiss Hotel
5 Shangri-La Hotel
6 MAS Office
7 Singapore Airlines Office
8 Sunday Market
9 Mini-Bus Terminal
10 Night Market
11 Sabah Bank
12 Sabah Parks Office
13 Tourist Information (TDC)
14 Kampong Air (Restaurant)
15 New Capitol Hotel
16 Immigration Office
17 Fortune Hotel
18 to the Sabah State Museum
19 to the Sabah State Mosque
20 Express Buses
22 Parking Lot
23 City Buses
24 Main Post Office
25 Fish Market
26 Boat Landing for the Islands

To get a complete view of the city, go up *Signal Hill*. The road up goes from behind the old *post office* or the clock tower. The best view of the city used to be from the rotating restaurant at the top of the 32-story *Sabah Foundation Complex*. But its lack of popularity finally forced it to close at the end of 1987. It might open again soon, so it is worth checking. You can see the 100 m glass cylinder from the city, even though it is 4 km out of town.

If the strict regularity of KK's streets gets you down, you can go for a short walk through the remains of the water village, *Kampong Ayer*. It seems peculiar how, when you cross Jalan Laiman Diki, a major thoroughfare, suddenly the mainland ends and the regularity just stops. Over here, all the houses are made of wood, and rest on stilts above the water. All the paths are made of wooden planks, with smaller paths leading off main ones to individual houses.

Markets:

The *Central Market* is located on Jalan Tun Fuad Stephens. Aside from the usual market goods, many local handicrafts are also sold. It's opposite the Sabah National Park Headquarters. Many of the vendors are Filipino. It is often cheaper here than at the *night market*, which takes place every evening between Lorong Jesselton, Jalan Tun Fuad Stephens and Jalan Datuk Chong Thain Yun.

Kota Kinabalu's *Sunday Market*

begins every Sunday at 6:00 am. By Saturday evening, the streets between Jalan Pantai and Jalan Gaya are already closed to traffic as hundreds of merchants start their trading early.

Accommodation

As the capital of Sabah, Kota Kinabalu naturally has a large assortment of hotel rooms. Unfortunately, most of the assortment is in the higher price ranges. There are no double rooms under M$ 25 in the city and the cheapest rooms are sometimes not worth the trouble. You must plan on at least M$ 25 to 35 a night.

●*White Water Adventures & Travelers' Rest House*, Block L, 4th floor, lot 5, 6, STPC Building, Sinsuran. Run by Jon Rees and his wife, from Sabah. Both are very friendly and they run one of the most pleasant and clean hostels in all Malaysia. In addition, they run wilderness trips, including activities such as white-water rafting, mountain climbing, cave exploration, four-wheel drive safaris, etc. They have a lot of experience and know a great deal about Sabah. Dorm: M$ 15; deluxe dorm: M$ 20 / 25 with A / C; DR 28 / 34 or 36 / 42 with A / C; all prices include breakfast. Tel. 231892.

●*Hotel Rakyat*, Block 1, Sinsuran Komplex, from M$ 30. Tel. 211100 / 3.

●*Islamic Hotel*, Jalan Perpaduan, from M$ 25, pretty seedy. Tel. 54325.

●*Swiss Hotel*, Jalan Sentosa, from M$ 34 (single rooms are big enough for two, but they will probably try and rent you a more expensive room), very clean, A / C. Tel. 210632.

●*New Capital*, Jalan Laiman Diki 7, from M$ 24 for a single. Tel. 53011.

●*Kin Fah Hotel*, Jalan Haji Yaacub 7, from M$ 25. Tel. 53833.

●*Fortune Hotel*, Bandaran Berjaya, from M$ 33.

●*Cecilia B&B*, Jalan Saga Mile 4 ½ Likas, from M$ 20 (dorm), rest house with family atmosphere. Tel. 35733.

●*Hotel Kinabalu*, Bandaran Berjaya, from M$ 84. Tel. 53233.

●*Shangri-La*, Bandaran Berjaya, from M$ 120. Tel. 212800.

●*Hyatt Kinabalu*, Jalan Datuk Salleh, from M$ 200. Tel. 221234.

Food

The selection of **restaurants** is about the same as in other Malaysian cities, though the prices are much higher. Plan on spending between M$ 3-4 for a simple *nasi goreng*.

●In Segama, there are both **Chinese and Malay restaurants**, but in Sinsuran, the selection is mainly Chinese.

●As always, there are the standard Western **fast food restaurants**, which are incidentally no more expensive than in the rest of Malaysia.

City Transportation

Within Kota Kinabalu, almost all places are accessible on foot. For further destinations, like the airport or the Sabah State Museum, there are buses, minibuses and taxis.

●The city **bus** station is at the intersection of Jalan Tugu and Jalan Merdeka. City buses also go outside to neighboring towns like Tanjung Aru and Penampang. Trips cost between 80 *sen* and M$ 1.50.

●**Minibuses** go around the city and the neighboring areas. Do not try and get on one anywhere, as you have to go to the station in the small square between Jalan Pantai and Jalan Gaya. The cost is M$ 1.

●There are **taxi stands** near the minibus station and at the corner of Jalan Perpaduan and Jalan Tugu near the Islamic Hotel.

Important Addresses

●**American Express** is represented by Discovery Tours, Tel. 57735.

●**Forest and Nature Protection Agencies:** You have to register to visit Kinabalu Park at the Sabah National Parks Headquarters on Jalan Tun Fuad Stephens.

Bring your passport, your exact dates of travel and an international student ID, if you have one. Tel. 211585, 211652, 211881.

●**Changing Money:** There are a number of big banks in Kota Kinabalu. As in the rest of Malaysia, you have to pay a fee for travelers' checks. The best rates, the lowest fee of 15 *sen* per check and the fastest service are at Sabah Bank on Jalan Tun Fuad Stephens next to the Park Headquarters office.

●**Immigration:** To get a visa extension, go to the immigration office in the administration building on Jalan Tungku Abdul Rahman. Plan on spending an hour answering a lot of questions.

●**Information:** The TDC has an office in the Bandaran Sinsuran part of town. It is located in the Old Post Office. The Senior Tourist Officer, Abd. Halim Mohd Anuar, was very helpful. Tel. 211732, 211698.

●**MAS** has an office on Jalan Gaya, Tel. 53560. As in other MAS offices, you can plan on a nice, long wait. It is better to do your business with a travel agent, if possible. Sarawak Travel Service is very good, in the Sabah Handicraft Center, Lot 49, Ground Floor, Bandaran Berjaya, Tel. 221230 / 1 / 3.

●**Royal Brunei**, Jalan Tun Fuad Stephens, Tel. 53211.

●**Singapore Airlines**, Jalan Pantai, Tel. 55444.

●**Cathay Pacific**, Jalan Gaya, Tel. 54733.

●**Philippine Airlines**, Jalan Pak Satur, Tel. 57870.

●**Post Office:** The old GPO on Jalan Gaya has been replaced by a new one. The old building is filled with colonial charm, and the new one is the complete opposite, a giant complex opposite the city bus terminal on Jalan Tun Razak. You can receive mail *Poste Restante*.

●**Police:** Jalan Balai Polis, next to the bus station.

●**Hospital:** The Queen Elizabeth Hospital is out of town on the road to Penampang, opposite the Sabah State Museum.

●**Feri Malaysia:** Represented by Jarrisons & Crawford, Tel. 215011-246, 52057. Travel agents in the city also sell tickets.

●**Indonesian Consulate:** Jalan Sagunting, Wing On Life Building, Tel. 54100.

Around Kota Kinabalu

Tanjung Aru

is the weekend getaway for Kota Kinabalu. There are beaches, promenades, restaurants, food stalls and even a big hotel. To get there, take the No. 12 or 13 bus, which also go to the airport, for 60 *sen*. Taxis from the city are around M$ 5. Unfortunately, Tanjung Aru is the only cheap place to go in the vicinity of Kota Kinabalu.

Tuaran

is a Kadazan town, about 40 minutes by bus from Kota Kinabalu.

Every Sunday, there is a Tamu, but it is smaller than the one in Kota Belud. It is only interesting for people with very little time.

Tunku Abdul Rahman Park

This island **national park** in the bay of Kota Kinabalu is good for swimming and diving. To get there, you will have to rent a boat, which can be quite expensive. The park includes the islands opposite Kota Kinabalu: **Pulau Gaya, Pulau Sapi, Pulau Mamutik** and **Pulau Manukan**. The park has a total area of 4900 hectares.

Because of its rich vegetation and coral reefs, the park is a protected area. There are trails on the islands that lead through the jungles as well as good beaches for swimming and sunbathing. Especially fine (and on weekends, crowded) is Police Beach in Bulijong Bay. The police used to practice shooting on the beach, thus the name. The coral reefs offer very good snorkeling and diving. On weekends, there are tours in glass-bottomed boats which offer a nice view of the coral for anyone who doesn't want to get wet.

What to See: The vegetation of the island is tropical rainforest. It is a good place to experience a jungle without having to go too far from the city. There is a large variety of animal life, from monkeys and squirrels to rats and wild pigs. The land animals are complimented by a wide variety of birds. If you really want to see animals on your visit, do not go on a weekend, when there is

simply too much activity for them. There is no need to register in advance of your visit.

Getting There: There are regular boat connections only on weekends and holidays. The boats leave hourly between 7:00 and 10:00 am to Pulau Sapi and Police Beach. The trip costs M$ 10. During the week, you will have to rent a boat. Boats can take a maximum of 12 passengers and cost around M$ 190.

Agree on the price before you go anywhere and beware of operators who will try and extort high prices even on weekends.

Accommodation: There are really no places to stay on the islands, as such. There are campsites, but you will have to bring all your own food and supplies. There is fresh water available. Due to the strong demand, there are plans to construct bungalows on the islands. Ask in the TDC office.

Further Travel

Fligths

From Kota Kinabalu, there are regular **international flights** to Brunei, Singapore, and the Philippines. There are also a number of daily **domestic flights** within Sabah and Sarawak, as well as to Peninsular Malaysia.

The **airport** is in Tanjung Aru, 8 km out of town. During the day, there are mini buses for M$ 1 that go there. A taxi would cost around M$ 12, after some hard bargaining, especially at night.

The **airport tax** is, as in the rest of Malaysia, M$ 3 for domestic flights, M$ 5 for flights to Brunei and Singapore and M$ 12 for other international flights.

International Flights:
- *Singapore* – M$ 346.
- *Bandar Seri Begawan* – M$ 65.
- *Manila* – M$ 490.

Domestic Flights:
- *Kenigau* – M$ 38.
- *Kuching* – M$ 198.
- *Kudat* – M$ 50.
- *Labuan* – M$ 43.
- *Lawas* – M$ 47.
- *Miri* – M$ 82.
- *Sandakan* – M$ 69.
- *Sibu* – M$ 156.
- *Tawau* – M$ 80.

Those traveling to Kuala Lumpur or Johor Baru on *Peninsular Malaysia*, should ask about the YAP Fare (Advance Purchase Excursion Fare) to Johor Baru and the YN Fare (Night Tourist Fare) to Kuala Lumpur. For example, a normal one-way from Kota Kinabalu to Kuala Lumpur costs M$ 380, but the YN fare is M$ 266. A ticket from Kota Kinabalu to Johor Baru normally costs M$ 301, but the YAP fare is M$ 256. These fares are subject to certain conditions: the YN fare is only good for night flights and is valid for three months; the YAP fares must be purchased 14 days before departure and any change carries a 15% penalty.

Ships

There are regular **ship connections** between Kuching on Tuesdays and Kuantan and Port Klang on Peninsula Malaysia on Fridays, with the ships of Feri Malaysia, Tel. 215011-246. For prices, see the section on Getting to Sabah and Sarawak. There are daily **ferries** to Labuan at 8:00 which take 3 hours and cost M$ 28.

Train

Between Kota Kinabalu, Beaufort and Tenom, there is a **train connection**. The train station is not in Kota Kinabalu proper, but in the nearby town of Tanjung Aru. Diesel locomotives make the trip daily. The stretch from Kota Kinabalu to Beaufort is very long and not very interesting, while the trip from Beaufort to Tenom offers spectacular scenery.

Bus

As in the rest of Malaysia, the most important means of transportation are **express buses** and **long-distance taxis**. The central station is on Jalan Balai Polis. Buses and taxis leave from there to everywhere. There are good roads between Kota Kinabalu and Beaufort, Kudat and Ranau, though they can still be quite tiring. If you are going to *Sandakan* or farther south to Lahad Datu or Tawau, you should fly, if possible. The trip to Sandakan is about 10 hours over dreadful unpaved roads. From time to time, there are landslides that block the road for hours. This trip costs M$ 35. The flight direct from Kota Kinabalu to Sandakan takes 45 minutes and costs M$ 69, and you get a bird's eye-view of Mount Kinabalu.

- *Kinabalu National Park* – M$ 7.
- *Keningau* – M$ 18.
- *Kota Belud* – M$ 6.
- *Kudat* – M$ 15.
- *Beaufort* – M$ 6.50.
- *Ranau* – M$ 12.

Ranau

Ranau is a small town at the foot of Mt. Kinabalu. It's on the road to Sandakan. From here, you can get to Poring, a part of Kinabalu Park. Normally, Ranau is more a place you pass through than a place you go. You change here from bus to taxi if you are going to Poring, and vice-versa if you are coming from the park.

The people here are very friendly. There is a big *Tamu* on the first of every month, which attracts interesting people from all over. If you need more money for the national park, this is a good place to change some.

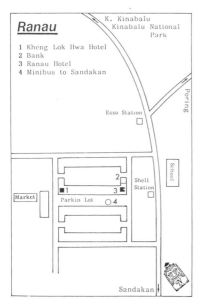

Ranau

1 Kheng Lok Hwa Hotel
2 Bank
3 Ranau Hotel
4 Minibus to Sandakan

K. Kinabalu
Kinabalu National Park

Poring

Esso Station

School

Shell Station

Market

Parkin Lot

Sandakan

If you are going to **Poring** during the week, you might have some problems. Ask around to see if anyone is heading in that direction. You might have to pay around M$ 20 for the trip. This is the normal taxi price, but many private vehicles travel the route as well. On weekends, pick-ups make the trip between Ranau and Poring regularly. Then it costs only M$ 4. If you are planing to go to Poring, do first check in the Park Office about the road. Sometimes it is in such bad shape that it becomes impassable and you will waste your time trying to arrange transportation.

Kinabalu National Park

This 754 sq. kilometer park is the main attraction of Sabah. It contains the highest mountain in Southeast Asia, Mount Kinabalu. The highest peak, **Low's Peak** reaches 4101 m or 13,451 ft. The mountain is part of the Crocker Range which runs through Sabah.

In 1962, the area around Mt. Kinabalu was closed to protect it. The park was opened in 1964, about a century after the first Westerner's ascent of the peak. That was by Sir Hugh Low in 1851, a British official on Labuan Island.

The park is popular with most of its visitors not because of its rich collection of flora and fauna, but because of its cool temperatures. At the Park Headquarters at 1558 m, the temperature varies between 13°C and 20°C. As you go higher, it gets cooler and temperatures of near freezing are common towards the summit at night.

Accommodation

• **Kheng Lok Hwa Hotel**, rooms for M$ 20.
• **Ranau Hotel**, better rooms at slightly higher prices, from M$ 25. Tel. 875351.
• **Mt. Kinabalu Perkasa Hotel** is outside the town, on a mountain. There is a good view of Mt. Kinabalu. Rooms from M$ 100. Tel. 889511.

Further Travel

Minibus

From Ranau, there is a daily minibus to **Kota Kinabalu**. It leaves as soon as there are enough people.

There is also a daily minibus to **Sandakan**, which leaves around 7:30. If you miss that one, if you are late coming out of the park, you can wait for one of the buses going from Kota Kinabalu to Sandakan, which arrive around 11:00 and 15:30. If you are lucky, they will have free seats.

The Park is divided into two regions:

1. The area around the Park Headquarters, which contains numerous marked trails. This is where the ascent of Mt. Kinabalu begins.

2. Poring Hot Springs, which are only accessible from Ranau.

Arrival

From Kota Kinabalu, there are regular bus connections to **Ranau**. the buses leave daily between 7:30 and 12:30 and cost M$ 8.50 per person.

Tell the bus driver to let you off at the Park Headquarters, about 30 minutes from Ranau. It is recommended you take an early bus, since the trip takes around 2.5 hours. That will give you enough time to prepare everything for your climb the next day.

Registration

To visit Kinabalu National Park, you must register in Kota Kinabalu. The Sabah National Park Headquarters is on Jalan Tun Fuad Stephens, next to the Sabah Bank. Or write to: The Director, Sabah Parks, PO Box 10626, 88806 Kota Kinabalu, Sabah, Malaysia, Tel. 211585, 211652.

When you register, you must state the exact dates of your travel, book all your accommodation, including those along the climb, show your passport and pay the fees in cash. If you have an international student ID card (ISIC), do bring it, as it can make things much cheaper.

Save all receipts and papers you get in the park office, as you will have to produce them again in the Park Headquarters.

You will also have to buy a **climber's permit** in the park for M$ 10 or M$ 2 for students.

Accommodation

Since the park is very popular with city residents, there is a large assortment of accommodation to choose from. The first price given below is for a room during the week, the second for weekends and holidays:

- **Kinabalu Lodge** (8 pers.) M$ 270 / 360.
- **Double Storey Cabin** (7 pers.) M$ 180 / 250.
- **Single Storey Cabin** (5 pers.) M$ 150 / 200.
- **Duplex Chalets** (6 pers.) M$ 150 / 200.
- **Annex Rooms** (4 pers.) M$ 100 / 160.
- **Twin Bed Cabins** (2 pers.) M$ 50 / 80.
- **Basement Rooms** (2 pers.) M$ 50 / 80.

All of the above are comfortable, some with complete kitchens and refrigerators. They are all near the Park Headquarters.

You can stay in cheaper **Hostels** and **Mountain Huts**, which have dormitories. They all have shared bathrooms and shared kitchens. The hostels near the Park Headquarters have warm blankets, while the huts rent sleeping bags for M$ 2 per night. Booking in advance is not essential. The prices in parentheses are for students.

- **Old Fellowship Hostel** (46 pers.) M$ 10 (M$ 3).
- **New Hostel** (52 pers.) M$ 15 (M$ 4).

Mountain Huts: (approx. 3350 m)
- **Waras Hut** (12 pers.) M$ 4 (M$ 1).
- **Panar Laban Hut** (12 pers.) M$ 4 (M$ 1).
- **Gunting Lagadan Hut** (44 pers.) M$ 4 (M$ 1).
- **Laban Rata Rest House** (52 pers.) M$ 35.
- **Sayat Sayat Hut** (10 pers.) M$ 4 (M$ 1).

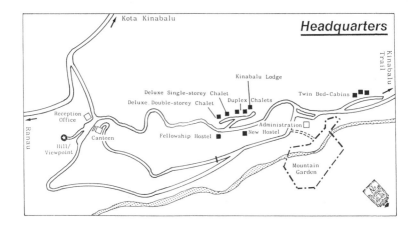

Park Headquarters

The Park Headquarters is at a height of 1558 m. In addition to registration and administration, there are exhibition halls, two restaurants, and many lodging alternatives nearby. Almost all tourists stay in this area and it is particularly crowded on weekends.

As soon as you arrive, you should register with the park administration. Show your permit and room reservations from Kota Kinabalu. This is also where you get a Climber's Permit to hike on the mountain. It is also where you hire a guide. If you are starting out the nextday, you might want to take a short hike in the area of the park headquarters. For example, from behind the headquarters to the nearby viewpoint, which offers a surprisingly good view of the area, including Mt. Kinabalu.

The administration building has an exhibition room with information about indigenous flora and fauna. On weekends from Friday to Monday, at 7:30 in the morning, there are films and lectures about the area.

Adjoining the administration building is a small Mountain Garden, which has a few paths which go past all sorts of local plants.

Other trails near the park headquarters vary between 45 minutes and several hours (see map). Every morning at 11:15 (check with the office for exact information), a park ranger leads a walk along one of these trails, pointing out interesting sights and giving advice on how to look for animals. This is very valuable!

Before the Ascent

Before you attempt to climb Mt. Kinabalu, a few preliminary considerations are in order.

To begin with, take careful heed of the sign in the Park Headquarters saying that the trip is not for those with any kind of health problems. That includes high blood pressure, stomach problems, arthritis, etc.

The climb takes you above 3500 m relatively quickly.

That means some people might experience a mild form of altitude sickness, a sickness which is caused by exertion in air which has a low concentration of oxygen. Symptoms include headaches, dizziness, nausea, etc. The proper way to treat altitude sickness is to monitor the symptoms very carefully, and ascend very slowly. If the symptoms worsen, go back down to a comfortable altitude to rest. Do not take medicine, such as aspirin, that alleviates the symptoms.

Good physical condition is a further necessary preparation and can make the difference between a wonderful experience and a nightmare.

Equipment

In assembling your equipment, bear in mind that you must carry everything with you. Good shoes, a comfortable shirt and good long trousers are important. Since the nights get very cold, be sure to take a warm sweater. You can rent sleeping bags in the park, but they are not always very clean. If you have your own sleeping bag liner, bring it. A hat and sunglasses offer protection against the sun. You must bring all your own food. Instant meals are a good choice since you can cook them very quickly. Uncooked snacks include potato chips, chocolate, nuts, raisins and candy.

Since it rains regularly on the mountain, be sure to bring some waterproof clothing, like a light raincoat or poncho. Also, when everything you have on is wet, you will certainly appreciate a change of clothes.

The parks department recommends taking a pair of gloves, but this is probably not necessary for Europeans and North Americans used to colder climates. Gloves could be useful for climbing when everything is wet and slippery, so if you have them, you might as well take them.

You will be able to fill your water bottle at every shelter along the way. A good

flashlight is essential, since on the second day, you will have to break camp in the middle of the night in order to catch sunrise at the summit.

If you are about to take off and then suddenly realize you have forgotten something, there is one last chance. There is a small store in the restaurant that sells essentials like food, candy, gas cartridges for stoves, batteries, etc.

The Guide

Every group is required to hire a guide for the trip. Each morning, men who are available as guides register with the park rangers. When you stop by the office, they will be able to pair you with a guide for the next day.

It is possible to make the trip down without a guide, so that you only have to pay him for two days of a three-day trip. The price depends on the size of the group: M$ 25 per day for up to 3 people; M$ 28 per day for 4-6 people; M$ 30 per day for 7-12 people which is the maximum group size. The best size for a group is around 3 people.

The Ascent

Climbing the mountain takes about three days, two for the ascent and one for the descent. This pace is slow enough for you to enjoy the many varieties of vegetation along the way. The following is a rough timetable for the hike. Experienced hikers will probably go faster.

- Kinabalu Headquarters to the Power Station: 1 hour or 15 minutes in a pick-up.
- Power Station to the Komborongoh Telecom Station: 1.5 hours.
- Komborongoh Telecom Station to Layang-Layang: 1.5 hours.
- Layang-Layang to the Pakka Cave: 1.75 hours.
- Pakka Cave to the Laban Rata Resthouse: 0.75 hours.
- Laban Rata Resthouse to Sayat-Sayat: 1.5 hours.

Trails Near the Park Headquarters

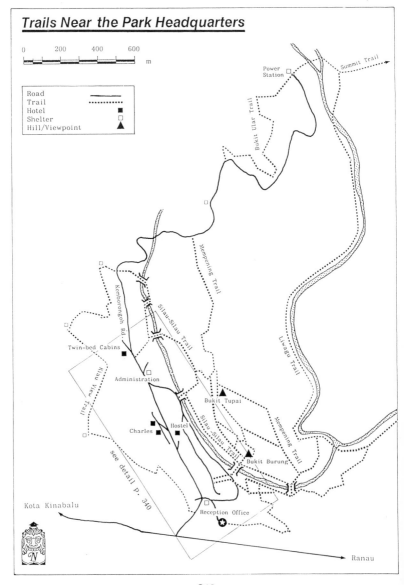

• Sayat-Sayat to the summit: 1.5 hours.

The hike begins at the Park Headquarters, at an altitude of approximately 1550 m.

From here, a road goes to the **Power Station**. You can walk the 4 km, but the road is very hard. It is better to take a pick-up, which costs M$ 20 for up to 6 people. The **Summit Trail** really begins here at 1829 m. Along the way, you will see small signs with numbers written on them, like 50, 150, etc. These count the chains, or distance hiked. 50 chains equal one kilometer, 80 chains one mile.

Shortly after the Power Station, you come to **Carson's Fall**, a waterfall named after the first administrator of the park. The path gets steeper after the waterfall. You reach the first shelter at an altitude of 1951 m. These shelters are designed for protection from the rain. They all have fresh water cisterns nearby. On a clear day, you can see from here to the road to Kota Kinabalu.

After a short time, you come to the second shelter at 2134 m. From here, the trail goes to the **Kamborongoh Telecom Station** at 2225 m. Right before you get there, the path forks off. Visitors are not permitted on the grounds of the station. Shortly after the fork is the third shelter.

After that, the path splits again and the path to the left leads to Layang-Layang, or the Field of Swallows. There is a television station here.

The right path continues up to the summit. It goes through a bamboo forest to the fourth shelter, at a height of 2651 m. It is a bit further to **Carson's Camp**, a camp for park rangers. From here, it is a steep hike to the fifth shelter at 2896 m. The sixth shelter is at 3109 m.

From here, one path forks off to a helicopter landing pad and another to the **Paka Cave**. The cave is formed by a rock overhang. In the past, it was used by hikers as the last protected campsite before the summit. From this point, you should have a good view of Kinabalu, weather permitting.

At 3353 m, you come to **Panar Laban**. In the Dusun language, this means something like Place of Sacrifices. There are places to

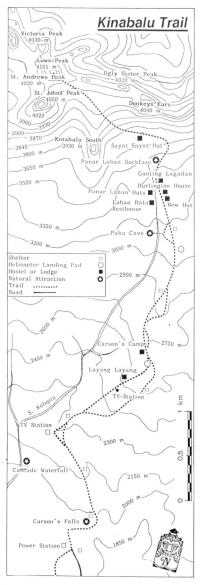

343

Rest of the Weary: Laban Rata Resthouse at 3300 m.

stay here including the Laban Rata Resthouse and the Gunting Lagadan Hut. You can rent sleeping bags in these huts. The rooms in the Laban Rata Resthouse are comfortable and heated and there is a restaurant and a radio connection to the Park Headquarters. Bunting Lagadan Hut seems to be falling down as most of the windows are broken. They have a gas stove, but do not sell food.

The summit ascent comes in the morning. The guides usually suggest leaving around 3:00 in order to catch the sunrise at the summit. Many hikers prefer to leave around 5:00, since the summit is often shrouded in fog at dawn anyway, and the climb is much easier when you can see. There are ropes to assist you for much of the way up, but they are not easy to use with only the light of a flashlight.

The vegetation zone ends shortly after Panar Laban and the trail continues over rocky ground. The next rest spot is *Sayat-Sayat Hut* at 3810 m. This tin hut offers shelter for 10 people. There is water and agas stove. It is rudimentary at best and pretty dirty, with chilly winds, rats, etc.

The slowly ascending summit plateau begins after the hut. You will pass by the various rugged peaks of Mt. Kinabalu on your way to the highest, *Low's Peak* at 4101 m. This is the highest point in Southeast Asia. There is a sign here congratulating successful hikers. The sign also asks that you sign your name in a book and not on the rock. Though there has been no book there for some time, we would also make the same request.

Looking out from Low's Peak, you can see the other peaks including *St. John's Peak, Donkey's Ear* and *Victoria Peak*. Right below you (c. 1000 m) is *Low's Gully*. *Sacrifice Pool* is just below the summit. Animal gods used to be honored here.

From Low's Peak, you can either go straight back to the Park Headquarters which takes one day or stay a night in Sayat-Sayat Hut. Cold and filthy though it is, the peace and quiet and the view make it worthwhile.

Vegetation in the Park

On Mount Kinabalu, there is a wide range of vegetation zones, some of which are home to plants not normally found in the tropics, like pine trees.

The vegetation below 1000 m is *tropical rainforest*. It has the greatest variety of plants. Over half the trees are of the *Dipterocarpaceae* family, and this type of forest is often called a Dipterocarp Forest. It is known for its huge trees, the highest of which are over 50 m tall. At altitudes above 600 m, there is a kind of Rafflesia only found on Kinabalu. It is a parasitic plant that lives in the branches of other plants usually trees and has one flower, up to 1 m across, that grows on the jungle floor. There are only Rafflesia in the area around Poring.

At altitudes between 1000 m and 1800 m around the Power Station, the jungle starts to fade. There are still a few Dipterocarps and highly prized meranti trees.

In the area around the Park Headquarters around 1550 m, the vegetation is given over to **Mountain Rain Forest**. Oaks, chestnut trees, pine trees, laurels, giant ferns and epiphytes (plants that grow on other plants,

All the Way Up: On top of Victoria Peak

but are not parasites, like orchids) are all found here. There are around 1100 varieties of orchids in the park.

From 1800 m, the vegetation becomes **mountain forest**. The trees get smaller and deformed. Huge ferns overshadow the path. Rhododendrons (blooming between October and early February) and bamboo make the forest seem impenetrable. The constant humidity causes a rich growth to flourish on the forest floor. Everything, including tree roots, is covered with moss and lichen. There are also a lot of **orchids**. Certainly the most interesting carnivorous plants here are the **pitcher plants**. These plants have leaves that form a pitcher. In the pitcher is a digestive fluid that works on insects that get caught in it. The edges of the pitcher are brightly colored, and this is what attracts the insects. But there is a slippery surface on the edges which makes them lose their footing and fall into the

pitcher to be digested. The 16 different varieties in the park all have different sized pitchers including one up to 35 cm long in the *Nepenthes rajah*.

The mountain forest extends up to 3300 m around Panar Laban. The vegetation continues to get less diverse and smaller. Shrubs like myrtle and rhododendron, and mosses account for most of the growth at higher altitudes.

The **Alpine zone** begins at 3300 m. Only grasses, lichens and mosses grow here. There are still some white orchids (*Coelogyne papillosa*) near the Sayat-Sayat Hut at 3810 m. They bloom in November, and from a distance, they look like small clumps of snow.

In the **summit region**, there is no vegetation at all.

Fauna

Normally, there should´be a large diversity of animal life in an area as large as Kinabalu Park. But due to the number of tourists coming through, a lot of the larger animals have retreated further into the jungle.

The **orang-utan**, which used to be very common here, is now seen only in remote areas. The most common mammals in the park are rodents like the **Kinabalu rat** (*Rattus baluensis*). Generally, you will encounter **birds** far more often than other animals.

Poring Hot Springs

This is a separate part of the park. The "bathtubs" built by Japanese troops, are a great place to rest weary bones. There are many paths that go through the rainforest and along the river. The biggest botanical attraction is the *Rafflesia*, which grows in this area. It blooms between the end of July and September.

Registration

You have to register to visit the park, usually in Kota Kinabalu. If you are not sure whether or not you will go to Poring, you can also register in Kinabalu Park. This can be problematic if you want to visit the park on a weekend or holiday. The advantage of going to Kinabalu Park first is that the rangers there will know if theroad to Poring is passable. Anyone not spending the night in Poring must pay a day fee of M$ 1 per person or 50 *sen* for students.

Getting to Poring

Although Poring is part of Kinabalu Park, to get there, you have to leave the park and then reenter it through **Ranau**. There are regular connections from Ranau only on the weekends. At other times, you will have to rent a taxi. See the section on Ranau for more precise information.

Accommodation

There are fewer places to stay in Poring and some of these are quite luxurious and expensive. The rates are lower during the week than on weekends and holidays:
- **Old Cabin** (6 pers.), M$ 75 / 100.
- **New Cabin** (4 pers.), M$ 60 / 80.
- It is far cheaper to stay in the **hostel** or to rent a **tent**. The prices in parentheses are for students with an international student ID (ISIC).
- **Poring Hostel** (24 pers.), M$ 8 (2).
- **Campground**, M$ 2 (1).

Sandakan

Around 300 km east of Kota Kinabalu, Sandakan used to be the capital of Sabah. Today, the city is an important business center, mainly for export products like rattan, hardwood and palm oil.

Like Kota Kinabalu, Sandakan was entirely destroyed during the

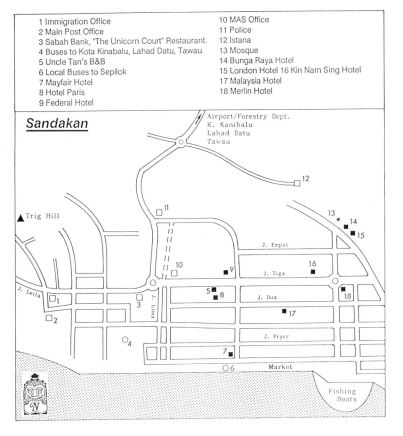

1 Immigration Office
2 Main Post Office
3 Sabah Bank, "The Unicorn Court" Restaurant.
4 Buses to Kota Kinabalu, Lahad Datu, Tawau
5 Uncle Tan's B&B
6 Local Buses to Sepilok
7 Mayfair Hotel
8 Hotel Paris
9 Federal Hotel
10 MAS Office
11 Police
12 Istana
13 Mosque
14 Bunga Raya Hotel
15 London Hotel 16 Kin Nam Sing Hotel
17 Malaysia Hotel
18 Merlin Hotel

Sandakan

Airport/Forestry Dept.
K. Kanibalu
Lahad Datu
Tawau

Trig Hill

J. Empat

J. Tiga

J. Leila

J. Lima

J. Dua

J. Pryer

Market

Fishing
Boats

Second World War. The new city is based on a parallel grid along the Sandakan Bay. In the center of the town, the streets do not have names, just numbers like Jalan Dua, Jalan Tiga.

There is really nothing to see in the city except long straight blocks of anonymous housing. It might be interesting to sit by the bay and watch the variety of ships go by. You can also see giant logs from the interior being loaded onto cargo ships. There is a huge **market** right next to the water. Everything imaginable is sold here. And a trip up *Trig Hill* is a good way to spend an afternoon. From this hill above the city, there is a great view of the bay and offshore islands.

Accommodation

Sandakan is the most expensive city in Sabah. There are no cheap hotels anywhere. The least you will pay for a relatively clean room is M$ 30, but count on paying more.

•The only exception is the **Hotel Paris**, which charges M$ 26.25 for a single room big enough for two. It is centrally located and all rooms have their own bathrooms.

•**Uncle Tan's B&B**, Taman Khong Lok, clean house with a private atmosphere and good food. They offer interesting tours. M$ 15 / person with breakfast. Tel. 669516.

•**Federal Hotel**, Jalan Tiga 3, from M$ 38. Tel. 219611 / 7, 219637.

•**Malaysia Hotel**, 32 2nd Avenue, from M$ 38, Tel. 42277 / 8.

•**Mayfair Hotel**, Jl. Prayer 1 / F 24, good and clean, but often full since it is near the bus station, from M$ 32. Tel. 45191 / 2.

•**Kin Nam Sing Hotel**, Jalan Tiga 51, from M$ 40, some rooms with A / C. Tel. 3244.

•**New Sabah Hotel**, Jalan Singapura 18, from M$ 40 for a huge bed and bathroom.

•**Hsiang Garden Hotel**, from M$ 110.

Food

As usual, there is a big assortment of places to eat. There are a number of good **Chinese restaurants** on Trig Hill. There is an excellent Chinese restaurant, *The Unicorn Court*, in the middle of the city, in the Sabah Bank building. You have to enter through the garage of the bank building and take the elevator to the 17th floor. There are a number of food and drink stalls on the roof terrace for those who want to enjoy the view.

Around Sandakan

Since there is nothing to do in the city, it is worth taking some side trips. Animal and nature lovers will want to visit the **Sepilok Sanctuary**, a reserve for orang-utans.

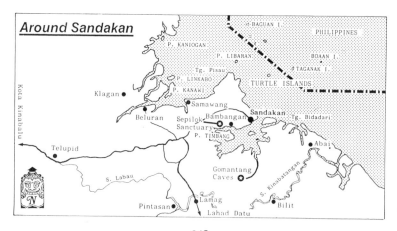

348

Orang-Utan Sanctuary

This 4049 hectare reserve is covered mainly by tropical rainforest. There are around 450 different types of trees. Along the coast, the rainforest gives way to mangroves.

In this sanctuary, *orang-utans* that have been captured illegally are set free in a controlled environment to get them used to life in the wild again. Many of the animals have illnesses or psychiatric problems that would make it very difficult for them if they were immediately set free in the wild. Also, most of them have not yet learned to care for themselves. There is a program underway to teach them these necessary skills. After a period of quarantine, newly-arrived animals are let loose in the area around the station and cared for a few times a day. Soon they learn to climb, and their food is put on platforms high up in trees farther and farther away from the station. The next step is for the animals to move out of the sanctuary and back into the wild.

There are usually about 15 orang-utans in the area around the station. This area is, unfortunately, much too small for this many. At the same time, the habitats for the animals outside of the reserve are rapidly diminishing. For this reason, it is doubtful whether this kind of program will ever really work.

In addition to the orang-utans, there are a number of hikes you can go on in the park. Along the main path, many of the trees have their Malay and scientific names noted on a small sign. An especially interesting 2 hour walk goes through the *mangrove swamp*. There are over 200 species of birds to see here. If you are lucky, you might get a look at some other animals like gibbons, Malay bears, crocodiles, etc.

There is an **exhibition** in the park with information about the animals and plants. It focuses on the problems with and importance of maintaining Sabah's tropical rain forests. There are also daily films about the project with the orang-utans.

●*Times to Visit:* The station is open from 9:00 to 16:00. Feedings are daily at 10:30. If you want to see a feeding, be there at 9:30, since the feeding site is a 20-30 minute walk from the station.

●*Getting to the Park:* Since there is nowhere to stay in the park, you will have to start from Sandakan. Buses from the Labuk Road Bus Company go in the direction of the park. Other buses, Batu 16, 17 and 30, also go there. However, you will have to get out along the main road and walk the remaining 3 km.

Getting there:

There is a direct bus No. 14 every hour from the Sandakan bus station. The 25 km trip takes just under an hour and costs M$ 1.20.

●*Registration:* No need to register.

Gomantong Caves

Another interesting side-trip is to the Gomantong Caves, on the other side of the bay, some 30 km from Sandakan. Like in the Niah Caves in Sarawak, swift's nests are collected here to be used in Bird's Nest soup. The only problem with this otherwise worthwhile trip is the expense of getting here. People who are not pressed for funds can take a tour with one of the travel agencies in the city that goes regularly for about M$ 80 per person. Those with less money, but who know something of the language, can try and go with the nest collectors on their next trip. You can find them at the market. The boats leave across the bay very early, between 5:00 and 6:00 from Sandakan for around M$ 5. Next, you can take a taxi, and then walk the final 5 km up a mountain.

You will need a **permit** for the trip. You can get one in the Forestry Department, nearly 10 km out of town. Take a No. 6 bus to the Government Complex.

Sukau

If you are already on the other side of the bay, you can take a taxi to Sukau on the Kinabatangan River. It takes 50 minutes. From here, you can rent a boat for around M$ 35 and go up the river. Here, there is a very good chance of seeing one or more proboscis monkeys *(Nasalis larvatus)*. The chances of seeing one here are better than almost anywhere outside of a zoo, and just one can make the entire trip worthwhile.

Green Turtle Island,

30 km from Sandakan, in the bay. The real name of the island is Pulau Selingan, but since a national park was established here with the goal of protecting the turtles, the island has been better known by its new name. In addition to the turtles, there are also some good beaches.

Registration: A permit is necessary to visit the island. You can get one for M$ 30 in the Sabah Parks Office (Tel. 273453), in the Federal Building, nearly 10 km out of the city. Take a taxi or bus Batu 14, 16, 17 or 30.

Getting to Green Turtle Island: There is no regular transportation to the island. You can either rent a boat for around M$ 100, or try to get on the park administration boat. Ask when you register. If that does not work, try asking the people on the boat directly.

Accommodation: There is only one place to stay on the island, taken care of by the rangers. This may or may not still be the case, so it is best to find out when you register. It costs only M$ 2, but you have to bring everything you'll need, including bedding and food. Usually, there is drinking water on the island, but it sometimes runs out, so it's best to bring your own.

Further Travel

From Sandakan, there are **buses** and **land cruisers** to points all over Sabah. The central bus station is near the market. There are daily buses to:
- **Kota Kinabalu** – M$ 35.
- **Ranau** – M$ 27.
- **Lahad Datu** – M$ 14.
- Because of the bad roads, there is only a land cruiser to **Tawau** – M$ 25.

Sandakan has an airport, daily **flights** to:
- **Kota Kinabalu** – M$ 69.
- **Lahad Datu** – M$ 40.
- **Kudat** – M$ 54.
- **Semporna** – M$ 50.
- **Tawau** – M$ 61.

All are Twin Otter flights, with a free baggage allowance of only 10 kg. Get tickets from travel agencies around the city or directly from MAS, Jalan Tiga, Tel. 273966.

Lahad Datu

The **green turtle** *(Chelonia mydas)*, is considered a delicacy by some people. Its cartilage (not its meat) is used to make turtle soup.

The shell of the green turtle can reach a length of more than 140 cm. It is completely herbivorous, which supposedly makes it tastier than other omnivorous turtles. Its powerful body is well-suited to swimming-underwater. The green turtle is found in all warm waters, but particularly near algae and seaweed growths.

Females lay their eggs on flat, sandy beaches. They have been known to swim hundreds of kilometers to lay their eggs in a particular spot. Since they always return to the same spot, sometimes whole groups of them are seen together. Individuals lay eggs every third year.

They bury their eggs in the sand and then swim off. The heat from the sun incubates the eggs and finally the little turtles hatch.

On Green Turtle Island, this natural process of laying eggs is helped along by man to promote the growth of the species. At night, the beach is patrolled by park personnel, who collect any eggs that have been laid that night and bring them to a protected area until they hatch. Once the young turtles are hatched, they are released out at sea off a boat, so they are not eaten on the beach.

Very few tourists make it as far as Lahad Datu, some 130 km southeast of Sandakan. The town of 25,000 is the local commercial center. There is nothing to see in the town, but it is the gateway to the islands in the Darvel Bay. These islands have beautiful beaches and coral reefs.

We have to point out that the city, and the islands in the bay, are not always very safe. According to our contacts in Sabah, the city or the islands are very often attacked by pirates with automatic weapons. We ourselves were never held up, but in early 1988, we arrived just after an attack. Between January and April 1988, there were 5 pirate attacks in the area around Lahad Datu reported in the paper.

The **Danum Valley Field Center** is near Lahad Datu. Research into the effect of logging on forest animals, the regeneration cycles of plant life, and the availability of useful forest wood is conducted here, funded by the World Wildlife Fund. There are supposed to be many orang-utans in the area. On Mondays, Wednes-

days and Fridays, there is an administration bus that goes from the Yayasan Sabah Office to the park. It usually leaves around 15:00 but ask first. There is a place to stay in the park for M$ 10 a night as well as a restaurant and a place to cook.

Accommodation / Food

Although the town is not often visited by tourists, there are a few hotels. Unfortunately, they are not cheap.
●*Government Rest House*, near the airport, about 1 km out of town. Ask the bus driver to let you off. Very good. From M$ 12. Tel. 81177, 81536.
●*Ocean Hotel*, Jalan Timur, from M$ 40, mid-range, clean and good. Tel. 81700.
●*Perdana Hotel*, Jalan Bajau, from M$ 35, rooms with A / C and bath from M$ 65. Tel. 81400.
●*Lahad Datu Hotel*, Jalan Kemboja, from M$ 31.50. Tel. 81100, 81101.
●*Venus Hotel*, from M$ 32. Tel. 81900 / 1.
●*Mido Hotel*, 94 Main St., from M$ 90, best place in town. Tel. 81800.

Food: As in other trading centers, Chinese food is probably your best bet and there is a big selection.

Further Travel

The road between Sandakan and Lahad Datu is only paved in sections. Despite this, and other worse roads, there are **buses** to:
●*Sandakan* – M$ 14.
●*Tawau* – M$ 22.
●*Semporna* – M$ 12.
●*Kunak* – M$ 7.
Land cruisers are often used instead of buses for trips in the direction of Tawau.

In addition, there are **flights** to:
●*Tawau* – M$ 40.
●*Sandakan* – M$ 40.
The MAS office is in the Mido Hotel Building, Ground Floor, Tel. 81707, 82767.

Boats leave Lahad Datu daily for Semporna for M$ 14, at around 8:00 and to Kunak for M$ 7, at around 11:00. They leave from the wharf behind the market. Get tickets there.

Semporna

Semporna is about halfway between Lahad Datu and Tawau. From here, you can get to **Pulau Gaya**, which has very good diving. It is, however, very expensive to get to (a boat will cost around M$ 150). There is a beautiful, kilometer-long coral reef right off the coast, which is ideal for diving and snorkeling.

There is also good diving off Pulau Sipadan. For information, contact Mr. Ron at the Semporna Ocean Tourism Center, PO Box 6, Tel. 089-781088.

There is an **oyster farm** just off the coast. It can sometimes be visited, but ask first.

Accommodation

There are two big hotels and also a few guest houses from around M$ 15, which are really just mattresses in a room, in Semporna.
●*Island View Hotel*, from M$ 40.
●*Semporna Hotel*, from M$ 55.

Further Travel

Buses travel the route between **Lahad Datu** and **Tawau** and it costs M$ 12 to either. Sometimes there are only land cruisers to Tawau. They carry fewer people. In addition, there are flights to:
●*Sandakan* – M$ 50.
●*Tomanggong* – M$ 40.

Tawau

Tawau is the commercial center of the southeast. All exports from the interior, including cocoa, hardwood, rubber, and copra are shipped from here. The city has remained very much a provincial town and still retains a bit of charm.

Tourists usually only get a fleeting glimpse of this as they pass through on their way to Kalimantan. However, traveling to Nunukan, either by land or sea, is forbidden for foreigners. All points in the city are easily accessible on foot.

A side-trip to one of the huge cocoa plantations outside the city might be interesting, especially for people who only know cocoa in the form of a powder that goes into milk. The cocoa beans grow in big green pods hanging from the tree branches.

Accommodation

Since the town is a big trade center, there are quite a few hotels, none though has rooms under M$ 25.
●*Foo Guan Hotel*, 152 Chester St., from M$ 25 with fan. Tel. 771700.
●*Kuhara Hotel*, Jalan Kuhara, from M$ 29. Tel. 771200.

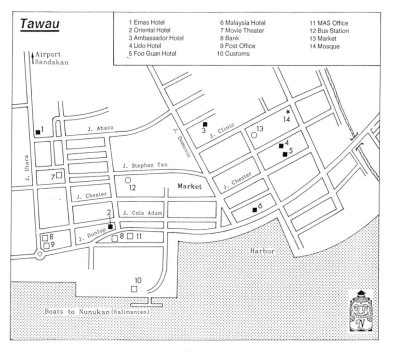

Tawau

1 Emas Hotel	6 Malaysia Hotel	11 MAS Office
2 Oriental Hotel	7 Movie Theater	12 Bus Station
3 Ambassador Hotel	8 Bank	13 Market
4 Lido Hotel	9 Post Office	14 Mosque
5 Foo Guan Hotel	10 Customs	

Airport Sandakan

J. Abaco

J. Domenic

J. Clinic

J. Utara

J. Stephen Tan

Market

J. Chester

J. Chester

J. Cole Adam

J. Dunlop

Harbor

Boats to Nunukan (Kalimantan)

●*Lido Hotel*, Jalan Stephen Tan, from M$ 30, M$ 50 with A / C. Tel. 74547.

●*Wah Yew Hotel*, 117 Jalan Chester, from M$ 30, good. Tel. 771300.

●*Malaysia Hotel*, 37 Jalan Dunlop, from M$ 31.50. Tel. 772800.

●*Ambassador Hotel*, 1872 Jalan Paya, from M$ 30, with bath. Tel. 772700.

●*Oriental Hotel*, 10 Jalan Dunlop, from M$ 68, all rooms with A / C and bath. Tel. 771500.

●*Far East Hotel*, Jalan Masjid, from M$ 45 with A / C. Tel. 773200.

●*Emas Hotel*, Jalan Utara, from M$ 105, a higher standard. Tel. 773300.

●*Marco Polo Hotel*, from M$ 125 to 1000, luxury hotel. Tel. 777988.

Further Travel

There are daily **taxis** and **land cruisers** to Semporna and Lahad Datu. Taxis leave for **Semporna** around 8:30 for M$ 12, and around 7:00 for **Lahad Datu** for M$ 25. Land cruisers leave around 7:15, but do not leave every day, so check the day before. Land cruisers to **Semporna** cost M$ 9; to **Lahad Datu** (minibuses too) the cost is M$ 20.

There are also irregular **boats** to Semporna and Lahad Datu. For more exact information, check at the wharf.

The airport is 1 km out of town. There are **flights** to **Sandakan** for M$ 61 and to **Lahad Datu** for M$ 40. The MAS office is at Lot 1 A, Wisma SALSCO, Fajar Complex, Tel. 772659, 772703 / 4.

Kota Belud

Kota Belud, which means, Mountain Fortress, is the main town in the Bajau region.

The main attraction for tourists here is the big market, or **Tamu**, that takes place every Sunday. All kinds

of people come from all over to take part. The Kadazan and Bajau are the biggest groups, but there are also Malay, Chinese and sometimes a few Indian traders as well. The market is not in the town itself, so do not be surprised when the bus lets you off at the small town market, but behind a hill in· a small depression. To get there, either ask the way, as everyone knows it, or figure it out yourself. The best way to get there is to follow the main street in the direction of Kudat. At the intersection at the foot of the hill, goright in the direction of Ranau. After about 100 meters, there is a flight of stairs that goes up the hill to the left. On top, there is another road, which you follow to the right. After 100 meters, there is a small path that goes up the hill, which leads to a wooded depression. The Tamu takes place here, under the trees. Don't miss the buffalo market at the edge of the Tamu.

The Tamu begins early in the morning and ends between 11:00 and noon. The vendors then sell whatever they have leftover in the city market. Try and get there very early (this is not possible from Kota Kinabalu) or even better, on Saturday.

This market is probably not the best place to look for handicrafts. We have found little of interest here, save for some Rungu artifacts. The Tamu in Sikuati on the Kudat Peninsula is better for that. If you can't make it there, almost everything is available in the Sunday market in Kota Kinabalu.

If you arrive in Kota Belud on Sunday morning and do not want to spend the night, you will have to do something with your bags, or else carry them around all day with you. Fortunately, the generous police officers at the station on the road to Kota Kinabalu are often kind enough to look after a few backpacks during the day. Ask politely.

Accommodation

There are two hotels in town, as well as a resthouse, which is a bit removed:
●*Hotel Kota Belud*, 21 Jalan Francis, from M$ 36, A / C, common shower with hot water. Tel. 976576.
●*Government Resthouse*, M$ 12, normally only for government employees, but you can ask politely if they have room. Tel. 67532.

Further Travel

There are daily **bus** connections to Kota Kinabalu, Kudat and Tamparuli to connect for Kinabalu Park and Ranau. On Sundays, there is a lot of additional transportation – just about anything that moves. Ask if they have room, and agree on a price beforehand.

Buses to *Kota Kinabalu* are M$ 6, to *Kudat*, M$ 10, and to *Tamparuli*, M$ 3. The trip to the national park is an additional M$ 10.

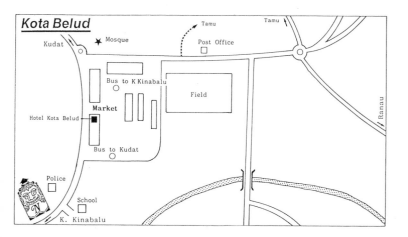

Kudat

Kudat is roughly in the center of the Rungu area. People here used to live in long-houses and you still see them here and there. The entire Kudat peninsula is supported by banana plantations, rice fields and coconut palms. There are some long sandy beaches and coral reefs that see almost no tourists.

Unfortunately, there is one major drawback to this beach paradise. The beach closest to Kudat, Bak Bak, is more than 10 km away. Since there is no place to stay there, you have to make it a day-trip and travel by taxi as there are no buses. The trip out is quite cheap at around M$ 5 per person, but the trip back can be more than twice that. The beaches near Sikuati, which are even more beautiful, are almost inaccessible. There are buses, but because of the great distance, you would have to turn back immediately, since there is no place to stay there either. There was a TDC resthouse, but it burned down in 1986.

If you have enough money, time and language skills, you can go from Kudat to Pulau Banggi. There are wonderful beaches and undisturbed jungle on this island. Since there are no regular boats, you have to ask around and, the boats only make the trip in good weather. With a bit of luck, you can stay in a village on the island.

There is a Rungu *Tamu* every Sunday morning in Sikuati, on the west coast of the Kudat Peninsula. There, you can see women wearing traditional black sarongs, strings of pearls and brass rings.

Accommodation

Although Kudat is a small town, there are a few hotels and even a government resthouse.
●*Greenland Hotel*, the best in Kudat, from M$ 35. Tel. 62211.
●*Sunrise Hotel*, from M$ 29.40, more expensive rooms have bath and A / C, good restaurant. Tel. 61517.
●*Kudat Hotel*, Little St., from M$ 30, with A / C, from M$ 40 with bath, clean. Tel. 616379
●*Hotel Kinabalu*, 1 Block C, Sedco Shophouse, from M$ 65, the best in town. Tel. 62693.
●*Government Resthouse*, M$ 12, normally only for government employees, so ask politely if they have a room. Tel. 61304.

Further Travel

There are regular **buses** from Kudat to **Kota Kinabalu** for M$ 15 and to **Kota Belud** for M$ 10. Since the road to Kota Kinabalu is quite good, there are also taxis available.

There are **flights** to **Kota Kinabalu** for M$ 50 and to **Sandakan** for M$ 54. If you are going to Sandakan, it is very strongly recommended that you fly, since you will save yourself a day of travel over grueling unpaved roads and spend only M$ 5 more. Buy tickets at the General Sales Agent, Lo Cham En, Tel. 61399, at the airport.

Beaufort

Beaufort is about 100 km from Kota Kinabalu. It is named after an old director of the North Borneo Company. There is nothing to interest the tourist here. The town is merely a stop on the way to Sarawak or the interior.

Accommodation

There is really no need to stay here, as it is almost always possible to organize further travel. Just in case though, there are two hotels:
●*Foh Lodging House*, at the train station, from M$ 15, dormitory-like rooms.
●*Padas Hotel*, near the bus station, from M$ 23, very clean. Tel. 211441.

Further Travel

From Beaufort, there are **buses** to **Kota Kinabalu** for M$ 7 and to **Sipitang** in Sarawak for M$ 8. Buses leave from the market; when trains arrive, they leave directly from the train station.

There are **taxis** as well. They travel the same routes as the buses and leave from the same places. Taxis take bus passengers when there are not enough people to fill a bus. This happens quite often on the trip to Sipitang. You have to pay only the bus fare in this case.

Between Beaufort and Tenom there is a slow **train**, which is one of the biggest attractions in Sabah. The train creeps through a ravine, often right up against the stone wall. There is a typical jungle river flowing below which has meandering sections as well as rapids. The train passes a big water power plant that supplies the area with power. From time to time, it passes stations that are nothing more than clearings in the jungle. The rails are almost completely covered over by grass, and the whole trip lasts two hours. Trains leave at 6:45, 10:50, 14:30 and 16:05. It costs M$ 2.75.
●There is also a much faster train to Tanjung Aru, leaving at 10:38.

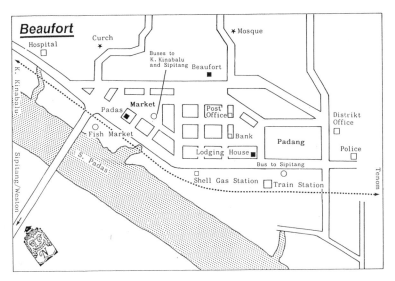

Tenom

Tenom is the endpoint of the railway line into the interior. The **Murut**, the only nomads in Sabah, live in this area. There is very little to see here. If you arrive with the train from Beaufort, you will have to spend the night here before your return to Beaufort, or trip to Tomani, or to Kota Kinabalu by way of Keningau.

The only rock paintings in Sabah are near Baku. From Tenom, take a minibus to Tomani for M$ 4, and from there, take a four-wheeler to Bakuku for M$ 5. There is a resthouse where you can stay for free, but it is in awful shape. Hire a guide for about M$ 10 for the 45-minute walk to the paintings.

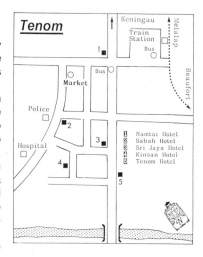

Tenom

1. Namtai Hotel
2. Sabah Hotel
3. Sri Jaya Hotel
4. Kinsan Hotel
5. Tenom Hotel

Along the way, in Kemabong between Tenom and Tomani, you can see the longest suspension bridge in Sabah.

Accommodation

Of the few hotels in town, we like the Sri Jaya and the Sabah Hotel the best. The Tenom Hotel is falling down. The Sabah Hotel has good Indian food.
● **Sri Jaya Hotel**, on the main street, from M$ 31.70 with A / C.
● **Sabah Hotel**, opposite the police station, from M$ 20.
● **Kin San Hotel**, shophouse No. 58, from M$ 30, TV and A / C. Tel. 735485.
● **Nam Tai Hotel**, on the main street, from M$ 20.
● **Tenom Hotel**, on the main street, from M$ 20, completely neglected.

Further Travel

From Tenom, there are **buses** to **Keningau** for M$ 4 and **Kota Kinabalu** for M$ 15.

There is no exact schedule, but they usually leave sometime between 7:30 and 9:00. The best thing to do is ask at the bus terminal the night before. Daily **pick-ups** go to Tomani for M$ 4. They also leave around 8:00. There are also **taxis** to **Keningau** for M$ 40 and **Tomani** for M$ 40. All of these leave from the main street.

There are **trains** to **Beaufort** and **Kota Kinabalu**. They leave at 6:40, 7:30 (direct to Kota Kinabalu), 8:00, 13:40 and 16:00, Monday to Friday. Sunday schedule: 7:20, 7:55, 12:10 (direct to Kota Kinabalu) and 15:05 for M$ 8.35.

Labuan

The island of Labuan used to be part of the Straits Settlement, along with Singapore, Malacca and Penang. Today it maintains the status of a free port.

To get from Sabah to **Brunei**, you can go overland through Sarawak or take a ship to Labuan from Menumbok and then a speedboat to Brunei.

Since there is really nothing on Labuan except a cemetery for soldiers from World War II and very expensive hotel rooms, we would not recommend a stop here.

Accommodation

There are some very expensive hotels on the island, but most of them are not of the standard one might expect, given the price.
●**Kim Soon Lee Hotel**, 141 Jalan Okk, Awang Besar, from M$ 50. Tel. 42554.
●**Victoria Hotel**, Jalan Tun Mustapha, from M$ 50. Tel. 412411.
●**Emas Hotel**, 27-30 Jalan Muhibbah, from M$ 50. Tel. 413966.
●**Labuan Hotel**, Jalan Merdeka, from M$ 98. Tel. 412502.

Further Travel

There are daily **boats** between the island and **Brunei (Bandar Seri Begawan)** for M$ 24 and to **Menumbok**, on the Sabah mainland for M$ 7.

There are also daily **flights** to Sabah and Sarawak:
●**Kota Kinabalu** – M$ 43.
●**Lawas** – M$ 31.
●**Long Pa Sia** – M$ 54.
●**Miri** – M$ 57.
●**Bintulu** – M$ 95.
●**Kuching** – M$ 173.

Sindumin / Merapok (Sarawak)

Sindumin is the **border crossing** between Sabah and Sarawak. You get there by bus or taxi from Sipitang. Most people take the bus to Sindumin and then a taxi to Lawas.

The border town is quiet, to say the least. The part in Sabah is called Sindumin and the part in Sarawak, is called Merapok. There are very few houses along the road, which might lead one to think that the border is simply in the middle of the wilderness.

If you are crossing the border, tell the bus driver early enough that you want to go to the **immigration post**. You get off outside what seems to be a private house. There is a sign – *Immigresen* – and sometimes even a state flag. Inside, they will ask a few simple questions: Do you know Bruno Manser? Do you have plane tickets? Are you a journalist, biologist or ecologist? Where are you coming from and where are you going? Everything is very friendly and one gets the distinct impression these questions are being asked only as a form of entertainment, since the employees here do not see much excitement. Once the whole procedure is finished, you get an exit stamp from Sabah on your passport. Then they take your immigration card, give you a new one to fill out, and you get an entry stamp for Sarawak. Unfortunately, this does not automatically extend your visa.

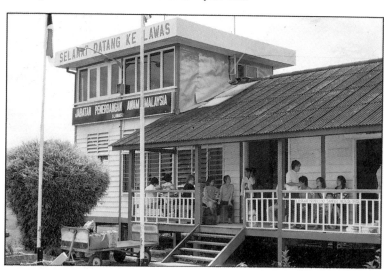

Around 15:00, there is a bus from the border to **Lawas**. If you don't want to wait, then you can walk to Merapok and try and get a pick-up from there. To get there, walk about 500 meters straight down the main road to a police post, where they have plenty of time and seemingly little to do. You will have to show your passport again and answer the same questions they just asked at the immigration post.

Diagonally across from the police post is the turn off for the road to Lawas. 50 meters past the intersection is the bus stop. On each side of the street, there is a small store selling drinks and snacks. There are always people here heading to Lawas, so your chances of getting a ride are pretty good.

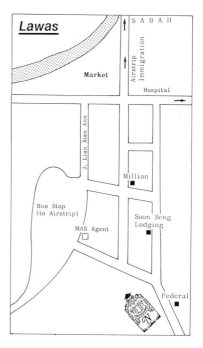

Lawas (Sarawak)

Lawas is a small town in Sarawak, about 30 km from the Sabah border. From here, most travelers head to Brunei, and there is a variety of transportation available.

Immigration: There is an immigration office in Lawas where you can extend your visa. The office is located on the main road to Sabah, right at the edge of town.

Accommodation

There are no cheap rooms in Lawas. Good, large clean rooms cost at least M$ 38.
●*Million Hotel*, DR with A / C, from M$ 40, nice and clean.

●*Federal Hotel*, SR with A / C, from M$ 38, expensive, but good.
●*Soon Seng Hotel*, dirty rooms with three beds from M$ 20.

Further Travel

To get to Brunei, you can take a combination of bus or taxi and boat. There are also *buses* and *taxis* to Sindumin in Sabah.

There is an early *speedboat* every day at 7:00 to Bandar Seri Begawan. It takes around 2 hours and costs M$ 25.

From the small airstrip, there are *Twin Otter flights* to Sabah, Brunei and other points in Sarawak. The airstrip is about 2 km out of

town on the road to Sabah. From 6:00, there is a city bus that goes there for 40 *sen* every two hours. You can also get to the airstrip by minibus, pick-up or taxi for M$ 3 per person. There are *flights* to:
- ●*Kota Kinabalu* – M$ 47.
- ●*Labuan* – M$ 31.
- ●*Limbang* – M$ 25.
- ●*Miri* – M$ 59.
- ●*Bakelalan* – M$ 46.

There are two places in town that sell and reconfirm MAS tickets. We recommend *Eng Huat Travel Agency* , No. 2, Jl. Liaw Siew Ann, Tel. 5570 / 5368. They also sell tickets for Singapore Airlines.

Jungle Treks

Like Sarawak, Sabah has an interior that remains almost untouched by modernization and makes for exciting jungle trekking. Unfortunately, these trips can be expensive and time-consuming. Additionally, you will have to have at least some knowledge of Malay to get by.

One interesting tour starts in *Sapulot*. Get there by going from Kota Kinabalu or Tenom to Keningau and then take a pick-up from Keningau. Ask there about the exact schedule. After you get to Sapulot, find Mr. Lentia. He organizes trips to the interior, e.g. to the Murut. He also has information about boat tours up the Sungei Sembakung that go into Indonesia. Since there is no immigration post in the jungle, you will be in Indonesia unofficially, and must return to Sabah by the same route.

Mr. Lentia organizes everything, from the boat to the food. Such

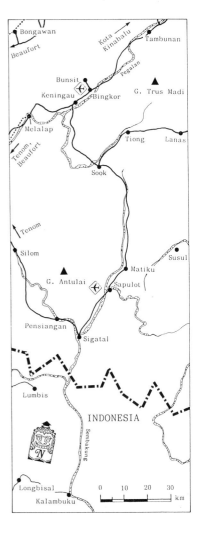

tours have their price, of course, so count on M$ 150-200 per person for a three-day tour.

Another possible tour is **between Kinabalu Park and Sandakan**. Start at Telupid. From here, there is one truck a day to Tanjod, where there is a resthouse for M$ 5. The next day, go to Kuamut along the Kinabatangan River. The easiest thing to do is catch a ride with someone who is going that way. There is also a resthouse in Kuamut.

From there, carry on to Kuala Kapamuh, where there is also a resthouse. On the way, near BK Geram, there are quite a few crocodiles, so it is best not to swim. If you do, stay only in areas with clear water.

The next day, take a boat from Kuala Kapamuh to Sukau. Here, in the mangroves, there are many proboscis monkeys.

From Sukau, you can get to Sandakan Bay by taxi in about 50 minutes, but they only travel in good weather. From there, you can get a boat to Sandakan. Each step of this trip takes about a day, but since you can never count on transportation going when and where you need it, leave your schedule open-ended.

We have not yet done this third trek ourselves, though others have told us about it. It is a somewhat unusual way to get from **Sabah to Sarawak**. First, go from Beaufort to Sindumin. From there, there is one truck a day to Maligan. Then it is a one-and-a-half day hike to Long Pa Sia. Supposedly, there is always someone in Maligan who is going to Long Pa Sia, but if not, you will have to hire a

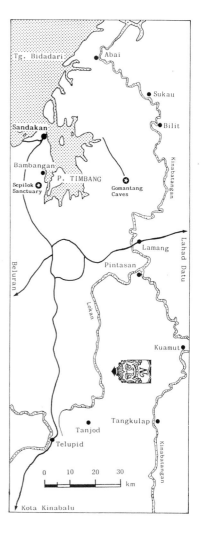

guide. From Long Pa Sia, it is another day's hiketo Long Semado, which is in Sarawak. You might run

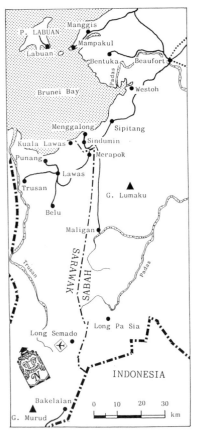

If you finally make it to Long Semado, you can fly from there to Lawas for M$ 40. The Co-Operative Multi-Purpose Society, Ltd. sells plane tickets.

into problems with the Sabah exit stamp and the Sarawak entry stamp. Before you set off, go to the immigration office in Kota Kinabalu and explain exactly what you are planning to do.

If you cannot make it past Long Pa Sia, you can always fly to Labuan for M$ 54. Puan Runang in Long Pa Sia sells tickets.

Singapore Land and People

The name **Singapore** used to have a certain exotic feeling to it, a feeling that even today is not entirely lost. In earlier times, it was the largest port in the Far East and the gateway to the interior of Asia. Today, the era of the big ships is more or less a thing of the past and over two million tourists fly into Singapore every year. This city-state, however, is more of a point of transit than a destination. Visitors come here almost exclusively for the city's attractive bargain shopping. Nevertheless, it is an interesting place with much to see even for those just passing through the Lion City – *Singha* means lion and *Pura* means city.

Singapore is a colorful pastiche of people and cultures from all over Asia. Next to Chinatown is the Indian quarter, where you might forget that you are in Southeast Asia and instead imagine yourself somewhere on the Indian subcontinent. European culture is written large in the city's luxury hotels.

In terms of cleanliness, the city really stands out. Littering of any kind, including tossing cigarette butts or soda cans, is strictly punishable by a fine of S$ 500. It is likewise forbidden to cross a street within 50m on either side of a crosswalk, traffic light or pedestrian bridge. Doing so will cost you S$ 50. These draconian regulations are taken seriously ever with regard to foreigners, so it is a good idea to be familiar with them.

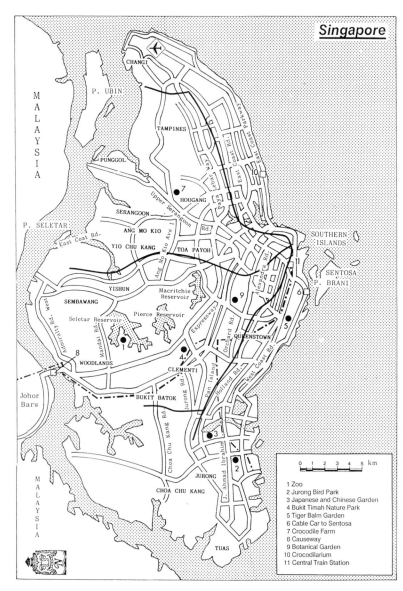

Singapore

MALAYSIA

CHANGI

P. UBIN

TAMPINES

PUNGGOL

Upper Serangoon

7 HOUGANG

Pan Lebar Way

East Coast Rd.

East Coast Parkway

SERANGOON

P. SELETAR

East Coast Rd.

ANG MO KIO

YIO CHU KANG

Ang Mo Kio Ave 1

TOA PAYOH

Rd.

SOUTHERN ISLANDS

SENTOSA
P. BRANI

11

YISHUN

Macritchie
Reservoir

SEMBAWANG

Pierce Reservoir

Seletar Reservoir

Admiralty Rd.

Mandai Rd.

Expressway

9

Alexandra Rd.

Orchard Rd.

6

5

QUEENSTOWN

West Coast Rd.

West Admiralty Rd.

8

WOODLANDS

CLEMENTI

4

Jurong Rd.

Pan Island

Holland Rd.

Johor
Baru

BUKIT BATOK

Choa Chu Kang Rd.

MALAYSIA

3

JURONG

J. Ahmad Ibrahim

2

CHOA CHU KANG

TUAS

0 1 2 3 4 5 km

1 Zoo
2 Jurong Bird Park
3 Japanese and Chinese Garden
4 Bukit Timah Nature Park
5 Tiger Balm Garden
6 Cable Car to Sentosa
7 Crocodile Farm
8 Causeway
9 Botanical Garden
10 Crocodilarium
11 Central Train Station

Geography

The island nation of Singapore lies 130 km north of the Equator, 1° north and 103° east, at the southernmost tip of the Southeast Asian mainland.

The country has an area of 620 sq. kilometers of which the main island occupies 570 sq. kilometers. The remainder is divided among 54 smaller islands.

Since the 1920's, a causeway has connected Singaporewith Malaysia, its closest neighbor. At the island's north-western most point, the distance to Malaysia is only 600 meters.

Topographically, the main island is divided into three regions. A hilly region dominates the center and contains the highest point, Bukit Timah, 175 m above sea level. The hills continue into the northwest, but descend into lowlands in the east. The best-known hill is Mount Faber at 120 m which offers an uninterrupted 360x view.

Climate

Singapore is located within the tropics. Temperatures range from 20°C at night to 32°C during the day. This pattern varies only during the time of the northeast monsoon from the end of October to the beginning of February, when it rains regularly. The greatest monthly rainfall comes in December with approximately 270 mm. During the rest of the year, it also rains relatively often. As a result, the humidity is constant at about 80% year-round.

In the city of Singapore, the daytime temperature can indeed get much warmer as the hot air gets trapped between gigantic buildings. High temperatures coupled with exhaust fumes have cut short many a shopping spree.

Best Time to Visit

Outside of the monsoon season (see above), there is no particularly good or bad time to go to Singapore. For those coming only to shop, the monsoons do not pose much of a problem either, as the big shopping centers can be reached comfortably by public transportation.

Though there are masses of tourists descending on Singapore throughout the year, European vacation times and Western holidays like Easter and Christmas are particularly bad. Those seeking peace and quiet should plan to visit Singapore at other times than these.

Population

The population of Singapore is primarily Chinese, but many other ethnic groups, in particular Indians and Malays, are represented. The total population is around 2.6 million, or about 4000 people per sq. kilometer. 76% of the population is Chinese, 15% Indian and 7% Malay. The remainder are European and Eurasian.

The Malay population is mostly descended from theoriginal residents, while the Chinese and Indians are descended from immigrants who arrived in the 19th and 20th centuries, mainly as a result of British colonial politics.

The **population growth** is maintained at 1.2% annually. An active family planning policy has successfully contained a population explosion. The ideal family is considered to have no more than two children. There are even financial penalties for having more than that. In 1987, the birthrate was 16.8 per thousand the death rate was 5 per thousand. Infant mortality was 7.4 per thousand live births.

Language

Singapore has four official languages: English, Malay, Mandarin Chinese and Tamil. The national language is Malay, but the most commonly used language in public is English.

There are problems today in getting the Chinese population, most of whom speak southern Chinese dialects like Hokkien, Cantonese, and Hainan to convert to Mandarin. The government has conducted an intensive *Speak Mandarin* campaign over the last few years, as posters all over the city attest. All four languages are used in schools and parents can choose which one their children will use.

History

The history of Singapore has been very closely linked with that of Malaysia. In the *13th century*, Prince Sang Nila Utama founded the Kingdom of Temasek, the city on the sea. According to legend, he named the city Singha Pura, because he saw a lion there when he first arrived.

Sir Stamford Raffles

Thomas Stamford Bingley Raffles was born in 1781, the son of a sea captain. In 1795, at the age of 14, he began his career with the East India Company. He learned quickly and by 1805, he was promoted to assistant secretary of Penang.

In the following years, he became comfortable with the Malay culture and language.

In 1811, he led an expedition to Java, with the intention of driving out the Dutch. Among other things, he discovered the Borobudur Temple. For his skill and bravery, he was knighted in 1817.

Throughout his career, he was a staunch advocate of social reform in the colonies, and as a result, he fell out of favor at home. He was tucked away in Bencoolen, a poor part of Sumatra. From here, he tried to establish a new port to protect British shipping from the Dutch. In this, he was supported by the Resident of Malacca, Major Farquhar. The two of them finally got permission from the governor general to outfit an expedition to search for a port. Raffles' eight ships landed on Sentosa on January 29, 1819, and from there, went on to Singapore. He established a trading post here on February 6, 1819. In 1824, the island was given over to the British.

Up until 1822, Raffles visited Singapore several times, but only for short visits. The last of these was in 1822, on the way back to England. He lost his family to malaria on Sumatra, and he, himself, was sick. He spent several months recovering on what is now Fort Canning Hill.

In 1823, he left Singapore for England. During the voyage, his ship burned, and though he was saved, Raffles lost all his drawings of the natural phenomena of the area. He reached England in 1824, where he died on July 5 at the age of 43.

In *1377*, the city was destroyed by soldiers of the Javanese Majapahit Kingdom.

In *1819*, Sir Stamford Raffles, an agent of the East Indian Company, first visited Singapore. He immediately saw the potential value of the island as a port and trading post. On February 6, 1819, he established an outpost here.

In *1824*, the Sultan of Johor, Hussein Mohammed Shab, signed the land over to the British.

In *1826*, the Straits Settlements, consisting of Penang, Malacca and Singapore were established to control trade between Europe and Southeast Asia. In *1871*, Singapore became a British colony.

In *1877*, the first rubber tree seedlings were brought to Singapore and from there, spread out over the entire Malaysian Peninsula. An Englishman, Wickham, managed to smuggle 100,000 seeds from Brazil to England. They were planted in England and then shipped to Singapore. This broke the long Brazilian monopoly on rubber production, which benefited Portugal, who had colonized Brazil.

Until 1914, the city grew very rapidly, becoming the most important port in Southeast Asia. Tin and rubber from Malaysia were shipped to Europe out of Singapore. At the start of World War I, most of the British troops were called away to fight in Europe. After the war, many of them were sent back as Japan began to build up its military presence in the area.

The first bombs fell on Singapore in *1941*. The Japanese captured and occupied Singapore and Malaya.

The British returned in *1945*, following the Japanese defeat. Parties favoring Singaporean independence were formed at this time.

The city-state was given its independence in *1959*. Lee Kwan Yew, the head of the **People's Action Party (PAP)**, was elected prime minister in this year.

In *1963*, the Malaysian Federation, including Singapore, was established. This was encouraged by the British, as Singapore was the only state that was dominated by a left-leaning government. That time is now long gone and the PAP has since become quite conservative.

Following differences with the Malays, Singapore quit the Federation in *1965* and became a sovereign nation, recognized by the Commonwealth and the United Nations.

Singapore joined ASEAN in *1967*. On June 12, Singapore issued its own currency. The PAP, which continues to rule Singapore today, helped transform the city-state into one of the most important Southeast Asian nations. In *1972*, the PAP won all 65 seats in the parliamentary elections.

1976: On May 31, the PAP resigned from the Socialist Internationale, after being threatened with removal due to accusations of human rights violations. In the elections on December 23, the PAP again won all the seats in parliament. In *1980*, the PAP won all the seats in parliament, now 75, yet again.

In *1981*, an opposition candidate, Joshua B. Jeyaretnam, the head of the Workers' Party, won a seat in parliament. In the *1984* elections, the PAP won 77 of 79 seats. The other two were won by the leaders of the Workers' Party and the Democratic Party.

In *1985* the president, Devain Nair gave up his position due to alcoholism. He was replaced by Wee Kim Wee. In the *1988* elections on September 9, the PAP won 80 seats with 61.8% of the vote. The only opposition seat was won by the Democratic Party. In *1990* Prime Minister Lee Kuan Yew stepped down after leading Singapore for over 30 years.

About the State

Singapore is a republic, with a parliament of 79 elected members. There are secret and universal elections every 5 years. Since 1984, the opposition parties that do not win seats in parliament, have been given three additional seats. There are 16 ministers in the cabinet. The official head of state is the president.

Economy

After Japan, Singapore has the highest standard of living and the highest per capita income of any nation in Asia.

Singapore owes much of its success to its strategic location, which makes up for its paucity of natural resources, as even drinking water is imported. It is the finance, trade and manufacturing center of the region. Singapore is becoming more and more well-known as a manufacturer of electronic devices. It also offers foreign investors the benefits of comparatively cheap labor and widespread fluency in English.

Media

The media in Singapore primarily serves commerce. They have had *television* since 1974. Programs are broadcast in English, Malay, Chinese and Tamil. Most shows are from America. There are commercials as well.

The *radio* broadcasts of the state-run Singapore Broadcasting Corporation are also in four languages. They feature mainly light entertainment.

There are also *newspapers* in all four languages. The English ones are THE

SINGAPORE MONITOR and THE STRAITS TIMES. Check them for special rates in the big hotels or sales at electronics stores, it can save you lots of footwork.

Religion

Due to the ethnic variety of the city, there are many religions represented here. In addition to the Chinese religions of Confucianism, Buddhism and Taoism, there is Islam, Hinduism and Christianity. The constitution guarantees freedom of religion.

Holidays and Festivals

So many cultures in such a small place leads to a great assortment of holidays and festivals. Many of the dates are based on the lunar calendar, so they change from year to year according to the Western calendar.

Hindu Holidays

The most important Hindu festival is *Thaipusam*, which takes place in January or February, or in the tenth month, Thai of the Hindu calendar under the constellation of Pusam. The festival honors the god Subramanian, son of the god Shiva. The major celebrations are at the Chettiar Temple on Tank Road, the Sri Mariamman Temple on South Bridge Road, and at the Vinayakar Temple on Keong Saik Road. Thousands of believers flock to the temples to honor the god, to ask for favors and to make good on oaths. Some pilgrims wear wooden or metal harnesses on their heads. These harnesses are called Kavadi and are held in place by metal hooks puncturing the skin. The harness represents a peacock, the mount of Shiva. In a trance, some pilgrims insert spears or stakes through their lips or cheeks or walk over hot coals. Miraculously, they are unhurt. This self-inflicted suffering is forbidden in India.

The Hindu harvest festival, *Thaiponggal* takes place around the same time. Rice cakes are baked to honor the spirits of the rice harvest. People decorate their houses with sugar cane and various leaves. The rice cakes are symbolically offered to the sun god and then distributed among family and friends. Perumal Temple on Serangoon Road is the center of this four-day celebration.

The Hindu festival of lights, **Deepavali**, takes place in October or November. House doors and windows are opened and decorated with lights to welcome in Lakshmi, the goddess of prosperity. Temples are similarly decorated and sacrifices are offered. The main ceremony takes place in Perumal Temple.

The **Thimithi Festival** takes place in October. It honors the goddess Duropadai. According to legend, the goddess was taken by Prince Arjuna after he defeated her father. Arjuna's mother ordered him to share Duropadai with his four brothers. Every year, she appears in the house of a different brother. At the end of the year, she must prove her innocence by walking barefoot over hot coals.

A few days before the ceremony, a pit is filled with wood at the Sri Mariamman Temple. The wood is burned to charcoal so that the pit is filled with hot coals on the day of the ceremony. The worshipers then walk over the hot coals barefoot, just like the goddess.

Islamic Holidays

The birthday of the prophet Mohammed is celebrated in the first month of the Islamic calendar. This holiday, **Mauloddan Nabi**, is marked by readings from the Koran and processions.

The end of the fast month of Ramadan is celebrated in the tenth month of the Islamic calendar. This festival, **Hari Raya Pusa**, is the most important Islamic holiday for Malay Moslems because they can now partake of everything they have given up. Prayers of thanks, friendly invitations to one's home and processions are all part of the two day holiday, celebrated all over the Islamic world.

Hari Raya Haji takes place in the twelfth month of the Islamic calendar. It is the time of the pilgrimage to Mecca.

Buddhist Holidays

The **Songkran Festival** takes place in March or April. It marks the Buddhist new year. During this two-day festival, Buddha images are removed from their temples and bathed with cool water, along with friends and family. If you do not mind getting wet, you can participate in the ceremonies in the Ananada Metyrama Thai Temple on Silat Road and in the Sapthapuchaniyaram Temple on Holland Road.

The Buddha's birthday, **Vesak Day** is a big celebration in May. There are celebrations at all the city's Buddhist temples.

Chinese Holidays

Chinese New Year is in either January or February. The 15 day festival begins with a big family dinner. Gifts and food are all part of the celebrations, as are lion and dragon dances and visits to temples. Small red paper packets containing money, *ang pows*, are distributed to children. After 15 days, the festival ends with the Chap Goh Meh, one last parade.

For fireworks Singaporeans go to Johor Baru, because it is prohibited in Singapore.

The **Qing Ming Festival** takes place in April or May. On this occasion, people visit the graves of their ancestors and make offerings to their spirits. It is by no means a sad holiday. Rather, it is a time for families to get together to go to the cemetery, make their offerings, have a picnic and enjoy the day. When families return from the cemetery, they hang branches from their doors to ward off any evil spirits that might have followed them home from the cemetery.

According to Chinese belief, the spirits of the dead return to the earth for one month a year during the **Festival of the Hungry Spirits** (August / September). During this time, offerings are made in the form of fruits and sweets, and often, complete meals. You might see small altars with food on them in the streets. They are for the spirits that do not have any living ancestors. There are also ceremonies carried out to communicate with the spirits.

The **Moon Cake Festival** is celebrated sometime in September or October. It is a day of good luck commemorating an important victory over the Mongols. Small round cakes are baked to honor the Man in the Moon. These cakes were used to hide messages in during the Mongol occupation. Houses are decorated, children join in lantern processions and family differences are forgotten. Many marriages take place at this time.

The **Birthday of the Monkey God**, T'se T'ien Tai Seng Yeh, is celebrated in February or March and September or October. Processions honor him and men go into trances, and stick spears through their cheeks and tongues. The main place to see this is in Eng Hoon Street.

The **Birthday of the Guardian of the Poor** is celebrated in February or March at the White Cloud Temple on Ganges Avenue. There is a procession and some people go into trances and temporarily mutilate themselves.

The **Dragon Boat Festival** in May or June honors the memory of the Chinese minister Chu Yuan. Chu opposed the corruption among civil servants during the Zhou Dynasty. As a result, he was banned from the palace and drowned himself in the Mi Lo River. Fishermen tried to save him, but arrived too late. In old China, there was a day to honor him on which fish were fed with rice to appease his soul. This traditional feeding has since developed into the Dragon Boat Festival, which is marked in Singapore by an international regatta off the East Coast Parkway. As a reminder of the original meaning of the holiday, people eat sticky rice, *chang* or *zong zi*, with their families and friends.

The **Festival of the Seven Sisters** comes in August or September. On this day, all unmarried women ask the gods for a good husband. They make offerings to help give their requests favor.

The **Festival of the Nine Emperor Gods** in October or November honors the gods that grant wealth and longevity. For nine days, prayers and processions are offered in the temples.

To honor the god Tua Pek Kong, there are **boat trips to Kusu**, an island in the south of Singapore, from September to November. People come here to ask for prosperity and health. According to a legend, the island was created when a sea turtle saw a ship sinking and turned himself into the island to save the people on board.

National Holiday

Singaporean independence is celebrated on August 9. Parades and dances mark the day. The big celebrations are on the Padang, between the Esplanade and St. Andrew's Road. In the evening, there are fireworks over the harbor, visible from Queen Elizabeth Walk. All businesses and shops are closed.

Behavior

Although Singapore is very Westernized and Singaporeans are used to having foreigners around, it pays for the tourist to learn a little about proper conduct. This will help you from inadvertently offending anyone. Of course this is not as simple as it may seem, since some things that Westerners consider normal are considered impolite here.

●Above all, politeness towards the person you are speaking to is very important. Be careful to speak softly, even when you are making a point that you want to stress. Try not to let strong negative emotions, especially anger, creep into your speech. If a person shows anger, he loses face and appears foolish and weak.

●As among Westerners, compliments are greatly appreciated, but be careful not to compliment children. To do so will arouse the jealousy of the gods, many people believe. After their children are complimented, many parents will not rest easily again until the gods are appeased through elaborate ceremonies.

●Touching people upon greeting, such as shaking hands or hugging, is frowned upon. Singaporeans normally only touch close friends, and then only lightly.

●If a Westerner is having trouble being understood, he will naturally start using gestures to communicate with. This is fine, but bear in mind that it is considered quite rude to point your finger at someone. If this is unavoidable, it is preferable to use your thumb.

●It is also considered rude to motion to someone, for instance a taxi driver, with one finger, the way we do in the West when we mean, "Come here." The way to do this in Singapore is to wave with your whole hand, with your palm facing down. Just watch people on the street calling cabs.

●To put your hands on your hips while talking is a sign of anger. To hit your hand with your fist is an obscene gesture.

●In general, the same rules of behavior apply to both Malaysia and Singapore.

In Singapore

Arriving from Neighboring Countries

Singapore is the hub of Southeast Asia. You can get there by land, sea or air. *From Southeast Asia*, there are a number of possibilities.

●From Thailand, Malaysia and Indonesia, there are dozens of daily *flights* to Singapore.

●*Ships* arrive from Java and Sumatra in Indonesia and Kuala Lumpur, Kuching and Kota Kinabalu in Malaysia.

●*Overland travel* is possible from Thailand and Peninsular Malaysia. There are taxis and local buses from Johor Baru and express buses and long-distance taxis from every major town on the Peninsula. There are also buses from Bangkok and Hat Yai in Thailand. In addition, the train line runs all the way to Bangkok, though you will have to change trains at Butterworth (Penang) if coming from Thailand.

Here are some current prices:

Flights from Asia:
●from *Jakarta* – US$ 125
●from *Medan* – US$ 95
●from *Pekanbaru* – US$ 86
●from *Bangkok* – US$ 240, round-trip
●from *Kuala Lumpur* – M$ 98

Ships:
●from *Port Klang* – from M$ 99
●from *Kuching* – from M$ 200
●from *Kota Kinabalu* – from M$ 310

Buses:
- from **Bangkok** – US$ 45
- from **Johor Baru** – M$ 1
- from **Kuala Lumpur** – M$ 17
- from **Kuantan** – M$ 15

Entry Regulations

Upon arrival, holders of valid passports will be allowed entry for 14 days. This permission may be withheld if you do not have a ticket to leave or if you do not have enough money to support yourself during your stay. Normally, they do not check.

To stay any longer, you will have to extend your visa at the Immigration Department. The length of an extension is usually three months, but varies by nationality.

Visa Extensions are always made into a complicated bureaucratic affair. This hassle can be easily avoided by quickly popping over to Johor Baru, turning around, and picking up another 14-day visa upon reentering.

As in all of Southeast Asia, it helps to be well-groomed and presentable upon arrival at the border. It can help save you time and hassles. Write legibly on your immigration card.

If you will be entering Singapore several times, be sure to pick up a few immigration cards and fill them out in advance so that you can avoid the long lines next time you enter. They are free at all border crossings, except if you are coming from Johor Baru by bus, in which case they cost 20 cents.

Drugs: As in Malaysia, there are very harsh penalties for possession of drugs, including marijuana and hashish. Possession is punishable with long prison terms and all convicted dealers are executed. "Dealing" means not only selling, but even the possession of more than 15 g. Do not carry drugs, or carry anything for anyone you do not know!

Customs

There is no limit to the import or export of foreign or domestic **currency**.

Every visitor may bring in goods for personal use. This includes a camera with film, a radio, a typewriter, sports equipment and jewelry. Also duty-free are one liter of spirits, one liter of wine or beer and 200 cigarettes, 50 cigars or 250 g of tobacco.
- To bring in a car or other vehicle, you must obtain a *carnet de passages*.
- It is forbidden to bring in any weapons or ammunition, living or dead animals, meat products, plants, poisons and vaccines or blood serum without special permission.

The prohibition against **weapons** is important for people coming from other Southeast Asian countries who might have picked up weapons as souvenirs.
- **Blowpipes** and **kris** both count as weapons here. Upon arrival, declare these things immediately with customs. The agents will take the weapons, store them up to several months and give you a receipt to claim them when you leave. If you really do not want to part company with your dear souvenirs, or will be leaving Singapore through a different point of entry, you will have to get a **permit** to transport your weapons through the city. Do so by taking your receipt to the **Department for Arms and Explosives**. They will charge you S$ 10 for a seven-day permit. If you will be staying longer, you need only get a permit for the very end of your stay. Let customs store the weapons for you until then. With the permit in hand, you can go to your first point of

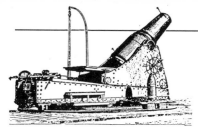

entry and reclaim your weapons. Always carry the permit on you or you could get into real trouble.

If, for example, you pick up a blowpipe in Malaysia, then go through Singapore to Indonesia and then back to Singapore to fly home, Singaporean customs will store your blowgun for you the whole time you are in Indonesia. Very nice of them isn't it?

Singapore — No Smoking!

Singapore is probably the cleanest city in the world. There are steep and strict fines for smoking in any no smoking area. The same applies for tossing cigarette butts in the street. There is no smoking in the following areas, to name but a few:

● Air-conditioned restaurants and bars with restaurant licenses.
● Air-conditioned rooms that are open to the public including lobbies, theaters, ballrooms and conference rooms.
● Air-conditioned supermarkets and other food markets.
● Sports and recreation areas like stadiums, bowling alleys, billiard halls and fitness, aerobic and health clubs.
● Public libraries, museums and art galleries.
● 27 large department stores.
● Elevators.
● MRT stations and trains.
● Doctors' offices.
● These conditions can be quite a shock to anyone who is accustomed to smoking wherever they like. But they are very serious about the fines, so do be careful.

Transportation

From the airport, there are taxis running round the clock. The 20 km trip costs between S\$ 13-15, and there is a 50% surcharge between midnight and 6:00. The SABS Airport Bus goes to the city for only S\$ 4. The cheapest way to get to the city is by bus. The No. 390 goes from the ground floor of the airport building to Orchard Road. To get to Bencoolen Street, get out at the corner of Bras Basah Road and Victoria Street. This trip costs 80 cents.

From the train station, there are a number of buses into town. The No. 1 goes to Orchard Road, the Nos. 97, 125, 146 and 163 go to Bencoolen Street for 50 cents.

The No. 125 goes from the International Plaza Terminal on Anson Road, at the end of Prince Edward Road about 400 meters from Finger Pier to the intersection of Middle Road and Bencoolen Street.

Money

Singapore is the easiest country in Southeast Asia in which to change money. Every bank exchanges foreign currency, though there are very high surcharges of up to 10% for travelers' checks. To avoid these, or to change money when the banks are closed, you can go to one of the many money changers in the shopping complexes or along Orchard Road, Serangoon Road, or near the GPO. Though their rates are not as good as the banks', you might do better there with travelers' checks.

Credit cards are widely accepted in Singapore, both by businesses and by banks for cash advances. It is also very easy to arrange to have money sent to you from home.
Inquire at banks.

The ***costs*** of accommodation and food are somewhat higher in Singapore than in the rest of the region. A bed in a dormitory, including breakfast, will cost S\$ 5 per person. The cheapest double rooms cost between S\$ 20 and S\$ 55. Even the YMCA costs S\$ 55. If you are after luxury, you will have no problem spending hundreds of dollars.

Cheap food is available from the hawkers all over the city, with dishes costing between S$ 2 and 3. Restaurants are more expensive; plan on upwards of S$ 10.

Health

If for some reason you should become ill, the medical care in Singapore is excellent, on par with that in the West, and in some cases, better. Everything must be paid for on the spot, so if you have insurance, be careful to get complete receipts for whatever you spend.

If you wear glasses, you might want to have an extra pair made here. The prices for both frames and lenses are quite a bit less than what they cost in the West.

Vaccinations

There are no special vaccinations required for Singapore, except for those coming directly from Africa or South America, in which case a yellow fever vaccination is required.

As with other Southeast Asian countries, it pays to check on the health situation in Singapore just before you go, either with your doctor, or preferably, with an institute of tropical medicine.

Singapore is a good place to check up on the situation in neighboring nations. The information there is likely to be more up-to-date than in the West. You can also get whatever shots or other medicines you need like malaria prophylactics.

Security

Though it is quite safe compared to other Southeast Asian cities, there are pickpockets and thieves in Singapore, so take the same precautions as you would anywhere else. Whenever possible, carry your valuables on you and put whatever you cannot in a hotel safe and get a receipt. Only carry as much cash as you need. You can always find a place to cash a travelers' check.

If you are trying on clothes or an imitation Rolex, keep an eye on your own clothes and watch. It won't do you any good to divide your money among various pockets if your trousers are stolen outright.

If anything should be stolen, contact the police immediately and fill out a report which is necessary for insurance, if you have it. If your passport is stolen, contact your embassy.

Note: If you are using Singapore as a base for visiting other Southeast Asian countries, consider leaving luggage like camping equipment and souvenirs that you won't be needing at the airport. There is a *left luggage desk* in the arrival hall. It's near the information and rental car booths. They will not, however, take any responsibility for anything fragile. If you do have fragile luggage, you are better off taking it to the departure hall. The main left luggage desk is in the corner on the right as you enter. If you ask, they might let you put your bags on the shelf yourself, or at the very least, ask them to put them at the very top. That way, they will probably not be moved again until you pick them up. You might want to get some "fragile" stickers from one of the airlines. Storage costs S$ 3 a day per bag.

Hours: In the east wing 7:00-22:30; in the west wing 24 hours. Tel: East, 5418861; West 5418860.

Accommodation

Like any world-class city, Singapore has all levels of accommodation, though it is a bit top-heavy. If you want, you will have no trouble spending thousands of dollars a night on a fantastic suite.

It might be a bit more difficult to find a cheap place to stay, and even then these are more expensive than in the rest of Southeast Asia. Rooms under S$ 20 are rare indeed. The cheapest places are guest houses with dormitories. They usually cost around S$ 5, sometimes with breakfast included. There should be a place to leave your bags safely during the day.

A few years ago, there were quite a few cheap hotels in the area around Bencoolen St. Unfortunately, since then, whole rows of housing have been torn down, and the hotels along with them. The same thing has been happening in other areas, like Mackenzie Road. The best thing to do is to ask other budget travelers about the current situation before you arrive.

If you are not looking for a dirt-cheap place to stay, you might want to book, from abroad, a short-term special package in a luxury hotel, such as 2 nights with meals for S$ 205. The papers in Kuala Lumpur have a lot of these, but make sure you read all the fine print. If you are flying with a major airline, check to see if they have a stop-over program. This will often include a huge discount on a first-class hotel, some meals, airport transfers, a city tour, and some discounts on shopping.

Cheap Places include the following:

● *Travellers' Centre*, 27 Bencoolen St., 7th floor, in Bencoolen House, very central, cheap rooms, a bit seedy; up to S$ 25, dormitory S$ 8. Tel. 3381206, 3391576.
● *GOH's Homestay*, 173E Bencoolen St., 6th floor, central, not very clean; up to S$ 25, dormitory S$ 10. Tel. 3396561.
● *Kian Hua*, 81 Bencoolen St, clean, but loud; up to S$ 25. Tel. 3383492.
● *Bencoolen Hotel*, 12 Bencoolen St., not worth the high prices; up to S$ 125. Tel. 3370034.

There are dozens of other places around Bencoolen St. and Bras Basah Rd., all similar to the ones described above.
● *Sim's Resthouse*, 114A Mackenzie Rd. Next to a small restaurant. Some rooms have no windows and are quite dirty, outside rooms are expensive but have

windows and some have A / C. They will hold your valuables. Good information about the city and region. Often full. Up to S$ 40, dormitory S$ 7.
● *Backpack Accommodation*, 15A Mackenzie Rd., make breakfast yourself, very nice people; up to S$ 35, dormitory S$ 7 (ac). Tel. 3361458, 2989867, 3374338.
● *Shang Onn*, Beach Rd. / Purvis Rd., nice people; up to S$ 25. Tel. 3384153.

Mid-range places include:
● *Majestic*, 31 / 37 Bukit Pasoh Rd., up to S$ 65. Tel. 2223377.
● *Station Hotel*, Keppel Rd., up to S$ 80. Tel. 2221551.
● *YMCA*, 70 Palmer Rd., with swimming pool, from S$ 55. Tel. 2224666.
● *Metropolitan YMCA*, 60 Stevensons Rd., from S$ 55. Tel. 737755.

There are also quite a few **luxury hotels** in the city, many of them along Orchard Rd. Plan on at least S$ 250:
● *Raffles Hotel* (to reopen in 1991), 1 / 3 Beach Rd., Tel. 3378041.
● *Dynasty*, 320 Orchard Rd., Tel. 7349900.
● *Holiday Inn*, 11 Cavenagh Rd., Tel. 7338333.
● *Oberoi Imperial*, Jalan Rumbia, Tel. 7371666.
● *Hyatt Regency*, 10 / 12 Scotts Rd., Tel. 7331188.

Food

The selection of food in Singapore is legendary. The supermarkets sell absolutely everything and there are restaurants serving every type of cuisine imaginable. The decision on what to eat depends only on your desires...and your wallet.

A good place for an evening drink (what else but a Singapore Sling for S$ 9) is the Raffles Hotel, a relic from the colonial era at the corner of Bras Basah Road and Beach Road. White-clad doormen with pith helmets are still there to welcome the guests as they

Bencoolen Street

1 Sim's Resthouse
2 Backpack Accomo-
  dation (Stanley's)
3 Endstation 'Bus 171'
4 U–Bahnstation
  'Viktoria'
5 Hotel Bencoolen
6 Hotel Strand
7 Plaza Singapura
8 U–Bahnstation
  'Dhoby Ghaut'
9 National Museum
10 Raffles Hotel
11 Raffles City
12 U–Bahnstation
  'City Hall'

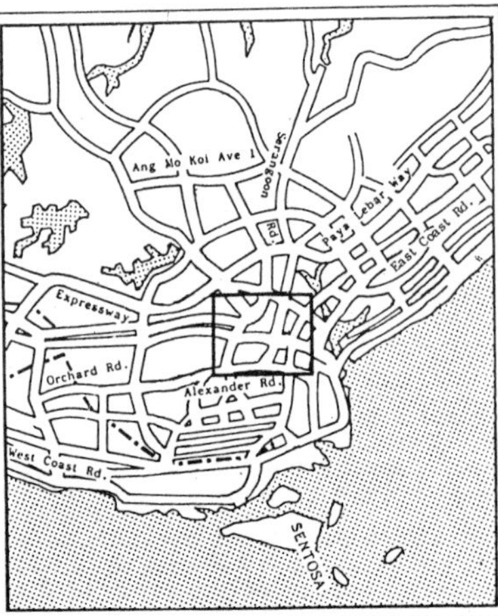

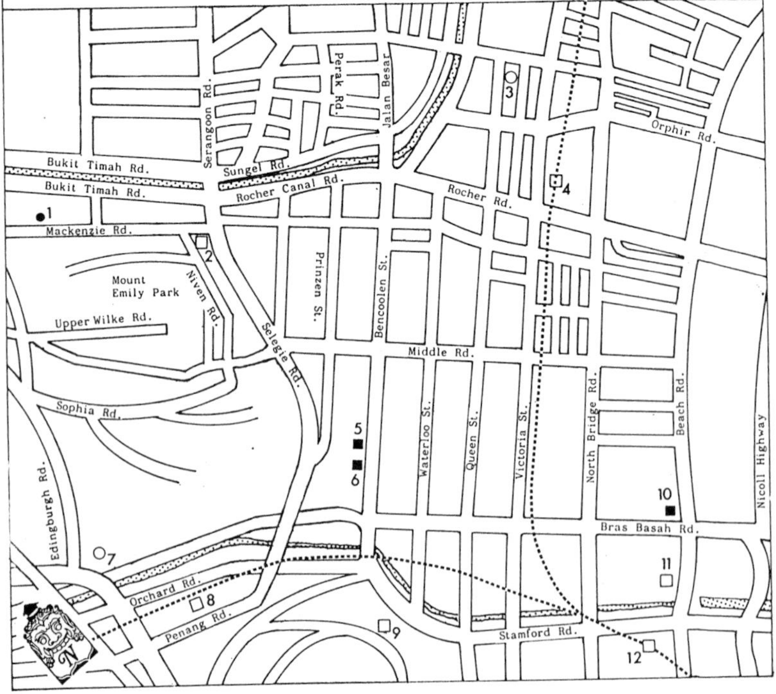

The Raffles Hotel

were when it first opened in 1887. It was known as the meeting place for Europeans in colonial Singapore and at one time was home to, among others, Somerset Maugham, Joseph Conrad and Rudyard Kipling.

The cheapest, and often the best food can be had from any of the thousands of **hawkers** in the city. Often, you will find a number of them grouped together in a kind of co-operative. This springs from Singapore's stringent health regulations, as the larger areas are easier to keep clean than individual stalls.

So there is little to worry about – the food is safe, as is the tap water, which is chlorinated. Many hawkers offer fruit and wonderful fresh fruit drinks. There are good hawkers in Merlion Park and in the Food Center opposite the Albert Complex, between Waterloo and Queen Street.

There is good Chinese food on Cuppage Rd., between Centrepoint and Orchard Point. Dishes cost around S$ 10. For the truly adventurous, there is crocodile on a hot plate for S$ 20-30.

The incredible variety also extends within each different cuisine. Here there is not just Chinese food, but each different Chinese province's own specialties.

Most Chinese Singaporeans are from **Hokkien**. The specialty is *Hokkien Mee*, a noodle dish cooked with shrimp and vegetables. Restaurants: *Beng Thin Hoon Kee*, OCBC Centre, Chulia Street; *Beng Hiang*, 20 Murray Street; *Prince Room*, Selegie Complex, Selegie Road.

Teochew is known for its beef soups with vegetables, eggs, fish or lobster. Braised goose is also well-known. Restaurants: *Ban Seng Restaurant*, 79 New Bridge Road; *Chui Wah Lin*, 46 Mosque Street; *Golden Phoenix*, YIC Building, Shenton Way; *Hung Kang*, 38 North Canal Road; *Swatow Restaurant*, Centrepoint, Orchard Road.

Everyone knows about **Peking** duck, but there are also stuffed breads and dumplings and noodles. Restaurants: *Eastern Palace*, Supreme House, Penang Road; *Pine Court Restaurant*, Mandarin Hotel; *Jade Room Restaurant*, 36 Newton Road.

Szechuan food is usually very hot, with lots of peppers and garlic. Try the duck. Restaurants: *Dragon City Restaurant*, Novotel Orchard Inn; *Golden Phoenix Restaurant*, Equatorial Hotel; *Meisan Restaurant*, Royal Holiday Inn Hotel; *Min Jiang Restaurant*, Goodwood Park Hotel; *Omei Restaurant*, Hotel Grand Central.

Shanghai food is a cross between Pekingese and Cantonese. There is a lot of fish with soy sauce. *Temasek Restaurant*, Temasek Club, Portsdown Road is good.

Cantonese food is mild, and is the most common kind of Chinese food in the United States and Europe. Try *dim sum* for lunch. Restaurants: *Hillman Restaurant*, 159 Cantonment Road; *Kelong Thomson Restaurant*, Thomson Plaza, Upper Thomson Road; *Majestic*, 31 Bukit Pasoh Road; *Mayflower Restaurant*, DBS Building, Shenton Way and Changi Airport; *Li Bai Restaurant*, Sheraton Towers Singapore, 39 Scotts Road; *Shang Palace*, Shangri-La Hotel; *Tsui Hang Village Restaurant* Hotel Asia; *Tung Lok Sharks Fin Restaurant*, Liang Court, River Valley Road; *Union Farm Eating House*, 435 Clement Road.

Since the **Hakka** people were originally nomadic, their food is flexible and not elaborate, featuring lots of fishballs and tofu. Restaurants: *Moi Kong Restaurant*, 22 Murray Street; *New Moi Kong Restaurant*, International Plaza, Anson Road; *Plum Village*, 16 Jalan Leban.

Hainan dishes include chicken rice, roast pork and beef soup. Restaurants: *Swee Kee*, 51 / 53 Middle Road; *Yet Con Restaurant*, 25 Purvis Street.

Hunan dishes like pigeon soup, steamed fish and mussels are available at the *Apollo* in the Apollo Hotel, Havelock Road.

In addition to Chinese food, there is **Indian food** all over Singapore. Curries are a main part of Indian food. Cooked mostly out of vegetables, they might also have lamb, chicken, fish or prawns added. They are often very hot. Southern Indian food is traditionally eaten with the right hand off of a banana leaf.

Breads are also an important part of Indian cuisine, and they may be eaten alone or with curries.

Roti is a particular kind of flat bread, making it is an art in itself. The cook forms the dough into a sausage shape and then rolls it out flat, like a tortilla. Then it is thrown onto a hot grill and cooked very fast. The whole process takes place in a flash. *Roti canai* are served with curry sauce. *Roti telur* are made with egg. *Chapati* is another kind of flat bread. *Murtabak* is a stuffed bread cooked in a pan, with eggs, vegetables and perhaps meat.

Not surprisingly, there are Indian restaurants all over Little India. Try the *Zam Zam Restaurant*, 699 North Bridge Road; the *Banana Leaf Apollo*, 56 Race Course Road; the *Islamic Restaurant*, 791 North Bridge Road; the *Omar Khayyam*, Hill Street; the *Bilal Restaurant*, International Plaza, Anson Road.

Malay and **Indonesian food** is also very popular. The main element is rice (*nasi*) or noodles (*mee*). See the section on Malaysia. Restaurants: *Aziza's Restaurant*, 36 Emerald Hill Road; *Rendezvous*, 4 Bras Basah Road; *Satay Club*, Queen Elizabeth Walk; *Sanuir*, Centrepoint; *Tambuah Mas* Tanglin Shopping Centre.

Nonya Food is a cross between Chinese and Malay food. The ingredients are typically Chinese, like pork, but they are cooked in a Malay style, with a lot of coconut milk, fresh spices, etc. Try *satay babi* for an appetizer. Restaurants: *Bibi's*, Orchard Road and *Keday Kopi*, Peranakan Place.

Thai food is very spicy with a lot of fresh vegetables and seafood. Try grilled fish, chicken cooked in banana leaves and the soups. Good places include the *Parkway Thai Restaurant*, Centrepoint, the *Haad Yai Restaurant* at 467 Joo Chiat Road, and *Her Sea Palace* in the Forum Galleria on Orchard Road.

Korean food is also spicy and features a lot of grilled meats like chicken, pork and beef. Seafood dishes include prawns and oysters. There are a few Korean places on Orchard Road. Try the *Go Ryeo Jeong* in Orchard Plaza or the *Han Do* in the Orchard Shopping Centre.

Vietnamese food is an art in itself, something (though not quite) like a mixture of Thai and Cantonese. Try the *Saigon Restaurant* in Cairnhill Place or *Pare'gu* in Orchard Plaza.

Japanese food is growing in popularity. Many restaurants have prepared or plastic dishes on display. Try the *Kobe* in Tanglin Shopping Centre, the *Nadaman* in the Shangri-La Hotel, the *Kampachi* in the Hotel Equatorial, the *Shima* in the Goodwood Park Hotel or the *Suntory* in the Delfi Orchard on Orchard Road.

In addition to all the Asian food, there is *Western food* available including the now ubiquitous *fast-food chains*: *The Baron's Table*, Royal Holiday Inn; *La Taverna Marco Polo*, Hotel Grand Central; *Movenpick*, Scotts Shopping Centre; *Shashlik Restaurant*, Far East Shopping Centre; *Jack's Place Steakhouse*, Yen San Building, Orchard Road; *Maxim's de Paris*, Pavilion Intercontinental; *Elizabethan Grill*, Raffles Hotel.

What to See

Despite what you might have heard, there is a lot to see in Singapore. There are the old parts of town, like Chinatown and Little India, famous buildings and museums and a whole range of outdoor places, including a zoo and a bird park.

Chinatown

Today, Chinatown occupies only a small area between New Bridge Road and South Bridge Road. The original area was much larger, defined by the Singapore River, New Bridge Road, Clemenceau Avenue and Tanjong Pagar Road. Now that area is filled with big office towers, which house major international banks.

The *morning market* is at the corner of Smith and Trengganu Street, in the Kreta Ayer Complex. Everything you can imagine in an Asian market, from fish to fruit, to live animals is on sale here every morning.

In the evening, take a stroll through the *Pasar Malam* or night market, around Smith, Temple and Trengganu Streets. There is interesting handiwork on sale here.

Also in Chinatown is the most important Hindu temple in Singapore, the *Sri Mariamman Temple*, at the corner of Pagoda Street and South Bridge Road. It was built between 1830 and 1843 to honor the goddess Sri Mariamman, who protects Hindus against illness. Look out for the five-story tower above the entrance which is decorated with likenesses of various deities. Among other things, the Thimithi Festival is held here. Remember to take off your shoes when you visit a temple.

There are also two mosques in Chinatown, the Jamae Mosque on South Bridge Road and Mosque Street and Al Abrar Mosque on Telok Ayer Street. The *Jamae Mosque* was built in 1926 by south Indian Muslims or Chulias. It is especially holy for those seeking good health.

Al Abrar Mosque was built in the 1850's. It is a typically Indian mosque in that it has no dome and is quite plain in decoration.

The *Thian Hock Keng Temple* is the oldest Chinese temple in Singapore. It is mainly used by Taoists from Hokkien Province in China. The temple was built before 1840 as an expansion of a Joss House, built to thank the gods for a successful voyage from China to Singapore. The old shrine is now located on the main altar, protected by two guardian statues, Chien Li Yen, who can see for 1000 miles, and Soon Fong

Chinatown

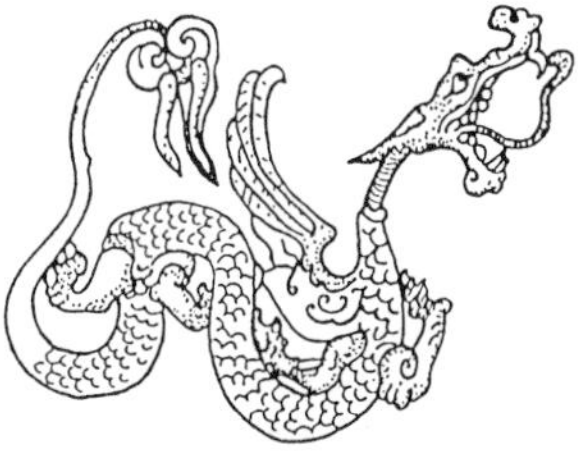

1 Melaka Mosque
2 People' Park Complex
3 Jamae Mosque
4 Sri Mariamman Temple
5 Morning Market
6 Kreta Ayer Theater
7 Al Abrar Mosque
8 Wak Hai Temple
9 Shell Building
10 to Merlion Park
11 Thian Hock Temple
12 Police
13 General Post Office

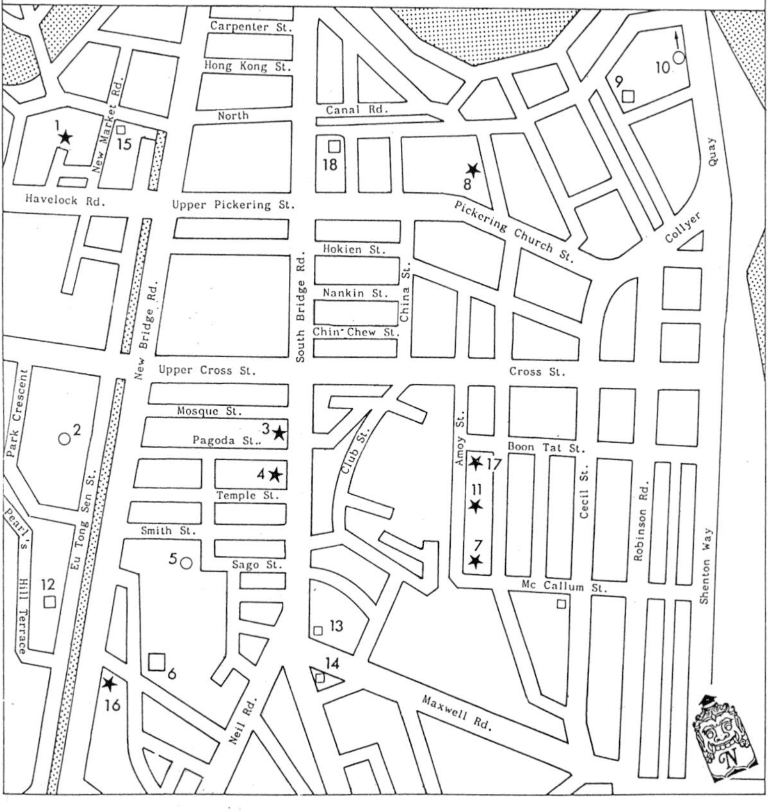

Er, who can hear for 1000 miles. The outside of the temple is quite attractive, and typical of Chinese classical architecture, with exquisitely decorated columns and roofs.

In addition to its cultural wealth, Chinatown offers the opportunity to enrich yourself materially as well. The **People's Park Complex** is a giant shopping center on Eu Tong Sen Street. It seems as if every electronic gadget ever made is on sale here. Make sure you do some comparison shopping.

The Harbor and the Government Quarter

The symbol of the city, the **Merlion** is right at the mouth of the Singapore River, which is almost 3 km long. This fantastic creature, half lion and half fish, commemorates Prince Utama. The park where it is situated is a nice quite place to escape the hustle and bustle of the city for a few hours. There are two good food centers here as well.

If you are interested in a **tour of the harbor**, go to Clifford Pier, on Fullerton Road. There are a number of groups that run day tours as well as evening tours on refitted junks, which include dinner on the deck. These trips cost around S$ 30.

The **Telok Ayer Market** is located on Raffles Quay, on the site of the first market established by Stamford Raffles. The present market was built in 1894 in the Victorian style. It has an interesting 8-sided form. Today, it is no longer a market, but a food center. Right nearby is Change Alley, named for its plethora of money changers. Boat Quay, known for its variety of food stalls, intersects Change Alley.

Right across the river is one of the several monuments to Raffles around the city, the **Sir Stamford Raffles Landing Site**, the spot on what is now North Boat Quay where Raffles first set foot on Singapore in 1819. Many old Victorian buildings are located in this area: **Victoria Memorial Hall, Victoria Theater and Concert Hall, Parliament House** and **City Hall**.

The **Padang**, or sports field, is located between the Singapore Recreation Club and the Singapore Cricket Club, the most exclusive club in town. It is used for various competitions as well as parades, rallies, etc.

St. Andrew's Cathedral, the Anglican cathedral, is no longer the glorious monument it once was. It is interesting to contemplate the huge skyscrapers which now form its background, but which were inconceivable when it was built in 1856. The combination makes an interesting visual parable to the modern history of Singapore.

Raffles City is a new business and shopping center between the church and Raffles Hotel. In addition to many stores, the 72-story tower contains the Westin Stamford Hotel, the Singapore Tourist Promotion Board and an office of Singapore Airlines.

Raffles Hotel, the unofficial symbol of colonial Singapore, is located on Beach Road. The Singapore Sling was invented at the bar here in 1915, by the bartender Ngiam Tong Boon. The bar is a popular spot for tourists. If you are looking for a bit of peace and quiet, try the Writers' Bar. There is a strict dress code, so look neat and don't wear rubber sandals or flip-flops.

The 125 year-old ***Empress Place Building*** on the Singapore River has just recently undergone a huge renovation. It is now used as an exposition center. Check to see what is going on as there is often something interesting.

Indian Quarter

Little India is the area around Serangoon Road. This area is very different from the rest of Singapore. A walk around here, and you could be forgiven for believing you really are in India. There are hundreds of tiny shops, some of which only sell spices, and dozens of aromatic Indian restaurants and colorful temples. Few people in this area wear Western clothing, preferring instead traditional Indian garb.

Sri Srinivasa Perumal Temple, on Serangoon Road, is 100 years old, though it was completely renovated between 1961 and 1970. It now appears fairly new. The central temple honors Vishnu and there are many statues and paintings of him near the Perumal Shrine. The two smaller buildings are dedicated to Vishnu's wives, Lakshmi and Andal. The temple is the starting point for the Thaipusam procession.

The ***Sri Veerama Kaliamman Temple*** was built in 1881 by Bengali workers to honor their maternal deity Kali. Since then, it has been torn down and rebuilt. The relief sculptures of the gods are worth looking at.

The ***Sri Vadapthira Kaliamman Temple*** is also dedicated to Kali. There are quite a few giant statues here that show the different sides of Kali: maternal, war-like, bloodthirsty and all-powerful as evidenced by her many arms.

The ***Temple of 1000 Lights*** (Sakya Muni Buddha Gaya Temple) is on Racecourse Road, which runs parallel to Serangoon Road. It was founded in 1927 by a Thai Buddhist monk. There is a 15 m high statue of a seated Buddha. Every evening the temple is lit up with 1000 lamps. Inside the base of the Buddha, in the back, is a room containing a reclining Buddha. The life of Buddha is illustrated with English explanations. At the entrance to the temple is a very good reproduction of the footprint of the Buddha, based on the one found on Adam's Peak in Sri Lanka.

Islamic Quarter

The Islamic Quarter is located in the area around Beach Road, North Bridge Road and Arab Street. Muslims from Malaysia, Java and India live here. There is a big market and several smaller ones in the area. Also there are some small shops that sell interesting imported handicrafts like batik, hand-made wicker baskets and weaving.

The **Sultan Mosque** built in 1924, is the most important mosque in the city. It is on North Bridge Road. It was built to replace the first mosque in Singapore, which was financed by Stamford Raffles. The architecture is Moorish, particularly the decorations around the windows and doors. You can visit the mosque, but not during prayers. Do dress respectfully, with no short pants or skirts, or shirts that do not cover the shoulders. Take off your shoes.

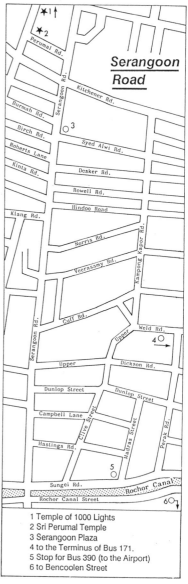

1 Temple of 1000 Lights
2 Sri Perumal Temple
3 Serangoon Plaza
4 to the Terminus of Bus 171.
5 Stop for Bus 390 (to the Airport)
6 to Bencoolen Street

Nearby on Java Road is the smaller *Hajah Fatimah Mosque*. It was built by Hajah Fatimah from Malacca in 1845. The interesting part of this mosque is the minaret.

Other Things to See

The *National Museum* on Stamford Road has good exhibits on the history, ethnology and archaeology of Singapore and some information about the rest of Southeast Asia. The neoclassical building was built in 1887. There is a collection of art by Southeast Asian artists, the University Art Collection, a historical section, a collection of coins and a section on the ethnology of Southeast Asia. Also a Young People's Gallery, a Singaporean Art Gallery, and a collection of jade, financed by the Aw Brothers, the tycoons of Tiger Balm. There are 385 pieces of jade, all very beautiful and some quite old.

The museum is open from 9:00 to 17:30 during weekdays, and until 19:00 on weekends. Admission is free. On weekdays, there are free tours in English at 11:00. There are daily audio-video shows at 10:15, 11:15, 14:15 and 15:15.

The *Van Kleef Aquarium*, on River Valley Road, has a big collection of fresh-water and salt-water tropical fish. If you missed them in the wild, you can see sea turtles and sharks here. It is open daily from 9:30 to 21:00. Entry costs S$ 1. From the aquarium, you can walk through *Central Park* to Canning

Hill.   Here you will find the remains of *Fort Canning*. There is also a good view of the city over Fort Canning Reservoir.

The *Singapore Zoo* is located in the north of the island. There are 1600 animals of 170 species. It is very good, as far as zoos go, and all kinds of indigenous animals are well-represented. If you are dying to see a crocodile in the jungle, first look at them here to see how big they really are – it might quench your thirst for adventure. The zoo conducts an orang-utan program to help preserve and propagate this endangered species. There is also a pair of Komodo dragons, known for their speed and frightening appetites. You can ride an elephant and have your photo taken with a giant snake around your neck. To get there, take bus No. 171 for 80 cents. Open daily from 8:30-18:00. Admission S$ 3.50, S$ 1.50 for children.

Mandai Orchid Garden is right near the zoo on bus No. 171. They have some of the largest orchids in the world, and a stunning variety. Open daily from 9:00-18:00.

If you do not want to go all the way to the zoo, you can see quite an impressive variety of orchids and other plants in the *Singapore Botanic Garden*, on Napier Road, an extension of Orchard Road.

Jurong Bird Park in the west is a 20 hectare park with a wide selection of Southeast Asian bird life. A big

attraction is the flight show, daily at 10:30, in which various birds of prey fly right over the heads of the audience. Another attraction is a small valley with a waterfall which has a net stretched over it. Visitors can go underneath and watch birds feeding from quite close up. The park is open daily from 9:00-18:00. Admission is S$ 3.50.

Right next to the Jurong Bird Park is the **Jurong Crocodile Paradise**, which houses thousands of the creatures in a very well-made environment. There is a glass tunnel from which you can observe the animals from underneath, as well as an area for deformed crocodiles. There are shows throughout the day. Open from 9:00 to 18:00. Entry is S$ 4.50, S$ 2.50 for children.

To get to both parks, you first have to go to the Jurong Interchange with bus No. 198 from Bencoolen Street and then take bus No. 250.

Tiger Balm Garden (*Haw Paw Villa*) on Pasir Panjang Road, is dedicated to the world of Chinese mythology. It is on 3 hectares near the ocean. The garden was built by the Aw Brothers,

who got rich from marketing Tiger Balm. Though Westerners might find the giant, colorfully painted statues to be kitschy, they are well-liked by Singaporeans, who come to the park on weekends and holidays. It is open daily from 8:00 to 18:00. Admission is free. To get there, take Bus CSS 2 for 40 cents from Orchard Road or Bus CBD 1 for 50 cents to Clifford Pier and then change to Bus 10, 30 or 97 for 80 cents.

In the Jurong district, there is a **Chinese Garden**, based on the one in the summer palace in Beijing. It is filled with pagodas and pavilions from the time of the Song Dynasty. There is a **Japanese Garden** next to the Chinese one. It is the largest one outside of Japan and very beautiful. Both are open from 9:00 to 18:00. To get there, take bus No. 198 from Bencoolen Street to the Jurong Interchange and then take bus No. 242 from there for 30 cents, or take the subway to the Chinese Garden station.

Sentosa Island was developed into a big leisure park in the 1970's. There is a lagoon where you can swim and rent paddle boats, a Coralarium, a Maritime Museum, a Wax Museum and the ruins of an old fort. The Surrender Chamber in the Wax Museum is interesting. It recreates the scene when the Japanese invaders surrendered to General Mountbatten at the end of World War II. In front of the Corala-

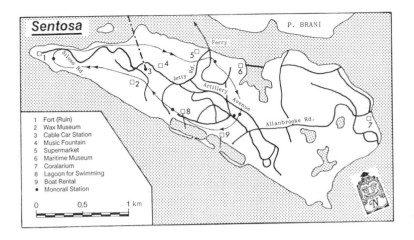

Sentosa

P. BRANI

Ferry

Siloso Rd.

Jetty Rd.

Artillery Avenue

Allanbrooke Rd.

1 Fort (Ruin)
2 Wax Museum
3 Cable Car Station
4 Music Fountain
5 Supermarket
6 Maritime Museum
7 Coralarium
8 Lagoon for Swimming
9 Boat Rental
• Monorail Station

0   0,5   1 km

rium, there is a large pool that holds a few sea turtles. From time to time, there are also sharks in the pool. All the attractions on the island are accessible by foot, bus or monorail. There are three kinds of tickets:

•1. *Regular ticket:* S$ 4.50, S$ 2.50 for children, good from 8:00-22:00. It includes the ferry to and from the island, and all attractions on the island except for the Coralarium and the Wax Museum.

•2. *Composite ticket:* S$ 7.00, S$ 3.50 for children, includes admission to the Coralarium and Wax Museum.

•3. *Afternoon ticket:* S$ 3.00, S$ 2.00 for children, which is the same as a regular ticket, but is only good from 17:00 on.

You can reach Sentosa from the **World Trade Center** by ferry. Also by the Swiss Cable Car from the WTC or from **Mount Faber**, the 115 m hill that offers a good view of the city. The ferries go daily between 7:30 and 22:45 (until 23:00 Friday through Sunday). The cable cars run from 10:00 to 19:00 (Sunday 9:00 to 19:00). From Bencoolen Street, take bus No's. 97, 125 or 146 to the World Trade Center for 80 cents.

•*Note:* There are several construction sites on the island. The works are in progress till 1994.

From the World Trade Center, there are also ferries going to **Kusu** and

St. John Islands. St. John is known for its beaches. Kusu has a Chinese temple and is the site of the annual Kusu boat pilgrimage.

Reptile lovers will want to visit the ***Crocodilarium*** on East Coast Parkway or the Crocodile Farm in Upper Serangoon Road. Hundreds of animals are raised here for their skins. Both are open daily from 9:00-17:30. Admission is S$ 2 or S$ 1 for children at the Crocodilarium and free at the Crocodile Farm. Before you decide to buy handbags, belts, or even worse, baby crocodile

feet, remember that the import of crocodile products is prohibited in many Western countries. And keep in mind that these animals are kept and raised only for their valuable skins.

To get to the Crocodile Farm, take bus No. 11 from Orchard Road for 80 cents, Selegie Road or Serangoon Road. To get to the Crocodilarium, take the airport bus No. 390 from Orchard Road, Dhoby Ghaut or Selegie Road for 80 cents.

There are some good jungle walks in the ***Bukit Timah Reserve***. The 60 hectare tropical rainforest reserve has marked paths, a walk through will give you a brief impression of what the rainforest is like. Sometimes, you can even see monkeys. From Orchard Boulevard or Scotts Road, take bus No. 171 or 173 for 80 cents to Bukit Timah Shopping Centre and then walk from there.

If you are ending your trip and have forgotten to pick up some souvenirs or if you are just starting out and want to see what's available, look though the stores at the ***Singapore Handicraft Centre*** on Tanglin Road. Merchants from different countries sell their wares here. On Wednesdays from 18:00 to 22:00 and on weekends from 16:00 to 22:00, there is a night bazaar here, organized by the Singapore Tourist Promotion Board. They also have demonstrations of techniques at these times. Naturally, everything is more expensive than in the country of origin.

Shopping

Singapore is known throughout the world as a shoppers' paradise. The tourism industry promotes this image with books and pamphlets featuring detailed information about what, where and when to buy. All city maps show shopping centers along with hotels and sights. Singapore is a great place to let money burn a hole in your pocket. It is a good thing it's so easy to get money wired here.

Singapore is a free port, which means that there is no import duty on most goods. Usually, that means that things are cheaper here than abroad, but even in Singapore, there is no such thing as a free lunch. The prices are all in relation to the US dollar, so depending on how your own national currency is doing against the US dollar, things will vary in price. (E.g. if the Canadian dollar is doing well against the US dollar, Canadians should be able to find some good bargains in Singapore.)

Also bear in mind that there are customs duties in most other countries. If you buy a lot in Singapore, you will have to pay duty when you bring your purchases home. In the United States, you are normally allowed to bring in US$ 400 worth of merchandise duty-free, after that, the rate is a flat 10% for the next $1000.

If you are looking for a specific item in Singapore, make sure you know how much it will cost you at home. If the difference is not great, I would advise that you buy it at home since it will be easier to get the product serviced, should anything go wrong. Make sure that anything you buy comes with a complete, fully-documented international guarantee. And get it when you make your purchase; do not give anyone any money for something that does not include the guarantee at the time of purchase.

The best buys in Singapore are cameras, including video-cameras, stereo equipment, TV's, electronic household items, textiles, sports equipment, leather, eye · glasses, watches, cosmetics and jewelry.

You will have to bargain in almost every store in Singapore. The only exceptions are supermarkets and shops of internationally known brands like Rolex, Esprit, and others.

The **main shopping district** is the area around Orchard Road. The shopping centers there are truly amazing, each containing scores of small stores that seem to carry almost everything. Most tourists shop here and some of the prices can be very high. In general, the farther you get from Orchard Road, the lower the prices. Try the corner of Scotts Road.

In 1988, there were good prices in the Far East Plaza on Scotts Road. There were good deals on **jewelry** at Swank Marketing, 03-62, Overhead Bridge and at Enshine Jewellery, 02-72, Ground Floor. **Cameras** were also a good buy there.

The Far East Shopping Centre on Orchard Road opposite the intersection of Scotts Road has a good selection of **clothes** like jeans and shirts in G 2000, 01-12, Ground Floor.

There is a huge selection of **books** in MPH-Bookstore in the Peninsula Plaza and the Centrepoint. If you are interested in buying or trading used books, go to Bras Basah Road, between Selegie Street and Bencoolen Street.

Cosmetics are very cheap in the small Indian shops on Serangoon Road.

There are all sorts of **imitation** brand-name watches and shirts for sale in the big shopping centers. Obviously, they are not as high quality as the originals, but you should only have to pay a fraction of the original price. Be careful not to buy too much, since most countries forbid the import of such fakes and they could be confiscated at customs when you return home.

If you are buying a **watch**, pick up a few and get an idea of their weight. Supposedly, the heaviest ones are the best.

Developing **film** is very cheap in Singapore as is purchasing new film. If you are shooting movies, it is better to have the film developed at home.

In case you missed anything, there is a whole slew of Duty-Free Shops at the **airport**, which might lead you to wonder how much cheaper duty-free can be in a free port. At any rate, the prices there are fixed and the best thing to do is to pick up

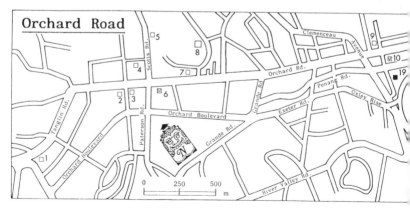

Orchard Road

a copy of the Shopping & Eating Guide at the airport when you arrive. It has a listing of the prices at the airport, so you will know what to pick up in town and what can wait until you leave. In general, the prices at the airport are more expensive.

Public Transportation

If you are staying in the downtown area, it is pretty easy to walk everywhere. The traffic is so bad during rush hours, from 7:00 to 9:00 and from 16:30 to 19:00, that it will certainly be faster to walk. If you have a lot of distance to cover though, you will want to take public transportation.

Private cars that drive in the downtown area, the so-called Central Business District or CBD, are surcharged S$ 5 a day. This is intended to limit the vehicular chaos in the CBD.

Taxis:

There are more than 10,000 taxis in Singapore, each of which can take up to four people. They stop in the city at taxi stands. The fares are fixed, and you pay according to the meter. The base price is S$ 1.90 for the first 1500 m. Then, up to 10 km,

it is 10 cents per 300 m. Over 10 km, it is 10 cents per 250 m. In addition, there is a 10 cent charge for every 45 seconds of waiting time, including traffic jams and lights. For three people, there is a 50 cent surcharge and for 4 people, it's a dollar. There is a dollar charge for each bag that must be put in the trunk. Between midnight and 6:00, there is a surcharge of 50%.

From the airport, there is an additional S$ 3 charge. There is a S$ 2 charge to enter the CBD from 7:30 to 10:15 and a S$ 1 charge to leave it between 16:00 to 19:00. You can call a taxi by dialing 4525555. There is a S$ 1 charge for this.

Sample prices for 2 persons:
- From the GPO to Lucky Plaza on Orchard Road, S$ 5.10 in the morning.
- From Mackenzie Road to Raffles Hotel, S$ 3.80 in the afternoon.
- From the airport to Bencoolen Street, S$ 12-15.

Buses:

The SBS or Singapore Bus Service goes just about everywhere in the city. You can get a bus map at newsstands for S$ 1. Fares are between 40 and 80 cents, depending on how many fare stages you go through. Get a ticket from the conductor when you get on.

1 Singapore Handicraft Centre
2 Far East Plaza
3 Orchard Subway Station
4 Lucky Plaza
5 Elizabeth Hospital
6 Singapore Plaza
7 Dhoby Ghaut Subway Station
8 YWCA
9 YMCA
10 National Museum
11 Van Kleef Aquarium
12 Raffles Hotel
13 Raffles City / Tourist Information
14 Merlion Park
15 Main Post Office
16 Parliament

In addition, there are **OMO Buses** (One Man Operator). These have no conductor. The fare is listed on the outside of the bus, or ask the driver if you are unsure. There is a box next to the driver where you deposit your exact change (!) when you get on and get a ticket. Bus 390, to the airport, is one of these.

Bus stops are marked with a red sign, but they only stop if you flag them down from the curb. In most of the big hotels, you can buy a Singapore Explorer Ticket which entitles you to ride all bus lines for one day for S$ 5, or three days for S$ 12.

Subway:

Altogether, the MRT or Mass Rapid Transit encompasses 42 stations over 67 km. It can save a lot of time inside the city. Outside the city, some lines of the train come above ground, to the Chinese Garden, for example. Tickets cost between 50 cents and S$ 1.80.

There are shopping arcades in the spotless subway stations. Buy your ticket from a machine (there is a price guide on it), and if you do not have enough change, there are change machines right nearby. You have to put the ticket in a slot to get through the turnstile, and then pick it up again once you get through.

The stations are all air-conditioned, and there is a glass wall with sliding doors that seals off the tracks. When the trains come, they always line up exactly with the doors, so that you are always in a safe, air-conditioned environment. When you get off, you will once again have to use your ticket to get through the turnstile, so do not throw it away!

● Subway stations are marked with MRT.

Important Addresses

American Express
● UOL Building 02-02, 96 Somerset Rd., and Lucky Plaza 01-06, 304 Orchard Rd., Tel. 2358133, open Monday-Friday, 8:30-17:00, Saturday 8:30-12:00.

Train Station
Singapore Railway Station, Keppel Rd.

Information
● Tourist Information Centre, Raffles City.Tower 01-19, Tel. 3300431 / 2.
● Tourist Information, Singapore Handicraft Centre, 163 Tanglin Rd., Tel. 2355433 / 4, open Monday-Friday 8:00-17:00 and Saturday 8:00-13:00.

Medical Help
● Alexandra Hospital, Alexandra Rd., Tel. 635222.
● General Hospital, Outram Rd., Tel. 2223322.
For more addresses, consult the Yellow Pages. Hospitals are listed under "hospitals" and "clinics." Doctors are under "medical practitioners" and dentists are under "dental surgeons."

Post Offices
● General Post Office, Fullerton Rd., Tel. 5323753.
● Orchard Point Post Office, Orchard Rd, Tel. 7374483.

Police / Emergency
●Beach Rd. Police Station, Beach Rd.
●Emergency, Police 999, Ambulance / Fire 995 – just dial, no need to put in money.

Passenger Ship Lines
●Yang Passenger Ferry Service, 407 Jalan Besar, Tel. 2972231.
●P.T. Bintan Baruna Sakti, Tel. 2200555 and 2227849.

Government Offices
●Immigration Department, Empress Place.
●Department of Arms & Explosives, 3 Kinloss House, Lady Hill Rd., Tel. 7344162.
●Director of Primary Production, 40 City Veterinary Center, Kampong Java Rd., Tel. 2511203.
●Customs House, Maxwell Rd.

Embassies

●*Australia*, 25 Napier Rd., Tel. 7379311.
●*Austria*, 1 Scotts Rd., 22-04 Shaw Center, Tel. 2354088, open Monday-Friday 8:00-16:00.
●*Bangladesh*, Thomson Rd., Goldhill Square, Tel. 2506323.
●*Brunei*, 7a Tanglin Hill, Tel. 4743393, open Monday-Friday, 8:30-12:30 and 13:30-16:30.
●*Burma*, 15 St. Martin Drive, Tel. 2358704, open Monday-Friday, 9:30-13:00 and 14:00-17:00.
●*Canada*, Faber House, Orchard Rd., Tel. 7371322.
●*Denmark*, Thomson Rd., Goldhill Square, Tel. 2503383.
●*Germany*, 545 Orchard Rd., 14-01 Far East Shopping Center, Tel. 7371355, open Monday, Thursday, Friday, 8:00-14:00 and Tuesday, Wednesday, 8:00-13:00 and 14:00-16:30.
●*India*, 31 Grange Rd., Tel. 7376809.
●*Indonesia*, 7 Chatsworth Rd., Tel. 7377422, open Monday-Friday, 8:30-12:30 and 14:00-16:30.
●*Japan*, 16 Nassim Rd., Tel. 2358855.
●*Malaysia*, 301 Jervois Rd., Tel. 2350111, open Monday-Friday, 8:30-15:15.
●*Netherlands*, 541 Orchard Rd., 13-01 Liat Towers, Tel. 7371155, open Monday-Friday, 9:00-12:00 and 13:30-15:00.
●*New Zealand*, 13 Nassim Rd., Tel. 2359966.
●*Philippines*, 20b Nassim Rd., Tel. 73733977, open Monday-Friday, 9:00-12:00 and 14:00-16:30.
●*Sweden*, PUB Building, Somerset Rd., Tel. 7342771.
●*Thailand*, 370 Orchard Rd., Tel. 7372644, open Monday-Friday, 9:00-12:30 and 14:00-17:00.
●*UK*, Tanglin Rd., Tel. 639333.
●*USA*, 30 Hill St., Tel. 3380251.

Airlines

●*Aeroflot*, 100 Orchard Rd., Meridien Shopping Centre 02-15, Tel. 2355282.
●*Air India*, UIC Building, 5 Shenton Way, Tel. 2205277.
●*Air New Zealand*, Ocean Building, Collyer Quay, Tel. 918266.
●*Air Lanka*, Crosby House, 75 Robinson Rd., Tel. 2236026.

- **Bangladesh Biman**, Fidvi Building, 97-99 Market St., Tel.912155.
- **British Airways**, International Building, Orchard Rd., 7371422.
- **Cathay Pacific**, Ocean Building, Collyer Quay, Tel. 911811.
- **China Airlines**, Lucky Plaza, 304 Orchard Rd., Tel. 7372144.
- **CSA**, 25 Scotts Rd., Royal Holiday Inn 04-05, Tel. 7379844.
- **Garuda**, 101 Thomson Rd., Goldhill Square 01-68, Tel. 2502888.
- **Japan Airlines**, Hong Leong Building, Raffles Quay, Tel. 2202211.
- **KLM**, 333 Orchard Rd., Mandarin Hotel Arcade 01-02, Tel. 7377622.
- **Lufthansa**, 19 Tanglin Rd., Tanglin Shopping Centre 03-01, Tel. 7379222.
- **MAS**, 190 Clemenceau Ave., Singapore Shopping Centre 02-09, Tel. 3366777.
- **PIA** (Pakistan), Hilton International, Orchard Rd., Tel. 7373233.
- **Pan Am**, Hong Leong Building, Robinson Rd., Tel. 2200488.
- **Philippine Airlines**, 35 Selegie Rd., Parkland Shopping Mall 01-10, Tel. 3361611.
- **Qantas**, 333 Orchard Rd., Mandarin Hotel 01-05, Tel. 7373744.
- **Royal Brunei Airlines**, 400 Orchard Rd., Orchard Towers 04-30 / 31, Tel. 2354672 / 3.
- **Singapore Airlines**, Orchard Rd., Mandarin Hotel, Tel. 2297291; North Bridge Rd., Raffles City Shopping Centre, Tel. 2297128.
- **Swissair**, 435 Orchard Rd., Wisma Atria 18-01, Tel. 7378133.
- **Thai International**, 1333 Cecil St., Keck Seng Towers 08-01, Tel. 2249977.

Further Travel

Changi Airport is a huge international hub located about 20 km out of the city. There are taxis all day and night going into the city for around S$ 12 for 2 people. The cheapest way to get into town is with Bus 390 for 80 cents from Rochor Road.

There is an **airport tax** charged on departure of S$ 5 for flights to Malaysia and Brunei and S$ 12 for all other flights.

There are all sorts of **cheap flights** to be had in the various travel agents. German Asian Travel has some good offers. It is at 9 Battery Road, 15-03 Straits Building, Tel. 5335466. If you are flying to Malaysia, it is worth a short trip to Johor Baru to check out the prices there. It is often much cheaper, since it is only a domestic flight from there, and things are generally cheaper in Malaysia anyway.

Sample prices:
- **Bangkok** – S$ 438.
- **Jakarta** – S$ 345.
- **Kuala Lumpur** – S$ 98.
- **Kuching** – S$ 179.
- **Kota Kinabalu** – S$ 346.

To Malaysia: The cheapest way to get there is to take SBS Bus 170 from Queen Street for 80 cents to Johor Baru. There is also a Johor / Singapore Express for S$ 1.50 which does not make any stops. The 170 bus can be very hectic. It first goes to the Singaporean part of the border. You have to get out here with all your bags since the bus does not wait, get an exit stamp and then line up for the next 170. In the meantime a conductor will check to make sure you still have your ticket, so do not lose it. The next bus takes you to the Malaysian part of the border, where you get out with your bags, fill out a form, go through customs and then wait for another 170 bus. This one will take you to Johor Baru.

There are also **taxis** to Johor Baru from next to the bus station. They cost between S$ 25 and 30.

There are **express buses** from the station at the corner of Lavender Street and Jalan Besar to Kuala Lumpur for around S$ 17, to Malacca for around S$ 9 and to Kuantan for around S$ 13.50.

There are several daily **trains** to Kuala Lumpur. The ticket office at the train station is open daily from 9:00-12:30 and from 14:00-19:00. Get to the station with Buses 1, 20, 30, 97, 125, 146, 176 and 186.

To Sabah and Sarawak: There has been a passenger ship connection since 1986. the Muhibah leaves Port Klang every other Saturday and gets into Singapore on Sunday at 8:00. At 14:00, it leaves Singapore for Kuching, Kota Kinabalu and then Kuantan. The next week, it leaves Kuantan on Saturday and goes to Kota Kinabalu, Kuching and onto Singapore, where it arrives around 16:00 on Thursday. It leaves Singapore Thursday at midnight for Port Klang. The price for Singapore-Port Klang is S$ 99, or S$ 210,

depending on class. Singapore to Kuching costs S$ 200 or S$ 355 one-way. Singapore to Kota Kinabalu costs S$ 310 or S$ 620.

To Thailand: From Singapore, there is a **train line** that goes all the way to Bangkok and beyond. It costs about S$ 90. There are also **express buses** to Haad Yai and Bangkok, which are cheap, but painful. The bus station is on New Bridge Road.

To Indonesia: Small boats travel daily between 8:15 and 16:15 from Singapore to Batam for S$ 40. From there, you can make a connection to Pekanbaru, Sumatra by boat, or fly to other points in Indonesia. Get tickets at Dino Shipping Pte. LTD, Tel. 2200555, 2227849 or at Yang Passenger Ferry Service, 407 Jalan Besar., Tel. 2972231.

The boats leave from Finger Pier. To get there from Bencoolen Street, take Bus 125, 146 or 163 for 50 cents. Get out at the Treasury Building, between Maxwell Road and Prince Edward Road. Turn left and walk the remaining 200 meters to the pier. Buses 10, 20, 30, 79, 94, 97, 100 and 107 all go directly to Finger Pier. Buses 1, 8, 50, 75, 189, 196 and 131, 172 and 175 from Bencoolen Street all go one station past Finger Pier. Get off there and walk 250 meters back and then turn right.

YANG PASSENGER FERRY SERVICE
FERRY AUTO BATAM
TEL. 2239902-2239908

DEPARTURE TIME
SINGAPORE — BATAM (SEKUPANG)
8.15a.m. 10.15a.m. 12.15p.m. 2.15p.m. 4.15p.m.

DEPARTURE TIME
SINGAPORE — BATAM — TG. PINANG
10.00a.m.

Appendix

Information

Singapore Embassies

Australia 81 Mugga Way. Red Hill, Canberra ACT 2603.
Hong Kong 19th Floor, Wang Kee Building, 36 Connaught Rd, Central
India 48 Golf Links, New Delhi 110003
Indonesia 23 Jalan Proklamasi, Jakarta; 3 Jalan Suryo, Medan
Japan 12-2 Roppongi, 5 chome, Minato-ku, Tokyo
Malaysia 5th Floor, Straits Trading Building; Lebuh Pasar Besar, Kuala Lumpur
New Zealand 17 Kabul St, Khandallah, Wellington
Philippines 6th Floor, ODC International Plaza, 217-219 Salcedo, St. Legaspi Village, Makati, Rizal
Sweden Banergathan 10, 5 Tr S-11522 Stockholm
Thailand 129 Sathorn, Tai Rd. Bangkok
United Kingdom 2 Wilton Crescent, London SW1
USA 1824 R St NW, Washington DC 20009

Singapore Tourist Promotion Boards

Australia 60 Margaret St., Sydney, NSW 2000; 55 St. George's Terrace, Perth, WA 6001
Canada 175 Bloor St, No 1112, Toronto, Ontario M4W 3R8
Japan Yamato Seimei Building, Tokyo 100
New Zealand Walshes World, 87 Queen St, Box 279, Auckland
United Kingdom 126-130 Regent St, London W1 R5FE
USA 333 North Michigan Ave, 818, Chicago, IL 60601; 590 Fifth Ave, 12th Floor, New York, NY 10036

Malaysia Embassies

Australia 7 Perth Ave, Yarralumia, Canberra ACT 2600
Canada 60 Boteler St, Ottawa, Ontario KLN 8Y7
Hong Kong 24th Floor, Lap Heng House, 47-50 Gloucester Rd, Wanchai
India 50M Satya Marg, Chanakyapuri, New Delhi 110021; 23 Khader Nawaz Khan Rd, Madras
Indonesia 17 Jalan Imam Bonjol, Jakarta; 11 Jalan Diponegoro, Medan
Japan 20/16 Nempedai Machi, Shibuya-ku, Tokyo
The Netherlands Adries Bickerweg 5, The Hague
New Zealand 10 Washington Ave, Brookly, Wellington
Singapore 301 Jervois Rd, Singapore 1024
Thailand 35 Sathorn Tai Rd, Bangkok; 4 Sukhum Rd, Songkhla
United Kingdom 45 Belgrave Square, London SW 1
USA 2401 Massachusetts Ave NW, Washington DC 20008

Malaysia Tourist Development Corporation (TDC)

Australia 65 York St, Sydney, NSW 2000
Hong Kong 47-50 Gloucester Rd, Wanchai
Singapore 10 Collyer Quay, Ocean Building, 0104
Thailand 315 Silom Rd, Bangkok 10500
United Kingdom 57 Trafalgar Square, London WC2N 5DU
USA 818 West 7th St, Los Angeles, California 90017

A Few Words and Phrases: Bahasa Malaysia

Some courtesies and a few questions

selamat datang welcome
selamat pagi / tengahari / petang /
malam
   good   morning / midday / afternoon
(evening) / night
selamat jalan / tinggal
   goodbye (said when leaving) / goodbye
(said to a person leaving)
apa khabar? how are you?
maaf(kan) sorry (pardon)
sila(kan) please
terima kasih thank you
ya yes
tidak no, not
baik / bagus good / that's fine
tidak baik no good
sila ulang satu lagi
   please can you repeat that once more
...ta'boleh faham
   ...I cannot understand
siapa nama saudara?
   what is your name?
nama saya... my name is...
berapa how much? how many?
berapa harga what is the price?
wang / duit money

Time

bila? when?
jam pukul berapa?
   what time is it?
pukul lima 5 o'clock
jam hour
minit minute
sa'at second
hari day
minggu week
bulan month
tahun year
pagi morning
tengahari midday / noon
petang afternoon

malam evening / night
hari ini today
tiap-tiap hari everyday
besok tomorrow
lusa the day after tomorrow
kelmarin, semalam yesterday

Days of the week

Hari Ahad Sunday
Hari Isnin Monday
Hari Selasa Tuesday
Hari Rabu Wednesday
Hari Khamis Thursday
Hari Jumaat Friday
Hari Sabtu Saturday

Getting Around

ada ka bas ke...?
   is there a bus to...?
bila cuti bas? what time does the bus
leave?
teket ke...berapa?
   how much is the ticket to...?
saya mau pergi ke...
   I want to go to...
bank bank
pejabat pos post office
immigrasi immigration
kedai shop
bas bus
kereta api train
kelas dua second class
stesen, stesyen railway station
teksi taxi
tempat teksi taxi stop
tempat duduk seat
kapal terbang aircraft
lapangan terbang airport
pelabuhan harbor
kapal(laut) ship
utara north
timor east

selatan south
barat west
hutan jungle, forest
ladang field (plantation)
padi rice field
sungei river
tasik lake
laut sea
pantai beach
polis police
kereta car
motosikal motorcycle
basikal bicycle
jalan street
simpang crossing, intersection

Getting a room

ada ka bilik kosong? do you have a room?
untuk dua orang for two people
untuk tiga malam for three nights
katil bed
mandi bath *sabun* soap
tandas toilet
lelaki / laki2 men
perempuan women
kunci key
tingkap window
tikus rats
nyamuk mosquito
lipas cockroach

Eating and drinking

makanan ini apa ada?
what kind of food is it?
saya mau makan...
I would like to eat...
ada ka...? have you...?
makan / minum apa?
what would you like to eat / drink?
saya mau bayar I would like to pay
sedap / enak delicious
(*sedap* is for everyday usage)
makanan food
minuman drink
susu milk
susu lembu
cow's milk (specify or you'll get condensed milk)

air minum drinking water
air batu ice
air...
(name of fruit) ...juice (also general word for liquid)
teh tea with milk and sugar
teh o tea without milk or sugar
kopi coffee with milk and sugar
kopi o coffee without milk and sugar
teh / kopi ais
iced tea / coffee with milk and sugar
masak cooked
goreng fried
rebus boiled
nasi goreng fried rice
nasi putih boiled rice
mee goreng fried noodles
mee kuah noodle soup
daging meat
lembu beef
kambing mutton (goat or sheep)
babi pork
ayam fowl (usually chicken)
itik duck
ikan fish
udang prawns / shrimps
ketam crab
telur egg
sayur-sayuran
vegetables (also vegetarian)
buah-buahan fruit
kelapa (muda) (young) coconut *limau*
kapas lime
limau manis orange
limau puting lemon
nanas pineapple
tembikai watermelon
mangga mango
pisang banana
tebu sugar-cane

Numbers

kosong	0
satu	1
dua	2
tiga	3
empat	4
lima	5
enam	6

tujuh	7
(di)lapan	8
sembilan	9
sepuluh	10
sebelas	11
dua belas	12
tiga belas	13
dua puluh	20
dua puluh satu	21
tiga puluh	30
empat puluh	40
empat puluh lima	45
seratus	100
dua ratus	200
seribu	1000
dua ribu	2000
juta	million
setengah	half
satu pertiga	third
suku	quarter

Outdoor Activities

Addresses of organizations and clubs.

For those with a bit more time to devote to outdoor activities, here are some organizations that might be worth contacting. I cannot guarantee that the contacts and phone numbers are still valid.

Mountaineering Association of Malaysia
(*Persatuan Mendaki Malaysia*).
No. 2, Jalan SS4A / 3 Kelana Jaya, 477301 Petaling Jaya, Selangor.
●Activities: Hiking (almost every Sunday on Bukit Takunin Templer Park, 20 km north of Kuala Lumpur), jungle trekking, spelunking, boat and river trips, snorkeling, community and environmental projects.

The Malaysian Society of Marine Science
(*Persatuan Sains Lautan Malaysia*).
●Activities: Monthly meetings, newsletter, seminars, protecting the marine environment, initiating protected marine areas, photo contests, etc.
Offices in Penang, Selangor and Kuala Terengganu.

Orienteering Association of Malaysia
(*Persatuan Orienteering Malaysia*).
Pusat Penyelidikan Perhutanan Kepong, 52109 Kepong, Selangor.
●Activities: Orienteering courses for beginners and advanced levels.

Malayan Nature Society (*Persatuan Pencinta Alam*).
MNS PO Box 10750,Kuala Lumpur.
3000 members with offices in Johor, Kelantan, Malacca, Negeri Sembilan, Pahang, Penang, Perak, Sabah, Selangor, Terengganu and Singapore.
●Activities: Meetings, slide lecture, mailings, expeditions, bird watching, spelunking, jungle trekking, photo trips, environmental action projects, furthering public interest in nature, nature camps for children, etc.

Wilderness Adventure Camp
Teluk Batik, 32200 Lumut, Perak, Tel. (05) 935559
●Activities: Courses (weekends, 6 days, 10 days,. etc.), jungle trekking, hiking, rock climbing, kayaking, bicycle touring, camping, etc. Courses cost from M$ 35 (adults), M$ 30 (students) and M$ 25 (children).

Malaysia Boardsailing Association
c / o Mr. Warrick Sdn Bhd, 17-B Jalan 14 / 20, PO Box 1119, 46100 Jalan Semangat, Petaling Jaya, Selangor.

Skydiving
Mr. Samsuri Suradi, Tel. (03) 2308833 (office), Mr. Mohmd. Amin Pilus, Tel. (03) 2611040 (office).
●Activities: Among others, two day introductory courses in skydiving.

Malaysian Inflatable Boat Association
Mr. Fadzil / Zainal, 22 SS 4D / 2, Peoples Park, 47301 Petaling Jaya, Selangor, Tel. (03) 7032886.
●Activities: Inflatable boat trips and information about boating.

Persatuan Penyelam Samudera Malaysia
(Diving Club)
  P.P.S.M., Secretariat, Majlis Rekreasi
Fizikal Nasional, no. 159 Jalan Tun Razak,
50400, Kuala Lumpur, Tel. (03) 2417373 /
272.
●Activities: Scuba diving and snorkeling.

Hash House Harriers
  John Duncan, Tel. (03) 4569660, or David
Maugham, Tel. (03) 2425693.
●Activities: The H.H.H. meet every Monday
at 6 pm (only the men as the Harriers and

Harriettes have different meeting times) at
the edge of the city and run a route around
the countryside, including jungle. The route
changes every week.
  Guests are welcome for M$ 7 a run (the
same applies in Ipoh, where I am a member.) Word has it that there are several
meetings a week in Kuala Lumpur now. The
office in Kuala Lumpur can give you
information about clubs all over Malaysia,
including groups in Penang, Taiping, Ipoh,
etc.

Literature

Culture and Everyday Life - Malays, Chinese and Indians

●Munan, Heidi: *Culture Shock! Borneo*. Times Books Intl., Singapore, 1988. About the customs of the people of Borneo.
●Winstedt, Richard: *The Malay Archipelago — A Cultural History*. Singapore, 1981. 1st published in 1947. The classic cultural history of Malaysia with a contemporary afterword.
●Haji Mohtar: *Federal Cultural Series*. Kuala Lumpur, 1979. Five easy to read, illustrated stories.
●Knappert, Jan: *Malay Myths and Legends*. Kuala Lumpur, 1980. Easy to read.
●Sheppard, Mubin: *Taman Indera: Malay Decorative Art & Pastimes*. Kuala Lumpur, 1972.
●Sulivan, Margaret: *Can Survive, la — Cottage Industries in Highrise Singapore*. Singapore, 1985.
●Lee Kip Lim: *Emerald Hill — The Story of a Street in Words & Pictures*. Singapore, 1985.
●Durai Raja Singam, S.: *Place-Names in Peninsular Malaysia*. Kuala Lumpur, 1980.

Orang Asli Literature

●Carey Iskandar: *Orang Asli — The Aboriginal Tribes of Peninsular Malaysia*. Kuala Lumpur, 1976. The standard work on the Orang Asli.
●*Ethnic Groups of Mainland Southeast Asia*. Human Relationship Area Files Press, New Haven, 1964.
Articles on the Semang, the Senoi and the Jakun.
●Evans, I.H.N.: *The Negritos of Malaya*. Cambridge, England, 1937.
●Werner, Roland: *Mah Meri — Art & Culture*. Kuala Lumpur, 1973. Details the art and culture of a small Orang Asli society, with bilingual explanations of myths and masks, many illustrations. For sale in the National Museum.

History

●Hall, D.E.G.: *A History of Southeast Asia*. London, 1964. The standard work, albeit a bit dated.
●Comber, Leon: *13 May 1969 — A Historical Survey of Sino-Malay Relations*. Kuala Lumpur, 1983. A good account of ethnic relations in Malaysia, focusing on the race riots of 1969.
●Chapman, F. Spencer: *The Jungle is Neutral*. London, 1949. The three year jungle war at the end of World War II.
●Miller, Harry: *Jungle War in Malaya: The Campaign against Communism, 1948-1960*. England, 1972 and 1981. An informative, though biased view of the Emergency.
●Hua Wu Yin: *Class & Communism in Malaysia: Politics in a Dependent Capitalist State*. England, 1983. An analysis of domestic politics from a socialistpoint of view.
●Mahathir: *The Malay Dilemma*. Singapore, 1977. The Prime Minister's view of the nation's racial problems.

Guide Books

●Insight guide to *Malaysia*. Apa Productions.
●Insight guide to *Singapore*. Apa Productions. Good photographs in both guides.
●Wheeler, Tony: *Malaysia, Singapore and Brunei: A Travel Survival Kit*. South Yarra, Australia, 1982. Backpackers' favorite; brief.

Miscellaneous

●Bock, Karl: *The Headhunters of Borneo*. Jena 1887. A naturalists travel account. Some very good drawings.
●Geddes, W.R.: *Nine Dayak Nights*. Oxford 1973. A scientific account of the life of the Land Dayaks.

List of Photos

The photographers' initials are given in parentheses: Martin Lutterjohann (ML); Eberhard and Klaudia Homann (Ho); Gerold Suffner (GS); Wolfgang Wask (WW); Rainer Krack (RK); Gunda Urban (GU); Peter Rump (PR); Klaus Nitschke (KN); Frank-Peter Herbts (FPH).

24   A dentist's sign in Penang (GU)
26   Bamboo shades become advertisements (GU)
27   Funeral offerings – Even the dead don't miss out on TV (ML)
28   Typical room in a guest house (ML)
29   Malaysia has its share of luxury hotels (ML)
31   Street vendors, or hawkers, often have delicious cuisine. Shown here in Penang (ML)
33   Chinese food can be bought everywhere (ML)
34   Serving tea with milk as a performing art (ML)
37   Orang Asli wood carving (ML)
41   You never know what to expect driving through the forests (ML)
45   Pushing a car in Penang (ML)

49   View from the Gunung Tahan trail (ML)
50   Bukit Takun in Templer Park near Kuala Lumpur (ML)
51   The Perak River (ML)
54   Ipoh under water – no rarity during the rainy season(ML)
56   A rest stop in Taman Negara (ML)
56   An 20 cm wing span: An Atlas Falter (PR)
57   A giant liana in Taman Negara (ML)
60   The Orang Asli village of Suleh I, 15 km from Ipoh
61   An Orang Asli village in the Cameron Highlands (ML)
62   Above: T-shirts, worldwide fashion (ML); below:
       Decked out as "King and Queen for a day" (ML)
64   Absolutely no hawkers (GU)
64   Just to be safe, a sign in four languages (GU)
65   Prehistoric cave paintings near Ipoh (ML)
68   Portuguese presence in Malacca: Porta de Santiago (ML)
69   Dutch presence in Malacca: Tombstone (ML)
74   Tin mines near Ipoh (ML)
75   An especially thick rubber tree (PR)
80   The roof of the Guan Yin temple in Georgetown (ML)
81   The fantastic roof decorations on Indian temples are known as Sikara (ML)
88   Dragons can be seen everywhere during the Chinese New Year celebrations (WW)
89   Qing Ming in the Chinese cemetery near Ipoh (ML)
90   Giant sticks of incense, taller than 2m (KN)
91   No blood, no pain – Thaipusam in Ipoh (ML)
94   Loud, colorful and exotic: Chinese opera (ML)
96   *Baju kurung* – traditional Malay clothing (ML)
98   Pork is shunned by Muslims, but remains a favorite with the Chinese (ML)
100   Visiting an Indian family (ML)
102   A light tent is useful for jungle trekking (ML)
119   One of Langkawi's many beaches (ML)
122   In Kedah, the rice bowl of Malaysia (ML)
123   The resthouse on Gunung Jerai (ML)
124   The restored ruins of a Hindu temple near Merbok (ML)
127   Sun blinds in front of shops on Chulia Street in Georgetown (ML)
130   A trishaw station (KN)
134   The Penang skyline seen from Butterworth (ML)
135   Kek Lok Si temple: Above, holy turtles; Below, a view of the pagoda (both PR)
136   The Buddhist Association of Penang (GS)
140   Snakes! (GS)
143   Arriving in Penang with the bridge in the background (ML)
157   Cave paintings in the Perak Tong and statues of monks in Ipoh's Thai temple (both
       ML)
161   A view of Ipoh (ML)
162   The Rafflesia, the largest flower in the world (ML)
163   Kellie's Castle near Batu Gajah (ML)
164   Inside Kellie's Castle (ML)
166   A boat trip to Pangkor (ML)
169   Swimming on Pasir Bogak with a view of Pangkor Laut (ML)
170   A tree-fern (ML)
171   Like a green carpet – tea plantations (ML)

172 Near Brinchang (KN)
174 An Orang Asli with a blowgun (ML)
176 There are waterfalls all over the Cameron Highlands (ML)
179 The Friday Mosque in front of skyscrapers (ML)
179 A "white elephant" (ML)
184 The Royal Selangor Club on the *padang* of Kuala Lumpur (ML)
185 Old and new Kuala Lumpur (ML)
187 Art and kitsch inside the Central Market (ML)
190 Food at the night market (ML)
191 The Mall, a palatial shopping center (ML)
194 The Batu Caves, near Kuala Lumpur (KN)
198 Bukit Takun in Templer Park: two views (ML)
205 Classic, and still occupied (GU)
210 A view of Malacca from St. Paul's Hill, with Santiago Gate to the lower right (ML)
211 Dutch architecture in Malacca (ML)
212 Live Portuguese folk dancing (ML)
213 Kampong Hulu Mosque (ML)
215 Rubber plantation (KN)
217 Advertising and film posters in Malacca (ML)
231 A traditional pastime, flying kites (TDC)
236 Fun on the beach with a baby shark (ML)
238 A typical fishing village, built on stilts (ML)
239 Accommodation on the beach in Marang (ML)
243 Giant turtle laying eggs in the sand near Rantau Abang (ML)
260 Shhh! (ML)
261 Boats at the dock in Kuala Tahan (ML)
266 Seven Up around the World (ML)
267 Guides know how to dress for the trail (ML)
269 Resting on the bank of the Tahan (ML)
270 Rafflesia on the edge of the "path" (ML)
280 Rainy season (Ho)
288 Resting in the woods (ML)
289 A Punan shelter (ML)
290 A Dayak woman with tattooed "gloves" (Ho)
292 A Punan community near Bario (ML)
298 A Dayak totem pole (Ho)
301 A shopping street in Kuching (Ho)
303 An overland bus (Ho)
305 A pitcher plant, bright green with red stripes (Ho)
308 Bathing in a village (ML)
309 River taxi (Ho)
317 In the Niah Caves (Ho)
371 A house pet (ML)
330 The Tamu at Kota Belud (Ho)
333 View of the city from the pedestrian bridge, looking right (Ho)
334 Looking left (Ho)
334 The market of Kota Kinabalu (Ho)
341 The ascent begins on the road (ML)
344 One of the highest hotels in Asia (Ho)
345 Victoria Peak, not for beginners (ML); Pitcher Plants (ML)
349 Orangutans in the rehabilitation center (Ho)

351 K. Homann in a "supply center" (Ho)
354 Women in the market (Ho)
359 The best way to get around Borneo – the Twin Otter (Ho)
359 A station on the Beaufort-Tenom Railway (Ho)
360 The Lawas airport (Ho)
370 A Thaipusam pilgrim in Singapore (Ho)
380 Fast-food in Malay – roasted bananas (Ho)
384 Shops in Chinatown (WW)
389 The Sentosa monorail (Ho)
390 The source of handbags and shoes (PR)
391 Orchard Rd. – A shopper's paradise (Ho)

Help!

This book is packed full of information, addresses, prices and advice. Only by visiting the individual sites can this information be checked, updated and corrected.

Over time, things change – prices go up, hotels get better or more run -down, restaurants open, close, and change cooks, etc.

The authors of this book are constantly traveling and are planning to publish a new edition every two years, but they can't go everywhere and do everything without the help of fellow travelers.

Write to us and let us know what's got better, what's got worse, what's changed and what hasn't. We can only keep our books up-to-date with your help. The writers of the most useful letters will earn a free copy of the next edition and will receive a mention in the credits.

Write to the publisher directly: P.R. Publishing, Hauptstrasse 198, D-4800 Bielefeld 14, Germany. ***Thanks!***

Rainer Krack

Thailand
Handbook

The complete guide
for the modern adventurer

This guidebook is packed with nearly 400 pages of practical
ideas for the do-it-yourself adventurer. Some information has
never been published before in any guidebook in any language.
- From Bangkok and Ko Samui to the Golden Triangle and the
  steamy jungles along the Malaysian border.
- History, people, religion, festivals, traditions, and forgotten
  legends.
- Suggestions for trekking, rafting, and diving.
- Remote exotic islands, and the finest beaches.
- Over 1,000 hotels and restaurants.
- Up-to-date prices and schedules for trains, buses, planes,
  and boats.
- Over 100 maps and 150 photographs, many in color.
- Indispensable for long- and short-time visitors.
- ISBN 3-89416-330-5
  Peter Rump Publishing Co., D-4800 Bielefeld 14

Flight Prices (in M$)
Twin Otter Flights in Sabah and Sarawak

from-to	one-way	return	overweight luggage per kg
BAKELALAN to			
Lawas	46	92	0.70
BARIO to			
Marudi	55	110	0.80
Miri	70	140	1.00
BELAGA to			
Kapit	47	94	0.70
Sibu	76	152	1.10
BINTULU to			
Mukah	44	88	0.65
KAPIT to			
Belaga	47	94	0.70
Sibu	48	96	0.70
KENINGAU to			
Kota Kinabalu	38	76	0.55
KOTA KINABALU to			
Keningau	38	76	0.55
Kudat	50	100	0.75
Labuan	43	86	0.70
Lawas	47	94	0.70
Miri	82	164	1.30
Pamol	55	110	0.80
Sandakan	69	138	1.00
KUCHING to			
Mukah	90	180	1.35
KUDAT to			
Kota Kinabalu	50	100	0.75
Pamol	48	96	0.70
Sandakan	54	108	0.80
LABUAN to			
Kota Kinabalu	43	86	0.70
Lawas	31	62	0.45
Long Pasia	54	108	0.80
LAHAD DATU to			
Sandakan	40	80	0.60
Tawau	40	80	0.60
Tomanggong	35	70	0.50
LAWAS to			
Bakelalan	46	92	0.70
Kota Kinabalu	47	94	0.70
Labuan	31	62	0.45
Limbang	25	50	0.40
Long Semadoh	40	80	0.60
Miri	59	118	0.85
LIMBANG to			
Lawas	25	50	0.40
Miri	45	90	0.65
LONG LELLANG to			
Long Seridan	35	70	0.50
Marudi	46	92	0.70
Miri	66	132	0.95

from-to	one-way	return	overweight luggage per kg
LONG PASIA to			
Labuan	54	108	0.80
LONG SEMADOH to			
Lawas	40	80	0.60
LONG SERIDAN to			
Long Lellang	35	70	0.50
Marudi	42	84	0.60
Miri	57	114	0.85
MARUDI to			
Bario	55	110	0.80
Long Lellang	46	92	0.70
Long Seridan	42	84	0.60
Miri	29	58	0.45
Sibu	100	200	1.45
MIRI to			
Bario	70	140	1.00
Kota Kinabalu	82	164	1.30
Lawas	59	118	0.85
Limbang	45	90	0.65
Long Lellang	66	132	0.95
Long Seridan	57	114	0.85
Marudi	29	58	0.45
Mukah	55	110	0.80
Sibu	75	150	1.10
MUKAH to			
Bintulu	44	88	0.65
Kuching	90	180	1.35
Miri	55	110	0.80
Sibu	30	60	0.45
PAMOL to			
Kota Kinabalu	55	110	0.80
Kudat	48	96	0.70
Sandakan	40	80	0.60
SANDAKAN to			
Lahad Datu	40	80	0.60
Kota Kinabalu	69	138	1.00
Kudat	54	108	0.80
Pamol	40	80	0.60
Semporna	50	100	0.75
Tomanggong	42	84	0.60
Tawau	61	122	0.90
SEMPORNA to			
Sandakan	50	100	0.75
Tomanggong	40	80	0.60
SIBU to			
Belaga	76	152	1.10
Kapit	48	96	0.70
Marudi	100	200	1.45
Miri	75	150	1.10
Mukah	30	60	0.45
TAWAU to			
Lahad Datu	40	80	0.60
Sandakan	61	122	0.90
TOMANGGONG to			
Lahad Datu	35	70	0.50
Sandakan	42	84	0.60
Semporna	40	80	0.60

Fare Type Symbols: *F* = 1st Class, *Y* = Economy, *S* = Fokker Friendship, *YSP / SSP* = Specially Advertised Price, *FN* = 1st Class / Night, *YN* = Economy / Night, *YE* = Excursion Fare, *FU* = only 1st Class, *YU* = only Economy, YAP = Advance Purchase Excursion Fare

MAS Domestic Flights

from-to	fare type	one-way	return	over-weight luggage per kg
ALOR SETAR to				
Kota Bharu	F	84	168	0.90
"	Y/S	59	118	0.90
Kuala Lumpur (Direct or via KBR)	F	134	268	1.40
"	Y/S	94	188	1.40
" (Direct)	FN	87	174	1.40
" (Direct)	YN	61	122	1.40
B.S. BEGAWAN to		BS	BS	BS
Kota Kinabalu	F	93	186	1.00
"	Y/S	65	130	1.00
Kuala Lumpur (Direct, via BKI or KCH)	F	528	1,056	5.30
"	Y	372	744	5.30
"	YE30	–	595	5.30
Kuching	F	275	550	2.80
"	Y/S	192	384	2.80
BINTULU to				
Kota Kinabalu	S	110	220	1.60
Kuching	S	97	194	1.40
Labuan	S	96	192	1.40
Miri	S	57	114	0.90
Sibu	S	53	106	0.80
IPOH to				
Johor Bahru (via KUL)	Y/S	132	264	1.90
"	Y/S	119	238	1.90
Kota Bharu (via PEN)	S	113	226	1.60
Kuala Lumpur	S	55	110	0.80
Penang	S	41	82	0.60
JOHOR BAHRU to				
Ipoh (via KUL)	Y/S	132	264	1.90
"	Y/S	119	238	1.90
Kota Bharu (via KUL or W. Coast)	F	233	466	2.40
"	Y/s	163	326	2.40
Kota Kinabalu	F	428	856	4.30
"	Y	301	602	4.30
"	YE14	–	542	4.30
"	YAP	256	512	4.30
Kuala Lumpur	F	110	220	1.10
"	Y	77	154	1.10
"	S	64	128	1.10
"	YSP	70	140	1.10
"	SSP	58	116	1.10
Kuala Terengganu	F	233	466	2.40
"	Y	163	326	2.40
"	S	132	264	2.40
Kuantan (Direct or via KUL)	F	110	220	1.10
"	Y/S	77	154	1.10
Kuching	F	209	418	2.10
"	Y	147	294	2.10
"	YAP	125	250	2.10
"	YE14	–	265	2.10
Penang (via KUL)	F	210	420	2.10
"	Y/S	148	296	2.10
KERTEH to				
Kuala Lumpur	S	80	160	1.30
Kuala Terengganu	S	40	80	0.60
Kuantan	S	32	64	0.50
KOTA BHARU to				
Alor Setar	F	84	168	0.90
"	Y/S	59	118	0.90
Ipoh (via PEN)	S	113	226	1.60
Johor Bahru (via KUL or W. Coast)	F	233	466	2.40
"	Y/S	163	326	2.40
K. Lumpur (Direct or via W. Coast)	F	123	246	1.30
"	Y/S	86	172	1.30
" (Direct)	FN	87	174	1.30
" (Direct)	YN	61	122	1.30
" (Direct)	YSP	72	144	1.30
Penang	F	103	206	1.10
"	Y/S	72	144	1.10
KOTA KINABALU to				
B.S. Begawan	F	93	186	1.00
"	Y/S	65	130	1.00
Bintulu	S	110	220	1.60
Johor Bahru	F	428	856	4.30
"	Y	301	602	4.30
"	YE14	–	542	4.30
"	YAP	256	512	4.30
Kuala Lumpur (Direct, via JHB or SIN)	F	540	1,080	5.40
"	Y	380	760	5.40
"	YAP	323	646	5.40
" (Direct)	YE30	–	599	5.40
" (Direct)	FN	378	756	5.40
" (Direct)	YN	266	532	5.40

from-to	fare type	one-way	return	over-weight luggage per kg
KOTA KINABALU to				
Kuching	F	282	564	2.90
"	Y/S	198	396	2.90
Labuan	F	62	124	0.70
"	Y/S	43	86	0.70
Lahad Datu	S	88	176	1.30
Miri	F	128	256	1.30
"	Y	90	180	1.30
"	S	82	164	1.30
Sandakan	F	98	196	1.00
"	Y/S	69	138	1.00
Sibu	S	156	312	2.30
Singapore	F	492	984	5.00
"	Y	346	692	5.00
Tawau	F	114	228	1.20
"	Y/S	80	160	1.20
KUALA LUMPUR to				
Alor Setar	F	134	268	1.40
"	Y/S	94	188	1.40
"	FN	87	174	1.40
"	YN	61	122	1.40
B.S. Begawan (Direct, via BKI or KCH)	F	528	1,056	5.30
"	Y	372	744	5.30
"	YE30	–	595	5.30
Ipoh	S	55	110	0.80
Johor Bahru	F	110	220	1.10
"	Y	77	154	1.10
"	S	64	128	1.10
"	YSP	70	140	1.10
"	SSP	58	116	1.10
Kerteh	S	80	160	1.30
Kota Bharu (Direct or via West Coast)	F	123	246	1.30
"	Y/S	86	172	1.30
" (Direct)	FN	87	174	1.30
" (Direct)	YN	61	122	1.30
" (Direct)	YSP	72	144	1.30
K. Kinabalu (Direct via JHB or SIN)	F	540	1,080	5.40
"	Y	380	760	5.40
" (Direct or via JHB)	YAP	323	646	5.40
" (Direct)	YE30	–	599	5.40
" (Direct)	FN	378	756	5.40
" (Direct)	YN	266	532	5.40
Kuala Terengganu	F	123	246	1.30
"	Y	86	172	1.30
"	S	80	160	1.30
Kuantan	F	87	174	0.90
"	Y/S	61	122	0.90
Kuching (Direct, via JHB or SIN)	F	329	658	3.30
"	Y	231	462	3.30
"	S	211	422	3.30
" (via JHB)	YAP	197	394	3.30
" (Direct)	YE30	–	369	3.30
" (Direct)	FN	231	462	3.30
" (Direct)	YN	162	324	3.30
Labuan (Direct or via BKI)	F	540	1,080	5.40
"	Y	380	760	5.40
" (Direct)	YAP	323	646	5.40
"	YE14	–	570	5.40
Langkawi	F	159	318	1.60
"	Y/S/T	112	224	1.60
Miri	F	522	1,044	5.30
"	Y	367	734	5.30
Penang	F	123	246	1.30
"	Y	86	172	1.30
"	S	80	160	1.30
"	FN	87	174	1.30
"	YN	61	122	1.30
Singapore	F	180	360	1.80
"	Y	130	260	1.80
"	FU	145	304	1.80
"	YU	103	216	1.80
Tioman	T	100	200	1.45
KUALA TERENGGANU to				
Johor Bahru	F	233	466	2.40
"	Y	163	326	2.40
"	S	132	264	2.40
Kerteh	S	40	80	0.60
Kuala Lumpur	F	123	246	1.30
"	Y	86	172	1.30
"	S	80	160	1.30
Kuantan	S	55	110	0.80
Penang	S	80	160	1.20
KUANTAN to				
Johor Bahru (Direct or via KUL)	F	110	220	1.10
"	Y/S	77	154	1.10
Kerteh	S	32	64	0.50

Ship Fares

From Peninsular Malaysia to Sabah and Sarawak

Prices in M$	Standart-Cabine		Deluxe-Cabine		Suite	
	one-way	return	one-way	return	one-way	return
from Kuantan						
to K.Kinabalu	265	530	380	760	550	1100
to Kuching	160	320	235	470	350	700
from Kuching						
to K.Kinabalu	140	280	195	390	300	600
to Kuantan	160	320	235	470	350	700
to Singapore	200	400	270	540	355	710
to Port Klang	160	320	235	470	350	700
from K.Kinabalu						
to Kuching	140	280	195	390	300	600
to Kuantan	265	530	380	760	550	1100
to Singapore	310	620	445	890	620	1240
to Port Klang	265	530	380	760	550	1100
from Singapore *						
to Kuantan	99	198	140	280	210	420
to Kuching	200	400	270	540	355	710
to K.Kinabalu	310	620	445	890	620	1240
to Port Klang	99	198	140	280	210	420
from Port Klang						
to Singapore	99	198	140	280	210	420
to Kuching	160	320	235	470	350	700
to K. Kinabalu	265	530	380	760	550	1100

* Prices in S$; discounts: Children under 2,90%;children under 12, 50% students, 25%.

Train Fares (in M$)

KTM

From Kuala Lumpur

	Class: 1	Class: 2	Class: 3
Padang Besar	$ 65.60	$29.60	$18.20
Alor Setar	$ 57.10	$25.80	$15.80
Butterworth	$ 47.40	$21.40	$13.20
B. Mertajam	$ 46.20	$20.80	$12.80
Taiping	$ 36.50	$16.50	$10.10
Ipoh	$ 25.50	$11.50	$ 7.10
Tapah Road	$ 18.90	$ 8.50	$ 5.30
Kuala Lumpur	–	–	–
Seremban	$ 9.00	$ 4.10	$ 2.50
Tampin	$ 15.20	$ 6.90	$ 4.20
Gemas	$ 21.90	$ 9.90	$ 6.10
Segamat	$ 25.50	$11.50	$ 7.10
Kluang	$ 35.30	$15.90	$ 9.80
Johor Bahru	$ 45.00	$20.30	$12.50
Singapore	$ 48.60	$21.90	$13.50
Kuala Lipis	$ 49.80	$22.50	$13.80
Krai	$ 75.30	$34.00	$20.90
Wakaf Bahru	$ 83.80	$37.80	$23.20
Tumpat	$ 86.20	$38.90	$23.90
Haadyai	$ 69.10	$31.50	–
Bangkok	$128.20	$59.00	–

From Butterworth

	Class: 1	Class: 2	Class: 3
	$ 20.70	$ 9.30	$ 5.80
	–	–	$ 3.50
	–	–	–
	$ 1.50	$ 0.70	$ 0.50
	$ 11.70	$ 5.30	$ 3.30
	$ 22.50	$10.20	$ 6.30
	$ 29.20	$13.20	$ 8.10
	$ 47.40	$21.40	$13.20
	$ 57.10	$25.80	$15.80
	$ 62.00	$27.90	$17.20
	$ 69.20	$31.20	$19.20
	$ 71.70	$32.30	$19.90
	$ 82.60	$37.20	$22.90
	$ 92.30	$41.60	$25.60
	$ 96.00	$43.30	$26.60
	$ 96.00	$43.30	$26.60
	$122.70	$55.30	$34.00
	$131.20	$59.10	$36.30
	$132.40	$59.70	$36.70
	$ 24.20	$11.20	–
	$ 83.30	$38.70	–

From Singapore

	Class: 1	Class: 2	Class: 3
Padang Besar	$113.00	$50.90	$31.30
Alor Setar	$105.70	$47.60	$29.30
Butterworth	$ 96.00	$43.30	$26.60
B. Mertajam	$ 94.70	$42.70	$26.30
Taiping	$ 83.80	$37.80	$23.20
Ipoh	$ 74.10	$33.40	$20.50
Tapah Road	$ 68.00	$30.70	$18.90
Kuala Lumpur	$ 48.60	$21.90	$13.50
Seremban	$ 40.10	$18.10	$11.10
Tampin	$ 34.00	$15.40	$ 9.50
Gemas	$ 28.00	$12.60	$ 7.80
Segamat	$ 24.30	$11.00	$ 6.80
Kluang	$ 14.00	$ 6.30	$ 3.90
Johor Bahru	$ 3.40	$ 1.60	$ 1.00
Singpore	–	–	–
Kuala Lipis	$ 54.70	$24.70	$15.20
Krai	$ 81.40	$36.70	$22.60
Wakaf Bahru	$ 89.90	$40.50	$24.90
Tumpat	$ 91.10	$41.10	$25.20
Haadyai	$116.50	$52.80	–
Bangkok	$175.60	$80.30	–

All pricesare for one-way tickets!

Sleeper Supplement on KTM	
1st Class	M$ 10
1st Class with AC	M$ 20
2nd Class (lower)	M$ 8
2nd Class (upper)	M$ 6

International Express

From   **Kuala Lumpur**

	Class: 1 AFC	Class: 2 ASC	Class: 2 SC	Class: 3 TC
Butterworth	$54.00	$28.00	$25.00	$17.00
Bukit Mertajam	$53.00	$27.00	$24.00	$16.00
Taiping	$43.00	$23.00	$20.00	$14.00
Kuala Kangsar	$39.00	$21.00	$18.00	$13.00
Ipoh	$32.00	$18.00	$15.00	$11.00
Kampar	$27.00	$16.00	$13.00	$ 9.00
Tapah Road	$25.00	$15.00	$12.00	$ 9.00
Kuala Lumpur	–	–	–	–
Seremban	$15.00	$11.00	$ 8.00	$ 6.00
Tampin	$22.00	$13.00	$10.00	$ 8.00
Segamat	$32.00	$18.00	$15.00	$11.00
Kluang	$42.00	$22.00	$19.00	$13.00
Johor Bahru	$51.00	$27.00	$24.00	$16.00
Singapore	$55.00	$28.00	$25.00	$17.00

From   **Butterworth**

	Class: 1 AFC	Class: 2 ASC	Class: 2 SC	Class: 3 TC
Butterworth	–	–	–	–
Bukit Mertajam	$ 8.00	$ 7.00	$4.00	$ 4.00
Taiping	$18.00	$12.00	$ 9.00	$ 7.00
Kuala Kangsar	$22.00	$14.00	$11.00	$ 8.00
Ipoh	$29.00	$17.00	$14.00	$10.00
Kampar	$33.00	$19.00	$16.00	$11.00
Tapah Road	$36.00	$20.00	$17.00	$12.00
Kuala Lumpur	$54.00	$28.00	$25.00	17.00
Seremban	–	$32.00	$29.00	$19.00
Tampin	–	$34.00	$31.00	$21.00
Segamat	–	$39.00	$36.00	$23.00
Kluang	–	$44.00	$41.00	$26.00
Johor Bahru	–	$48.00	$45.00	$29.00
Singapore	–	$50.00	$47.00	$30.00

All pricesare for one-way tickets!

From   **Singapore**

	Class: 1 AFC	Class: 2 ASC	Class: 2 SC	Class: 3 TC
Butterworth	–	$50.00	$47.00	$30.00
Bukit Mertajam	–	$49.00	$46.00	$30.00
Taiping	–	$44.00	$41.00	$27.00
Kuala Kangsar	–	$43.00	$40.00	$26.00
Ipoh	–	$40.00	$37.00	24.00
Kampar	–	$38.00	$35.00	$23.00
Tapah Road	–	$37.00	$34.00	$22.00
Kuala Lumpur	$55.00	$28.00	$25.00	$17.00
Seremban	$47.00	$25.00	$22.00	$15.00
Tampin	$40.00	$22.00	$19.00	$13.00
Segamat	$31.00	$17.00	$14.00	$10.00
Kluang	$20.00	$13.00	$10.00	$ 7.00
Johor Bahru	$10.00	$ 8.00	$ 5.00	$ 4.00
Singapore	–	–	–	–

Sleeper Supplement on International Express

1st Class	M$ 11.80
1st Class with AC	M$ 19.00
2nd Class (lower)	M$ 9.10
2nd Class (upper)	M$ 6.40

Abbreviations

AFC	– 1st Class with A/C
ASC	– 2nd Class with A/C
SC	– 2nd Class without A/C
TC	– 3rd Class (only for Expres Rakyat)

General Index

accommodation, Singapore 376
accomodation 27
airlines, Singapore 395
airplanes 38
airport tax 20, 197
airports 18
Ang Pow 89
animal kingdom 55
Animism 82
arts 92
Bahasa Malaysia 64, 401
Bajau 328
behavior 95, 244
behavior, Singapore 371
birds' nest soup 318
blowgun 174
boat people 237
boats 48
British 69
Brooke, Charles 286
Buddhism 79, 371
Bumiputeras 59
bungalows 28
buses 40
cash 22
Changi Airport 396
Chinese 63, 79, 88, 97, 371, 379
chinese food 33
Chinese Opera 94
cholera 12
Christianity 82
circumcision 85
climate 52
climate, Singapore 367
clothing 14
clubs 27
Coat of Arms 73
colonialism 68
costs 12, 23
credit cards 22
culture 92
currency 22
customs 21, 83
customs, Singapore 374
Dayak 286, 288
discos 27
distances 42
domestic flights 38

Dutch 68
economy 74
economy, Sabah 327
economy, Sarawak 287
embassies 192
embassies, Malaysia 400
embassies, Singapore 395, 400
employment 21
entry regulations, Singapore 374
equipment 14
eurochecks 22
Europeans 68
exchange rate 23
fauna 54, 260, 284
festivals 87
flora 54, 284
food 30
food, Singapore 377
geographical terms 51
geography, peninsular 49
geography, Sabah 325
geography, Singapore 367
gifts 283
government offices 25
government resthouse 29
guest houses 27
Hari Raya Puasa 88
head of state 72
head-hunter 290
health 13, 24
hepatitis 12
Hinduism 81, 370
history 64
history, Sabah 326
history, Sarawak 286
history, Singapore 368
hitchhiking 44
holidays 87
hotels 29
income levels 77
independence 70
Indian dance 94
Indian food 34
Indians 64, 81, 90, 99, 381
individual states 103
Indonesian 381
inflation rate 23
Islam 77, 371
Japanese 70
jungle gear 270

jungle trekking 264, 362
Kadazan 329
karst formations 50
Kellie's castle 163
language, Malaysia 64, 401
language, Singapore 367
leatherback turtles 243
long-houses 289, 328
long-house tours 301
malaria 13
Malay dance 93
Malays 61, 381
Malaysia Tourist Development Corporation 400
manners in a long-house 291
Manser, Bruno 293
maps 15
marine parks 57
measurements 25
media 26
medicine 24
medicine man 290
Minangkabau 205
minibuses 48
money 21
money, Singapore 375
money transfers 22
monsoon 53
movies 27
Murut 329, 358
national anthem 73
national parks, Sarawak 294
national symbols 73
newspapers 26
nightlife 27
Non-Bumiputeras 63
opening hours 25
Orang Asli 37, 59, 82, 174, 260, 404
Orang Asli Department 176, 193
orang-utans 284, 306, 346, 349
overcharging 25
overseas calls 26.
palm oil 75
Penyu Belimbing 243
people 59
people, Sabah 328
people, Sarawak 288
photography 15
pickpockets 24
pitcher plants 305
police 43

polio 12
political structure 72
politics 71
population, Singapore 367
Portuguese 212
postal rates 26
power 25
proboscis monkey 306
Proto-Malays 61
Punan 292
radio 27
Raffles, Sir Stamford 368
religion 77
religion, Sarawak 288
rental cars 41
rickshaws 48
road signs 44
rubber 74
rules of the road 43
Salanganes 318
sea turtles 244
security 24
security, Singapore 376
shadow puppets 93
shopping 36
shopping, Singapore 391
Sikhism 82
Singapore Tourist Promotion Boards 400
smallpox 12
snake bites 14
state holidays 91
superstitions 83
taboos 83
Taman Negara 259
Tamu 329, 354, 356
tattoos 290
taxis 40, 44
telephone 26
television 27
tetanus 12
Thaipusam 370
tickets 19
tin 74
tourism 100
tourist information 113, 188, 225
trains 39
transportation 38
travel routes 110
travelers' checks 21
trishaws 48

tropical fruit 35
tropical rain forest 284
turtle 350
turtle experience 242
typhoid 12
vaccines 12
vegetation 54, 345
video 27
visas 20
yellow fever 12

Geographical Index

Alor Setar 120
Anak Takun 194
Arau 114
Ayer Hitam 224
Ayer Keroh 215
Bako National Park 301, 304
Bandar Seri Begawan 279
Bandar Sri Aman 306
Bantal 268
Bario 313
Batu Caves 194
Batu Gajah 162
Batu Niah 315
Bau 301
Beaufort 356
Belaga 312
Bentong 257
Beremban 171
Beserah 250
Bidong Island 238
Bintulu 314
Brunei 278, 321
Bujang Valley 123
Buki Teresek 264
Bukit Takun 194
Bukit Timah Reserve 390
Cameron Highlands 170
Carey Island 196
Cave, see also Gua
Charah Caves 251
Cherating 246
Chinatown, Singapore 382
Chukai 245
Chuping 115
Danum Valley 351
Dendong Beach Park 238
Desaru 224
Dinding River 166
Dusun 329
Endau Rompin 268
Endau Rompin Park 252
Fraser's Hill 255
Gadek Hot Springs 217
Genting Highlands 193
Gerik (Grik) 149
Gomantong Caves 349
Green Turtle Island 350

Gua Cerita 118
Gua Langsir 119
Gua Musang 231
Gunung Angsi 201
Gunung Beremban 175
Gunung Besar 253
Gunung Brinchang 176
Gunung Chali Pondok 176
Gunung Irau 176
Gunung Jasar 175
Gunung Jerai 122
Gunung Ledang 217, 218
Gunung Mulu Park 321
Gunung Murud 313
Gunung Ophir 218
Gunung Perdan 175
Gunung Raya 118
Gunung Siku 176
Gunung Tahan 267
Gunung Tapis Park 251
Gunung Telapak Burok 203
Gunung Yong Blar 176
Indian Quarter, Singapore 385
Ipoh 150
Islamic Quarter, Singapore 386
Island, see Pulau
Jeram Pasu Waterfall 231
Jerantut 259
Jerejak 141
Johor 108
Johor Baru 220
Johor Lama 223
Kajang 196
Kaki Bukit 114
Kampong Kuantan 177
Kampong Ru Muda 241
Kampong Sega Benuh 301
Kangar 114
Kapas Island 241
Kapit 311
Kedah 103
Kedah Peak 122
Kelang 196
Kelantan 108
Kemaman 245
Kenyir Dam 238
Kinabalu National Park 338
Kinta Valley 160
Kledang Hill 160
Kong Kong 224

Kota Baru 226
Kota Belud 354
Kota Kinabalu 330
Kota Tinggi 223
Kuah 117
Kuala Besar 230
Kuala Dungun 245
Kuala Gula 177
Kuala Gula Bird Preserve 147
Kuala Kangsar 147
Kuala Kedah 122
Kuala Lipis 257
Kuala Lumpur 106, 178
Kuala Perkai 268
Kuala Perlis 115
Kuala Selangor 177, 196
Kuala Selangor Nature Park 177
Kuala Tembeling 263
Kuala Terengganu 232
Kuantan 248
Kubaan 313
Kuching 295
Kudat 356
Kukup 224
Kustu 389
Labuan 359
Lahad Datu 351
Lambir Hill National Park 319
Langkawi 115
Lata Berkoh 268
Lawas 361
Lembaga Penapsis Air 218
Limbang 324
Lombong Waterfalls 223
Long Lellang 313
Low's Peak 338
Lubuk Antu 307
Lumut 165
Lundu 301
Lutong 319
Malacca 66, 106, 206
Marang 239
Merapoh 231
Merapok 360
Merit 312
Mersing 224, 252
Mimaland 193
Miri 318
Mount, see also Gunung
Mount Ophir 218

Muar 217
Negeri Sembilan 106
Niah National Park 313, 316
Nyireh Island 246
Padang Besar 114
Padang Masirat 118
Pahang Darul Makmur 109
Pa'Longan 313
Pangkor 166, 167
Pantai Cenang 118
Pantai Rhu 118
Pantai Tengah 118
Pasir Hitam 118
Pasoh 203
Pa'tik 313
Pa'Ukat 313
Pekan 251
Penang 104, 125
Pengkalan Kempas 204
Perak 104
Perlis 103
Pernu 217
Petaling Jaya 194
Poring Hot Springs 346
Port Dickson 201, 204
Port Klang 196
Pulau Besar 217
Pulau Bidong 237
Pulau Dayang Bunting 119
Pulau Duyong Besar 233
Pulau Jong 230
Pulau Perhentian 237
Pulau Pinang 125
Pulau Rawa 252
Pulau Redang 236
Pulau Sembilan 166
Pulau Tenggol 246
Pulau Tioman 252
Rajah Pulau 241
Ranau 337
Rantau Abang 241
Raub 257
Ringlet 171
Sabah 325
Sandakan 346
Santubong 300
Sapulot 362
Sarawak 285
Sarikei 308
Segamat 253

Sekayu Waterfall 239
Selangor Darul Ehsan 105
Selepong 307
Sematan 301
Semporna 352
Sentosa Island 388
Sepilok Sanctuary 348
Seremban 199
Serkam 217
Shah Alam 195
Sibu 308
Similajau National Park 314
Sindumin 360
Singapore 365
Skrang River 307
Sri Menati 201
St. John Islands 390
Sukau 350
Sungai Dungun 246
Sungai Karang 250
Sungei Kemana 314
Taiping 144
Taman Negara 259
Tanah Rata 171
Tangkak 218
Tanjung Aru 335
Tanjung Rambutan 160
Tasek Bera 258
Tasek Chini 250, 259
Tatau 312
Tawau 353
Telagah Tujuh 118
Teluk Chempedak 250
Temerloh 258
Templer Park 194
Tenom 358
Terengganu 109
Tioman 254
Tuaran 335
Tumpat 230
Tunku Abdul Rahman Park 336
Ulu Lepar 259

Maps

Alor Setar 121
  Around Alor Setar 125
Around Bandar Sri Aman 307
Bako National Park 304
Batu Niah 316
Beaufort 357
Bencoolen Street 378
Bintulu 315
Brunei 278
Cameron Highlands 173
Central Malaysia 256
China-Town 383
Domestic Routes (MAS) 38
East Coast/Middle 246
East Malaysia 275
Georgetown Hotels 128
Georgetown 132
Getting to Malaysia 19
Getting to Sabah and Sarawak 276
Gunung Ledang 218
Gunung Mulu Park 322
  Around Gunung Mulu Park 223
Ipoh 152
  Around Ipoh 159
Johor Baru 221
  Around Johor Baru 223
Jungle Trekking 265, 362
Kangar 114
Kapit 312
Kinabalu Headquarters 340
Kinabalu-Trail 343
Kota Baru 228
Kota Belud 355
Kota Kinabalu 332
Kuah 118
Kuala Kangsar 148
Kuala Lumpur 182
  Around Kuala Lumpur 193
Kuala Selangor 177
Kuala Terengganu 234
Kuantan 249
Kuching 296
  Around Kuching 302
Langkawi 116
Lawas 361
Lumut 165
Main Roads 44
Malacca 208

Around Malacca 216
Marang 240
Miri 320
Natur-Trails, Kinabalu 342
Niah National Park 316
Northeast Coast 226
Northwest Coast 113
Orang Asli 59
Orchard Road 392
Pangkor 168
Penang 139
Peninsular Malaysia 48
Protected Marine Areas 58
Ranau 338
Sabah 327
Sandakan 347
  Around Sandakan 348
Sarawak 286
Sentosa 389
Serangoon Road 386
Seremban 200
  Around Seremban 202
Sibu 310
Singapore 366
Southeast Coast 247
Southwest Coast 178
States 107
Taiping 145
Taman Negara 262
Tawau 353
Tenom 358
Tioman 254

Temperature

To convert °C to °F multiply by 1.8 and add 32
To convert °F to °C subtract 32 and multiply by 0.55

Length, Distance & Areas

	multiply by
inches to centimetres	2.54
centimetres to inches	0.39
feet to metres	0.30
metres to feet	3.28
yard to metres	0.91
metres to yards	1.09
miles to kilometres	1.61
kilometres to miles	0.62
acres to hectares	0.40
hectares to acres	2.47

°C	°F
50	112
45	113
40	104
35	95
30	86
25	75
20	68
15	59
10	50
5	41
0	32

Weight

	multiply by
ounces to grams	28.35
grams to ounces	0.035
pounds to kilograms	0.45
kilograms to pounds	2.21
British tons to kilograms	1016
US tons to kilograms	907

A British ton is 2240 lbs, a US ton is 2000 lbs

Volume

	multiply by
Imperial gallons to litres	4.55
litres to imperial gallons	0.22
US gallons to litres	3.79
litres to US gallons	0.26

5 imperial gallons equal 6 US gallons
a litre is slightly more than a US quart, slightly less
than a British one

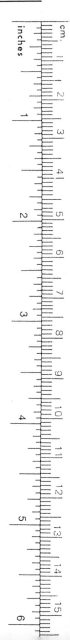

The Authors

Martin Lutterjohann, born in 1943, is a psychologist specializing in addictive behavior, on which he has written a dozen books. During 1987 and 1988, he was the director of a small institute that trains addiction therapists in Ipoh, halfway between Kuala Lumpur and Penang. During that time, he became familiar with the day to day life of Malaysia and her people.

He has spent many days swimming and snorkeling Malaysian waters from Langkawi in the northwest to Desaru in the southeast, on Penang and all along the east coast. He has climbed mountains and visited caves, bird sanctuaries and waterfalls. A member of several nature organizations, he has spent considerable time in the jungles of the Peninsula, and also on Borneo. He has hiked the formidable Mount Kinabalu in Sabah and spent time with the Penan in Sarawak.

Malaysia is only one of more than 50 countries visited by the author, but other than his native Germany, he has never spent so much time in any one.

Klaudia Homann was born in Gütersloh, Germany in 1961. She studied pedagogy in the Bielefeld University. *Eberhard Homann* was born in Bielefeld in 1959. He studied biology and pedagogy and currently works in Bielefeld University, researching primates.

The two have been traveling together since 1979, first as backpackers and auto tourists in Europe (France, Italy, Yugoslavia and Greece). Their first visit to Malaysia was in 1983, and since then, they have been drawn to the region like a magnet. In 1984, they spent several months in Malaysia and Indonesia and in 1986, they returned to Malaysia, on their first visit to Sarawak. In 1988, they returned to Malaysia to spend almost two months in Sabah. Together they have also written a guidebook to Sarawak.